# GENIUS, GRIEF and GRACE

A Doctor looks at Suffering and Success

Dr. Gaius Davies

CHRISTIAN FOCUS PUBLICATIONS

ISBN 1-85792-630-7

Expanded and extended edition,
published in 2001, reprinted 2003
by
Christian Focus Publications, Geanies House,
Fearn, Ross-shire, IV20 1TW, Scotland.
www.christianfocus.com

Cover design by Alister MacInnes

Printed and bound by
Bell & Bain, Glasgow

This book was previously published as *Genius and Grace* in 1992 by Hodder and Stoughton/Hodder Headline plc, 338 Euston Road, London, NW1 3BH, England.

# Contents

to
Rev. Emyr Roberts
and
Dr R. Geraint Gruffydd

## Original Preface

It is never easy to be sure where a lifelong interest began. Perhaps my parents, by welcoming a number of unusual figures as visitors to our home, helped me most; I came to accept that gifted eccentrics, owing much to their experience of grace, were in no way unusual. David Bentley Taylor, in three lectures on Luther and Erasmus, enabled me to see that a medical student could find such men fascinating. The late Dr Douglas Johnson gave me books like *Nature and Grace* in 1947, and they influenced my reading about people such as John Bunyan and William Cowper. It was, for me, a special privilege that DJ, as that enthusiastic and learned man was known, read and criticized a good deal of this book as it took shape. For forty years and more, in second-hand bookshops, catalogues and libraries, I have been picking up books related to the theme of grace and personality. Now I can call it research.

I have had many teachers and colleagues in the psychiatric field who taught me much and helped me to apply the knowledge to people very much like the men and women studied in this book. As always seems to be the case, it was patients, rather than textbooks and journals, who taught me most.

I am grateful to many who have helped me by reading and making suggestions about the chapters, in part or whole. My family have borne the heaviest burden, and I thank my wife Nest for allowing each of the characters sketched in the book to share our bed and board for long periods. I thank my children Ruth, Carys (whose computer expertise made using a word-processor possible), Bethan and Jonathan for all their help. Dr J. I. Packer made many suggestions and read a number of chapters. Professor R. M. (Bobi) Jones applied his scholarly attention to the manuscript; to have a real live poet comment on other poets was, for me, a rare gift. Professor R. Geraint Gruffydd read many drafts, without complaint, and was a constant source of help and cautious encouragement; Geraint and his wife Luned were often consulted by telephone at critical points, but accepted the benign harassment with grace. The Rev. A. P. Baker, our

Reformed pastor, was a great help. Dr Oliver Briscoe was an invaluable friendly critic and support.

Other friends read parts of the book: Dorothy Allin, Ann Desmond, Andrew Ferguson, Eric Hamilton, Lily Jacobs, Major Clifford Kew, Robert Langley, Stuart Meyer, Iain Murray, Mary Nayler, Heather Nunnerly, Chris Olsen, Pauline Pitt, W. B. R. Saunders, Susannah Stanley, and Neil Yorkston. I am grateful to them and others (who made valuable suggestions) for help and encouragement.

The libraries of Bromley, the Institute of Psychiatry, and the University of London were most helpful. The Bethlem Royal and the Maudsley Hospitals' study leave committee were kind enough to grant me two weeks of study leave.

Ann and Edward England were especially helpful. I am grateful to Carolyn Armitage for all her editorial work from beginning to end, together with that of her colleagues.

I began to learn to write in 1959 when my editor, the late Rev. Emyr Roberts, persuaded me to do so. With him and Dr Geraint Gruffydd I served on the editorial board of *Y Cylchgrawn Efengylaidd* for ten years. They taught me much about writing to some purpose, in my own language and idiom. In those days Emyr had not won the Prose Medal, and Geraint had not sat in either of his two professional chairs, or been made National Librarian, or been elected Fellow of the British Academy. It is a pleasure to remember working with Emyr and Geraint, long before they attained their deserved distinctions, as two men who kept the faith and were faithful friends: to them the book is affectionately dedicated.

# Preface

This book is mainly a reprint of *Genius and Grace*. I am grateful to all the reviewers who were kind enough to praise it when it first appeared. Those who wrote to tell me of the enjoyment and help they obtained from it were a great encouragement to me.

I am most grateful to Christian Focus and to Mr William Mackenzie and his staff, for agreeing to publish it in its new form. I thank Hodder for releasing, without charge, the manuscript they first published, and enabling me to give it to Christian Focus. I thank Errol Hulse, a reformed pastor and friend, for suggesting Christian Focus as a publisher.

Special thanks go to Professor James I. Packer for his help and his foreword: we have known each other since student days, when he first persuaded me in 1953 to speak at a Puritan Conference and then arranged for Professor F. F. Bruce to publish the paper that I gave. His ministry of encouragement and support is much appreciated. His suggestions about the new title for this book, and about adding chapters on Frances Ridley Havergal and Dr Martyn Lloyd-Jones will, I trust, prove happy ones which will add to the book's interest and value.

The Rev. Dr John R.W. Stott was asked for a few words of recommendation, and wrote a foreword: I can only be grateful for his generous misunderstanding of the publisher's request. Since my first book on *Stress: the Challenge to Christian Caring* came about because of a lecture given to John Stott's project (with Miss Myra Chave Jones) called *Care and Counsel*, I hope his friendly and helpful words will help some to overcome their doubts about buying a book on suffering and success.

Two other friends are owed a debt of gratitude: Professor R. Geraint Gruffydd for his reading, suggestions and support and Dr E. Wyn James, Senior Lecturer at Cardiff University, for helping me with his detailed knowledge of material in the two new chapters.

My aim remains the same as I have expressed elsewhere in this book: to make a contribution to the stretching of our minds and the enlarging of our hearts by helping to make sense of the suffering that good people have experienced and describing something of the joy that makes such suffering worthwhile.

Dr Gaius Davies

# Foreword

This book is a celebration of grace, of God's grace which transforms even those who suffer painful handicaps and disabilities.

Dr Gaius Davies introduces us to eleven distinguished – even heroic – Christian people: Luther in the sixteenth century, Bunyan in the seventeenth, William Cowper in the eighteenth, Lord Shaftesbury, Gerard Manley Hopkins, Christina Rossetti and Frances Ridley Havergal in the ninteenth, and Amy Carmichael, J. B. Philips, C. S. Lewis and Dr D. Martyn Lloyd-Jones in the twentieth. In each case he begins by giving us a brief but fascinating biographical sketch, including a careful analysis of his of her particular trial, and then indicates how grace operated in each. For each could be described as a triumph of grace.

Having had twenty-five years clinical experience as a Consultant Psychiatrist, Gaius Davies is well qualified to investigate the frailties of the people he writes about. His purpose is emphatically not to debunk them, however, but rather the reverse, namely to show how divine grace transformed their human weakness. His particular focus is on their 'obsessive-compulsive disorders', including anxiety, depression, guilt, darkness and doubt. In doing so, he displays the integrity of the Bible, which does not conceal the foibles and failures of its great characters, and goes on to describe God's gracious dealings with them.

Fundamental to Gaius Davies' thesis are two convictions about the operation of God's grace.

First, 'grace does not change us as personalities'. To be sure, we are 'a new creation' (2 Cor. 5:17). Grace changes our outlook, ambitions, motives and behaviour, but not our inherited temperament. If, therefore, before experiencing the new birth, we were extroverts, we will be extroverts afterwards, but we will be easier to live with! If, on the other hand, we were introverts before, we will still be the same, but we will find it easier to live with ourselves!

Secondly, grace does not render us immune to either physical or mental illness. Nor does God promise healing in every case. There is a tendency in some Christian circles to declare it inappropriate for Christians ever to fall sick. 'You have no business to suffer from depression', some say. But no. Although God can and does heal, and indeed all healing is divine healing, he often leaves us to struggle with disability and to bear pain. For example, the deprivation of parental love during childhood may result in permanent psychological damage.

What I specially admire about Gaius Davies' book is his honesty and realism. He offers no glib remedies. He tells us the truth, that some of God's heroes and heroines have been eccentric and neurotic, and have suffered repeated breakdowns. He is well read and his book is well written. Its message in the end is Christ's word to Paul: 'My grace is sufficient for you, for my power is made perfect in weakness' (2 Cor. 12:9).

John Stott

## To the reader

I am delighted that this book is being reprinted. It has been one of my favourites since it first appeared.

Why does it please me so? For six reasons at least.

First, Dr Davies can write, and, like you, I enjoy what is well-written.

Second, he writes knowledgeably about some fascinating individuals – gifted, troubled Christians, whom he brings brilliantly to life. Such people always grab my interest, and I think these particular ones will grab yours.

Third, his focus is on their griefs and pains, their struggles and their sufferings: how they faced temptations that temperament within as well as circumstances without had sharpened, and how they gave themselves to serving and honouring God despite their own felt weaknesses. From inside stories of this kind flow the truest benefit of Christian biography, and these testimonies to the grace of our Lord Jesus Christ (for that really is what they all are) are narrated with outstanding insight into the things that make Christian people tick.

Fourth, Gaius Davies is a psychiatrist with a particular concern for believers whose minds, for whatever reason, are working less than well. With specialist expertise he diagnoses his subjects clinically and pinpoints pastorally the roots as well as the fruits of the out-of-shapeness that he sees in them. He knows about depression, bipolar mood swings, obsessive-compulsive disorder, and the destructive pitfalls of perfectionism, and puts his knowledge to good use in profiling these lovers of the Lord. Thus he gives us a three-dimensional understanding of their humanness in a way that hagiography cannot do, and that big biographies of his chosen characters often fail to do. I greatly value this feature of what he has put together.

Fifth, Davies appreciates poetry as the concentrated verbalizing of personal vision, and so as a profound revelation of its writers as well as of what they are looking at and thinking about. Whether narrative, descriptive, or meditative in form, poems are always a personal 'take' on something, communicating not just from head to head but from heart to heart. Davies' profilings of Hopkins and Rosetti in particular are illuminating just because he discerns so clearly how poems express and enrich life, for Christians no less than for unbelievers.

Sixth, Davies' authoritative exploration of his subjects' psychological makeup (a road less travelled in Christian biography) yields an enhanced sense of their stature – their integrity, bravery, and as we say sheer guts, in coping with calamity while cleaving to Christ. Rubbing shoulders with them, as I meet them here, becomes a source of strength under God for my own life.

So I commend this book with enthusiasm, and wish it a readership worthy of its wisdom.

J. I. Packer

# Introduction

## Sweet are the uses of adversity

This is a book about suffering and success; about how adversity may lead to achievement. In one way it is about how to be a successful failure. Each person described in it was, in some way, gifted to the point of genius. Each person described had crucial experiences of grace. Their faith became the most important factor in their lives. None of them was exempt from a share of distress; but it seems to have *driven* them to serve, rather than been a hindrance. Their service has often been of a most distinguished kind.

Winston Churchill used to speak of his 'black dog': he survived though he was dogged by depression for much of his life. It is said that only because Churchill had faced his own black periods was he able, at sixty years of age, to rally those who felt overwhelmed by the Nazi threat. His own experience of adversity enabled him to be a leader who helped to save the world from the darkness of tyranny.

Many heroes, men and women of genius who achieved so much, did what they did in spite of much suffering: many have said that their special trials and troubles *enabled* them to succeed in the way they did. We may find it upsetting that such heroic figures were flawed. We may be willing to admit privately that our leading characters have feet of clay. It is another thing for it to be made public, discussed freely, and for the larger-than-life figures thus, somehow, to be diminished.

It was the great hero Achilles who had his vulnerable heel: that, it will be recalled, was blamed on his mother, since she held him by the heel while dipping him as an infant in the magical waters.

In the Jewish and Christian tradition one of the great archetypal figures is that of Jacob. His very name means one who supplants or undermines; a twister. Yet Jacob became Israel: a name meaning a prince with God. He was permanently affected with a limp after his thigh was touched in his encounter one night, as he wrestled with the angel of the Lord. It is a short step to suspecting that perhaps, every heroic figure has his hidden weaknesses with which he has to struggle.

The burning questions for Christians are: How did such heroic figures overcome their weaknesses, and what role did their faith, God's grace and the power of his Spirit play in their achievement?

**Heroes who suffered**

I have selected a number of people who are, to me and many others, heroic figures. In writing about them I have worn two hats: that of a doctor who has specialized in psychological medicine for the last twenty-five years, and that of a Christian believer.

All the heroes are from the Christian tradition, even when their influence extends well beyond that tradition. I respond to them first with my heart and my affections: I grew to love them. It has been my experience that my faith and understanding are enriched by contact with people like Bunyan, Luther, Amy Carmichael and C. S. Lewis.

Just as early Christians in the period of the New Testament looked back on a cloud of witnesses, so can we. To do so is full of interest and offers much we can learn and enjoy. I have relished trying to share my admiration and love for these figures whose temperament and lives I have sketched.

Wearing my other hat, as a consultant psychiatrist I am curious to know what sort of people they were. What made them tick? I am drawn to some, like William Cowper, Gerard Manley Hopkins, Lord Shaftesbury and Christina Rossetti, because I know they suffered from much anxiety and depression.

It is a pity that some maverick psychiatrists and psychologists have been seen as enemies of both genius in general, and of those who are Christian or religious in particular. It is only too easy to try to explain away the towering achievements of great men and women. To do this is almost always misguided. It often reflects more on those who try to do it than on those whose work they attack.

What a psychiatrist has to offer, in my view, is not to reduce things to illness, or sexual frustration or whatever is currently in vogue, but rather to propose ways of understanding and obtaining insight. By this I mean learning as much as we can about how people's personalities are formed, and how they function in God's purpose. Where there is suffering, illness or distress, I hope to bring the best of modern knowledge to bear in the process of teasing out the many strands in their problems, while trying to avoid speculation.

When I see modern Christians, coming reluctantly for help with their problems, I feel like comforting them by saying that some of our illustrious forebears suffered just like them. They were men and women of like passions as we are. They were not afraid to admit it, nor were they ashamed of being anxious or depressed.

## Grace and personality

I must confess to another motive that led to my study of these heroes: a great curiosity about the relation between personality and the way God's grace works in the heart. The subject is mysterious, and yet the results of the interaction between grace and personality form the subject matter of much Christian biography and, indeed, of most religious experience.

The question of how temperament and faith are connected is, of course, brought to the fore in every conversion experience. We cannot understand Methodism without knowing something of how John and Charles Wesley found faith and assurance in 1738. Both found Martin Luther a great catalyst: John through Luther's work on Romans, Charles through Luther's Commentary on St Paul's letter to the Galatians.

Every Christian who seeks to find faith and to grow in grace is bound to wonder how the whole process works. We may consider one example in the form of a question: Does every believer, in the process of repentance and faith, have to go through his or her own Slough of Despond as described in Pilgrim's Progress? Is John Bunyan right in making so much of conviction of sin? I believe it was necessary for him, because he was a special case. Unique examples can teach us general principles, yet not every Christian has to be introduced to the faith in as harsh and difficult a way as Bunyan.

## Saving grace and common grace

Grace means different things, depending on the context. I take it to mean the unmerited favour God shows to men and women in Christ. It includes his mercy and his love shown in the great acts of redemption which make forgiveness and new life possible.

In these sketches I try to consider how this saving grace, mediated by God's Spirit, works in the hearts of men and women. The differing backgrounds against which salvation came to the figures sketched here are the result of what is sometimes called *common grace,* part of the ecology of grace. This aspect of grace is not to do with salvation: it is part of God's general goodness and kindness to undeserving men. I believe it is what is referred to in the Gospels as the rain that falls on the just and unjust. It was wittily described by Lord Bowen:

> The rain it raineth on the just
> And on the unjust fella;
> But more upon the just because
> The unjust stole the just's umbrella.

Those lines touch upon the problem many feel about the unfairness of God's goodness: why should the wicked flourish as the green bay tree? The grace which restrains corruption by blessing us with law, education, medicine and the arts is a part of God's goodness: it deserves our praise and thanks.

I see the 'natural' gifts of many of my heroes as part of God's common grace in action. These gifts, too, come down from the Father of lights. They formed and made their special characters, making them fit vessels for their Master to use in his work.

**Reflecting and refracting God's grace**

I have found it helpful to think of saving grace as light, and the human personality as a prism through which it shines and is diffracted into all the colours of the spectrum.

We are accustomed to thinking of mirrors, since both the apostles Paul and James encourage us to do so. God's word is spoken of as a mirror in which we may see ourselves in the light of the law, and go and act by it, not forgetting what we have seen. More daring is the image of St Paul: 'We all reflect as in a mirror the splendour of the Lord; thus we are transfigured into his likeness, from splendour to splendour; such is the influence of the Lord who is Spirit' (2 Cor. 3: 18, NEB). It is a bold figure of speech, to explain part of the way grace works in us.

Grace is described using many images, and light is surely one of the best. It is used from beginning to end in the Bible, starting with the primeval 'Let there be light' and ending with the final scene in the holy city where the glory of God is its light, and the Lamb is its lamp.

When the light of God's grace shines in a human heart, the way it is diffracted is surely related to the personality in whom that grace is at work. When a prism breaks light down into its constituent parts it shows a rainbow-spread of all the colours: a spectrum of promise. It illustrates the manifold grace of God. In some lives *faith* is the outstanding part of the spectrum of grace that we see: Martin Luther is such a person, for whom it was always *Sola fide,* by faith alone. For Amy Carmichael *love* was the most important thing: she emphasised Calvary love, surely quite rightly.

Shaftesbury might have said that for him *faith working through love* was the hallmark of grace, or at least of grace in action. For Gerard Manley Hopkins the emphasis was on *praise* and seeing God's *glory.*

It will be my intention to try to show that even the flaws in the prism of personality may demonstrate, in a special way, aspects of God's grace. For grace is made perfect in weakness, and its treasure is in earthen vessels which are frequently flawed and cracked. We all know examples of broken earthenware, and may sometimes feel we are examples of this ourselves.

**The temperaments**

In writing these biographical sketches to illustrate how grace works in our lives, I have tried to establish the facts, and to be cautious with explanations. I have taken the best historians I can find as my guides, and where possible I have used the words of those who have written their own accounts in diaries, letters and journals.

I have tried not to speculate, but to tell it as it was. Everyone, however, has a hidden model of personality and temperament. My problem was: which should I choose?

I was tempted to follow Professor Ole Hallesby, the well-known Lutheran writer from Norway. In his book, on *Temperament and the Christian Faith,* he uses Galen's ancient model based on the four humours: the sanguine, the melancholic, the choleric and the phlegmatic.

It is fascinating to observe his method: the apostle Peter is *sanguine:* warm, buoyant and lively. John is the apostle chosen as *melancholic:* dark, gloomy, full of feeling and suffering. Paul is the apostle he chooses to show the *choleric:* hot, quick and active. Hallesby offers no example of the *phlegmatic* person: slow, cool and sober. The phlegmatic folk, with the melancholic, are seen as the solid nucleus of the living Church.

Hallesby's method is to describe the strengths and weaknesses of each temperament, and the problems that each offers in counselling. To his great credit he does not want Christians to deny their temperament and lose all real, individual character. Instead, an individual's temperament should be disciplined, modified and sanctified – but still remain his own.

My decision to abandon the four temperaments was inevitable. The shades of Jung and the way Professor Hans Eysenck had made Jung's views applicable in a scientific way were good reasons for abandoning the four humours. *Extraversion* and *introversion,* with their variants, are much more easily understood. And yet no theory of personality does justice to the complexity of each individual character.

**'Speak of me as I am'**

I have settled for trying to describe the distinguishing traits of personality in my heroes and heroines. To be a slave to any system would be to do violence to their temperaments, to force them to fit a Procrustean bed or a fancy framework. I certainly do not wish to put anyone into a psychiatric strait jacket. I have therefore adopted Othello's suggestion:

> Speak of me as I am, nothing extenuate
> Nor set out aught in malice.

Sometimes an *obsessional* trait stands out, as in the scrupulous perfectionism of Luther or Bunyan in early life. Sometimes a *paranoid* tendency to see enemies (as Shaftesbury saw them, often without reason), emerges under stress. In others the histrionic traits, a tendency, like old-fashioned *hysterics,* to make a drama out of a crisis, is very evident. Sometimes there is much *psychosomatic illness.* The *depressive* tendency, the melancholy in William Cowper, can be dissected carefully and understood in terms of his early experiences and the life events that preceded his attacks.

What of the 'fruits' of suffering? 'Sweet are the uses of adversity,' says the Duke in *As You Like It.* 'It was good for me that I was afflicted,' says Cowper, quoting Psalm 119. The Christian statement of it was made at different times by the apostle Paul: 'We must go through many hardships to enter the kingdom of God.' Our Lord had promised: 'In this world you will have trouble. But take heart! I have overcome the world.'

The waters of Marah were bitter after the Israelites had crossed the Red Sea and started the long desert trek. Moses was shown a piece of wood which, after he had thrown it into the water, made it sweet. Such has been the experience of many Christians, notably those I have, almost at random, chosen to sketch in these pages. Many others, who kept few diaries and may have been less distinguished than those described here, might well add their testimonies.

The experiences of those I have chosen may, I hope, be a source of comfort and encouragement, quite apart from their intrinsic interest and importance in our Christian heritage. Their experience, in some respects, was well described by George Herbert in his poem 'Bitter-sweet':

> Ah my deare angrie Lord,
> Since thou dost love, yet strike;
> Cast down, yet help afford;
> Sure I will do the like.
> I will complain, yet praise;
> I will bewail, approve:
> And all my sowresweet dayes
> I will lament, and love.

I also write to counteract the tendency to paint a picture simply of peace and joy in believing; for there can be painful suffering as well as all the pleasures.

**The transforming power of grace**

The transforming power of grace works at different levels. Luther and Bunyan emphasized how remarkably grace changes our *status*. They reflect the New Testament teaching that we are moved from the dominion of darkness to that of light, to the kingdom of the Son. This basic change has many consequences. We become, in a special way, children by adoption and grace. And as children we become heirs. One of my many reasons for writing is to remind myself, and anyone willing to read on, that our forebears entered into this inheritance on earth while we sometimes live like paupers. The riches of grace can be ours as they were to these heroes of faith.

Grace does not change us as personalities. The bodies, intelligence and natural aptitudes remain the same. Grace does not change temperament. The new life, the new creation, expresses itself through the same old personalities. Some readers may find this a harsh and a wrong judgement, as if I were attempting to make light of the wonder of all things being new when a person is 'in Christ'. But for Amy Carmichael and Christina Rossetti being 'in Christ', union with him by faith, was an important part of how grace transformed them.

How, then, do the changes produced by grace happen? Lifestyles may be completely different, because *behaviour* is changed. Some things are dropped immediately because they are not appropriate for Christians. Other forms of behaviour, more ingrained in the past pattern, may take longer to change. To establish new patterns of living we all need examples to follow, now so often called role-models. Our role-model is Christ, and being conformed to Christ means we are in all things to grow up into him (Eph. 4:15; 5:1; Col. 2:6).

This implies a learning process, something which, to me, stands out throughout the New Testament, as it does in the lives of our heroes. Many Christian heroes can say, as the apostle Paul said: 'You became imitators of us and of the Lord, in spite of severe suffering' (1 Thess. 1:6). Imitative learning has an honourable place in Christian history.

*Attitudes and motives* change. It has often been noted that some people *appear* to get more intelligent after they become Christians. They seem to read more difficult books, because they have a new reason for using their minds. For many different reasons great periods of religious revival are marked by a return to reading basic texts which explain and apply the Bible to our lives. A simple way of describing this is that when we have come to know the Author we wish to read his books and learn more about him. The new life is to do with knowing and loving Christ: wanting to know more of the one we love is a powerful motivator. Our faith, too, needs to grow by knowing more: we exercise newly discovered mental muscles. The faith and love lead to obedience: to wanting to live better lives, more like Christ's own obedience to his Father.

Yet if I am good with words but not with numbers, it is unlikely that grace will turn me into a computer buff. If I can use my head but am clumsy with my hands, I may want to be a carpenter but may find it harder to knock in a nail correctly than to read about the design of chairs.

*Traits*, easily measured by psychologists, are aptitudes which are part of what we inherit and develop because of our genetic potential. Our faith in Christ, and his grace working in us, enables us to use them in new ways. But to try to change our basic personalities, rather than accepting them as part of what we are given, seems to me to lead to endless problems. It is to look for magic, not the miraculous changes that grace brings. It is like looking for spiritual cosmetic surgery, or a brain transplant.

When we are filled with God's Spirit, are we not filled to the capacity that we have been given? The gifts of the Spirit may likewise function within the limits of the natural capacity with which God has endowed us, and he is the Father who knows our frame and remembers that we are but dust. But, of course, exceptional feats may follow such filling with the Spirit. In this area I apply the words of the apostle Paul in Romans 12:3: 'Do not think of yourself more highly than you ought, but rather think of yourself with sober judgment, in accordance with the measure of faith God has given you.'

All things become new, certainly. But they are perceived using the old eyes, the old mind: and therefore the eyes have constantly to be opened to see new things out of God's law; and the mind has constantly to be renewed.

## More than conquerors

While making much of the transforming power of grace, we may also appreciate the human achievement involved. And yet, overcoming the problems posed by our personalities might lead to a pride that is not warranted; that is why the Christian wants to give God the glory. One of Lord Shaftesbury's favourite phrases in his diary was *Non nobis, Domine,* 'Not unto us, O Lord.' He was keen to ascribe all praise to God, as in the famous Reformation watchword *Soli Deo Gloria.*

We wish to magnify God's grace, but we may also observe that some work out their salvation in better ways than others. This is not to advocate an elitism of the select few, but to recognize that in the Gospels and the letters of the New Testament we are made responsible for building on rock not sand, on Christ as the one foundation. We are urged to be careful of how we build, as in the passage which speaks of choosing gold, silver and precious stones to build with, rather than using wood, hay and stubble (1 Cor. 3:12-13).

Thus grace in Christ lays the only foundation, and *enabling* grace allows us to choose how we may build upon it. God graciously gives the talents, one, five or ten, and we are responsible for how we trade with them; how we use our gifts is a matter for audit, both as we go along our pilgrim way and also in a final audit: 'the Day will bring it to light. It will be revealed with fire, and the fire will test the quality of each [person's] work.'

Genius is said to be an infinite capacity for taking pains. What makes the heroes of faith endearing to me is this painstaking, persevering quality of their work and daily lives. It may be considered a failing in them that they were, in some sense, workaholics. Not one seems to have been famous for *play* as opposed to work; leisure did not seem to be very attractive to them. Their lives were full, and a change of occupation seems to have been therapeutic to them. They found a change was as good as a rest, often enough.

They shared with Henry Martyn a fear of trifling, and a wish to be in earnest. Martyn, the young scholar-missionary who worked in India and Persia, died young, having wished to 'burn out for God'. In that same earnest spirit the heroes and heroines here studied tackled their personality problems, accepted or fought their symptoms and illnesses, and triumphed over them in many ways. Amy Carmichael gave Old Testament names to her different pains, and felt it was then easier to fight and to bear them, with wit and humour as well as patience.

Those for whom scrupulous obsessionality might have become a lifelong crippling disorder (as it so often is), seem to have learned to conquer much of it by putting their obsessional anxieties to use, as if it were the water that could drive a mill-wheel. Even depressive thoughts and symptoms could often be utilized, as William Cowper found to his own enrichment, and ours.

But those who are more than conquerors do not have to be perfect: they fall, but are not utterly cast down. They have their scars in front, and are not injured while running away from the fight. That is why Amy Carmichael's poem 'Hast Thou no Scar?' is so profoundly moving. Perhaps it is all a reflection on the greatness of persevering grace, as much as on prevenient grace – the love that God shows in going before us, preparing the way and enabling us to be patient to the very end. Gerard Manley Hopkins, in his darkest moments, is able to express some of these facts magnificently.

At times, in the phrase that C. S. Lewis used to Sheldon Vanauken when his young wife was dying in Oxford, it is a *severe mercy.* Under that mercy any part of our lives may be transfigured, even when we have to march on using the same old body, the same temperament, and fighting the same old nature which militates against our new life in Christ. Not all the heroes and heroines lived to old age; some, like Hopkins, succumbed to typhoid fever in their forties. Yet each one would have joined in the words of Philip Doddridge about his own life:

> His work my hoary age shall bless
> When youthful vigour is no more;
> And my last hour of life confess
> His love has animating power.

**The threefold cord**

I would like to think that it is the animating power of love which is the main strand which runs through the lives of the characters I have sketched. It is seen most clearly in their personal and private lives, but it motivates their public careers too. If it is true that a cord of three strands is not easily broken, it seems to me that their faith in Christ and the hope that he inspires are the other two strands in the gold cord that we may trace.

At their best, these heroes of the faith remind us to 'fix our eyes on Jesus, the author and perfecter of our faith, who for the joy set before him endured the cross, scorning its shame' (Heb. 12:2). They all, in their different ways, admitted that they were pilgrims and strangers, soldiers in an alien land. But they also knew something of the joy set before them: it is a joy of which all Christians, of whatever persuasion, may have that occasional foretaste which makes some sense of their sufferings, and makes their work worthwhile.

*Further Reading*

Anthony Storr, *Churchill's Black Dog* (London: Collins, 1989); O. Hallesby, *Temperament and the Christian Faith* (Minneapolis, MN: Ausburg, 1962); J. Rapaport, *The Boy Who Couldn't Stop Washing* (London: Collins, 1990); William James, *The Varieties of Religious Experience* (originally published 1902, republished Hamondsworth: Penguin Books, 1985).

# 1

# By Grace and Faith Alone: Martin Luther (1483–1546)

> Martin Luther the Reformer is one of the most extraordinary persons in history and has left a deeper impression of his presence in the modern world than any other except Columbus.
>
> Ralph Waldo Emerson, 1835

> I consider myself convicted by the testimony of Holy Scripture, which is my basis; my conscience is captive to the Word of God. Thus I cannot and will not recant, because acting against one's conscience is neither safe nor sound. God help me. Amen.
>
> Martin Luther at the Diet of Worms, 1521

> I did not learn my theology all at once, but I had to search deeper for it, where my trials and temptations took me . . . Living, nay rather dying and being damned make a theologian, not understanding, reading or speculation.
>
> Martin Luther, *Autobiographical Preface,* 1545

Luther's turbulent life (1483–1546) spanned the ending of the Middle Ages and the beginnings of our modern world. It illustrates the struggle to find faith, and shows how grace may affect a man's temperament and then work through it. Luther led the way to the Reformation which, in turn, changed the world.

At twenty, Luther had not seen a Bible. Yet, in the monastery he became a biblical scholar. He tells us that he was a doctor of theology and yet he did not know that he could not expiate his own sins. As Professor of Biblical Theology he struggled for years to know for himself what grace meant. Then he found faith: the trust in Christ that made him 'right' in God's sight. Before Luther, grace had become almost an object, some kind of substance infused by the Church into the believer through the sacraments. After Luther, as has been well said, grace was restored to being a matter of relationship – relationship with a gracious God, made possible through the love and mercy of Christ, and his Spirit who created faith and trust in men and women.

Luther fought passionately to defend this truth once he had found it, in the Bible and in his experience. He believed the honour and glory of God were at stake. He took enormous risks. If we try to understand his temperament, his suffering and illnesses, we may begin to see why he became the pioneer leader in the reform of the Church; the events of his life may explain why his fellow reformers saw him as the foremost prophet of their time.

I believe, with many others who have studied Luther, that it was not only his great ability in many fields, but also his personality and his capacity to suffer anxiety and depression, that helped him to do so much for the Church and for the world.

**What Luther learned**

Luther has been attacked and abused (as well as praised) for four centuries. Only now do Catholics and Protestants begin to agree on his immense strengths, as well as his failings. At a time when the modern world was beginning to take shape, he found out for himself what grace meant.

A panic decision, taken during a storm, led him to become a monk. In the monastery his skill and hard work marked him out. He entered in 1505 at the age of twenty-three, and seven years later became a doctor of theology. Tortured with doubts about himself and his beliefs, he accepted an appointment as Professor of Biblical Theology. How did this professor find salvation? We shall follow his road of discovery. He remained a simple Augustinian friar, for all his fame, until his superior allowed him to leave the order.

No one listening to Luther lecture to sleepy students would have guessed that he was to challenge both Pope and Emperor. He did this simply because he found in the Bible truths about God's grace, and faith in Christ, which lit up his whole mind and compelled his conscience. It was a solitary and painful experience: it led to a lonely stand which began the Protestant Reformation.

What made him such a fighter? Was it just how he was, violent in his swings of mood, sometimes very low and sometimes elated? In his youth, by contrast, he was obsessive and full of scrupulous anxiety.

He went through a period of doubts, vigils and intense study, changing from a man crippled with indecisiveness and perfectionism to a man of action.

His stubborn and strong mind stood up to many tough tests. Both the Emperor and the Pope wanted to silence the obscure monk, Luther. The papal bull named him 'the wild boar who has entered our vineyard': such animals should be searched out and destroyed.

His moods do not by any means explain everything about him. Consider how he was kidnapped by friendly soldiers and put in a safe house, for ten months, in the castle of the Wartburg. There, his isolation and deprivation called for survival skills of a high order. It was a time of great stress. Yet he emerged with an almost complete translation of the New Testament into German. It was a version that any German (whatever his dialect) might read: the first such translation, and a version that has lasted for 400 years. If this was the fruit of a mere manic-depressive, we might well wish that others would have illnesses as productive.

Later Luther married one of the runaway nuns, Katherine von Bora. Together, they created a home in Wittenberg, where celibacy had once been the rule. Luther called marriage a school for character, and his wife and his friends cared for him in his many illnesses. For Luther, and even more for the future pattern of Protestantism, his marriage and home had far-reaching effects.

Luther was a pioneer. At a time when men and women had to pay money to the Church in order to obtain the grace or 'indulgence' of God, Luther dug anew the sources and the springs of the Christian faith, so as to make them available to his people. In this respect, he reminds us of the story of Isaac in the book of Genesis, on which Luther later loved to base many sermons. Isaac, it will be recalled, dug again the wells of water which had been dug in the days of Abraham his father, which the Philistines had stopped.

Luther made the Church an accessible home for the multitudes, who came to know free grace and costly faith. He may not have been an architect, erecting a system of thought and of church government, like John Calvin. But I think (with Professor Gordon Rupp) that he discovered a new world of grace and freedom. Other men may have made better maps of that new world, and taught people to read them, but Luther never lost the wonder of his discovery of the world of grace: he was indeed 'the first that ever burst into that silent sea'.

**Luther's family**

Hans Luder, Martin Luther's father, became a lessee of a coppermine owned by the counts of Mansfeld. He owed a lot of money to the firm that smelted the copper and fixed its price, for his business was subject to market forces in this period of early capitalism.

He has been blamed for the young Martin's nerves, his anxiety and obsessions. True, Hans frequently reminded Martin that he must honour his father, and he was angry that his bright son rejected the legal profession in favour of the monastery, thus exchanging possible wealth for certain poverty. But to say that Hans was the angry God whom Martin feared would be to carry a Freudian fundamentalism too far. When we examine the faces of Margaret and Hans Luder, in the portraits left to us by Lucas Cranach, we see the effects of their hard life; they look as if they did their best for him, as Luther later confirmed.

Eight children were born to them. Only three sisters and one brother survived with Martin. His mother has been characterized as a superstitious and ignorant peasant. The truth is that her family, the Lindemanns, were burghers who were keen on education. Their status, in fact, is thought to have helped Hans to obtain good credit in a risky industry. Their place in the world is illustrated by Martin's cousin, who became a court physician. Lindemann influence may have led to Martin having eleven years schooling and then a place at Erfurt University: an exceptional education for his time. Martin later remembered life with this large extended family as an educational experience in itself.

The stories of Luther's mother as a poor bath-house attendant are absurd. She was said to have had sex with the devil: thus making Martin demon possessed. Such ridiculous reports, retailed in diplomatic dispatches to the Vatican, persisted for three centuries.

Luther described the severe punishments his parents gave him: was this child abuse? His mother beat him till the blood came, for stealing a nut. He recalls his father giving him a whipping: 'I ran away from him; I was upset till he was able to overcome the distance.' Again Luther writes: 'The serious and austere life they led with me later caused me to enter a monastery and become a monk; but they meant it very well indeed.'

His parents' discipline was in keeping with the time. And Luther's early education in Mansfeld was equally severe. His teacher might strike him fifteen times in a morning. Weekends at school were watched over by an older pupil, and any violations of school rules were reported with a view to punishment.

At fourteen Martin was moved to Magdeburg. He was taught by a reforming group called the Brethren of the Common Life. Here he began to forget the tortures of Mansfeld. But his early training had certainly affected him: he was already set in rigid ways and was punitive with himself. After a year at Magdeburg he moved to Eisenach, where he remained for four years. He was a guest of a family friend (later Mayor of Eisenach), and it was this 'college experience' which prepared him for Erfurt, the third largest German university at that time.

Luther must have been a conscientious pupil. On first entering Erfurt he came thirtieth out of fifty-seven candidates in the examination results, but at the end of four years, in the examination leading to a Master of liberal arts, he came second out of seventeen. However, there was little, then, to indicate how Luther would change the future of Germany and the world.

## Luther's inheritance

His time at Erfurt University made him a philosopher, trained and moulded in medieval thought. 'My master Occam was the greatest dialectician,' he said, referring to the English philosopher William of Occam. Those who wish to attack Luther as unoriginal say he must have learned about grace from the great scholastic writers. He did indeed study scrupulously, and knew some writings on the sacraments by heart. But this did not make him happy. I think it was part of his obsessional temperament that he had to memorise the ritual and could only then hope (wrongly as it turned out) to be able to cope with it without anxiety.

Luther had to leave philosophy behind. He had to learn from the

Bible and from St Paul in particular. He turned to St Augustine. First he attacked Aristotle, calling Reason the 'Devil's Whore'. Then he turned to lecturing on the Psalms. It was at this time that he began, slowly and painfully, over a period of years, to find joy and peace in believing.

This experience came after he left the university and the study of law, and joined the Augustinian monastery at Erfurt as a result of his momentous decision in the thunderstorm, when he fell to the ground and prayed to St Anne, vowing to become a monk if he survived. Later, this occurrence was to be compared with the experience of Saul of Tarsus on the road to Damascus. But even without such comparison there was drama enough.

In deciding, during a storm, to become a monk, Luther acted as a child of his time. The end of the Middle Ages had its strong superstitions and belief systems. The cult of St Anne (the mother of Mary) was very powerful in young Luther's world, and in his mind. His was a built-in response to being caught in what he felt to be the life-threatening danger of the wild forces of nature. He believed that to honour his vow and become a monk was his sacred duty. Thus the imperatives of his world, where saints and superstition existed alongside learning and philosophy, drove him to seek acceptance in the monastery of the Augustinian friars.

**The young monk**

What sort of monk was Luther? There is no doubt about his devout intentions in seeking to follow the rules of his order. Before being accepted as a novice he would have been questioned in detail by the monks. At the appointed service, the prior would have asked: 'What do you seek here?' The reply set down for Martin, as for every novice, was that he sought 'the gracious God and his mercy'.

Luther's clothes would then have been taken away and exchanged for the 'spiritual habit'. The monk's clothes, which he was to wear for the next year, were the black robes of his outward habit. But he was to learn, painfully, a more important inner habit. The closed world he learned to live in, with its deeply conformist religious ways, greatly heightened the pressures he felt from his already sensitive conscience. I think he was already set in obsessional patterns of thinking and behaving, but the new monastic regime increased the demands made upon him. He tried, as he said later, 'to appease God by doing good works', and his 'heart trembled as to whether God would bestow his grace' upon him.

The first year passed. During the next year he would have to celebrate his first mass. Much has been made of this because of what is described as 'the fit in the choir'. Luther almost passed out at the altar where he was supposed to officiate. Some thought it was a kind of epilepsy, others just an attack of nerves. What really happened?

I think Luther was scrupulously conscientious. Although he had learned by heart most of the words (and teaching) of the office of the mass, he nevertheless suffered something that looked like stage fright. Just as his obsessive and compulsive disorder led him to feel an urge to blaspheme, so high anxiety played a *part,* but only a part, in this experience.

For a better understanding of what happened we must listen to Luther himself. Later in life he recalled the event clearly: 'I, ashes, dust, and full of sin, speak with the living, eternally true God. This cannot but cause one to tremble, as I did when I celebrated my first mass....' It was the tremendous mystery of God's holiness, the sense of the holy, the awful presence of the divine, which Luther felt on that occasion. In the same passage he went on to say, with rejoicing: 'Joyous faith, however, which rests on the mercy and the Word of God, overcomes the fear of his majesty ... and rises boldly above it.'

**Spiritual conflicts**

How did Luther come to joyous faith? He did not learn it all at once, but had to search along a path embattled with trials and conflicts. His own word was *Anfechtung,* meaning a special kind of temptation or test. The crisis when he first officiated at mass was the outward and visible sign of an inward spiritual distress from which he had suffered for years.

Luther recalls: 'After vigils, fasts, prayers and exercises of the toughest kind, with which as a monk I afflicted myself almost to death, yet the doubt was left in my mind, and I thought who knows whether these things are pleasing to God? ... The more holy, the more uncertain I became.' Doubt and unbelief were the ultimate temptations for him.

What was going on? Profound anxiety must have formed part of the life of someone who was as much of a perfectionist as Luther. It arose from what John Bunyan was later to call *'a bruised conscience'*. I think Luther learned painfully that he could not, by his own efforts, find what he so much wanted, namely, peace and joy in the presence of a loving and merciful God.

**Scruples and obsessions**

It used to be clear what 'scruples' and 'scrupulosity' meant, but nowadays these words may need to be defined. Oddly enough, they come from the Latin *scrupulus,* meaning a small sharp stone. Luther's sense of humour may have been tickled by this derivation when, in later life, his bladder and kidney stones were nearly killing him. He said then: 'It's the devil's fault, of course. He takes whatever he can to pester me with. He stoned Stephen with stones; he stones me with the stone.' But *scrupulum* also meant a small division of weight, which gives the further implication of a sensitive conscience, weighed down by minute matters.

A recent Catholic encyclopaedia defines 'scrupulosity' as 'habitual and unreasonable hesitation or doubt, coupled with anxiety of mind, in connection with the making of moral judgements'. A recent medical text compares it with obsessions thus:

| SCRUPULOSITY | OBSESSIVE-COMPULSIVE DISORDER |
|---|---|
| 1. Persistent concern with thought, word or deed. | 1. Persistent intrusive idea, thought, or impulse. |
| 2. Thoughts cause much uneasiness and distress. | 2. Ritual or thought causes distress, and is seen as alien to the person. |
| 3. Person compelled and obsessional. | 3. Thoughts or actions performed with a feeling of compulsion. |
| 4. Occurs in healthy person. | 4. Not due to another mental or physical disorder. |

(adapted from J. Rapaport, *The Boy Who Couldn't Stop Washing)*

We need to distinguish sharply between the obsessional but otherwise healthy personality, and an illness or *disorder* which causes the patient, and others around, much distress. The following checklist, compiled by the American Psychiatric Association for a diagnostic manual, is widely used in English-speaking countries. At least five of the following must be present, and cause problems, before a diagnosis of obsessive-compulsive personality disorder may be made:

1. Restricted ability to express warm and tender emotions.
2. Perfectionism that interferes with overall ability to see the needs of a situation.
3. Insistence that others submit to the person's way of doing things without awareness of how it makes others feel.
4. Excessive devotion to work to the exclusion of pleasure.
5. Indecisiveness to the point where decisions are postponed, avoided, or protracted (perhaps because of a great fear of making a mistake). Assignments may not get done on time because of ruminating about priorities.
6. Preoccupation with details, rules, lists or schedules to the extent that the major point of the activity is lost.
7. Overconscientiousness, scrupulousness, and inflexibility about moral and ethical matters.
8. Lack of generosity in giving time, money or gifts.
9. Inability to discard worn or worthless objects.

We must bear in mind that this list was produced after much discussion by many learned men, experienced in the field. One item, let us recall, is not enough – there must be five, together, and for a certain length of time, to qualify as a properly diagnosed personality disorder.

Such a brief excursion into definitions may be helpful, since John Bunyan, Gerard Manley Hopkins, J. B. Phillips and Christina Rossetti, as well as Luther, have all been described by themselves or by others as suffering from this disorder at some time or in some degree. We will return to a more careful description of the features as we proceed. It will be seen from these two lists that an obsessive-compulsive disorder is a serious and damaging condition. Many researchers believe it is more common than anyone thought. It is often well hidden by the secretive sufferers, and those who have it are often the last to recognize it, or to do something about it.

**Luther looks for help**

It seems to me that during his most obsessional years as a monk, Luther, like all obsessionals I have known, considered that everyone should be like him: perfection was, after all, the goal of any monk with a proper vocation.

In the next few years, although he was a devout monk who had a sense of living in God's presence, Luther's condition grew worse. Like many Christians before and after him, the God he then knew seemed to him to be a God of *wrath* and *judgement.*

It has been suggested that he was disillusioned with his calling as a monk. I think this was not so, for he strove to be a better monk. He felt he must fulfil, in all minute particulars, his vows of poverty, chastity and obedience. And he spoke up in protest when some brethren sought exemption from the strict Rule of the order. It was hard for Luther to know how he could further please God.

He turned to a favourite author, Gabriel Biel, whose words on the sacraments he had memorized. Biel saw the need for God's supernatural grace. But there were pitfalls. We must, in our own hearts, experience the indwelling love of God, said Biel. And he went on to say that there was no sure way of knowing if that love was present. We could not know if our love was real and genuine, or perhaps the false, feigned love of the hypocrite. Luther found little comfort in this.

He sought help from the mystics, for there was a strong German tradition based on the way of the mystic ladder. Might Luther thus ascend to God and find him? There was great appeal in the idea that he might give up striving, and instead surrender to the Everlasting, 'and in the abyss of Being find his peace'. At times this seemed to work and Luther felt uplifted and elated. But then would follow further darkness and alienation, and the emptiness which the mystic way said was to be expected. Luther became more desperate, as his words show: 'I was myself more than once driven to the very abyss of despair so that I wished I had never been created. Love God? I hated him!'

Help came through his spiritual director, whom he later called his 'father in Christ', John Staupitz. We all, at times in life, need someone (like Bunyan's Evangelist) to point the way to the wicket gate, or at least to yonder shining light. This wise, humorous, and experienced monk was also like an interpreter to Luther at this vital time of crisis.

**Staupitz: spiritual director**

It was Staupitz who encouraged Luther to study for a doctorate, and later appointed him professor to succeed himself. But he also had a much more important role: he guided Luther, like his spiritual child, in the faith. He told him that it was he, Luther, who was angry with God, and not God who was angry with him. Staupitz drew his attention to the facts about God's tender mercy, and tried to point Luther to 'the wounds of Jesus'.

Luther could see Christ only as his judge – a judge condemning him, always against him, never for him. The righteousness of Christ meant, for Luther, simply God's *demanding* justice: blaming, finding fault and never, never taking his side. All this made Luther lonely and frightened: it was a time of painful suffering.

Staupitz was very shrewd: he wondered if Luther was, in some way, actually enjoying his miseries. Luther, at that time, thought that his suffering was part of a process of inner attrition and contrition. If this was a process required of the devout Christian, why did it seem so endless? It was then that Staupitz did a strange thing. He appointed this young, unhappy, doubting monk Professor of Biblical Theology at Wittenberg.

Later, Luther would speak much of the need to 'plough oneself' as part of a preparation for repentance and faith. But before that 'ploughing' of mind and heart (which, for him, led to sowing and reaping in abundance) something else was necessary, namely, a deliberate turning away from his efforts at self-righteousness.

For Luther had a system of his own to help him in his devotions. It included remembering twenty-one saints, three for every day of the week. He would also, as a matter of unshakeable habit, pay his respects to any image of Christ such as a crucifix in a very unusual way – with a prayer to Mary. It was as if (to quote Roland Bainton) he was fleeing from the angry Son to the merciful mother.

How wise his director and confessor was! And he had to be obeyed. Luther was forced to turn from such devotional wrestling to contend instead with the Bible. Instead of the rituals, from morning to evening, and the frequent night-time vigils, in which he examined himself and tried thus to find some enlightenment, his task, as professor, was to find the words and message of a merciful God *in Scripture.*

Looking back on this experience, Luther was to see it as God's 'strange work'. Strange because God's law, as he experienced it, made him feel much *worse* at first, and better only afterwards. His own sense of sin and failure was very like that of the Slough of Despond as later described by Bunyan.

**A professor finds faith**

Luther does not speak of a *sudden* conversion in his life, as Calvin does. We know that for Luther conversion was a slow and lengthy process, spanning the three years in which he prepared and delivered his lectures on the Psalms and on St Paul's letter to the Romans.

It would be easy to think that it all happened while Luther was on a visit to Rome. His son tells how – while ascending the steps of St Peter's on his knees – Luther recalled the words, 'The just shall live by faith.' His trip to Rome (an important errand for his order, and an arduous journey by foot there and back) was indeed a very significant one. However, all it brought Luther was further disillusionment with the papacy. He was an innocent abroad, and to hear dissolute priests racing through their masses in Rome, the place which represented the very centre of his faith, was too much for him.

To get a truer picture of Luther's conversion, we must try and imagine Luther lecturing to sleepy students in those three years. While preparing for his early morning lectures, his own private struggle was proceeding. (The *public* drama of confrontation and conflict had not yet started.) By a splendid stroke of good fortune, we are helped by Luther's own Bible, which was found, lying in a showcase, in the Royal Library in Berlin. Scholars seized on the discovery. They could now trace his thoughts and experience in the copious notes written in those wide margins, for Luther had a special Bible printed for the purpose of his lectures.

We must ponder Luther's own words as he recalled his progress during these years of study:

> At last, God being merciful, as I meditated day and night on the connection of the words, 'the justice of God is revealed' and 'the just shall live by faith', I began to understand that the justice of God is *that by which the just live by the gift of God* .... This straightway made me feel as though reborn, and as though I had entered through open gates to paradise itself. From then on, the whole face of Scripture appeared different ... As much as I had previously hated the expression 'righteousness of God', I now loved and treasured it ... as that righteousness *through which we are made righteous.*

**Public debates**

Luther's new-found faith was in sharp contrast to what was going on around him in the Germany of his day and age. Johann Tetzel and the sale of indulgences are but one example. This friar with a genius for raising money was hawking indulgences all over Germany, and at that time was approaching Wittenberg. The practice of selling indulgences was based on the notion that the Church had a treasury of grace on offer. Even if this were true, Tetzel's debauched methods debased and dishonoured any teaching of grace. The friar would set up shop in a market-place, and letters were sold granting forgiveness for sins committed (or even *to be* committed in the future). Worse still, loved ones who had died could be 'bought out' of purgatory. A common rhyme, to help the sale of these letters of indulgence, was:

> As soon as the coin in the coffer rings
> The soul from purgatory springs.

It was a setting for a fight, and Luther nailed his ninety-five theses to the door of the castle church in Wittenberg, calling for a public debate on the issue of indulgences. It was a time-honoured academic procedure. Luther was questioning the doctrinal basis for these practices.

A year later (in 1518), there were public debates at the Heidelberg

Disputation and the Diet of Augsburg. The Vatican sent Cardinal Cajetan to demand that Luther recant; he would not. Luther's life was in increasing danger. Attempts were made to banish or extradite him. His patron, the Elector Frederick, protected him. He was released from his monastic vows by Staupitz, lest the Augustinian order might be asked to deliver him up for judgement and execution as a heretic. It was like a friendly, protective excommunication from the order.

The pressures mounted at the Disputation in Leipzig in 1519, and reached a climax at the Diet of Worms in 1521. Though trembling and fearful, Luther would not recant. The words 'Here I stand, I can do no other' have echoed often since Worms. We may read, in Luther's own hand, what he said to the Emperor Charles V in 1521: 'As long as my conscience is captive to the Holy Scriptures, which have furnished evidence for all my books, I cannot recant if I am not proven wrong.'

What a change in this obscure friar! The sad and scrupulous monk was now a fighter. To use a modern phrase, the worrier had become a warrior. That was one of the greatest effects of God's grace on Luther's character. Facing the worst that could happen to a heretic, he recalled the Bohemian John Hus who in 1415 was burned for his faith: 'We are all Hussites now,' he said.

He was not to die, but the Pope formally excommunicated him. The Emperor placed him under a ban, an edict at Worms forbade anyone to shelter Luther; he was to be seized and delivered to the authorities. The edict allowed twenty-one days' delay, and what followed is like an adventure of Robin Hood. Luther was returning from Worms to Wittenberg, slowly, pausing along the way to visit friends and to preach. Suddenly, while going through a wood, soldiers seized him, and took him to the castle of the Wartburg. The Emperor had sent friendly men to abduct him, and Luther was to spend ten months as a prisoner. During this time his hair and beard grew till he could appear as *Junker Georg,* his identity hidden by pretending to be a medieval knight.

So effective was the disguise that when he returned to Wittenberg it was said that his friend Cranach painted his portrait without recognizing him behind the beard and without the monk's tonsure. Looking at modern reproductions of that splendid portrait, it is hard to believe the story; perhaps Cranach was helping Luther to preserve his 'cover'. Later, two boys were allowed to accompany Luther, as pages, on outings to the woods around the castle. When on one occasion this 'knight' took out a book to read, his cover was nearly blown; in those early days of printing, books were a rare commodity, and few knights could read them!

Luther called the Wartburg 'my Patmos', disguising his whereabouts in his letters to friends. His room had a retractable staircase for greater security. Even the castle jailers had no idea of the identity of their distinguished prisoner. He busied himself with his studies and his writings, but suffered from a degree of sensory deprivation, the absence of the friends, students and colleagues who were so important to him. He became depressed, as we shall see.

**Luther's achievements**

Having translated the New Testament into German during his ten-month exile, Luther went on to translate the whole Bible. Of course other scholars helped him, including Philipp Melanchthon, the young Professor of Greek at Wittenberg. Yet it was Luther's Bible; his lasting gift to the German people was a unifying language for German Christians. His Bible is still in use 400 years later.

Luther's hymns might also merit a book to themselves. He wrote both the words and the music *(Ein'feste Burg,* 'A safe stronghold', became a kind of battle hymn of the Reformation). No translation can entirely do justice to the rugged German original, but Thomas Carlyle goes some way towards capturing its majesty in his memorable verses:

A safe stronghold our God is still
A trusty shield and weapon:
He'll help us clear from all the ill
That hath us now o'ertaken.
The ancient prince of hell
Hath risen with purpose fell:
Strong mail of craft and power
He weareth in this hour,
On earth is not his fellow.

With force of arms we nothing can,
Full soon were we down-ridden;
But for us fights the proper Man,
Whom God Himself has bidden.
Ask ye who is this same?
Christ Jesus is His name,
The Lord Saboath's Son;
He and no other one,
Shall conquer in the battle.

God's word, for all their craft and force,
One moment will not linger,
But spite of hell, shall have its course;
'Tis written by His finger.
And, though they take our life,
Goods, honour, children, wife,
Yet is their profit small;
These things shall vanish all;
The city of God remaineth.

George MacDonald, the Scots minister and writer so much admired by C. S. Lewis, translated all Luther's hymns into English. They show that he wanted to share his experience of grace, and used the Psalms (as many others have done) to express his faith in song. The old German hymns and folktunes provided him with a ready seed-bed, as it were, and out of the traditions sprang something new. It has been said that the sudden bursting forth of the Lutheran chorale is one of the most thrilling chapters in the history of the Reformation.

Three short books written in 1520 were Luther's manifesto. By their titles – *Address to the Christian Nobility of the German Nation, The Babylonian Captivity of the Church* and *The Freedom of a Christian* – they may not have seemed like books that would shake Europe. However, because of the invention of printing less than a century earlier, Luther's words spread swiftly. Their effect was incalculable: the way folk thought about faith, the Church and the state, all were affected. The sixty-one volumes in German (fifty-five in English translation) are a huge harvest, and a rich industry of Lutheran studies has grown up. This chapter owes a great deal to modern writers on Luther.

While many facets of Luther are brought out by recent scholars in their studies, millions who know nothing about him have heard his message sung to the music of J. S. Bach. For Bach, reared two centuries later in the shadow of the Wartburg, at Eisenach, was (as Professor A. G. Dickens put it) 'a deeply engaged Lutheran and by any sensible definition the greatest Evangelical Christian of his age'.

In his teaching Luther brought out his concept of the ordinary Christian's calling. George Herbert (owing much to Luther) wrote in his hymn:

> A servant with this clause
> Makes drudgery divine,

and we may all join in. And we do so because Luther removed religion from the cloister to the hearth, the kitchen and the ordinary home and household. As Professor James Atkinson described: 'his birth saw the death of the old world, and his death the birth of the new, the world we now live in, and more than any other person his life contributed to that change'.

Many historic events followed Luther's stand. He was a patriot rather than a nationalist. His effect on Europe was considerable. Partly as a result of his influence, sovereign nations were founded. A new capitalist economy emerged. Society and its classes were never the same again. Yet, for all this, Luther was not a politician. He was concerned with the gospel he had rediscovered. He was a servant of God's word. He stated all this explicitly:

> See how much he has been able to accomplish through me, though I did no more than pray and preach. The Word did it all. Had I wished I might have started a conflagration at Worms. But while I sat still and drank beer with Philipp and Amsdorf, God dealt the Papacy a mighty blow.

**Luther's unhappy legacy**

Luther was coarse in language. He attacked Jews, and hence the Nazis could quote him in support of their dreadful atrocities. It has been pointed out that Erasmus, the humanist, spoke even worse of

Jews, as did other eminent Christian leaders before him. But that does not excuse Luther in any way.

We must remind ourselves that it was the age of Rabelais, of coarse humour and dirty language, used and accepted by most; there was little sweetness and light. Enemies were attacked in arguments of vitriolic fierceness. When I read that John Wesley (that fastidious Fellow of Lincoln College, Oxford) loved Luther's 'good old earthy gospel', I wonder how far his reading went! All the images then current, from closet and privy, are present. Luther's writing is at times, as has been said, God's word in filthy language.

Those Freudians who see it all as 'the anal stage of development' (which is their way of describing an obsessional person) do scant justice to the times. Woodcuts from all sides of the discussions show similar lavatorial concerns. Luther used scatology to attack the Pope, other men and the devil: he was fighting for his life and for the truth.

Luther's most serious attacks on the Jews were in his later life. In his early years he had been known as a friend to Jews. He wrote of the guilt for Christ's death being ours, not simply theirs. Luther's tragedy is part of a wider one, namely the long history of enmity between Christians and Jews. The calls that Luther made to burn books and synagogues cannot be justified and must be deplored. In his later years Jews, Turks and infidels were all lumped together as enemies of the gospel.

Many might feel that Luther's part in the Peasants' War was also a deeply unhappy affair. The peasants had hoped he would support them, but Luther thought it his duty to support law and order. Many critics (then and since) have found the means he advocated hard to forgive.

In John Osborne's play *Luther* there is a scene where a dead peasant is wheeled on to the stage in a cart; the implied accusation is that Luther had failed to help the peasants as he should have done. The words of Gordon Rupp are more measured:

> Luther did not 'let down the Peasants', for, as they framed their cause, he had never taken them up, but he did read, as his critics never seem to read, the fanatic tracts of the peasant leaders who looked with pleasurable anticipation to disorder and anarchy, in the midst of which, as Luther well knew, the real matter of the Reformation would have been engulfed.

Some radical Christians (such as the Anabaptists) felt they were treated as stepchildren, and they turned away from Luther's reformation. They had to pursue their own, more radical reformation.

They wanted to owe less to the established churches and be more truly free and independent. Many of us may feel today that our hearts (and often our heads) are with these radicals: but Luther was wary of them, and had to defend what he had won. His is sometimes called the magisterial reformation, to distinguish it from the more radical reformation pursued by others like the Anabaptists.

**Two enemies**

In seeking a balance to preserve the faith (and also perhaps his own sanity), Luther had two special enemies. They were the philosophers and the ecstatics. Typical of the philosophers was Erasmus. There were others, like the heavenly prophets from Zwickau, who were among the fanatical enthusiasts of the day.

Erasmus seemed at first a friend to Luther. When his Greek New Testament arrived in Wittenberg it was welcomed by Luther. But when Erasmus wrote his book *On the Freedom of the Will,* it provoked Luther to write *On the Bondage of the Will.* These are both available today, and the debate is still alive. While Erasmus was dealing with one aspect of the will, Luther was concerned only with its relation to God's grace. It seems that Erasmus was less profound in his knowledge of both psychology and grace. He may have had a less solid knowledge of the texts also. Luther could not abide his scepticism: 'Take away assertions and you take away Christianity ... for the Holy Spirit is not a sceptic, nor has he written on our hearts our own doubts and opinions, but assertions far more certain and firm than life itself and all human experience.'

Luther wanted to show that grace was God's initiative, and that the human response was the work of his Spirit. He wanted all the credit and all the glory to be ascribed to God. Erasmus and he were arguing from different premises.

His fight with the ecstatics, the fanatics, was even more difficult. They saw Luther as an ally. Had he not recognized that reason was of no use, and that faith, the work of the Spirit in the heart, was of supreme importance? But Luther believed also that there was a great danger that (in the words of G. K. Chesterton) 'the inner light could lead to the outer darkness'. When the 'heavenly prophets' came to Wittenberg, Luther doubted their claims. He felt it his duty, after talking with them and discerning their spirits, to send them packing.

He saw their emphasis on special gifts of the Spirit, and associated claims to direct inspiration, as an attack on his work. A balance was needed between the word and the Spirit. There was an external testimony in Scripture, and an internal witness in the Christian believer's heart. Anything that upset the balance had to be fought, tooth and nail. Luther seemed to be perpetually engaged in fights.

**How ill was Luther?**

Luther was often ill in body, but was he mentally ill? His suffering from kidney stones has been graphically described. Perhaps the full significance of his kidney trouble has not been realized. A Danish psychiatrist, Paul Reiter, concludes that Luther was both a manic-depressive and an alcoholic. But his work has been censured by historians and biographers.

For instance, the effects of Luther's kidney troubles – as chronic as those of a renal failure patient nowadays kept alive by renal dialysis – are not allowed by Reiter. He considers that Luther shows evidence of presenile dementia at the age of forty-seven. Now we would judge the ill-effects of chronic kidney problems and consequent uraemia (a kind of chemical blood-poisoning) to be the cause, in Luther's case, of prolonged mental confusion, so easily mistaken for failing mental powers.

On one occasion, at a conference in Hesse, the blockage caused by kidney and bladder stones was so bad that Luther seemed near to death. There was retention of urine and gross swelling of his body, all remedies having failed to help. He insisted on going back to his native Saxony to die, and the Elector John Frederick encouraged him to travel along the mountain roads in his own ornate coach. The rough roads must have dislodged the stones causing the obstruction, for when the caravan stopped Luther was able to pass two gallons of urine and slowly recovered.

Such instances were repeated in milder forms, and one historian sees the kidney damage as causing typical symptoms of chronic renal failure: irritability, and difficulty in remembering and concentrating. Luther's worst personality traits came to the fore during his last nine years as a result of these transient states of confusion due to physical problems. This can happen in any confused state (and perhaps we should remember that Luther had angina, and presumably poor heart function as well). Few famous men have had students and friends write down remarks in casual, unguarded talk, as happened with Luther's *Table Talk.* To blame the exchanges disclosed here on alcohol or mental illness, when the symptoms were secondary to kidney problems, would be a serious error.

Reiter is criticised by historians on two further counts. First, he fails to grasp the essential nature of Luther's spiritual experiences. Second, he shows 'a singular and disastrous inability to comprehend, or make any sense of, Luther's theology'.

I think that only from within the household of faith can we ever begin to understand Luther correctly. His theology seems to me the most vital thing about him, and in essentials his experience is like that of the apostle Paul, St Augustine, and other Christian believers. Yet, even if we accept all that, we still have to decide what we are to make of his drinking, his personality and his mood disorder.

He certainly drank too much Wittenberg beer and wine on some occasions. There is no evidence of serious alcoholism. Beer may have helped him during times of anxiety and distress. It was (opium derivatives apart) perhaps the most effective drug he had available. After a few days in bed and the extra beer, he would recover. We must not strain or maltreat the evidence.

The young Luther seems, by general agreement, to have been full of scruples and a perfectionist. The negative side of an obsessional personality is that the anxieties can be great and the tendency to depression strong. The positive side of such a personality is the strength and devotion to detail; the meticulous scholarship of Luther shows this. For all his complaints and misery as a monk, he was evidently as strong as an ox. He coped with an enormous work-load of all kinds. He brought to all he did a strong and subtle intelligence. Had he the kind of rigidity that some obsessionals have, instead of the tough suppleness that enabled him to adapt, he might have had more breakdowns.

How serious was his mood disorder? I think nowadays he would have been diagnosed as having an affective disorder, with as much anxiety as depression in his periods of illness. What I mean by this is that Luther suffered panic attacks and severe symptoms of anxiety. He called his frequent sweating attacks 'the Devil's bath'. Perhaps a monk who was a professor, standing apparently against both the Pope and the Emperor at one and the same time, was entitled to feel a good deal of anxiety. But I think Luther describes *both* some quite understandable anxiety and depression, *and* attacks which he himself saw as part of an illness.

**His depression and his faith**

I believe there was a marked physical and constitutional element in Luther's tendency to depression. I do not see clear evidence that he was ever manic, elated or ill because of an upward mood swing. However, he might now be diagnosed as a cyclothymic personality, with many mood swings which, though significant, were never such as to cause a psychosis.

One illness is well described. In 1527 Luther was suffering both physically and with depression. He was forty-four. He collapsed physically and was expected to die. Two close friends were called to witness his faith on his deathbed. A professor of medicine was also called. The ice-cold Luther was wrapped in hot towels and after a few hours was declared out of danger. He was ill for a week or so, and then began to write accounts of the illness to his friends. Two pastors who attended him also recorded their own observations.

Luther saw this 1527 illness as partly physical and partly psychological. Three months after his collapse, he wrote to a friend asking him to pray for him, since he was 'haunted by anguish ... a miserable worm plagued by the spirit of sadness'. Of course Luther saw a spiritual aspect in his collapse, as he did in most life events. He thought it right to attribute it to an attack of the devil. We must repeat that there is no evidence that he was ill with depression in any *psychotic* way; that is to say, his reasoning powers were not affected. Whatever his illnesses, Luther would very soon be back on a punishing schedule of giving lectures and sermons and writing books, pamphlets and letters.

What of the legend that he threw an inkpot at the devil? An earlier account has the devil throwing the inkpot at Luther. To be locked up in the Wartburg castle entailed sensory deprivation similar to that described by prisoners and those who have taken part in experiments in small black rooms. Even quite normal folk, doing it for a fee, find that such periods of being deprived of company and sound and light may quickly (in as little as three days) produce hallucinations and delusions. A large element of the stresses of deprivation, even though it was not total or complete, must be allowed.

Tricks of the mind resulting from such loneliness are not signs of illness. At first Luther's captivity was strict, for his own safety. The anxiety of being a hunted man – hunted by Pope and Emperor – added to the strain. The most remarkable thing is that he produced letters, books and his German translation of the New Testament. Occupational therapy of a kind that has had lasting value resulted from his enforced isolation!

**The German Hercules**

The most remarkable thing about Luther was his strength. He was called the German Hercules, partly because of his work in cleaning up the 'stables' of Germany, and later of Europe. It is not surprising that, like his great hero the apostle Paul, he often experienced his inner strength as greater at times of physical weakness. He could say often, 'For when I am weak, then I am strong' (2 Cor. 12:9-10). He was aware of his moods, his bad temper and his aggressive attacks. They were all part of the way he lived, the way he was.

He died at the age of sixty-three, unexpectedly, while visiting Eisleben to sort out a disagreement between two families, which he succeeded in resolving successfully. He preached at Eisleben four days before he died. His young and gentle colleague Philipp Melanchthon was often teased by Luther for his devotion to astrology. But he praised Philipp for setting out in a masterly and systematic way in his famous book *Loci Communes* what Luther could express only with many words and much aggression. Luther freely admitted being both long-winded and always on the attack.

To Philipp fell the task of a brief funeral oration. He recalled finding Luther frequently on his knees, with tears running down his cheeks, praying for the universal Church. Recalling Luther's severe and harsh ways and remedies, he said:

> Some ... have complained that Luther was more vehement than need required. I will not dispute against any: but I answer thus; that Erasmus has often said: God has given this last age a sharp Physician, because of the great diseases of the same, and therefore ... in vain they quarrel with God.

For all his faults, Luther found in the plain meaning of the Bible a God who was there, and there for him, as a God of grace and mercy. Above all, he found Christ in all the Scriptures; God in Christ was *for* him, no longer *against* him. Referring to the words of Christ about searching the Scriptures, Luther translates: 'So that in it you discover Me, Me.' Christ became the centre of his world.

Grace was the love and forgiveness he could *never* merit. The righteousness of Christ was the robe that the Father had prepared for the prodigal son while that son was a great way off. And faith was the one thing needful: to trust, to accept and to experience the way that God himself had prepared to make us righteous.

Having been made right, justified by faith, the Christian knows and feels three things about himself, said Luther: *He is always a sinner, he is always penitent, and he is always justified.* At one and the same time and *always* he is both a sinner and also a person whom God holds, in Christ, to have been made right in his sight.

And of course this living faith must produce good works, as a tree that has been made good must bear good fruit. The person who has been reckoned by God to be righteous in Christ will strive to become more and more the person who *is* righteous and lives rightly. This faith, which cost Luther so much study and struggle, helped him to lose the anxiety and obsessiveness that dogged his younger years. It transformed him, and in turn became an experience shared by many other Christians.

**Loving and hating Luther**

More than many other prominent leaders, Luther seems to have divided people into two camps, those for and those against him. It is worth asking why.

Those who love him may be seen – in a series of snapshots – through four centuries. Hugh Latimer, for instance, describes in a sermon preached in 1552, how Luther's influence reached Cambridge in the 1520s. Luther's books had been burned there, but were so much loved by the Society of Christian Brethren that they imported them. His books, of which Cambridge wanted more and more, often arrived in bales of cloth from Holland, to supply a kind of 'forbidden book-of-the-month club', as Rupp described it. Latimer describes what happened after Thomas Bilney (who was a martyr years before Latimer himself) heard Latimer attack Melanchthon. Latimer writes:

> He came to see me afterward in my study, and desired me, for God's sake, to hear his confession. I did so; and, to say the truth, by his confession I learned more than before in many years. So from that time forward I began to smell the word of God, and forsook the school-doctors and such fooleries.

This is but one example, out of many from the 1520s, of men who learned from Luther, and came to love him for what he gave them; many died for the faith they found in Christ through him. John Bunyan, a hundred years later, is an outstanding example of how Luther's work lived on after his death, for Luther, far more than Calvin, made Bunyan what he was.

Moving on a further hundred years, to 1738, we glimpse John and Charles Wesley experiencing a faith made vital, clearer and more certain through Luther's writings. Thus it is evident that the truths Luther found with so much pain and labour were still highly persuasive. Methodism at its best owes a great deal to Martin Luther. Charles Wesley wrote 6000 hymns, putting many of Luther's doctrines into verse that millions sang, and still sing.

But today there is a danger that scholars and specialists will, as it were, take over Luther, staking out their claims and fencing in our Lutheran inheritance, just as the common lands of England were enclosed and made inaccessible to ordinary folk. Luther, great scholar that he was, loved preaching and teaching and counselling the ordinary men and women of his day, as much as he did princes and professors. We should reclaim Luther for the common Christian, and resist all attempts to make him more difficult to read or understand than he really is.

Yet Luther is hated. John Osborne's play *Luther* was based squarely (Osborne said) on the work of Erik Erikson, who gave a psychoanalyst's view of Luther. Osborne clearly dislikes Luther for his political stance during the Peasants' War. But he does not in my view understand Luther's great spiritual work or his profound experience of grace.

Paul Johnson, in his *History of the Jews,* has laid out very clearly and damningly the later Luther's part in the anti-Semitism of his day, and the way the Nazis used Lutheran ideas in their propaganda. We must deeply regret this aspect of Luther's life; no amount of understanding of his times or temperament can make those who link Luther with the Holocaust ever forgive him.

Others hate him for the coarseness of his language and life; but he cannot be transplanted from his time to a genteel Victorianism. His blunt speaking was part of the violent, virulent debates of his day. Life and death were the issues involved, as we have seen and Luther often risked his life to defend the cause he deemed right. His use of four-letter words and his preoccupation with excreta were not simply signs of bad breeding in an uncouth monk: it was how things were then.

We should heed such scholars as Heiko Oberman who say we should not turn away in embarrassed dislike, but see exactly how Luther was using his lifestyle and language in the service of the truth of the gospel as he found it.

I sometimes hear of devout and learned Roman Catholics who say they hate Luther even though they know they should not. For some of them, this is because he tore the seamless robe of Christian unity. They feel he attacked what seems dearest in their faith. Yet I believe there are many in the Roman communion nowadays, and not only scholars, who turn with fresh understanding to hear and see what Luther was saying and doing.

Perhaps one of the best reasons for admiring him is that, although he was a peasant's son, brought up in superstition and ignorance, Luther learned so much about Christ and his grace, and kept these central in his life, sharing his discoveries and fighting for them against all opponents.

Perhaps, in his frequent writing about the devil and demons, he retained some of the superstition in which he was brought up, prior to his conversion. It is worth pointing out, however, that he talks little of exorcism, but often speaks with the most acute perception of how spiritual realities are affected by evil powers. In most of his references to the devil, however coarse and unacceptable to our modern taste, he seems nearer to St Paul and the New Testament than most of us today.

Luther wanted every ordinary person to learn of Christ and of the mysteries of grace, and of life under the cross. He laboured to make more accessible the truths of the gospel, the vital teaching of its doctrines, and the Christian way of life which, for all his many faults and failings, he did so much to adorn and to honour.

*Further Reading*

Roland Bainton, *Here I Stand* (Tring: Lion, 1978) is a most readable masterpiece. Heiko Oberman, *Luther: Man Between God and the Devil* (New Haven, NJ: Yale University Press, 1989) is likewise both scholarly and readable.

The leading British Luther scholar, James Atkinson, has two studies in print: *Martin Luther and the Birth of Protestantism* (London: Marshalls, 1982; Harmondsworth: Penguin Books, 1968), and *Martin Luther: Prophet to the Church Catholic* (Grand Rapids, MI: Wm B. Eerdmans; Exeter: Paternoster Press, 1983), which is eloquent and challenging.

James M. Kittelson, *Luther the Reformer* (Minneapolis, MN: Augsburg; Leicester: IVP, 1989) is a good popular study. H. G. Haile, *Luther: A Biography* (London: Sheldon Press, 1981) gives a lively account, with special emphasis on Luther's illnesses. Heiko Oberman, *The Dawn of the Reformation* (Edinburgh: T. & T. Clark, 1986) is a splendid collection of essays. Erik H. Erikson, *Young Man Luther: A Study in Psychoanalysis and History* (London: Faber & Faber, 1958) is a classic, and was the basis of John Osborne's play *Luther* (London: Faber & Faber, 1961). Alister E. McGrath, *Luther's Theology of the Cross* (Oxford: Basil Blackwell, 1985) is masterly and profound.

For me, E. Gordon Rupp's *The Righteousness of God: Luther Studies* (London: Hodder & Stoughton, 1953) has a special place as a pioneering British study that first gave me an interest in Luther.

# 2

# Grace Abounding: John Bunyan (1628–1688)

Give me my scallop-shell of quiet,
My staff of faith to walk upon,
My scrip of joy, immortal diet,
My bottle of salvation,
My gown of glory, hope's true gauge,
And thus I'll take my pilgrimage.

'The Passionate Man's Pilgrimage',
attributed to Walter Raleigh, 1618

Christ's church is an hospital of sick, wounded and afflicted people.

John Bunyan

There was some books too.... One was *Pilgrim's Progress,* about a man that left his family it didn't say why. I read considerable in it now and then. The statements was interesting, but tough.

Mark Twain, *Huckleberry Finn*

The more I read Bunyan the more fascinating he becomes: in many ways his genius far outshines any other subject of these sketches, perhaps because he was a native genius, owing so little to nurture or formal education. Yet many readers of the sixty books by Bunyan might agree with the verdict Mark Twain puts into the mouth of Huck Finn: 'interesting, but tough'. For some people the word 'Puritan' is like a red rag to a bull. Puritans are accused of painting life in black and white colours, rather like the clothes that some of them wore. Yet the Puritan character was not all Bible-black, but colourful and often involved in dramatic struggles.

John Bunyan, coming at the end of over a hundred years of Puritan teaching in England, broke away from simply sermonizing, to dream and to write down his dreams. After writing over two dozen books like any other sermons (but a good deal livelier), he left that set form, and let his fancy roam. His imagination ran freely on the themes he had grown to love in the Bible and in the Christian life: the result was *The Pilgrim's Progress,* which has been translated into two hundred languages. The other two allegories, *The Holy War* and *The Life and Death of Mr Badman,* never achieved the success of his best-known book, but they were also works of Christian fiction.

How did a tinker, whose father also mended pots and pans for a living, become such a genius, especially in writing and expressing his Christian faith? It was not without great difficulty. His 'staff of faith, scrip of joy, and gown of glory', of which Raleigh's great poem speaks, were not picked up cheaply, at a market or a fair: they cost him dearly.

The suffering he went through because of his own personality, and the obsessional disorder that he endured for about five years of his early adult life, call for our close attention. His personal anguish helped in due course to fit him to be a great preacher and counsellor. Remarkably, it was almost certainly the time of further suffering as a prisoner in Bedford gaol for twelve years (one- third of his adult life) which consolidated his recovery from illness.

I doubt if he would have used this time in prison to such profit had he not been strengthened by his earlier experiences. One of my main aims is to show, from Bunyan's own autobiography *Grace Abounding,* how ill he was, and yet how this illness was at the same time part of an intense and prolonged spiritual crisis which resulted in huge benefits for him and for us all, as his readers.

Many men and women go through such periods of doubt, together with disturbing obsessional thoughts and compulsions, without telling a soul. Bunyan told the world, though I must say at once that *Grace Abounding to the Chief of Sinners* is not easy reading. One feels like saying, with Alice in Wonderland, 'What good is a book without pictures and conversation?'

*The Pilgrim's Progress*, on the other hand, is Bunyan's own story with pictures: arresting and illuminating scenes drawn from life and set down in clear and simple language. The writing is in vivid colours. The change in Bunyan's style is as great as the metamorphosis from caterpillar to butterfly. Perhaps for years in prison Bunyan was in some form of chrysalis till grace set him free, inwardly, to be a different kind of writer. The problem he faced was that many of his fellow Christians did not much like butterflies, and were deeply suspicious of a man who used his imagination, even when he was doing it for God, and for good.

That some of them objected strongly is shown by his long 'apology' at the beginning of *The Pilgrim's Progress*. Many religious folk of his time preferred truth to fiction; some thought that reading (let alone writing) fiction was wrong. Bunyan proves in *The Pilgrim's Progress* that fiction can be stranger than truth, and stronger in its power to affect the mind and will. The book is liberally sprinkled with dialogue, at which he had become a master. Dialogue became Bunyan's special hallmark in his later sermons too. Here it enabled him to slip much essential teaching into his account of Christian's journey, and that of his wife Christiana (in Part II).

My aim is to show how grace was at work in Bunyan's own long and painful journey. I hope that seeing the labour behind the familiar story will help us to appreciate the value of Bunyan's progress. After all, if Bunyan was gifted to express life's struggles in a manner beyond the ability of most of us who read him, we must bear in mind that his aim was to show that the same grace is offered to all of us who seek the 'straight gate' and 'narrow way' that he describes so well.

Christopher Hill, the historian who has done so much to make Bunyan's period of history come alive for his readers, points out that 'pilgrim' was a common name for vagabonds and tinkers (Bunyan was, like his father, a kind of odd job man), and that 'progress' was a word used in a special way to describe the customary manner in which a king or queen moved around the country in a 'royal progress'. We do not have to be fanciful, or to share all of Hill's Marxist views, to see the title as in itself a stroke of genius. For Bunyan wrote first for the poor, and saw the Christian hope as a spiritual reality: that Christ has made his people 'to be a kingdom and priests to serve his God and Father' (Rev. 1:6).

He saw this even while he was in Bedford prison for twelve years, and he created what is at once a ripping yarn and teaching about the gospel of grace. Such a move, from poverty and loss to sharing in Christ's kingdom, was the highest point in the believer's pilgrimage.

Like Bishop Hugh Latimer before him, Bunyan believed that 'The poorest ploughman is in Christ equal with the greatest prince that is.' Bunyan's writing often seems to me to echo to the strains of the song of Mary, the *Magnificat*: 'He has filled the hungry with good things but has sent the rich away empty' (Luke 1:53).

**Bunyan's life and times**

When Bunyan was born in 1628, King Charles I was about to assume his personal rule, without Parliament. Bunyan was to serve for two years in the first Civil War from the age of sixteen to eighteen. Just after his first marriage, the second Civil War began in 1648, and a year later Charles I was executed.

He lived through Oliver Cromwell's Commonwealth and was one of the congregation in Bedford who signed a petition asking Cromwell to refuse the Crown. Bunyan's first wife, who bore him four children, died in 1658, the same year as Cromwell.

Bunyan remarried the next year. By Elizabeth he was to have three children, during the years when he was allowed some freedom to leave prison for home, or even to preach for short periods. The year after his marriage, when Charles II returned to England, was the beginning of his twelve years as prisoner of conscience: he was arrested for preaching illegally, and would not undertake to stop preaching. That was the sum and substance of his offence.

He was elected pastor of the Bedford congregation in 1672 and was released from prison in the same year. He had already published some twenty-five books that were sermons expanded into book form, and in 1678 he published *The Pilgrim's Progress*. Bunyan shared in the intense persecution of Dissenters in the years 1681–5. He lived to see the death of Charles II and the accession of James II in 1685, after which the Declaration of Indulgence eased the persecution. Bunyan's unexpected death from fever while visiting London in 1688 happened some months before William of Orange arrived, whose reign led to the Toleration Act a year later.

To see John Bunyan thus, against a fast-moving pageant of historical change, may help us to recognize the enormous difficulties he and his own group of Christians, later to be called 'Nonconformists', were forced to endure. He could not publish some of his books because of censorship, and was even then very careful to avoid the political plots in which some of his fellow Christians became embroiled. His aim was to preach 'an awakening word' and to counsel and instruct his fellow men and women. He refused to join the many political agitators.

**Bunyan's early life**

Bunyan was born in the small village of Elstow, near Bedford, the town where he was to spend his whole life. He was baptized on 30 November 1628. His father, Thomas Bonnion, was a brasier, and Bunyan recalls that 'I was brought up at my father's house in a very mean condition ... the meanest and most despised of all the families in the land.' Perhaps he was exaggerating slightly, but we know that his forebears had sold off the land they once had, their house was exempt from hearth tax, and his father's will was signed with his mark.

John Bunyan's father was married three times, and John was the eldest child of his second marriage. The fact that his brother who died in infancy was named Charles has suggested to some that his father may have been a Royalist. His sister Margaret was to die tragically when John was sixteen, only a month after his mother also died, presumably of the same illness, one of the epidemics which so often killed in large numbers.

Bunyan describes his father as having taught him a wicked way of swearing, and his nightmares and compulsive swearing seem part of a pattern of growing into a roaring boy who 'played the madman, after my wonted manner'. His father sent him to school, but both the local grammar schools had a poor record. They were the subject of criticism at the time for neglect and cruelty towards the children by the masters. But Bunyan learned to read and write, even if there is little evidence of much love or nurturing in his childhood.

**Teenage tearaway**

Writing in later life, Bunyan draws a picture of himself as a wild and difficult adolescent. It is not hard to feel for him at the age of sixteen, grieving for the loss of his mother and sister and expressing it all in anti-social ways. He must have been very angry with his father for marrying again only two months after his mother died. Perhaps he was glad to leave home.

He was called up to the army, imprest in June 1644, and demobilized three years later, playing his part only in the first Civil War. Though we cannot be certain, the John Bunnion known to be at the garrison in Newport Pagnell is most probably the same man. Bunyan describes his time in the army briefly, saying that another soldier took his place on duty and was killed by a musket ball.

We may learn little about it from Bunyan, but a great deal is known about the army to which Bunyan belonged. It was a place where politics and religion were heatedly discussed. He would have heard not only the recognized Puritan chaplains but also those who belonged to the Quakers and the Ranters, two groups we shall meet later in his life and writings. The Quakers were then very different from today, and their leader George Fox visited Newport Pagnell. They were not yet pacifist in belief and practice, but they taught that the inner light of the Spirit was more important than the Bible, which they despised as a dead book. The Ranters went much further, and one of them, who espoused tempting Ranter views on the right to enjoy free love and a promiscuous sex life, almost got Bunyan to join him and the Ranter group.

The setting of the camp and garrison which Bunyan lived in was a rude, rough introduction to life during an English civil war. Food and pay were scarce. The men and women who were camp-followers offered plenty of drinking, wenching and rioting: we can only guess at Bunyan's part in it all. Religious and political ferment were part of his schooling. Bunyan found many of the ideas on offer very seductive, 'I being a young man and nature in its prime,' as he frankly admitted.

It is easy to think of him returning to Elstow at the age of nineteen as a man of the world. He was 'a brisk talker', he says of himself, who 'infected all the youth of the town ... with all manner of youthful vanities'. In the army Bunyan had suddenly found everything being questioned without taboos or censorship. Many wanted to turn the world upside down, and tried hard to do so, much to the distress of Cromwell and other more orthodox Christian leaders of the time.

The Bible, democratic equality, free love, new life-styles: these were all critically and loudly discussed, and traditional values challenged. These were the years of the Levellers, the Diggers and other radical groups. The old order seemed about to change dramatically. No wonder Bunyan became something of a wide boy and a tearaway.

But then he married at nineteen, and he tells us that he was chaste after his marriage. That first marriage was the beginning of his most intense period of spiritual change.

**First marriage: the turning-point**

Though we do not know his first wife's name, we do know that her influence was incalculable. This seems to be partly because of the two books to which she introduced Bunyan. Her father had been a devoutly Christian man, very different from Bunyan's own father. The two books he gave his daughter were read by Bunyan and his wife together.

Arthur Dent's book *The Plaine Man's Pathway to Heaven* may have been more important than the second, Lewis Bayly's *The Practice of Piety.* Both books taught Bunyan a very clear view of the orthodox Christian religion. They were enormously popular: Dent had run to twenty-seven editions by this time, Bishop Bayly to forty-seven.

Bayly may have led Bunyan to think of the changes in his life as being simply moral ones, or a matter of the outward form of religion. Dent's influence seems to have been deeper, and to have left its mark on some of Bunyan's best writing. For Dent's book is a narrative about an encounter between two sets of friends, two good and two bad. The dialogues are between a theologian and an honest man, on the one hand, and an ignorant man and a caviller, who doubts everything, on the other. The subjects covered in the dialogues are man's salvation, and the difference between the saved and the damned. Close attention is given to the Bible's teaching on God's initiatives through grace, to man's free will, and to his response of faith and trust. The doctrinal content is much like that of *The Pilgrim's Progress,* but without the action and excitement.

Inevitably, Dent deals with the thorny problems that surround the biblical teachings about God's election and predestination. These are, as is often pointed out, not Anglican, Puritan, or even Protestant doctrines, but Christian doctrines. It has been said that Bunyan became a thorough-going Calvinist because of John Calvin's emphasis on these doctrines. Yet it would be easy to show from the Gospels and the epistles of the New Testament that we must confront the fact of God's sovereign initiative in man's salvation, and that we love him because he first loved us.

But we must try and imagine how the powerful doctrinal statements about salvation in Dent (and to a lesser extent in Bayly) affected a young husband and father who was trying to learn to live a better life. I think they played a huge part in Bunyan's thinking and in the illness and spiritual crisis that followed, and which lasted almost five years.

I think the effect was like a time-bomb, ticking away in Bunyan's mind, to explode in a crisis of confidence and despair about himself. Or we can see these teachings as depth-charges such as ships use to try and destroy submarines: they sank into his mind, only to detonate when they reached levels of his personality of which he was barely aware.

Before we follow Bunyan's own account we must note that of his four children, the first, Mary, was born blind. This event, too, must have contributed to a young father's state of mind. When Mary was eight her mother died, in 1658. Did his first wife understand the torment of soul to which her father's books had given rise?

Some have thought that the description of Christiana in Part II of *The Pilgrim's Progress,* of 'her unbecoming behaviour towards her Husband ... all her unkind, unnatural and ungodly carriages to her dear friend, which ... did load her with guilt', is Bunyan's mature reflection on his first wife's attitude to his distress. It is equally possible that the remarks made by Christiana to her children ('For I hardened both mine own heart and yours against him, and refused to go with him on Pilgrimage') simply explain the loneliness which seems to have been an essential aspect of Bunyan's pilgrimage in Part I.

A year later Bunyan married his second wife, Elizabeth, when he was thirty-one and she was eighteen. By then he was an established preacher and writer. As we shall see, when he wrote Part II he seemed to unite all the best features of all the women he had known into the figure of Christiana.

**Becoming a Christian: Bunyan's illness**

Despite reading and rereading Bunyan's account of his life in *Grace Abounding,* it is difficult to be sure of many facts. We would dearly like to know which town his fellow soldiers were besieging when another soldier was killed in Bunyan's place, but he does not tell us. He skips many details, and blurs others, but the symptoms he suffered for nearly five years are fully described. It is of the agony of doubt and uncertainty, with occasional brief times of spiritual certainty, that he wants to tell: these are all very fully described. The vital thing for Bunyan is the traffic between God and his soul, not dates and places. He tells us why, frankly:

> I could have enlarged much in this my discourse, of my temptations and troubles for sin; as also of the merciful kindness and working of God with my soul. I could also have stepped into a style much higher than this ... but I dare not. God did not play in convincing of me, the devil did not play in tempting of me, neither did I play when I sunk as into a bottomless pit, when the pangs of hell caught hold of me; wherefore I may not play in my relating of them, but be plain and simple, and lay down the thing as it was.

He describes first his moral change after reading the two books his wife had brought with her, 'though we came together as poor as poor might be, not having so much household stuff as a dish or spoon betwixt us both'. He began to love going to church, but had no sense of sin. Later, in *The Pilgrim's Progress,* this period is described as going to the 'town of Morality'. For about a year his neighbours were amazed at the change from 'prodigious profaneness ... to outward reformation'. For a time, he says, 'I adored, and that with great devotion, even all things (both the High Place, Priest, Clerk, Vestments, Service and what else) belonging to the Church ... their Name, their Garb, and Work, did so intoxicate and bewitch me'. It was a sermon by the vicar, Christopher Hall, which made him realize that Sunday sport was wrong for him. Very slowly a sense of his own sin and need dawned on him, and he realized that he was simply playing the hypocrite.

A key experience when he was at his work in Bedford as a tinker was to listen to 'three or four poor women sitting at a door in the sun, and talking about the things of God ... they *spake as if joy made them speak'*. This was followed by what Bunyan calls a dream or vision. He sees these poor people of Bedford on the far side of a high mountain, enjoying the sun, while he shivers in the cold. He sees a wall with a narrow gap, and a passage through which, with great striving, he sidles into the light and heat of the sun.

Some, of course, see this as a kind of birthing experience, or a longing for a birth into a new life surrounded with warmth and joy, such as the women at the Bedford church had spoken of. I think it is Bunyan's version of the 'straight gate' that leads to the 'narrow way' in the Gospels. Bunyan interprets it as meaning that there is room for him if he is in downright earnest: 'for here was room for body and soul, but not for body and soul and sin'.

Then his doubts begin about whether God has chosen him to be a vessel of mercy. 'Therefore, this would stick with me, How can you tell that you are elected? And what if you should not? How then?'

It is then that Bunyan describes how ill he became. The dialogues and arguments that he had first encountered in Arthur Dent's book had come home to roost in his perplexed and despairing mind. In my view he suffered, for more than three years, from an obsessive-compulsive disorder. Before we look at this in detail, it is helpful to see what enabled him to come through to a Christian conversion and, later, to a full assurance of faith.

**John Gifford and Martin Luther**

Two men acted as counsellors or spiritual directors to Bunyan, one alive and one who had been dead for almost a century. John Gifford was the pastor of a 'gathered' Congregational church in Bedford: a community of believers closer to the Independent churches than to the Baptist ones. The women at the Bedford church who had so impressed Bunyan told Gifford about him, and Bunyan was invited to Gifford's home to hear him 'confer with others about the dealings of God with my soul'. Bunyan became worse for a time, but later spoke of 'holy Mr Gifford, whose doctrine, by God's grace, was much for my stability'.

Gifford's own story was remarkable.A Royalist major in the king's army, he was captured at a battle in Maidstone by Fairfax and his troops but, though condemned to death, escaped with his sister's help and came to Bedford where he began to practise as a doctor. Gifford lived a debauched life until suddenly, after heavy gambling losses, he became a Christian.

It was then that he began to form a small church based on 'faith in Christ and holiness of life ... by which means grace and faith was encouraged, love and amity maintained, disputings and occasion to janglings and unprofitable questions avoided, and many that were weak in the faith confirmed in the blessing of eternal life'.

It was to this remarkable band of pilgrims – a church nearer to a house-church than any formal chapel – that John Bunyan was to belong for the rest of his life; but only after further years of spiritual suffering.

Bunyan wanted to learn more, and he discovered Luther:

> Well, after many such longings in my mind, the God in whose hands are all our days and ways, did cast into my hand one day a book of Martin Luther, his comment on the *Galatians, so* old that it was ready to fall piece from piece, if I did but turn it over. Now I was pleased much that such an old book had fallen into my hand; the which, when I had but a little way perused, I found my condition in his experience, so largely and profoundly handled, as if his book had been written out of my own heart ... as most fit for a wounded conscience.

We may well ask what a letter like Galatians should do to help Bunyan so much. Is it not largely concerned with Abraham and his wife and the slave-woman Hagar, and the symbolic influence of the two children he had by these two women? Is it not largely about circumcision, and arguments about flesh and spirit? Perhaps so: but a recent commentator has described Galatians as spiritual dynamite. We may guess that Luther's long and laborious *Lectures on Galatians* helped Bunyan to see that freedom from rituals (like circumcision) and from the law through faith in Christ was the essence of the gospel of grace.

As we have mentioned, Calvin is blamed for some harshness in Bunyan: he applied his logic to teaching predestination and reprobation, and to some extent Bunyan followed him. But it was Luther who taught him most about how to apply first the law, and then grace, to his condition. Bunyan learned that 'the Law of Moses ... had a very great hand therein [that is, in his quest for certainty in faith,] which was at first very strange to me, but considering and watching, I found it so indeed'. It led directly to what many see as Bunyan's most important treatise, *The Doctrine of the Law and Grace Unfolded,* which he was to publish in 1659, when he was thirty-one.

Bunyan suffered like many other Christians of the Puritan period. There were many books written to help those troubled in their faith. Dr Richard Sibbes, a well-known preacher and comforter of those who were distressed about whether they were true Christians or not, had written a book called *The Bruised Reed.* Sibbes recalled how Staupitz had pointed Luther to the wounds of Christ, and he stressed that we should not enquire into questions about our own election or damnation, but rather start with God's love shown in Christ's cross.

It required a special sort of mind, a remarkable kind of personality, to benefit slowly and surely, as Bunyan did, from the help of Gifford and Luther. It is time to examine Bunyan's personality, and the disorder from which he suffered on his way to a full, healthy and rounded faith in Christ.

**In what ways was Bunyan ill?**

Having already considered Luther and his early scrupulosity and perfectionism, we may see the same features more clearly in Bunyan. In *Grace Abounding,* Bunyan describes his severe anxiety, and how it often drove him to despair. However, he was not a monk with hours to spend in the confessional. Unlike Luther, he was much more alone with the Bible, and struggled with difficult texts with little help, even allowing for John Gifford and the few books he could obtain. In the first years of his active search for Christ and faith, Bunyan was like the pilgrim, with his burden on his back and his Bible in his hands. He called himself 'an alone man': it was nearly three years before he found the fellowship of visible saints in the church, like Gifford, to help him by their counsel and teaching.

Yet, when Bunyan received some relief from a text of Scripture at this time of struggle, it only lasted for a few hours or days, and then he was back in the same turmoil. It is important to note that the same kind of conflict occurred after his conversion and his acceptance as a preacher in the Bedford church.

> I have gone full of guilt and terror even to the pulpit door, and there it has been taken off ... and then immediately, even before I could get down the pulpit stairs, I have been as bad as I was before.... Sometimes, again, when I have been preaching, I have been violently assaulted with thoughts of blasphemy and strongly tempted to speak the words with my mouth before the congregation.

There could be no clearer example of a severe obsessive-compulsive disorder at work. There are other examples of the same urge to blaspheme, so that he would want to hold his hand over his mouth, or plunge his head into a dung heap, rather than give in to the impulse. The above passage, in which Bunyan describes his condition at the end of the long period of time (probably five years, certainly more than three) spent in agonizing conflict, is quoted to show the extent to which he was concerned about the slow process of his regeneration. Conversion, the outward aspect of this process of grace, does not necessarily denote certainty, assurance of salvation, or peace of mind.

William James, the American professor of psychology who wrote *The Varieties of Religious Experience,* speaks of Bunyan at length. He points out that for some, like Saul of Tarsus on the road to Damascus, conversion is a *crisis.* The apostle Paul looks back on this and describes it more than once. For others, like Bunyan, it is a slow and gradual process of change (which James calls lysis). I think it is possible to make sense of much that happened to Bunyan if the time between 1650 and 1654, when he started preaching, is seen as a gradual process moving from unbelief to faith and, later, to a fuller assurance of faith.

**Understanding Bunyan's obsessions**

Bunyan was remarkable because he suffered so severely from obsessions; he would nowadays be diagnosed as being in need of treatment. He describes not only the symptoms he suffered, and how he obtained relief after his long struggle, but he also shows how great strength may result from overcoming a serious neurotic disorder. He is not, of course, using modern terms.

If we start with Bunyan's emphasis on his 'bruised conscience' we will not go far wrong. When we say that the obsessional person is over-conscientious, it is intended both as a compliment and as a way of describing the central problem. Conscience is working overtime because it is *afflicted* – full of self-accusations and the putting of oneself in the wrong – which is always unpleasant and threatening, and was especially so for Bunyan, who was alone and struggling with very little help in dealing with his shame and guilt and his wish for everything to be 'put right'.

His account has the hallmarks of his own personality: his striving for perfection, his ability to experience both hope and despair, as well as to be elated when he learns something new and good about the Bible and himself. Such experiences are shot through with uncertainty and indecisiveness until he arrives at a fuller, richer faith.

I will try and summarize the evidence for a serious neurotic disorder which in Bunyan mainly took the form of obsessional thoughts, compulsions, illusions and hearing voices. Associated with all this there was the most crippling anxiety and frequent bouts of despair and anguished misery. All this happened, let us not forget, while he went about his work as a tinker.

First let us note that an obsessional wants to get things absolutely *right* and that this perfectionism can show itself in many ways. In Bunyan the need for *certainty* was paramount. He wanted to know for sure that he was a Christian, one of God's elect. Eventually his intense studies of Scripture led him to feel 'my soul was led from truth to truth by God', and 'not one part of the Gospel of the Lord Jesus, but I was orderly led into it'. But the way it happened he describes further: 'first, to *suffer me* to be afflicted with temptation concerning them, and then reveal them to me', 'Now had I evidence, as I thought, of my salvation from heaven.'

The evidence is there in Bunyan's own words. His mental and spiritual suffering – when studied carefully – are two strands which may be disentangled. His *spiritual* suffering came about because he took the Christian message as he read and heard it with desperate intensity. The second strand, his mental torture, was worse because of his obsessional temperament.

I am not trying to reduce his spiritual experience to a mere illness (however severe), but rather am trying to show how the spiritual and psychiatric aspects, though separate, are inevitably intertwined. *Both* aspects are true and valid: Bunyan was ill with his unhappiness, and also, spiritually he was moving from darkness to light, from the City of Destruction to the Celestial City.

**Personality and illness**

*Control is* important for a person of obsessional temperament; loss of control, whether 'to be carried away as by a mighty spirit' or to be possessed of a devil, is dreaded. We all know how even the repetition of a snatch of song or a memorable phrase can be disturbing. The more awful disturbance (which Bunyan often experienced) was the intrusion of alien thoughts, against his will.

Because by this time his mind was soaked and impregnated with the text of the Bible, the form this problem took was 'the battle of the texts'. He would find himself thinking of the words 'I have loved thee with an everlasting love', but he would find his peace broken a hundred times that day: 'Oh the combats and conflicts that I did then meet with as I strove to hold by this word; that of Esau would fly in my face like to lightning.' (We will describe the Esau experience later.) He would feel 'set at liberty' for some days or a few weeks and then would sink into despair again, fearing that he might be deceived and destroyed.

He suffered from obsessive *ruminations,* as if he were chewing the cud over a text, but as likely with dread as with hope. The sequence I have described also shows how doubt and indecisiveness is part of the disorder. The French call it *folie de doute,* 'the doubting madness'. When you feel that your eternal destiny is involved, when that is your worry and not simply whether you have locked the door or turned off the gas, then the anxiety level is, by comparison, infinitely higher.

A small proportion of obsessional patients, of whom I think Bunyan was one, are pushed to the borders of psychosis, or madness. For Bunyan (as for many Christians since) 'Esau' was a code word. Esau had sold his birthright to Jacob and afterwards 'he was rejected. He could bring about no change of mind, though he sought the blessing with tears' (Heb. 12:17). He linked the Esau story with other texts, including those about unpardonable sin (e.g., Heb. 10:26), which he believed he had committed.

It is often found, in depression, that the patient feels such despair. Some, who have no idea what the New Testament means by 'sin', still feel they have sinned against the light, or against the Holy Spirit. It seems that Bunyan heard voices uttering biblical lines such as 'Simon, Simon, Satan has desired to have you'. Walking down a lane on one occasion, he believed that a human voice was calling after him. Such hallucinations, or delusions, are common in severe depression.

I think Bunyan's description of the devil 'pulling at his clothes' is not simply his vivid imagination or his concrete way of thinking, but a measure of how he felt his experience as a *physical* reality. His images are earthy and immediate, as if the truths about 'the Word made flesh' had to be felt as bodily sensations, because that is what they were for him.

**Some modern views**

Of all those psychiatrists who have sought to help us understand obsessional illness, Professor Sir Aubrey Lewis is perhaps the most learned. To him we owe the description that the obsessional experience is 'home-made but disowned'. In an obsessional disorder, a person's thoughts, ideas or images start in his or her own mind, and yet are resisted as if they were alien intruders. The person seems compelled to suffer the presence of thoughts and feelings that he or she would like to disown, but cannot. The sense of being compelled to think, feel, say or do something which seems silly or bad is the reason we nearly always see the two words 'obsessive-compulsive' linked together.

In his study of obsessional illness Lewis discusses a number of classic examples. He uses Luther and Bunyan to show that the obsessional character need not be a 'social invalid' or a 'contented weakling'. He writes:

> But I have not brought in Bunyan and Luther just to provide brief pathographies and still less do I wish to attempt to reformulate their profound and far-ranging religious experiences as symptoms of psychiatric illness – such a devaluing

> transformation serves no purpose. What I want to emphasize is that we have here, in two men of genius, a malady, well known to theologians and psychiatrists alike, which is most painful, whether we view it from the religious or the medical standpoint, which goes with or precedes phases of utter despair, and is yet compatible with a life of the utmost vigour and practical activity.

I agree with Lewis' magisterial judgement on the matter.

Henry Maudsley, an illustrious predecessor of Lewis, puts it thus:

> ... there is no real derangement of mind: there is only profound pain of mind.... The impulse is bad enough, but the essence of the misery is not always so much the fear of actually yielding as the haunting fear of the fear.... It is not easy to persuade him who suffers in one or other of these ways that he is not doomed to madness.

Many will have read the explanations of Freud and some of his followers that obsessionality derives from problems in early toilet training, the so-called anal character traits being cleanliness, punctuality, and meanness with money. A number of people trained in the Freudian approach have abandoned it because the old formulas do not fit with modern knowledge. Yet, by an odd quirk, since he wrote so much about it, Sigmund Freud was himself a good example of the obsessional temperament. His wife became quite tired of his insistence on being at the station in Vienna four hours before the train was due to leave. Another aspect was Freud's irrational fear of some numbers, and his fascination with the number 62. He felt sure he would die at the age of 62, and when the last two digits of his telephone number were 62 he became very frightened about it.

There are many other clear examples among great achievers. Dr Samuel Johnson is one of the best known, since he suffered severe obsessional symptoms for many years. Ignatius Loyola may have been one of the first to describe how his religion, and that of the Jesuit order which he founded, was affected by his obsessionality. His systematic, rigid and detailed *Spiritual Exercises* still forms a staple part of many Catholic retreats. Those exercises helped Ignatius; it does not follow that the same obsessional approach would help every Jesuit or Catholic.

Because of shame and secrecy, the true extent of obsessional distress is not known. Let me emphasize that it is far more common than most people think. Sometimes it is simply a question of temperament, sometimes of illness; the two things must be kept separate.

## Religious mania

It is not, of course, necessary for every Christian to have gone through Bunyan's intense experiences. But his capacity to suffer in the way he did gave him a unique ability to understand how grace works in the heart, and then to help others when he became a pastor and a counsellor.

During his lifetime he would have been accused of religious mania by many who wanted to write off the whole of Christian experience, as when the apostle Paul was told that much learning had made him mad. Bunyan is describing himself in the portrait of Christian in *The Pilgrim's Progress*, and puts into the mouth of the character called Obstinate the argument so commonly used, that becoming a Christian means suffering 'religious mania'. Obstinate is the character who says: 'Who knows whither such a brain-sick fellow will lead you? Go back, go back, and be wise,' and who sees Christian as one of 'a company of crazed-headed coxcombs'.

That Bunyan realized his case was especially severe is indicated by his words in a sermon later in life: 'Perhaps God will deal more gently with you than with me; if so thank him for it.' He was to recover from his inward trials, but went on to suffer many years of persecution and uncertainty which involved not just prison, but slanderous attacks on his character. These pressures from a hostile outside world were as vital for his growth in grace as the earlier intense spiritual conflicts.

An anvil with 'J.B.' inscribed on it was found in Bedford. Whether or not it was actually his, Bunyan knew well that hammer blows on heated metal shape the iron for use. It was what he gloried in: that he had been able to suffer in the fires of affliction and persecution in order to be a vessel fit for his Master's use. He felt that all the dishonour that was heaped upon him was nothing compared to the honour and glory that he brought to his Master's name.

**'Thou must live upon the Word'**

Just as the Bible had formed his faith, so it was the Bible which he went on to teach, preach and explain. Like John Wesley, he became a man of one book. Though he wrote sixty books, one for every year of his life as his first editor put it, he made a bold claim: 'I have not for these things fished in other men's waters; my Bible and my Concordance are my only library in my writings.' What about Luther's commentary? Bunyan must have read much, and we know he loved his *Book of Martyrs* by John Foxe. What he meant was 'though I am not skilled in the Hebrew tongue, yet through grace, I am enlightened into the Scriptures'. The Scriptures were indeed the head and fount of all his learning.

The Bible verses which he memorized developed a life of their own: 'that Scripture fastened on my heart', it was 'as if the Scripture had said, Take me, take me'. These are commonly used phrases in his account in *Grace Abounding.* Thus, as with many Christians who feel that God speaks to them, some verses of the Bible would come vividly to his mind – so vividly that he felt he was receiving a special message.

**Guarding the essentials**

But Bunyan was soon in conflict with those who thought differently. The Quakers and Ranters whom we met earlier were only a few of those who despised the written Word, the Scriptures Bunyan valued above all else as the source and record of revelation. Two of his most important books are attacks on the Quakers, including his first book, *Some Gospel-Truths Opened.* In these he insists on the historical facts that Jesus was both man and God, was crucified and is risen. Bunyan thought that the Quakers, by stressing Christ 'crucified within ... risen again within', were virtually denying the importance of what they called the Jerusalem Christ.

Thus Bunyan asks the Quakers: 'Is that very Man crucified on Mount Calvary between two thieves, whose name is Jesus, the Son of Mary, I say, is he the very Christ of God, yea or no?' He of all men had learned, slowly and painfully, the vital part that an inward work of the Spirit played in coming to faith in Christ. He fought, with no holds barred, against losing the balance between believing in the historic events on the one hand, and having an inward enlightenment of the Spirit on the other. For Bunyan, as for Luther, to say that *all* that mattered was the inner light, the ecstatic certainties, the fine feelings, was the way to disaster.

He deployed many debating skills in his attack on those who wished to throw away the Bible and to rely instead on immediate, exciting spiritual revelations. We must bear in mind that for three days, not far from Bedford, George Fox had led a festival where thousands were enjoying thrilling religious experiences. Converts were drawn to Fox from churches round about, including Bunyan's in Bedford. Fox himself was to attack Bunyan's writing in his book *The Great Mistery of the Great Whore Unfolded* (1659).

This fact may serve to remind us that *The Pilgrim's Progress* did not appear until after Bunyan's first twenty-five books had been published. Some say his wit and his gift for language were sharpened and polished in his first years of writing. He attacked his opponents vigorously, and perhaps he was at times unfair to them. It seems clear, however, that his aim was 'to contend for the faith once for all entrusted to the saints', as Jude 3 indicates we should do.

Bunyan was a courageous fighter, and many of his shorter works were written because he thought the best form of defence was attack. While explaining the Christian truths as he saw them in Scripture, he felt bound to attack misinterpretations and heresies. Some of these flourished as they do now, and indeed always have done in one form or another in Christian times.

**The liberals and 'prosperity' believers**

He attacked the liberal, rational, middle-of-the-road men who are sometimes called Latitudinarians, sometimes 'Broad churchmen'. The diarist Samuel Pepys reports sermons by such men in London, in which they said that 'righteousness is a surer moral way of being rich than sin and villainy' and 'sanctified riches were marks of favour from God'.

Such 'prosperity' theology was linked to an emphasis on natural religion and a firm opposition to grace as understood by the Reformers and Puritans. This easy-going religion not only emptied faith of what Bunyan thought was its saving and supernatural content, but it fitted in easily with the life of a turncoat and trimmer. Bunyan hated this mainly because of its wilful ignorance and contempt for the essentials of faith. A number of the characters he later sketched – Mr By-ends, Mr Worldly Wiseman, and particularly Ignorance – resembled the liberals with whom Bunyan took issue.

**Fighting with friends**

Bunyan also fought with his fellow believers who shared his biblical understanding of Calvinism – though less aggressively. He says: 'I saw my work before me did run in another channel even to carry an awakening word; to that therefore did I stick and adhere.'

He did not believe that baptism was essential for the admission of an adult to the Church. He wanted to stick to essentials and be detached from everything secondary.

After twelve years in prison he wanted, as he wrote, 'To weigh and pause, and pause again, the grounds and foundations of those principles for which I thus have suffered.' Long experience of grace had made him more conciliatory. He wanted to unite all Christians, that is, all those who accepted the Bible's authority without human additions, and he wanted to do this in love, so that Christians could together concentrate on spreading the gospel of grace.

**The loneliness of the long-distance pilgrim**

'As I walked through the wilderness of this world, I lighted on a certain place, where was a den; and I laid me down to sleep: and as I slept I dreamed a dream.' So begins the book which, next to the Bible itself, has been the greatest in influence and in number of translations. Is it read today? Not as much as it used to be, certainly: yet in London the BBC considered it worthwhile to package it as audiotapes. *The Pilgrim's Progress* is still influential. The music to Vaughan Williams' setting of the words is still available, and was recently performed in Manchester to considerable acclaim. A musical on the same theme is being written in the United States of America.

The stories of pilgrimage that antedate Bunyan have been endlessly analysed. It is probable that the popular romances had some influence on Bunyan's choice of style. In the seven-page 'Apology' for the book which serves as a preface he gave his own answer to most of the objections and doubts raised about the book:

Thus I set pen to paper with delight,
And quickly had my thoughts in black and white.
For having now my method by the end,
Still as I pulled it came.

C. S. Lewis, another best-selling Christian writer of allegories, says these words describe better than any others he knows 'the golden moments of unimpeded composition: *It came*. I doubt if we shall ever know more of the process called inspiration than those two monosyllables tell us.'

In his 'Apology' Bunyan counters objections that *The Pilgrim's Progress* was not as clear as his sermons had been. Some people said, 'It is dark', where they expected 'Scripture light'. Others said, 'But it is feigned', objecting to the fictional element. In reply Bunyan showed that Holy Writ uses types, shadows, metaphors, figures and parables. His quotation on the original title page of 1678 is from Hosea 12:10, 'I have used Similitudes'. My view is that the struggles in his own spiritual life form the basis from which the content of *Pilgrim's Progress* is drawn. Thus I think that the Slough of Despond, Giant Despair and Doubting Castle are written out of his own experience of depression. One such experience – the Slough – follows from a conviction of sin.

This may seem so obvious that it does not need stating. It seems to me that Christians quite often believe it is somehow a denial of their faith to be depressed. Bunyan would not agree. His discussions of suicide in the passages about Doubting Castle are a model of how suicidal thoughts in depression can be countered to some extent by argument. His fellow prisoner Hopeful acts as his counsellor, helping him to 'bear up with patience as well as we can'. Bunyan also describes how Christian finds for himself that 'the key called Promise' can get one out of suicidal despair and open any lock in Doubting Castle.

**Bunyan the teacher**

Bunyan's use of dialogue between Christian and the various characters that he meets on his pilgrimage reveals another vital part of his purpose. In these dialogues he is teaching Christian truths, attacking heresy and showing the dreadful consequences to oneself of twisting truth to one's own (short-sighted) advantage. It reminds us of Peter's comment about his fellow apostle Paul's writings, 'which ignorant and unstable people distort, as they do the other Scriptures, to their own destruction' (2 Pet. 3:16).

Bunyan's style has been much discussed: the plain language; the lively dialogue so close to the ordinary speech of his day; the almost indiscriminate use of Bible texts without reference to context. Even his use of allegory has been analysed for faults, as when he sometimes ceases to be allegorical in order to teach a truth or underline a point. But does any of this matter, from the standpoint of knowing how grace worked in and through him?

Perhaps it is true to say that Bunyan wanted 'by all means to save some', and cared comparatively little about purity of style or giving offence to some of his friends and admirers. I think grace helped him to be true to himself - warts and all - and he put all of himself, with as much of his understanding of the Bible as he could, into his writing.

A moving comment from his book *The Holy City* comes to mind: 'I with a few groans did carry my meditations to the Lord Jesus for a blessing which he did forthwith grant.' For, though it is true that Bunyan says about his great dream and allegory 'I did it my own self to gratify', his added comment tells much:

> It seems a novelty, and yet contains
> Nothing but sound and honest gospel strains.

Thus in the conclusion of *Pilgrim's Progress* he expresses his wish to the reader, 'See if thou canst interpret it for me', and more importantly, 'Do thou *the substance* of my matter see.'

It is evident that Bunyan worked very hard on his dream, and that the dream form was only a device that gave him freedom to describe the Christian journey in a way that would reach folk who would not otherwise hear what he so much wanted to say.

> Some said, 'John, print it'; others said, 'not so':
> Some said, 'it might do good'; others said 'no'.

His critics and assessors have been divided ever since. The praise of such writers as Sir Walter Scott, Lord Macaulay and Sir Charles Firth must be weighed against the appreciative criticism of Robert Bridges.

A liberal Nonconformist writing in the *Gentleman's Magazine* of 1714 said none of the characters spoke sense except Ignorance. But Bunyan cared little for critics, and wrote for the ordinary folk he loved. Those people who read his book 'with head and heart together' knew what and whom Ignorance represented. It is clear from Bunyan that the ignorance he is concerned about is that which invincibly and wilfully refuses to bow to revealed truth. In the story, the character Ignorance thinks he can get in at the Celestial Gate without going through the wicket-gate, or going to the cross to lose his burden. He also thought he could be a pilgrim without being clothed in the new coat (of Christ's righteousness) or receiving the mark on the forehead and the roll given to Christian.

Ignorance is the one who is bound and carried to a door in the side of the hill near the gates. There follow Bunyan's last awful words to end this part of his story: 'Then I saw that there was a way to Hell, even from the Gates of Heaven, as well as from the City of Destruction. So I awoke, and behold it was a dream.'

Would it have been better if he had ended with the simple words that close the previous paragraph? They conclude Bunyan's description of his glimpse of Christian and Hopeful entering the Celestial City: 'And after that, they shut up the Gates: which when I had seen, I wished myself among them.' The comment that C. S. Lewis makes on the fact that Bunyan feels compelled to describe the fate of Ignorance is: 'the choice of ways at any cross-road is more important than we think; and ... short cuts may lead to very nasty places'. In his own way Bunyan is saying that choices about Christ and his grace have eternal consequences. Reading the four Gospels, it is hard to see how we can reject Bunyan because he is not to our modern taste without rejecting the Gospels also.

### The spreading influence of Bunyan

It is remarkable how effectively such a mixture of adventure story, Scripture texts and dialogue conveys Bunyan's message. The story of *The Pilgrim's Progress* has crossed many barriers of language, time and culture, so much so that in a Japanese translation the Pilgrim is dressed as a Samurai warrior! Was it simply the zeal of missionaries which led to this diffusion of Bunyan world-wide? Not entirely.

The history of the Taiping Christian sect in China throws light upon this. The leader drew in hundreds of millions of people and came very near to conquering the whole of China. The leader's favourite books were the Bible and *Pilgrim's Progress*. Christopher Hill comments when recounting these facts that Bunyan might have been China's earlier little red book of revolution. That there were social and political aspects to Bunyan's writing is certain; but that is another question, and another story.

**Bunyan and Christiana: a more mature view?**

What of Part II of *The Pilgrim's Progress?* It was written some fifteen years after Part I. While Part I is an epic, Part II reads much more like a romantic novel. It describes Christiana, the wife left behind, deciding to take her children with her and follow her husband. They seem to have an easier time than Christian, but there is more to Part II than this. The fact that Christiana takes her sons and a neighbour called Mercy with her means that there is much more by way of family chat in Part II. But there is an attempted rape scene as well, and there are many dangerous situations which recall the courage of Christian in Part I. The communal talk is an important feature of the little group's stay at the Inn where Gaius 'mine host' (from Rom. 16:23) offers them entertainment. Marriages are arranged for Christiana's two sons. They sit at the table for a long time, and 'nuts' are cracked – meaning that difficult texts and riddles are explained.

It is part of our enquiry into Bunyan's way of thinking to ask why, in Part II, Giant Despair (and two other giants) are killed by Mr Great-heart (the conductor of pilgrims), Mr Honest and the other men. They take seven days to demolish Doubting Castle, and save two pilgrims who are found trapped there, Mr Despondency and his daughter Much-Afraid. Does this part of Bunyan's dream mean that he had learned something more about depression and anxiety since the writing of Part I? I think it does, and the presence of such people as Mr Great-heart and Mr Valiant-for-Truth reflects the value Bunyan had come to put upon spiritual leaders and counsellors. Perhaps we can see something of John Gifford and of Bunyan himself in those who look after the pilgrims in Part II.

Bunyan understands more, too, about 'the Reason why good men are so in the dark', as his margin note shows. He describes Mr Fearing as preferring doleful music and being often heavy-hearted: 'He had, I think, a Slough of Despond in his mind, a Slough he carried everywhere with him, or else he could never have been as he was.' Bunyan devotes many pages to his case-study of Mr Fearing. The Valley of Humiliation did not bother him, nor the Hill Difficulty. All this is a masterpiece of perceptive description: 'When we came at the Hill Difficulty, he made no stick at that, nor did he much fear the Lions. For you must know that his trouble was not about such things as those, his Fear was about his Acceptance at last.' These snatches of a long description show that, by the time he wrote Part II, Bunyan knew well the anatomy of melancholy. Who has not known, in Christian and other circles, how Mr Fearing feels and behaves? Perhaps all of us, to some extent, at some time, have been like him.

**Too much fear?**

Bunyan has been accused of three extraordinary faults by the many scholars who swarm around him like bees around a honey-pot. In *The Pilgrim's Progress,* they say, there is no progress, it is antiprogressive; then they say there is too much fear in it; and, thirdly, they say that Christ is not there in any obvious way.

To suggest that moving from death-in-sin to everlasting life is not progress is to miss the whole point of the story. But we may grant that the many difficulties that Christian meets on his journey do give the impression of slow progress. That, in my view, makes the account all the more true to life; the Christian life as described in the Bible in particular. Often Bunyan is describing mental states or, more properly, spiritual states, for he had come to know their importance. Going through the wicket-gate is a one-way progress; going to the cross and losing one's burden is another irreversible step forward. But the loss of the roll or certificate shows how Christians may lose their certainty and the enjoyment of their faith, and yet find them again. The final uncertainties that Christian experiences in the river (according to the margin note, 'Christian's conflict at the hour of death') are also realistic and true.

The fear that Bunyan describes so often in Part I is not, I think, overdone. Perhaps Bunyan knew more than most of us about fear because of his own earlier anxieties. In his book called *The Fear of God* he states squarely the biblical basis for the role that he attributes to fear. Fear is the beginning of wisdom. The fear of deceiving oneself (as Ignorance did) and the fear of grieving God's Spirit, and other functions of fear, are well described.

To say that Christ is not a real presence in Part I of *The Pilgrim's Progress* is a damaging criticism; but it is based on a glib and superficial reading. Certainly there is nothing to suggest that coming to Jesus is a simple matter. Bunyan wrestles with the problems of grace in the heart, and he does so on a broad canvas where Christ is the Lord of the Hill and the lover of poor pilgrims. One cannot go far without feeling the awesome presence of Christ. Consider how Christian sings when he wakes up in the Palace Beautiful:

> Where am I now? is this the love and care
> Of Jesus, for the men that Pilgrims are?
> Thus to provide! That I should be forgiven!
> And dwell already the next door to Heaven.

This is before Christian sets out to meet his many adversaries. After surviving them all, and while he wrestles with the fear of death in the river, Bunyan writes: 'And with that, Christian brake out with a loud voice, Oh I see him again! and he tells me, When thou passest through the waters, I will be with thee, and through the rivers, they shall not overflow thee.'

The passage he puts into the mouth of Mr Standfast seems to me even more moving:

> I have formerly lived by Hear-say, and Faith, but now I go where I shall live by sight, and shall be with him, in whose Company I delight myself. I have loved to hear my Lord spoken of, and where-ever I have seen the print of his shoe in the earth, there I have coveted to set my foot too.... His voice to me has been most sweet, and his countenance, I have more desired than they that have most desired the light of the sun.

It was this passage that made Helen Waddell, that remarkable

Christian scholar, take back everything she had said in criticism of Bunyan. Waddell's eminent mentor, Professor George Saintsbury, had told her that *Pilgrim's Progress* was 'one of the cheerfullest books in the world'. As a child Waddell had been haunted by the wicket-gate, and wished that Bunyan had made clear to her not only 'strait is the gate' but also 'I am the door'.

Much splendid writing comes in Part II of *Pilgrim's Progress*, with such characters as Mr Great-heart, old Honest, and Valiant-for-Truth. The description at the end, of how each member of the party crosses the river, is memorable. Who can forget Mr Valiant-for-Truth's farewell?

> Then said he, 'I am going to my fathers, and though with great difficulty I am got hither, yet now I do not repent me of all the trouble I have been at to arrive where I am. My sword I give to him that shall succeed me in my pilgrimage, and my courage and skill, to him that can get it. My marks and scars I carry with me, to be a witness for me that I have fought his battles who now will be my rewarder.' ... So he passed over, and the trumpets sounded for him on the other side.

**Many-sided gifts**

Bunyan's other allegory, *The Holy War*, is as ambitious as his first, but not so successful. It deals with the battle between God and Satan for Mansoul. It is full of interest in showing Bunyan's grasp of the human mind. Mansoul has five gates, named after the five senses (Eye Gate, Ear Gate, and so on). However, it shows that even an author of such great genius cannot always know how best to succeed.

Bunyan's verse is a vehicle for making plain words memorable. He does not seem to attempt poetry in his rhymes, although he often *achieves* poetry, without trying, in his prose. There are two passages of verse which I think are particularly beautiful. First, the song of the shepherd boy:

> He that is down, need fear no fall,
> He that is low, no pride:
> He that is humble, ever shall
> Have God to be his guide.

Two more stanzas follow. Secondly, Valiant-for-Truth sings a song which has become a well-known hymn:

Who would true valour see
Let him come hither
One here will constant be,
Come wind, come weather.
There's no discouragement
Shall make him once relent,
His first avowed intent,
To be a pilgrim.

The verses have often been changed to suit modern taste. But as with the text of Bunyan's other writings, it seems better to read what Bunyan wrote.

**Prisoner of conscience**

In 1991 millions of viewers and listeners were reminded of John Bunyan's imprisonment of twelve years' duration by Terry Waite, the Archbishop's envoy released after five years of appalling suffering chained in a room in Beirut. Waite was right to point out that in the Bedford county prison conditions were not altogether bad. Bunyan was allowed to see those who needed counsel, both inmates and others who came from some distance to see him as a spiritual counsellor. He was allowed to conduct a service and had an unusual captive congregation, who were often glad to hear him. Parole allowed him to go to London to preach, and doubtless look for friends to plead for him. As Waite reminded us, Bunyan had a table and chair and he could write.

Bunyan was arrested in November 1660; he was thirty-two, and had been preaching for some years. He had been indicted for preaching in 1658, and he said a year later that he 'saw what was a-coming'. Yet at the time preaching was not an offence. His offence (under an act of 1593) was for 'calling together the people' and 'holding unlawful meetings and conventicles'. He was to be in gaol until May 1672, when he was licensed to preach. His church at Bedford had chosen him as their pastor some four months earlier.

Without his enforced imprisonment he might never have written his three greatest books. His conscience, or rather his over-conscientiousness, had much to do with his going into and staying in prison. Bunyan was sure that preaching God's word was his calling. The divine vocation had to be obeyed; no human authority could avail against that imperative call.

As one reads the accounts of his trial and time in gaol, it is evident that Bunyan's rigidity and inability to compromise played a major part. Perhaps we can say that he was not willing to be as wise as a serpent. These personality traits had much to do with his decision to suffer.

He suffered much; his parting from his wife Elizabeth and his children was one reason for his distress. More severe in some ways was his shameful treatment at his trial. Only one judge had any sympathy for the Puritan cause: but he may have been upset by the bold and splendid words of Bunyan's wife, who later confronted the judge with the statement that no poor tinker could expect justice. Parts of the trial transcripts, or Bunyan's accounts at any rate, have an unintended humour more like pantomime. Thus the exchange with judge Kelyng (later Lord Chief justice), who says: 'we know the Common Prayer Book hath been ever since the Apostles' time'.

There was a grim reality of political enmity in the background. The same Kelyng, prosecuting Sir Henry Vane, obtained his execution as a republican. Bunyan was scrupulously careful not to give political offence, and to insist on his simple Christian duty (as he saw it) to preach.

At some times Bunyan expected perpetual banishment, since this had been the sentence on one occasion. The kinder justices who kept him in prison did so partly for his safety, and so as to avoid a sentence of transportation being carried out. Bunyan also feared the death sentence; death would mean martyrdom, and he prayed not to flinch. He hoped someone might be converted by his last words. His vivid imagination, and the experience of generations of saints who read Foxe's *Book of Martyrs,* led him to write: '... wherefore, thought I, I will leap off the ladder even blindfold into eternity, sink or swim, come heaven come hell, Lord Jesus, if thou wilt catch me, do; if not I will venture for thy name'.

Straw to sleep on, no fireplace to warm the prison, and the risk of fevers which could decimate a prison population – no one would choose such a life. But Bunyan could not give his bond not to preach. His conditions were made more severe later in his imprisonment. Though he was released in 1672 after Charles II signed the Declaration of Indulgence, this was repealed the next year. A warrant for Bunyan's arrest was issued in March 1675; somehow he eluded it. Had he, by this time, learned the craftiness of the serpent as well as the innocence of the dove? He was free till 1677, when an old Bedford enemy obtained a writ against him and he was put in prison again for six months or so.

John Owen, the distinguished Puritan Vice-Chancellor of Oxford University, worked hard for his release, and friends entered into a bond for his good behaviour. It was a measure of Owen's admiration for Bunyan that he told King Charles II that he would give all his learning to be able to preach like Bunyan. From a learned and godly statesman of Nonconformity, that was no mean praise.

As with so many who faced prison for their faith, the state may have had varying reasons for its policies during the fifteen years from the time of Bunyan's first arrest. I think, though, that whatever the changes in the political climate outside prison, it was a time when grace etched its work more deeply in Bunyan's character. His faith developed and grew stronger. It seems that at the end of this time he finally emerged successfully from the period of anxiety and depression which he describes so clearly in *Grace Abounding*. The title page of the second edition of his book *Christian Behaviour; or the Fruits of true Christianity* reads: 'By John Bunyan, a Prisoner of *Hope.'*

He had learned through the things that he suffered. He was a deeper, broader and wiser person. His humility prevented his new fame from going to his head. His fame certainly did not bring him much money: that went to his printers and (as with Luther) to those others who stole his work and produced pirated editions. When he died, the deed of gift to his wife Elizabeth shows very little property: it was worth some £42.

Fifteen more books were published after his death in 1688. Four months later, William of Orange landed in England and became king. The Toleration Act was passed in 1689, making publication less risky for fellow Christians who shared Bunyan's faith.

**To be a pilgrim: then and now**

Three hundred years later, how can we possibly expect Bunyan to be relevant to us, as he was to his contemporaries? It has been said that all that matters in Bunyan is his picture of a journey – as if he could agree that it is better to travel hopefully than to arrive! That was not Bunyan's view of pilgrimage. For some, the place of pilgrimage does not signify: whether Mecca or Benares, no matter. But for Bunyan it is not so. The Celestial City, arrived at after many dangers, is the goal and the reason for the journey.

The exact, historical basis of the Christian faith, the scandal of the particular, is disturbing to many people. But it is a part of Bunyan. If we try to make the faith universal and general by discarding aspects of the content, we may lose something vital. Let us start by separating out some of the elements that Bunyan considered essential.

First, the journey is above all an inward and spiritual toil; the outward aspects are only secondary. It begins when someone wakes from spiritual sleep, the sleep of death. Bunyan constantly refers to the eyes of the understanding: this is a matter of knowing oneself in the light of God's word. And the first thing to know in oneself is that one is dead in sin, and under the wrath of God. Hence Christian's initial 'lamentable cry, saying *What shall I do?*'

Bunyan dwells much on both God's law and his love. Self-knowledge becomes a burden on Christian's back because of the guilt attached to it and because of the sense of sin which knowing God's law produces. Pilgrimage is to do with relationships. The first is a new relationship with God in Christ, found through going by way of the wicket-gate and the cross where Christian can sing:

> Blest Cross, Blest Sepulchre, blest rather be
> The man who there was put to shame for me.

The second essential element is fellowship with others. The loneliness of the pilgrim can be overstressed. He is a man alone, going through the wicket-gate of necessity. At the same time, Bunyan thought very highly of belonging to a *band* of pilgrims; and in his other writings the *gathered* Church (of 'visible saints'), committed to love, learn and live *together,* is very important.

Bunyan stresses that the pilgrim is always in the process of learning; instruction, based on the Bible, is continuous. He is like the psalmist who delights in the law of the Lord and meditates on it day and night. Christian frequently breaks off to argue, discuss and instruct on his pilgrim's way, though some find this tedious and tiresome.

We are often reminded that the Way is 'as straight as a rule can make it'. But there are many by-path meadows, enchanted grounds and other traps to cause deviation from the narrow way. Bunyan knew the Ranters and Quakers of his day who could not abide the external light offered by the Bible and preferred their own inner light. He also knew the liberal, rational guides who turned away from the Bible for other reasons.

These are typical traps and diversions, and others are described in Bunyan's writings which are still with us today in various forms. We need to learn about them as Christian did in *Pilgrim's Progress* in order to avoid straying. We need to learn the same lessons.

**Striving for the truth**

One of Bunyan's constant fears was of being a hypocrite, that it might after all be a big 'act' – merely show and outward profession, without the real and inward work of grace which he considered the essential element.

What of the City of Destruction, which Christian leaves on this pilgrimage? We live in a global city with communications that are much more developed than in Bunyan's day. But those who are preoccupied by mushroom-shaped nuclear clouds and other dangers to our world are surely familiar with the threat of outward destruction. Such a threat lies behind all ecological movements and green politics.

Yet Bunyan, who had experienced an English civil war, was more concerned about destruction as a personal, spiritual possibility. For Bunyan, being separated from God meant hell, and being united with him through grace in Christ is heaven, and the most desirable aspect of salvation.

In his books Bunyan was of course also very concerned about 'working out' his salvation. In *I will Pray with the Spirit* he emphasized the need for personal growth in grace and inward development, and for not relying on mere outward forms, as in, for example, the liturgy.

He did not despise the blessings of being in God's natural world; on the contrary, his family was very important to him. He was indulgent with children, and he loved play and music. His hearty love of food appears often in his books; for instance, in the feasts that 'Gaius mine host' is made to produce for Christiana and her fellow pilgrims. He is said to have made a flute in prison, and to have played the fiddle too. His was a Puritanism very far removed from the false Victorian version.

I find it sad that after 1666 we lose sight of his inner life. Did his symptoms bother him much less as he grew older? I think living in prison with his thoughts and fears may have served as a kind of 'exposure treatment' which finally eliminated his phobias and his need for rituals. But this is speculation. His new role as a writer enabled him to expound his faith systematically (was his love of system a remnant of his former obsessionality?). His writing reached its classic best in prison. It must have helped him to write things down, since to make sense of one's experience by so doing is often therapeutic. The self-help aspect (often contrasted with the 'sent-help' in Bunyan's writings) was perhaps a by-product of his work as a writer.

Once a man of Bunyan's strength of heart and mind had found salvation in Christ, the Bible (some verses of which had been such a threat to him in early crises) became his delight. He loved the God whose grace had come to him, removing his burdens of guilt and sin. He 'lived upon the Word', and sought always to understand it better.

The fact that he had a priceless gift of imagination and was, in that sense, a dreamer, meant that he could give expression in his writings to the truth that he had learned so painfully and, in his own words, 'damnable hard'.

His death came suddenly, in his sixtieth year, on 31 August 1688. After going on a journey to reconcile a son in Bedford to his father in Reading, he rode on to London where he preached. He was soaked with rain on this journey, and ten days later he died of a fever. The thousands who heard him preach in London were to remember him mainly for the three books he wrote in prison. In the three centuries since, millions all over the world have benefited from his writing, with its unique blend of Scripture, experience and imagination.

*Further Reading*

The best person to read is John Bunyan himself. The late Professor Roger Sharrock made the editing of Bunyan's work one of his main tasks in life. His Penguin Classics edition of *The Pilgrim's Progress* (Harmondsworth: Penguin Books, 1987) is true to the original in a way many so-called modern editions are not; it costs little, and Bunyan's notes in the margins often explain obscure references.

*Grace Abounding* is available in many editions (Dent's Everyman's Library has it bound with *The Life and Death of Mr Badman).* George Offor's 1854 three-volume edition of *The Works of John Bunyan* was reprinted by Banner of Truth in 1991.

Christopher Hill, *A Turbulent, Seditious, and Factious People: John Bunyan and his Church* 1628–1688 (Oxford: OUP, 1989) is a remarkable account. Ernest W. Bacon, *Pilgrim and Dreamer* (Exeter: Paternoster Press, 1983) is a very clear and sympathetic brief account. Roger Sharrock's own *John Bunyan* (London: 1968) is one of the best and most balanced accounts. The classic study by John Brown, *John Bunyan* (1628–1688): *His Life, Times and Work,* was updated in 1928 by F. Mott Harrison. Harrison also wrote *John Bunyan:* A *Story of His Life,* a fictionalized life which was republished in 1964 by Banner of Truth. *The Pilgrim's Progress: A Casebook* (London: Macmillan, 1976), edited by Roger Sharrock, is a mine of information. Monica Furlong's *Puritan's Progress: A Study of John Bunyan* (London: Hodder & Stoughton, 1975) and her selection *The Trial of John Bunyan and the Persecution of the Puritans* (London: Folio Society, 1978) are helpful. Judith Gunn, *Bunyan of Elston,* (London: Hodder & Stoughton, 1985) is in the 'faction' style.

N. H. Keeble (ed.), *John Bunyan: Conventicle and Parnassus* (Oxford: OUP, 1988) is a helpful collection of tercentenary essays. George Wakefield's *Bunyan the Christian* (London: Harper Collins, 1992) is an expansion of his essay in that collection. The Open University has contributed two important books: A. Laurence, W. R. Owen and S. Sim (eds), *John Bunyan and His England* (1628–1688) (London: Hambledon Press, 1990), and Stuart Sim, *Negotiations with Paradox* (London: Wheatsheaf Press, 1990).

John Stachniewski, *The Persecutory Imagination: English*

*Puritanism and the Language of Religious Despair* (Oxford: OUP, 1991) is a learned attack on what the author calls 'a phenomenon as bizarre as belief in the Calvinist God'. In spite of his claim to use 'psycho-social understanding', I find little evidence in Stachniewski's account of any proper understanding of the quality of Bunyan's experience of grace: his findings are wholly negative.

A study by a French Catholic professor, Henri Talon, *John Bunyan: The Man and His Works* (London: Rockliff, 1951), is to my mind the best to whet the appetite for Bunyan himself.

# 3

# Darkness into Light: William Cowper (1731–1800)

I deliver'd thee when bound,
And, when wounded, healed thy wound;
Sought thee wand'ring, set thee right,
Turn'd thy darkness into light.

William Cowper, *Olney Hymns*

I am glad you love Cowper. I could forgive a man for not enjoying Milton, but I would not call that man a friend, who should be offended with the 'divine chit-chat of Cowper'.

Charles Lamb to S. T. Coleridge

It is a very consoling fact that so many books about real lives ... give one such an impression of happiness, in spite of all the tragedies they contain. What could be more tragic than the main outlines of Lamb's or Cowper's lives? But as soon as you open the letters of either, and see what they were writing from day to day and what relish they got out of it, you almost begin to envy them.

C. S. Lewis, to Arthur Greeves

Most of us know something written by William Cowper, at least if we are familiar with a hymn-book. Many of us know little of the man. 'God moves in a mysterious way' may be one of his most well-known hymns: there are many others, as well as two volumes of verse which made him the most popular poet of his day. He was more of a best-seller than John Betjeman in our days.

Cowper wanted to break the conspiracy of silence about depression, just as Betjeman did about his own melancholy experiences. Cowper was depressed first at the age of twenty-one, and from time to time thereafter for the next ten years. At thirty-one he had his first catastrophic psychotic breakdown, and at the time of his recovery from it he became a Christian. He was to have five more depressive illnesses before he died at sixty-eight: in between these times he was often amazingly productive as a letter-writer and poet.

In 1929 Lord David Cecil wrote a remarkable life of Cowper called *The Stricken Deer.* Elegant and eminently readable (it is still in print), it showed a considerable antipathy to Cowper's fellow Christians. Cecil evidently did not feel at home with the evangelical world of which he wrote, and he was also quite inaccurate about some of the most important features of Cowper's faith. We know more today about the depressive disorders which plagued Cowper at intervals through his adult life. It will be worth seeking to correct Cecil – and others – who blamed John Newton (and what was thought to be Newton's brand of Christian faith) for making Cowper worse.

There is much to enjoy in Cowper, as a man and as a poet. There is no darkness or shade without light and sunshine. There was much quiet joy, laughter and real pleasure in William Cowper, as well as tragic and sometimes unbearable sadness. A study of him answers C. S. Lewis' question: 'Perhaps the tragedies of real life contain more consolation and fun and gusto than the comedies of literature?'

Cowper is of exceptional interest for Christians, and for all those who are interested in human suffering. His life is also very relevant to today. In a special sense he shows what grace can do to a man's personality, and also what it sometimes appears *not* to be able to do. By this I mean that his experience points to a need for an honest explanation of non-healing, and the suffering that can go on and on.

For Cowper raises the question which has puzzled many: Why do so many Christians suffer from depression? It is not enough to call it spiritual depression, for it is more than that. It is partly physical, often chronic or recurrent as an illness, and it is not always removed by attempts to treat, cure or heal it. The extent of depression, and the need for Christians to understand it and care for sufferers from it rather than sitting in judgement upon them or condemning them – these aspects of the problem are all vividly illustrated in Cowper's life story.

John Newton was his friend. Cowper and Newton belong together because of their close links formed in the village of Olney, not far from Newport Pagnell, in Buckinghamshire. They produced the *Olney Hymns* together. Yet many know little about the facts in Cowper's case, even though Newton, the author of the hymn 'Amazing Grace', is so well known as the slave-ship captain who became a famous Christian minister in the City of London. There is much to be learned and enjoyed, as well as a good deal that attracts our sympathy and challenges us, in William Cowper's life.

**Sweetness and light – and shadows**

It is vital to stress one thing at the outset of this brief account. For most of his life Cowper was a sane, sensible and happy man. He was cared for by a series of friends: he was exceptionally happy in his carers. The episodes of depression, when they occurred, were awful and terrible. His delusions – depressive false beliefs – were at times intense, but for long periods they did not impair his daily life or his modest happiness in nature and his animals and garden. He was able, as we shall see, to enjoy close and loving relationships: his friends found his charm and loyalty to be qualities they valued highly.

His faith has been blamed for his illness: but a bare knowledge of the facts shows that his first depression and suicide attempt happened *before* his religious conversion. There may have been a few aspects of that time of evangelical enthusiasm which were inimical to his stability. But the *overwhelming* evidence is of how much his fellow Christians helped, supported and cared for him: and they cared for over three decades.

Cowper seems to have inherited a marked tendency to depression. Even when he was not ill (in the sense of psychotic or insane) he suffered from a melancholy disposition and a delicately anxious temperament. Yet his charm and humour, in his talk and in his hundreds of letters, were more evident than his sadness. We will seek to ascertain why, in spite of such great handicaps, Cowper achieved so much. Real fame came to him only in his late fifties, after his poem *The Task* was published. His working title for that poem was *The Sofa:* as we shall see, it was a strange way to be carried to fame.

**A Whig gentleman**

William Cowper was born in 1731 amid great expectations. The

Cowpers were a great family, whose estates spread over ten thousand acres in the centre of Hertfordshire. Although his father, the Rev. John Cowper, DD, may have been a relatively obscure rector of Great Berkhampstead, he was also chaplain to George II. William's grandfather was Spencer Cowper, a judge and a Whig Member of Parliament. Spencer's famous brother William was the first Earl Cowper, who had twice been Lord Chancellor. The law and politics were the life-blood of the family for generations on his father's side.

Cowper's mother died when he was aged six, in 1737. His mother, Anne Donne, traced her descent from noble families too, and Cowper loved going to his Donne cousins in Norfolk. Regrettably the earlier view that she was related to the poet John Donne is not true. The tortured mind of that Dean of St Paul's might have been fully capable of understanding William Cowper. The feelings that Cowper had about his mother are vividly recalled in a poem he wrote fifty years later, on being sent a copy of his mother's picture. Does he exaggerate the desolation he felt when he describes himself as a 'Wretch even then, life's journey just begun'? I doubt it: we know far more nowadays about the effects of a child losing a mother at that age. The risk of both depression and suicide in later life has been shown to be far greater in those who lose a parent before ten or eleven years of age. It is hardly possible to make too much of its effects on Cowper's personality. He needed mothering, and may only have found it later in 'My Mary' – Mrs Unwin. Her care for him (and his, later, for her) was a long and moving part of his life. The story of his relationship with Mary Unwin and her family is a remarkable one of compassion, care and catastrophe.

There were seven children, but only William and his youngest brother John survived into adult life. It was a few days after the birth of John that his mother Ann died. It is easy to imagine the distress that his father also suffered. Yet it is sad that the widowed father decided to send the six-year-old William away to school, seven miles from home.

The torment he endured from a fifteen-year-old bully led to the expulsion of the older boy, and the transfer of William to the care of an oculist. It may be too much to say (as Cecil does) that his nervous system was ruined for life. But it was certainly a horrid learning experience for Cowper. In his memoir he almost makes us see the buckled shoes of the tormenting bully, since he was too frightened to look up to and face him.

Mr and Mrs Disney were both oculists, and for the next two years he had some parental care from both, and began to enjoy the holidays at home too. Cowper recalls the Disneys without any affection, probably because staying with them meant separation from his father and his baby brother John.

Then came the decision to send him to Westminster School, in the shadow of the Abbey and Parliament. There it stands today, and the pupils still attend prayers in the adjacent Abbey. Whatever fears there may have been about going to London and to this new school proved unfounded: Cowper enjoyed it.

### Happy schooldays

Westminster School was the best in the land in 1742, when Cowper enrolled, and for the second time in its history it had a great headmaster. Eton had to take second place, and Cowper had to learn in the company of a large assemblage of sons of peers, many of whom would win fame as grown men.

Of course there was brutality and many features which Cowper would later attack in a famous poem. This work (Tirocinium) is said to have sowed seeds of change that led to Arnold's reforms at Rugby. The poem also says:

> Be it a weakness, it deserves some praise;
> We love the play-place of our early days.

Cowper joined 354 boys, and lived in one of the small boardinghouses in Little Dean's Yard run by a 'Dame'. Although Cowper shared a room and probably a bed with other boys, this particular house appears to have been well run. For Cowper there was a family atmosphere to enjoy.

He made friends, and became very fond of some of the masters, and he later remembered the care with which Dr John Nicoll, the headmaster, prepared the boys for confirmation. Cowper also remembered his first attempts at 'prayer in secret' and how Nicoll's teaching helped him. Many of his later characteristics became clear: his abilities in reading and writing, and in translating the classics from Greek and Latin, his love of pets, his pleasure in walking. He was to smuggle in a tame mouse, keep it in his bureau drawer, and be mortified when the mouse ate the six young mice it produced.

He won prizes and became what he himself called a 'typical Westminster-classical snob': many famous names in English literature had been on the rolls of Westminster School. Cowper was head of his house, and third in the sixth form. As well as that, he excelled at ball games, both football and the emerging game of cricket, at which he was a star performer. He was never a good horseman, and wanted an end to 'Jockeyship' (as he called the fashion in riding) for ever: he may have relished his later poem 'John Gilpin' for its 'horsey' humour.

It was the boys who taught each other more than the masters did, and Cowper may have been lucky in his school-friends who enjoyed the same literary and leisure tastes. There was barbarism and oppression among the boys, but Cowper seems to have escaped much of this; none the less he would not later advise his friends to send sons to Westminster. While he was there he enjoyed crossing the street to the House of Commons where boys might sit, in seats reserved for them, to listen to the debates. The London sights were to be visited, and this included Bedlam, the famous asylum. He was later cross with himself for watching the inmates who were on show at the Bethlem Royal Hospital.

We know a great deal about the boys with whom Cowper spent these formative five years. They came from similar families, many of whom were notable, and they shared the school interests: the classics, light verse, humour, the law as a possible career and (up to a point) an interest in religion. Cowper had been a scholar from childhood: his first books were Bunyan's *Pilgrim's Progress* and Gay's *Fables:* both most important early, and lasting, influences. As has been said by Charles Ryskamp: 'John Gilpin and John Calvin were part of him from the beginning.' During the last year of his life he was to translate Gay's verse, with its story of the hare caught by the hounds, into Latin. To him it had special meaning.

Cowper soaked up his reading of this time; he also had a good memory and recalled passages from borrowed books easily. He began to write, but none of his early poems has survived. They seem to be largely the kind of verse that was expected from the sons of gentlemen, and doubtless his juvenile verse was like the first that has survived, which was written when he was seventeen. Its title and style are redolent of the man and his time: 'Verses written at Bath, in 1748, on finding the heel of a shoe.' But soon the apprentice poet was to write differently.

**Young blade and first love**

Cowper was intended by his father to be a distinguished lawyer. He 'intended to beget a chancellor, and he begat instead, a translator of Homer. It is impossible for the effect to differ more from the intention,' wrote Cowper. He was a lazy lawyer, who never used his time or talents properly. He 'lost a legion of attorneys ... by never doing their business' after he was called to the bar. Though a lamentably failed lawyer, he still felt proud enough of it to write to his friend John Newton in 1781, 'announce me to the world by the style and title of William Cowper, Esquire, of the Inner Temple'.

In the years from leaving school in 1749 to 1763 he moved from articled clerk to Chapman, a London solicitor, to the Inner Temple, via the Middle Temple where he was actually first admitted in 1748. He was called to the bar in 1754, following a year of depression, which was not severe. The law may have formed the background to his London life, but the world he really enjoyed was very different. There was a group of young rakes, most of whom were old boys of Westminster. They formed the Nonsense Club, which met each Thursday to eat, drink and share some literary interests.

He was able to explore the world of women for the first time. This was made easier for him because he was welcome almost daily at the home of his uncle Ashley Cowper. There were three sisters. The eldest was Harriet, who as Lady Hesketh will reappear as one of two ladies so important in his Olney period. The younger sister was Elizabeth, but it was the middle sister, Theadora, with whom Cowper fell in love.

Thea and William formed a very strong affection for each other: she wrote to her sister that they saw each other daily for two years. Her sister in turn described Thea as a goddess to look at, and William was proud of her, very happily in love, and wrote many poems to her (where he addressed her as Delia). He describes how since knowing her he had improved at least in being less shy and more presentable:

William was once a bashful youth,
　　His modesty was such,
That one might say (to say the truth)
　　He rather had too much.

The women said, who thought him rough,
　　But now no longer foolish,
The creature may do well enough,
　　But wants a deal of polish.

At length improved from head to heel,
　　'Twere scarce too much to say,
No dancing bear was so genteel,
　　Or half so dégagé.

Now that a miracle so strange
　　May not in vain be shown,
Let the dear maid who wrought the change
　　E'er claim him for her own.

Was Thea's father, Ashley Cowper – brother to William's father – right in forbidding the marriage after a two-year courtship and engagement? I think he would have the support of any genetic counsellor today. Ashley himself had nervous fevers, but more important was Theadora's depression. Though able, cultured and in love, her melancholy nature and risk of illness were both known. The reasons given concerned Cowper's lack of money to support a wife.

A book could be written (and their mutual friend Haley wanted to write one) on *The Loves of William and Theadora.* She never married, and in fact suffered a serious illness and was admitted to St Albans under Dr Cotton, afterwards sharing the same physician as Cowper had in his later illness. Her letters show her devotion to Cowper into old age. She sent gifts and money to him anonymously, and was deeply hurt to read of his love for Mary Unwin when his poems to Mary were published. Theadora's letters after Cowper's death – and fifty-five years after they parted – describe her lasting love, sorrow and sadness. Cowper once recalled his happy days with Theadora and his other cousins in Southampton Row, saying he was 'constantly employed from morning to night in giggling and making giggle instead of studying the Law'.

Theadora had brought to Cowper not only love and some social grace and polish, as he wittily describes in the verses quoted: it was her close contact with him in a world dominated by his male friends which softened and civilized a wild time in his life. We know that his group lived as young rakes, proud of their hard drinking, their loves and their quest for fame.

At Theadora's there was some Christian influence (she was deeply religious), and on Sundays he joined the family in worship at a local Bloomsbury church. After the devastating loss of the girl he wished to marry, how much of a young blade and rake was Cowper? In a letter Cowper wrote in 1758 (five years after the break with Thea) he says he is 'tortured with love' because of a girl from the West Indies who was staying at Greenwich. It was also rumoured by Mr Unwin's former curate that 'Cowper's first derangement was occasioned by a love affair with the kept mistress of Lord Thurlow'.

Cowper and Thurlow were close friends, and the rumour must have been a very easy one to believe. Cowper had once predicted that Thurlow would be Lord Chancellor (which in fact he became), saying he should then provide for Cowper financially. He called the ladies with them at the time to bear witness to Thurlow's promise to that effect. Though estranged after the first 1763 breakdown, Thurlow helped obtain a pension for him later, and their friendship was resumed.

Years later Cowper told Mrs Unwin that in those days he could down four or five bottles of claret 'without sensible effect'. He was immersed in the gaieties and follies of his group, as witnesses relate. His pleasant and humorous personality made him welcome. He could make an amusing story out of nothing, and was much loved by his friends for his gentle satire of the ludicrous. He may have avoided the even greater excesses of his friends, but he was a very active man about town: inevitably, the effects on his legal career were bad ones.

**Failure: at law and in life**

Slowly and inexorably his real failures caught up with Cowper, leading up to a depression, attempted suicide and admission for treatment. The influence of the things we have already considered is evident. We must try to tease out the different elements now coming together.

We note the family tendency and the early losses. He never recovered as a person from the loss of his mother, and the loss of mothering care. This can be seen in his later life. But the broken engagement after two years must be seen as a major life event, leading to a good deal of grief at such a loss.

Another loss that aggravated Cowper's depressive tendency was the accidental death by drowning in the Thames of one of his best friends, Sir William Russell. He had known him since Westminster schooldays: 'Each dear companion of my voyage lost!' he wrote. 'My friend torn from me, and my Mistress lost.'

His grief at losing a woman he wanted to marry may not have been obvious: it was a depth-charge under the surface, ready to explode and sink him. It was significant that soon afterwards he left the family of Chapman, the solicitor with whom he had lived, and bought his first chambers at the Temple: there he was more lonely. The fact that he could see his life in the legal profession coming to nothing was an immediate cause of genteel poverty. More important was his failure to achieve anything worthwhile as a writer or as a poet.

Cowper depended on friends and relatives for money as well as affection and support. They sometimes objected to the ease with which he asked for and took money. A letter from Cowper to a friend embarking on a career in law puts his feelings well:

> The colour of our whole life is generally such as the three or four first years in which we are our own masters, make it. Then it is that we may be said to shape our own destiny, and to treasure up for ourselves a series of future successes or disappointments.... But three years misspent in an attorney's office were almost of course followed by several more equally misspent in the Temple....

His father's legacy was beginning to run out at this time: his friends were either moving on in their careers or getting married. Cowper was feeling lonely, and his melancholy was becoming something more than an understandable depression (resulting from the factors we have mentioned). He was still fencing and shooting, dancing all night, visiting the opera and the theatre, and drinking a good deal. His tailor was still seeing a lot of Cowper, for being elegantly dressed was then, as always, an important matter for him.

Though he was not thought to be ill at this period, Cowper recalls:

> I was struck not long after my settlement in the Temple, with such a dejection of spirits, as none but they who have felt the same, can have the least conception of. Day and night I was upon the rack, lying down in horror, and rising up in despair.

He turned to the works of George Herbert, the Christian priest and poet who had died at thirty-nine in 1632. 'This was the only author I had any delight in reading. I pored over him all day long; and though I found not here what I might have found – a cure for my malady, yet it never seemed so much alleviated as while I was reading him.'

### The constant friend

A visit to the coast, as to Southampton, might help his mood enormously. At his chambers at the Temple he would study and work sporadically. His study of law, though haphazard, stood him in good stead later in life when helping friends and neighbours. After four years he moved into better chambers in the Inner Temple. We must remember that the Inns of Court formed four small communities. It was said that the Inner Temple was for the rich and the Middle for the poor. Cowper was with many elegant bachelors who lived a life rich in entertainment of all sorts. How could he afford it?

A constant friend called Joseph Hill supplied much of the answer: for he gave money to Cowper on a regular basis. Hill was the son of an attorney and a close friend of all the Cowper family. Though his was a humbler background, Hill worked his way up from clerk to solicitor to very rich attorney, with a huge practice. He had no school or university background, but became Cowper's close friend and patron from the days he left Westminster until his death in 1800.

Hill would join the Cowpers on the excursions and holidays which did so much to prevent Cowper's spirits from falling into severe and psychotic depression, as they were to do in 1763. He paid Cowper's bills in London, and supplied him with funds when his own ran out. By a curious irony, Cowper had introduced Hill to Edward Thurlow, with whom he formed a close association. Thurlow became Lord Chancellor, and with the Woolsack in 1778 came many posts which were in his gift. Hill became, much later, Secretary of Lunatics.

Hill was to be the person who arranged for Cowper's care in the St Albans asylum, a small private nursing home run by Dr Nathaniel Cotton. Hill was one of the very few friends who helped Cowper through his first, serious illness.

**First illness and new life**

How did the first breakdown at last happen, after some years of feeling both very low in spirits and anxious about his inability to cope with his life and his work? To try and understand it we must learn about common eighteenth-century practices, in particular the offices and posts which were sinecures, calling for little or no work, but paying well.

His severe depressive breakdown of 1763 was to lead Cowper to an attempt on his life by taking opium and trying to hang himself. It took him finally out of London, to which he never returned. More than this: in St Albans he became a Christian. It was this evangelical conversion that brought him into a new life.

It was new because for the first time he came to believe and know as his most precious faith what had simply been vague to him before. His feelings were as involved as his intellect, and his way of life became totally changed. Eventually, by a strange road, it was to bring him a new impetus as a poet, a new career as a hymnwriter, and lasting fame.

It seems at first sight that the immediate cause of Cowper's severe depression was his fear of being examined publicly at the bar of the House of Lords. This was to decide if he was suitable for the post of Clerk of Journals there. Cowper was so shy of public appearances that his anxiety was dreadful. Yet the post had been his only hope of making enough money to live as a gentleman. He had doubts not only about his fitness for the post, but also about the way his cousin and uncle had obtained it for him in the first place.

Ashley Cowper, his uncle, had inherited a post of Clerk of the Parliaments which had been bought by his grandfather Spencer Cowper for £18,000. It gave the holder privileges in appointing all the clerks in the House of Lords. The Cowper cousins who now profited by these offices had been the subject of much criticism, leading to an inquiry. William Cowper knew that his uncle and cousins had made enemies by the way they corruptly managed posts. He hated the fact that these posts were the result of being bought earlier by political 'placemen'.

Cowper knew that the public examination would give those political enemies that the Cowpers had made a chance to make him the easy scapegoat. He dreaded the public humiliation. He began to long to be delivered from the crisis. For ten months he thought of how he might get out of an intolerable situation. He tried to go to the House of Lords, but could not get on with the job. His anxiety made concentration difficult, and he felt that going to work was like going to a place of execution. He dreaded the scandal his failure would cause all his friends and family.

Suicide came to preoccupy Cowper. He remembered how his father had once discussed with him a book on the ethics of killing oneself, and he seemed to think his father sided with those in favour of it; he found men in coffee houses talking of suicide; letters in the paper favoured it as a solution. When the recess came Cowper went to Margate for two months holiday, and afterwards seemed better. In October his misery and agitation returned and increased. His cousin Martin Madan tried to help, and his brother John came down from Cambridge to see him.

Madan had been to Westminster School, had also trained as a lawyer, and had become a hard-drinking rake until John Wesley had been the means of his conversion. Now Madan was a powerful preacher and a much-respected counsellor: but he failed to help Cowper, whose condition worsened.

On the eve of his public ordeal Cowper tried to take his life by drinking laudanum (a liquid form of opium he had bought some weeks before), but failed to take sufficient of it. He tried to pierce his chest with a knife and failed. Then he tried to hang himself by his garter, but fell and was discovered by a maid. His uncle Ashley brought in the celebrated Dr Heberden, who advised him to retire to the country. But Cowper's state of mind worsened and he showed for the first time clear signs of insanity. He had delusions that he was damned beyond hope. He abandoned the ideas of suicide, but sank deeper into a psychotic, deranged state of mind.

**Safety and salvation**

His brother John left his post as a Cambridge don and stayed with him in London. It became evident to John that his brother was now in need of proper care. The matter was discussed with friends, and Joseph Hill must have been foremost in assuring financial help. The family were consulted, and they agreed that this was not merely Cowper's constitutional melancholy but an illness needing treatment.

Dr Cotton's *Collegium Insanorum,* a spacious building near St Albans Abbey, was decided upon. Cowper was to stay there (with some four to ten other patients) for eighteen months. Within five months he was almost recovered, and it was after this that he experienced his conversion.

Dr Nathaniel Cotton was well known as an exceptionally well-trained physician who had studied under the renowned Doctor Boerhaave in Leyden. He was described as 'most amiable and engaging in his manners, and bearing the character of a skilful and experienced Physician'. It was exceptional in those days: 'the trade in lunacy', as the madhouses run for profit were called, created many scandals. It was rare to find a doctor both kind and well trained, whose patients were few and well cared for. The crowded private madhouses were usually very poorly supervised.

Dr Cotton had been a friend of the well-known dissenting minister and head of an academy in Northampton, the late Dr Philip Doddridge. His classic on *The Rise and Progress of Religion in the Soul* and other works by Doddridge were available to Cowper and became his daily bread later, with only the Bible being given precedence. Doddridge was an admirably balanced man, and his writings could never be seen as upsetting.

Five months after Cowper's admission, Dr Cotton found him able to tell stories with his usual wit and humour. When his brother visited him two months later, he seemed happier, but still believed he was damned. He began to hope there might be mercy for him, in spite of his persistent, depressive delusion about being damned. The actual moment of change is best told in his own words:

> I flung myself into a chair near the window, and, seeing a Bible there, ventured to apply once more to it for comfort and instruction. The first verse I saw was the 25th of the 3rd of the Romans: 'Whom God hath set forth to be a propitiation through faith in his blood, to declare his righteousness for the remission of sins that are past, through the forbearance of God.'
>
> Immediately I received strength to believe it.... In a moment I believed, and received the gospel. Unless the Almighty arm had been under me, I think I should have died with gratitude and joy.

His doctor was worried, for the next lines in Cowper's memoir suggest a switch from depression to mania:

> For many succeeding weeks, tears were ready to flow, if I did but speak of the gospel, or mention the name of Jesus. To rejoice day and night was all my employment. Too happy to sleep much, I thought it was but lost time that was spent in slumber.... My physician, ever watchful and apprehensive for my welfare, was now alarmed, lest the sudden transition from despair to joy should terminate in a fatal frenzy.... In a short time, Dr C. became satisfied, and acquiesced in the soundness of my cure.... He visited me every morning while I stayed with him, which was nearly a twelvemonth after my recovery.

In Cowper's own elegant prose the facts could hardly be better described. What happened? Was it the flicking of some hidden switch that changed the chemistry of his brain? Was it simply the endpoint of a long process of regeneration, the moment of grace in conversion? Might it have been an experience of assurance of salvation, as was John Wesley's in 1738 in Aldersgate Street?

Cowper states: 'Whatever my friend Madan had said to me, long before, revived in all clearness....' He saw it as the climax of a process, and the beginning of his new Christian life. He found salvation, and his subsequent life was to be a clear example of working out his salvation with fear and trembling.

My view is that two things happened at about the same time: his religious experience and a change in his mental state. His recovery from depression, and the beginning of a phase of elation and mild manic (or hypomanic) symptoms fits in well with his description. Equally, I think he had a true, and not unusual, form of Christian conversion.

It was unwise of nineteenth-century biographers to refer to religion as the cure of his depression. It was equally ill judged for Lord David Cecil to imply that he was madder with religious mania than he had been with religious melancholia. Of course his London friends and family feared for him: 'Enthusiasm' (whether Methodist or Anglican) was then seen as morbid and distasteful by most of those in Cowper's circle.

His modern editors commented wisely in 1980:

> Cowper's isolation during the next twenty years was largely self-imposed, and in part the consequence of poverty, but it was also a tacit recognition that to many of his former associates in that less tolerant age deliberate adoption of Evangelical Christianity seemed almost a worse lunacy than trying to hang oneself with a pair of garters.

Has the attitude of unbelievers to Christians changed much since Cowper's day? I think not. In his famous poem *The Task* Cowper described his experience with hindsight, in a memorable passage:

> I was a stricken deer that left the herd
> Long since; with many an arrow deep infixt
> My panting side was charged when I withdrew
> To seek a tranquil death in distant shades.
> There was I found by one who had himself
> Been hurt by th' archers. In his side he bore
> And in his hands and feet the cruel scars.
> With gentle force soliciting the darts
> He drew them forth, and heal'd and bade me live.

It is the same experience of grace that he celebrated in the hymn beginning 'Hark my soul it is the Lord', which is quoted at the head of this chapter:

Sought thee wand'ring, set thee right,
Turn'd thy darkness into light.

**Finding a new family**

Cowper left St Albans, taking with him a manservant he had acquired and a boy whom he had 'adopted'. His brother found him rooms in Huntingdon, and a horse on which William might ride to visit him at Cambridge. In Huntingdon Cowper soon found a new home with the Rev. and Mrs Unwin. Mary Unwin was to care for Cowper for over thirty years, and moved with him to Olney two years after his leaving hospital.

John Cowper was a remarkable scholar who died at thirty-three of dropsy. He had a remarkable conversion experience during the illness, and William was delighted to share his faith and assurance with his brother. John's death was a loss of 'the best classic and most liberal thinker in our University'. A brilliant linguist in six languages, he had won many distinctions for his learning, and his college made him Fellow and Bursar. Until his sudden illness and death he had a more robust nature than William. He had supported him, kept up a rhyming correspondence with him, and was an Anglican rector of the sort that combined sound learning with religion.

Cowper remained a gentleman: later, in Olney, he would be known as 'Sir Cowper' or 'The Squire'. His skills did not include money management. In Huntingdon he spent in a quarter the whole year's income. So, after five months, he was delighted to join the Unwin family. He wrote to Joseph Hill:

> ... the race of Unwins, ... father and mother, son and daughter ... are the most comfortable social folks you ever knew.... The son is twenty-one, unreserved and amiable ... the father a man of learning and good sense ... and the son designed for orders ... Mrs Unwin has a very uncommon understanding, has read much to excellent purpose.

The only thing Cowper missed was a ministry 'under the sound of the Gospel'. This soon became possible. The Rev. Morley Unwin died suddenly in 1767. A few days later there was the first meeting between Cowper and John Newton. The two men liked each other at once. Newton offered to settle them in Olney, and in the next month a house was found and the new Unwin family moved to Olney less than three months after Mr Unwin's death. Cowper was to stay in Olney for nineteen years, and as we shall see the arrangement led to some being offended or scandalized, and to Cowper being hurt. When Mrs Unwin's husband died there was gossip in Huntingdon. 'Black and shocking Aspersions ... Things which our soul abhors are imputed to us,' wrote Cowper. 'We are like mother and son,' wrote Mrs Unwin of Cowper. Her son (also called William) became very close to Cowper: a kind of adopted son to Cowper. When Mrs Unwin's son died unexpectedly Cowper was so upset by his sudden death that his breakdown of 1787 (his fourth) may well have resulted from this major loss.

His new family was of enormous importance to him: Mary Unwin was like a new mother. Newton was both a new father figure and a spiritual guide. For a time Cowper acted like a curate to John Newton in Olney. His settled family life was an important factor in allowing him to develop. Two volumes of his poetry were published. The second made him famous, and old friends began to visit Olney. His links with Newton produced the important volume of *Olney Hymns.* Wherever the Christian Church has met, the voice of Cowper has been heard in many hymns. His writings have had a great influence on the way many people speak, using phrases from Cowper that they never knew were first written by him. But his hymns were perhaps his most lasting and useful achievement.

## A tale of two ladies

There were three widows in Cowper's life, of whom Mary Unwin was far the most important. But the other two deserve some attention.

Lady Austen appeared as a bright butterfly on the Olney water-meadows, said one observer. She captivated Cowper, and a platonic affair ensued which Mary Unwin watched with pain. Lady Hesketh appeared later, and stayed in Cowper's life longer and with less threat to his and Mary's happiness. For Cowper's mother-son relationship with Mary had sustained them both: but it was vulnerable.

Anna, as he called Lady Austen, was visiting her sister when

Cowper saw her in Olney and asked Mary to introduce her to him. A firm friendship grew fast, and on her side seems to have been passionate, while Cowper was rather naively playing the part of the gallant poet. Lady Austen is important for us because she gave Cowper the ideas and inspiration to write. She told him the story of John Gilpin, which he turned into a ballad.

When he protested that he could think of no subject, she said he should write about the sofa. So began his greatest poem, *The Task.* When it was published together with 'John Gilpin' and his attack on public schools, the volume brought him fame. He became the talk of the town. His books were best-sellers. He was later offered the post of Poet Laureate, but of course refused it. Lady Austen and he, while she stayed in Olney, dined together daily. It could not last.

Cowper wrote in a lofty tone, saying their close relationship must end: Anna was furious. But she came back to Olney the following year and stayed in rooms at the Vicarage for eighteen months. William and Anna were again much closer, seeking to cultivate what they called a brother and sister relationship, and she did much to help Mary Unwin dispel the threatening gloom when he seemed sad.

As Cecil puts it: 'while still avoiding the boiling point of passion, Cowper still liked to keep the emotional temperature decidedly warmer than that of mere friendship'. After knowing each other for two years, Cowper wrote another letter to Anna, reproving her for indecorous advances. This time she left Olney for good. We next hear of her in the Paris of Napoleon, married to Count Claude Tardiff du Granger, who was also a poet. While they had both lived in a kind of Arcadia, Cowper had been able to begin to produce some of his best work in *The Task.* It had been the highest form of occupational therapy for him.

Lady Hesketh appeared five years after he met Lady Austen. She was his cousin Harriet (or Harriot), and was delighted with Cowper's new fame, sending presents, adding a hundred pounds a year to his income with gifts from her family, and bringing back memories of his youth. She made him laugh, and there was no hint of romance. Hers was a practical concern for his happiness, and she arranged a major move from Orchard Side to Weston Lodge. She also made new friends for Cowper: the Throckmortons, whose Roman

Catholicism alarmed John Newton in London. It all helped greatly to ease the burden of care that Mary bore, and improved the quality of their lives.

### 'My Mary': care and catastrophe

Mary Unwin bore these years well: she felt Cowper was better when he had more social contact. Yet Cowper loved the home atmosphere best of all. It is the way he celebrates this that is often remembered, as in 'The Winter Evening':

> Now stir the fire, and close the shutters fast,
> Let fall the curtains, wheel the sofa round,
> And while the bubbling and loud-hissing urn
> Throws up a steamy column, and the cups,
> That cheer but not inebriate, wait on each,
> So let us welcome peaceful evening in.

Mary Unwin was seven years older than Cowper, and she was to look after him for twenty-six years, until her first stroke. He did his best to look after her for the next five years, until her third stroke and death. It seems to me that the story of William and Mary itself deserves a chapter to show their devotion and love. Anyone who has cared briefly for a depressed person will know the enormous strain of it. To look after Cowper through four more serious relapses was a heroic task. How could she do it?

She was described as a 'sensible and accomplished though far from handsome woman' whose humour helped her to laugh easily. She was a draper's daughter from Ely, and married at eighteen: she was 'more polite than a duchess'. She made Cowper feel like a close relation at once, and intuitively understood him. She gave up her normal social life to look after him.

Five years after their move to Olney they became engaged, but this was followed by a severe depression, and they decided not to marry. But their relationship was a deep and special one. Cowper wrote a series of fourteen verses to her not long before she died. Two express the feelings present in all these stanzas:

The twentieth year is well nigh past,
Since first our sky was overcast;
Ah would that this might be the last!
My Mary!
And still to love, though prest with ill,
In wintry age to feel no chill,
With me is to be lovely still,
My Mary!

A sonnet written 'To Mrs Unwin' at the same time is one of his loveliest:

Mary! I want a lyre with other strings,
Such aid from Heav'n as some have feign'd to draw
An eloquence scarce giv'n to mortals, new
And undebas'd by praise of meaner things,
That ere through age or woe I shed my wings,
I may record thy worth with honour due,
In verse as musical as thou art true,
And that immortalizes whom it sings.
But thou hast little need. There is a book
By seraphs writ with beams of heav'nly light,
On which the eyes of God not rarely look,
A chronicle of actions just and bright;
There all thy deeds, my faithful Mary, shine,
And since thou own'st that praise, I spare thee mine.

Why did they not marry? Some have invoked the view that Cowper was not as other men, and had some 'intimate deformity', as one gossip maintained. I believe, together with those who have hunted out and destroyed this myth, that Cowper was normal sexually. He could not have survived Westminster School and the company of his fellow boys and young friends had he been some sort of androgyne or hermaphrodite – as was suggested.

After Theadora and his long depressive illness, he was afraid of passion, though he longed for love and affection. I believe it likely, as has been said, that he might have developed some depressive delusion about his body. He had many such physical (or hypochondriacal) beliefs about his body and his health. Part of his depressive anxiety was about a normal, close relationship with a woman. He preferred to be mothered and to enjoy a close companionship on which he could unfailingly depend. He was glad to return some care for Mary Unwin with his tender concern for her in the last years, when she had her three strokes.

**John Newton: blessing or bogeyman?**

I must declare my interest here: I think Newton was a great help to Cowper and cared for him deeply. Only in minor ways was it hard for him to avoid hurting such a sensitive plant as Cowper proved to be. Perhaps he was too strict a literary mentor to Cowper.

He has been attacked by many: by Walter Bagehot, by Sir James G. Frazer (of *Golden Bough* fame, who edited Cowper's letters), and notably by Lord David Cecil. They have demonstrated a marked dislike of all Newton was: a moderate evangelical whom the Calvinists called an Arminian and the Arminians thought a high Calvinist. In our days his hymn 'Amazing Grace' has achieved immense popularity. Perhaps also his achievements are now more widely known since a number of fine biographies have appeared.

His detractors make the silly and elementary error of not noticing that Cowper's depression – and even his religious delusions as part of it – appeared long before Newton was on the scene. He was depressed, and preoccupied with religious matters, for years before his contact with either his cousin Madan or Dr Cotton. It may be that the strictness of Newton's views was an aggravating factor in Cowper's case. But he had adopted very firm patterns of devotion before he met Newton. After Newton was asked to go to St Mary Woolnoth in the City of London, Cowper may have made a wider circle of friends, with some benefit.

These are minor points, which should not take away from the immense credit that Newton deserves. Their writing of the *Olney Hymns* was a great joint effort. We may feel that many of the hymns in it are relatively uninspired and are not only pedestrian but move with leaden feet. But the collection contains many gems. Many, both by Cowper and Newton, are in most hymn-books and are often sung. A few deserve to be better known. Almost at random we might look at one which is based largely on a paraphrase of the Song of Songs and starts:

To those who know the LORD I speak,
Is my beloved near?

It goes on, until in the last verse Cowper's own pain at not being able to feel any comfort from his faith is poignantly put:

Such Jesus is, and such his grace,
  Oh may he shine on you!
And tell him, when you see his face,
  I long to see him too.

Some will feel they cannot sing such words, just as others feel that they cannot sing the familiar hymn that begins:

Where is the blessedness I knew
  When first I saw the Lord?

We must respect such reticence, and perhaps wish for more fellow feeling for what is, to varying degrees, a common spiritual experience. Seldom has it been felt so deeply as by Cowper, and perhaps never so well expressed.

**To fame on 'The Sofa'**

While his hymns brought lasting fame, it was his second volume of verse that made Cowper a best-seller. He sold the copyright to the printer, who is said to have made a profit of £10,000 – an enormous sum. He gave the profits of the fifth edition to Cowper, but it did not signify much change in his genteel poverty.

In the half century after they were first printed, there were to be over a hundred editions of his two volumes of verse in Britain, and forty-eight in the United States. Why did such books sell so well for decades and bring him such fame?

*The Task* began when Lady Austen told him to write about the sofa. He chose the title because he was carrying out a task assigned to him. There are almost 300 pages, covering a wide variety of themes.

Many sections describe his delight in nature (like the 'Winter Walks', which John Betjeman read once a year).

There is much satire, with a cutting edge which is sharp though gently used. Some of it (like the passage on the stricken deer quoted earlier) is about his life. John Wesley thought it far too discursive, and dismissed it. Yet it was the revival of which Wesley and Whitefield were leaders which had created the readers for Cowper. He helped to educate, entertain and edify them.

His style was original: he was proud to have imitated none. There is a good deal of moral instruction and quiet effective teaching. The shy poet who could not face an audience now had a very great constituency to serve. The literary leaders recognized his gifts too, and he who loved the country was the talk of the town. The style was the man himself; how strange that the recluse should have such fashionable fame!

It becomes clear that if he was a kind of hermit, he was a happy one: his love of the home and its pleasures is obvious, and he returns to them after his many excursions into argument, lengthy description or long satire. The ordinary life he knew so well is observed faithfully. Much of it may seem dull to us today, but he served his own age well and left many veins of gold which have been mined in ordinary speech since. The current Oxford *Dictionary of Quotations* gives some five pages of familiar examples: few who refer to drinking tea as 'the cups that cheer but not inebriate' know that they owe such phrases to Cowper. There are many other phrases and frequently-used lines.

*The Task* has been seen by some as the way in which Cowper showed contemplation of nature to be a means of grace: in many ways he was expressing, in words his readers found helpful, much biblical teaching about nature as God's other book of revelation concerning himself. It is often said he cleared the way for William Wordsworth's verse, which owes him much.

'John Gilpin' had been successful long before, since it had been published anonymously in periodicals and had been recited publicly. Cowper explains that 'strange as it may seem, the most ludicrous lines I ever wrote have been written in the saddest mood, and but for that saddest mood, perhaps had never been written at all'. I cherish a modern King Penguin edition of *Gilpin,* with Ronald Searle's drawings of the rather mad horses. The diverting tale of the linen draper being urged by his wife to take their first holiday in twenty years is still enjoyable. Everyone has his favourite verse. One is that which follows his wife's promise to bring the wine with her:

John Gilpin kissed his loving wife,
  O'erjoy'd was he to find
That though on pleasure she was bent,
  She had a frugal mind.

The age he wrote in, as depicted by Hogarth, was extremely coarse and cruel: when Cowper heard that people were everywhere laughing at his poem he remarked that 'they do not always laugh so innocently, or at so small an expense ... a laugh that hurts nobody has at least the grace of novelty to commend it'.

**'Divinest melancholy'**

'It was good for me that I was afflicted,' said Cowper, quoting from the Psalms. Was his depression, terrible as it was, a secret blessing? Would he have thought – at least at times – with Milton:

Hail Thou goddess sweet and holy
Hail divinest melancholy?

One reflection on his time is that we recall very few of the other lawyers who were in the Inner Temple on a trajectory to fame when poor Cowper was trying to kill himself. Over thirty biographies of Cowper have been published: this interest is certainly partly because of the relationship between his illness and his immense powers of quiet, effective creation.

At the beginning we asked the question: Why was he not healed? Why should he have suffered six serious depressive breakdowns, several suicide attempts and endured so much mental pain? It is part of the larger mystery of suffering, and there cannot be a final answer. But good came out of the apparent evil of his distress.

We can go further, and say that a peculiar quality of strength comes out of his suffering. This point is well put by Ryskamp: 'Through all his trials Cowper maintained his amiable character, except when depression crushed him to silence. He was gentle and kind and sweet tempered; and out of this sweetness there would come forth strength.'

His gift for writing plain verse which spoke clearly to the reader lent itself to his beautifully simple hymns. It gave him a much greater chance to reach a multitude with his longer poems, with the same gift for seeing things clearly and expressing them skilfully by speaking directly from the heart. He was intellectually very well informed, and used an art that concealed itself.

The public face he came to present to the world hid his private agony. For his delusion that he was damned – and that (as he later thought) he was a kind of Isaac to be sacrificed – never fully left his mind. Most of the time he lived normally, with his delusions at the back of his mind, as if encapsulated.

Even when he was very depressed he might explain it pithily: 'I do not lose my senses, it is simply that I cannot make full use of them.' Then the melancholy fit would pass and he would use his considerable faculties to the full again.

After the success of his second volume of poetry he was given a commission to translate his beloved Homer, and this occupied much of his late years. For once he was well paid for it. The King had also given him a pension of £300 a year six years before he died. The *Iliad* and the *Odyssey* gave him special pleasure and fulfilment as a translator.

Much might be said of his declining years. With Mrs Unwin so ill, the figure of his young cousin Johnny Johnson from Norfolk looms large. He helped to look after Cowper and Mrs Unwin, and took them to his native Norfolk. Cowper loved to walk on the beach at Mundesley, where he had played as a childhood visitor to his cousins. He was able, after Mrs Unwin died in 1796, to revise his translation of Homer's *Odyssey* for the press. He wrote his famous poem 'The Castaway' in the year before he died. That poem has been used to illustrate many things, but it certainly shows that Cowper's powers as a poet were not diminished at the age of sixty-seven. He compares himself to a sailor lost in a storm, as recounted in *Anson's Voyages:*

> No voice divine the storm allay'd
> No light propitious shone;
> When, snatch'd from all effectual aid,
> We perish'd, each alone:

But I beneath a rougher sea,
And whelm'd in deeper gulphs than he.

It sounds pitiless and hopeless. A year later he developed dropsy and died after a short illness.

Nowadays we do not pay as much attention to death-bed scenes. Johnny had not realized his beloved Cowper had died until he noticed his expression had settled into one 'of calmness and composure, mingled, as it were, with a holy surprise'. I cannot help wondering if his devoted nurse Johnny thought of one of Cowper's loveliest hymns, which we still sing:

Sometimes a light surprises
  The Christian while he sings;
It is the LORD who rises
  With healing in his wings:
When comforts are declining,
  He grants the soul again
A season of clear shining
  To cheer it after rain.

May we not believe that his Christian life, real to him in spite of his great handicap of depressive illness, which often prevented him from enjoying it, led him into a final blessedness after walking so many of God's mysterious ways? Elizabeth Barrett Browning in her verses on the subject of Cowper's grave compares the lifelong fever of Cowper's depression to the delirium which may afflict a feverish child. Such a child, having recovered from its confused and febrile state, realizes that the mother who has nursed it has not deserted it. In a similar way (Browning suggests) it might be said of Cowper that 'after life's fitful fever, he sleeps well'. It is an act of faith to believe that he might then have fully known the reality of his Father's love, hidden so often behind a frowning providence.

*Further Reading*

The best single collection is Brian Spiller (ed.), *Cowper: Poetry and Prose* (London: Rupert Hart-Davis, 1968).

Earlier editions of Cowper's letters are patchy, expurgated, and of limited value. Much important knowledge is suppressed in them. The two men who worked on the five-volume Clarendon Press (Oxford) edition of the Cowper letters (1,306 of them, many previously unpublished) have put us all in their debt. Furthermore, each has written a fine biography: Charles Ryskamp's *William Cowper of the Inner Temple, Esq.* (Cambridge: CUP, 1959) takes us to 1768; James King's *William Cowper* (Durham, NC: Duke University Press, 1986) is the finest complete biography, using all known material.

David Cecil, *The Stricken Deer* (London: John Constable, 1929) is still in print, and has been described already. Norman Nicholson, *William Cowper* (London: John Lehmann, 1951) is also still in print, and is a good study of Cowper's life and his poetry. Hugh l'Anson Fausset, *William Cowper* (London: Jonathan Cape, 1928) is a study notable for all the liberal prejudices against Cowper and his faith current when it was first published.

Gilbert Thomas, *William Cowper and the Eighteenth Century* (London: George Allen & Unwin, 1948) describes his book as a labour of love, and it is the only brief life that gives a full and proper background, seeing how Cowper belongs in his Christian setting and century.

George Ella: *William Cowper: Poet of Paradise* (Darlington: Evangelical Press, 1996) gives a comprehensive account.

# 4

# Fighting Industrial Child Abuse: Lord Shaftesbury (1801–1885)

During a public life of half a century he devoted the influence of his station, the strong sympathies of his heart, and the great powers of his mind, to honouring God by serving his fellow-men, an example of his order, a blessing to this people, and a name to be by them ever gratefully remembered.

Inscription on the Eros Monument in London's Piccadilly, written by William Ewart Gladstone

Lord Shaftesbury would have been in a lunatic asylum if he had not devoted himself to reforming lunatic asylums.

Florence Nightingale

Few of those who sit on the steps around Shaftesbury's monument in Piccadilly can have any idea of the man whom Eros commemorates. Yet the name Shaftesbury crops up often in London, attached to the Avenue, Theatre and many other features of life. Youth centres were named after him. Societies and foundations to promote reform bear his name.

It may be surprising to learn of his fifty years of hard work in psychiatric reform, as Chairman of the Commissioners in Lunacy. Another of the many unexpected facts that come to light is that he pioneered the laws that made council housing possible. In his long career he touched many areas of life and usually became deeply involved. His was a *personal* crusade for social change, not part of any political party programme.

Anthony Ashley Cooper, the seventh Earl of Shaftesbury, is someone whose long life (1801–85) holds many surprises about his own temperament and how his personality may have affected his work and his enormous achievements in Britain. He was a high Tory who was drawn to sort out the cardboard cities of his day, and the lodging houses where one room might contain *sixty* people: it was all quite unexpected and it calls for some explanation. The puzzle of his personality presents a challenge to us.

He attracts opposite views and opinions. Two social historians, Barbara and J. L. Hammond, writing with little sympathy for his Christian beliefs, say that Shaftesbury changed the tone of his world by his noble life, and softened 'the savage logic of the Industrial Revolution'. They record the long list of what he did for those in factories, mines and agriculture, and show how greatly he improved their lot. His fight to improve the lunacy laws and other aspects of public health provision was a lonely one. While recognizing what a difficult man he was, they are unstinting in recognizing and praising him for what he did.

In his own time a hostile cartoon in *Vanity Fair* carried a legend which described him as a hypocrite. The comments made were that 'there are not wanting those who call Lord Shaftesbury's piety sanctimonious, his philanthropy foolish, and his consistency bigoted'. Quoting an unnamed MP, they said: 'like a Pharisee of old ... he called upon God to witness ... that he was not as other men were, for that he was never influenced by party motives'.

**Early deprivation**

His parents cared little for him. In one speech he said 'it would be better if children had no parents at all'. Two women gave him the care that his mother never tried to offer: a housekeeper called Maria Millis and the wife to whom he became devoted. Soon after his eighth birthday Maria Millis died, but she had by then taught Anthony the faith which remained the mainspring of his life.

His wife provided an oasis for him in a life which seemed a desert with few loving friends. Minny shared his faith and was one of the few people who could disagree with him and yet keep his affection. Before the marriage, her uncle expressed to her mother his disapproval of Shaftesbury's family and prospects: 'Three thousand a year ... which he will probably lose very shortly and which you and I both devoutly hope that he may. An odious father and four beggarly brothers. What has poor Min done to deserve to be linked to such a fate, and in a family generally disliked, reputed mad ...?'

If we believe modern medical opinion, the child who is deprived of parental care is likely to show less capacity to care for children of his own. The battering mother usually has a history of being battered herself in early life. We should therefore seek, in following Shaftesbury's early years, to find an explanation as to why he did *precisely the opposite.* He cared not only for his own children, but for thousands of others who were less fortunate.

What Anthony recorded in his diaries about his parents seems to be fact, confirmed by many other independent observers. Perhaps in that age most parents in his social class cared little for their children: they certainly saw little enough of them. I think it is evidently true that young Anthony was made to suffer much emotional and physical deprivation. At home he often starved and felt extremely cold, even at night.

In adulthood the price he paid for caring so much for children was high. Cardinal Manning, another eminent Victorian, described him thus: 'He took human suffering and human sorrow, and the helplessness of childhood, and the poor, as the end for which to live. He spent and was spent for it, and his own life was a suffering life like the Man of Sorrows going about doing good.' Even the brief sketch I am giving in this chapter should help us to decide how much of this description is high-flown exaggeration, and how much is plain fact.

## Trials of an aristocrat

Anthony Ashley Cooper was born in 1801, the eldest son. When his father succeeded to the peerage in 1811 he became Lord Ashley. In 1851 he succeeded his father as the seventh Earl, and he was known as Lord Shaftesbury till his death in 1885. He inherited debts which kept him a relative pauper, and he never profited from high office in government. Friends frequently helped him out with large gifts of money.

Lord Melbourne told the young Queen Victoria that Shaftesbury's parents both heartily disliked their children. The regime for all nine children was severe. Perhaps, as is often the case, the three daughters and five other brothers were less badly treated than Anthony was as the first born. Worse followed when he went to school at seven.

His mother was the daughter of the fourth Duke of Marlborough: both as Anne Spencer-Churchill and later as the Duchess she was a glittering socialite who presided over brilliant occasions as hostess. As a mother, her son described her in 1825 thus: 'What a dreadful woman our mother is! Her whole pleasure is in finding fault.' A little later he writes: '... away with her Memory! The Idea of such fiend-warmed Hearts is bad for a Christian soul ... The History of Father and Mother would be incredible to most men.' Yet, remarkably, his mother came to share her son's Christian faith later in her life.

His father was an able chairman of committees in the House of Lords, but that was all that most friends could say in his favour: his manner was hasty and brusque, and it was his rudeness that was remembered. It was an elder brother of his that inherited the title, but when this brother died without a son, Anthony's father inherited.

**Inherited talents**

That Anthony's father was of uncouth manners and indistinct speech should not make us forget his more distinguished lineage. The first Ashley Cooper was a noted politician, and the first letter of his name (A) was the second A in the first 'Cabal', the precursor of the modern cabinet. The five names were those of Clifford, Arlington, Buckingham, Ashley and Lauderdale: they signed the Treaty of Alliance with France in 1673. The word 'Cabal' has been used to describe a powerful clique ever since the poet Dryden invented it.

The third Earl was described by Voltaire as 'the boldest of English philosophers'. It was said by a reviewer of the Shaftesbury history that it showed that the genetics of the Shaftesbury family was like a river which went underground, emerging in the seventh Earl with all the best qualities that he had inherited made visible.

What Anthony recalled, however, was not to do with any genes that might later manifest themselves benignly: it was 'the very great severity, moral and physical, in respect of mind and body ... [used] to render a child obedient', and which kept it 'in a constant fear of its father and mother'. Ashley's father used to knock him down, and recommended that his tutor at Harrow do the same.

The abilities which Shaftesbury inherited were to show themselves slowly, and much later in his development. His first boarding school at Chiswick was barbaric, and he recalls it as 'bad, wicked and filthy; and the treatment was starvation and cruelty ... Nothing could have surpassed it for filth, bullying, neglect and hard treatment of every sort ... It was very similar to Dotheboys Hall.'

He was glad to move to Harrow, a school where he felt he learned little: he blamed himself, but it would appear that the school was not then very well organized. While at Harrow (he told a later headmaster) he witnessed a pauper's funeral which shocked him deeply. A plaque was later put up to note this early awakening to the plight of the poor. But some cautious biographers rightly point out that if Harrow Hill was his road to Damascus, he took thirteen years to decide to act upon his new-found concern. It was part of his very slow development.

**Shaftesbury the student**

At sixteen it seemed as if Anthony was taking two years out of his life before going to Oxford. His father sent him to live with a clergyman in Derbyshire who had married a cousin of his. He read nothing, learned nothing and day-dreamed of his future career. He was glad that a friend dissuaded his father from sending him into the army.

At Oxford he worked hard and gained a first in Classics, and a cousin, Edward Pusey, who was also at Christ Church, did the same. Pusey, a leading Anglo-Catholic in the Oxford Movement, was later to be an opponent and one of Shaftesbury's many enemies.

He made friends at Oxford and began to show he was a serious student. Science was a deep interest of his. In later years he knew and supported Charles Babbage (whose calculating machines might have brought us computers earlier) and tried to get him more money for his work. Later he was close to the astronomer John South: he tried to get Robert Peel (then Home Secretary) to provide funds for him to stay in England and not move his telescope to Paris. The glory of England was then, as always, important to him.

He was willing to study anything that came his way: it is interesting to learn that he studied Welsh and was made a Druid and a Bard. It happened that, while visiting his sister in Rowton Castle on the Welsh border, he visited Aberystwyth, where a parson persuaded him to stay for some weeks and learn Welsh. A year later he was asked to write the prospectus for the new *Cambrian Quarterly.* Like his fellow

Englishmen of that day he was something of a colonialist, and wrote of his 'residence among the natives'. A little later we find him learning Hebrew, though we shall see that his interest in Palestine was not colonial, but related to biblical prophecy. His was a keen, curious and searching mind, although this was more evident at this time than later.

Almost as a matter of course he became MP for Woodstock four years after leaving Oxford: it was the pocket borough of his uncle, the Duke of Marlborough. Wellington was his hero, and when 'Dukie' (as Shaftesbury referred to him) became Prime Minister and asked him to accept junior office he did so. He took his work at the India Board very seriously: it was another huge area for study, thought and action. Shaftesbury frequently refused office later, as he had also declined Canning's offer when he was Prime Minister before Wellington.

**Obstinate questionings of self**

Even more of his student instincts went into learning about himself. Self-examination and the keeping of a diary – a lifelong habit – took time. He showed 'a keen edge of ruthless and dispassionate self-awareness that partisan Evangelicalism was later to blunt', says Professor Geoffrey Best.

He engaged in much self-analysis, and reports in his diary for the first time in April 1826 that in the three previous years (when he was aged between twenty-two and twenty-five) he cured himself of several defects of character. He was aware of how he over-reacted to any coldness or indifference from his friends. He tried to curb his ambition and love of distinction.

Earlier, when he was twenty, his self-searching had extended to his depression: he wrote in 1821 that 'despondency fits have a tendency to exert their influence'. At twenty-six, a doctor whom he consulted told him he had never met a person with 'a more deranged system', and Anthony 'knew by my symptoms that my brain must be sadly loaded: enough to bring on any excess of bad spirits'. A year later he was glad he had 'acquired a more enlarged view of things', but he could not 'withstand despondency'.

## First signs of illness

At twenty-nine he writes that he felt 'a peculiar vivacity of... heart'. There was no special reason for this, and he knew he would pay for it by a 'corresponding dejection'. He wrote: 'how curious and uncertain is my character ... sometimes for a while in the wildest and most jovial of spirits; at others for a longer period in cruel ... despondency'.

For the next fifty years Shaftesbury was to use his diaries and journals to describe these mixed feelings. Later they were freely given to his first biographer, Edwin Hodder, to use for a three-volume *Life.* He often used them to record his feelings of intense anxiety and depression. His public life showed only the *results* of his inward struggles; their profound nature was never really known to the public that came to love and honour him for his work.

It seems as certain as it can be that he suffered from what would now be called a bipolar affective disorder, and what used to be called manic-depressive illness. A man who was a friend and admirer (the Hon. Henry Fox) may have observed early signs of this disorder when he knew Shaftesbury (or Ashley as he then was) in his early twenties. Fox wrote in his journal: 'Ashley's character seems quite unintelligible and can only be accounted for by a *dash of madness.'* Two years later Fox writes equally perceptively about Ashley that he has 'a much better opinion of his heart', but 'his understanding is so warped by the most violent prejudices, that he appears quite ridiculous whenever he finds opportunity to vent them'.

## Affairs of the heart

We have glimpses of Shaftesbury's sexual development before his marriage, and some full-length portraits of him as the young, handsome aristocrat in search of a wife. It is evident that he did not become known as an evangelical till his late twenties, when he is spoken of as 'almost a Saint' (the nickname of such Christians at the time).

Perhaps his first search was for a mother figure, and only then a wife. His Oxford friend, George Howard, took him to Castle Howard in the long vacations. It became (especially since he saw little of his father for some four years when he was a student) a kind of adopted home. It was Howard's mother, Lady Georgiana, who mothered him.

George told her Shaftesbury's feelings were 'very tender' for her. He spoke to her about the plight of his sisters, and she responded with care and affection. His letters to her (written later, when she became Lady Carlisle), show us how his relationships with younger women were progressing.

There were two other women who also became mother figures, and when he switched from Lady Morpeth to Lady Bathurst, the daughter of the former wrote that it 'made her feel half angry with him'. Such were the mothering and possessive feelings he provoked at this time.

In one letter Shaftesbury writes from Paris on holiday. He and his friend wish to 'improve their understanding by a steady course of French plays, fencing and whatever else is improving'. Lady Carlisle's sister writes saying they are 'behaving beautifully. I introduce him to the elegantes who think him *superbe, magnifique,* and he is much pleased.' Though he wrote of the 'dear, delicious women' he met in Paris, his diary records on his return: 'I hate France. It is a wicked country. It is the Devil's *pied-a-terre.'*

There is no hint of wild oats being sown, but of a young man, forbidden a home at this time by his father, visiting many friends and country houses where he was much liked and valued. A young woman writes of him (while he was visiting Scotland) as 'the handsomest young man I ever saw, full of fun and frolic, and his countenance radiant with youthful hope'.

Lady Holland was impressed too: 'he is very handsome and captivating, and young ladies are willing to be deceived and from their own vanity often exaggerate affections....' But when Ashley paid undue attention to her daughter Lady Holland was less approving: he was 'a male coquet, the cruellest of characters and the most cold-hearted'.

In Vienna, on a European tour that his father was happy to finance, he fell in love: 'Man has never loved more furiously and imprudently. The object was, and is, an angel but she was surrounded by and would have brought with her a halo of hell.' Shaftesbury was writing about Antoinette, the daughter of a Baron von Leykham who had married an Italian singer. The high aristocracy of Vienna looked on the actors and magicians who were often in Antoinette's home as immoral riff-raff. Shaftesbury suffered – 'A man loves fiercely but once; the next time is reason or convenience, or fancy, or plain matter of fact,' he wrote two years later. He heard of his 'Liebe' with another, more famous lover, Prince Metternich.

In 1829, three years after his return from Vienna, Princess Esterhazy told him that Antoinette had died a few days after giving birth to a child. His diary records his distress, how he took out a scarf of hers and mourned. But by then he was painfully aware of his want of a wife and was actively searching for a suitable spouse.

**Courtship and happiness**

Shaftesbury carried around with him on his social round an idealized picture of his fantasy wife: 'Methinks that if I could find the creature I have invented I could love her with a tenderness and truth unprecedented in wedlock. I pray for her abundantly; God give me this purest of blessings.' A number of young women failed to measure up to the ideal specifications. Then he found Lady Emily Cowper, and the story of their courtship and their intensely happy marriage is most remarkable. For her family, her mother and the presumed father (Lord Palmerston) were all a cause of great concern to the young Lord Ashley. He was still bruised from his failure with Lady Selina, whose father (Lord Liverpool) had put an end to his platonic affair and his hopes of marriage.

It was not just that Minny (as she was known because her mother was also Emily) sprang from a noted Whig family known for the free-thinking of the Lambs and their opposition to Ashley's religion. There were also well-established suspicions of her mother's infidelities. As Shaftesbury's diary put it: 'The mother herself has laboured under heavy suspicion of faithlessness to her marriage vows.'

Georgina Battiscombe writes: 'That shadowy character, Lord Cowper, was in all probability not her father. Who that gentleman might have been no one could say for certain, possibly not even Lady Cowper herself.' That is one biographer's view. The latest, Geoffrey Finlayson, considers it virtually certain that Lord Palmerston was the father. When he married Lady Cowper (ten years later, after Lord Cowper had died), Palmerston had a special affection for Minny which persisted to his dying day. On his deathbed Palmerston said,

'Come in Minny, you are a sunbeam.'

Those who knew Ashley felt he was making a fool of himself, but he fell in love with Minny, and she slowly responded to his intense wooing. His passion was tempered by doubts and hopes expressed in his diary: 'Have I not seen daughters the very reverse of their mothers, domestic, loving, faithful?' It really was no use anyone telling Ashley that he was thinking of marrying into 'one of the most profligate families in the kingdom, he being really as moral and religious a man as exists'. He thought Minny 'lovely, accomplished, clever, with an almost virgin indifference towards her admirers'. At Ascot it was said that 'all the men are more or less in love with Emily Cowper', and a diarist called Creevey said she was the leading favourite of the town. Three eligible suitors had been rejected, and Lord John Russell had also wanted to marry her.

**Happy marriage**

Ashley was no great catch, it was said, but Minny was both attracted and scared. She knew of his religious intensity and also about the 'dash of madness'. When he asked for an answer to his proposal, at first all she could say was that her delay was not a rejection, but repeated 'What a difficult situation!' We have already noted her uncle's feelings, and his opinion of Ashley's relative poverty, later to be fully confirmed.

In their small enclosed world everyone seemed to know both of his passion and his patience. He was pushed by her lack of response to threaten to resign and depart for America. He was perplexed by her hesitation, even when in love with him. Another factor was her family's opposition. Much could be said: but after a year they married. His father refused to attend the ceremony.

For all the doubts, the marriage was an extremely happy one. She was someone who was good for him, and was able to be herself – facetious as well as devoted, gay and good-humoured as well as steadfast and faithful. Her sunny disposition and her love helped him to be a little less stiff and defensive, and to grow and develop in the warmth she provided. He always praised her charm and beauty. He had found in Minny a wife, a lover, a companion and a friend such as he had never had before.

She came to share his faith and to be, as her husband said, 'a sincere, sunny and gentle follower of our Lord'. She may not have shared all his extreme views, but she seems to have understood them. She held her own in the discussion even when he was 'excitable and cruel' in what he said. There was, however, a period of coldness in their relationship, a time of difficulty perhaps inseparable from the pressures under which they both lived.

They had ten children: six boys and four girls. As one biographer says, 'He tried to make his home a model of his universal ideal, watching over the "kids" as he often referred to them, with tender vigilance ... with plenty of fun and freedom as well as principle and piety.'

His problems with his own eldest son, Anthony, may in fact show how hard it was not to repeat his own experience with his father. We will return to it later in trying to assess how much permanent damage his relationship with his parents caused Shaftesbury.

**Sixty years of hard labour**

To begin to outline what Shaftesbury did between his election as an MP in June 1826 and his death in October 1885 is a huge task. Much of his reforming work was done through Parliament, first in the Commons and then, after succeeding his father, in the Lords. Most of it was done as an independent rather than a party politician. We will list some of these achievements, but then we must record the many activities he took a lead in by promoting a number of movements and organizations *outside* politics. In some ways he became the conscience of the evangelical wing of the Church of England.

He helped Palmerston in the appointment of bishops, exercising great influence. This gives us sympathy for his wife, who once protested about the Jerusalem bishopric: 'You din this perpetually in my ears and it sets my back up against it.' So wonderful did Shaftesbury feel this work of bishop-making to be that he records his delight that his four sons gave some pence from their pocket-money for the new bishopric.

It is a curious fact that many of his ventures started by chance. The reform of the care of psychiatric patients is an example. Ashley was asked to second a motion in the House of Commons for his maiden speech, and was scarcely audible in the gallery. Yet his first Parliamentary work of importance, and his last, just before he died, was to do with the care of the afflicted in mind.

Better known is his work for the reform of factory laws. In this he did much to change the practices then prevalent for children, young persons and women. He once said that when he died the word 'Lancashire' would be found written on his heart.

The fight over those 'dark Satanic mills' was an epic struggle. Yet it started almost casually, with a request from a curate called Bull, from near Bradford, that Ashley should take the place of an MP who had lost his seat. Ashley agreed to deputize, and thus began a major life-work. It has been said that he hated the mill-owners because of his own rural interests. He was willing to believe that Mammon reigned in the mills but was happy to learn the full facts as he went along.

Children who climbed up chimneys to clean them were the subject of further scandal and concern. To read today that in evidence to Parliamentary committees it was said that 'a good age to choose was a child of six for this work since they were more trainable', opens a window on a terrible aspect of Victorian practice. The Chimney Sweeps' Act was a battlefield for him.

The coal-mines were full of children, both boys and girls, and also of women. They were considered absolutely essential to work the pits, to keep them open and to make a profit. The enlightened doctor who had a part in publishing the report of the Royal Commission on Children's Employment had the wit to have it illustrated. The pictures of a child or woman chained to a cart, pulling coal through passages not more than two feet high, added greatly to the impact of the report, which was so influential in producing a national wave of indignation.

Those who had listened to the defence of the mill-owners presenting their evidence to the Commission were told that the deformities of children in their factories were inevitable in the new profit-making age of capital. Once people knew the true facts they could not tolerate these bad conditions in the pits. The Mines Bill was an important step in obtaining support for Shaftesbury's reforming work: when it became law he had many new friends, and he was welcomed at meetings of those who would benefit from the reforms.

## What made Shaftesbury do it?

It is likely that those who heard or read Shaftesbury's speeches were surprised at his reasons for doing the work: 'We must keep before our eyes the undeniable but ill-considered fact that every child in these districts is an immortal being; and that another generation, neglected like the present, and left in ignorance and sin, will probably witness the final extinction of the British Empire.' He was no radical, and no friend of trade unionism. He ended, after the above words, by saying that he hoped he might one day see 'the restoration of *content* amongst all classes, the revival of good will between master and man, a blessing on every house, and a home for every labourer'.

Was Florence Nightingale right in saying it was his dash of madness that drove him? Readers of her biography will know that she was not really well-qualified personally to call attention to instability in others: but then the pot often calls the kettle black, and there was certainly some truth in what she said. Part of the truth has already been mentioned in the earlier description of his mood-swings.

Shaftesbury's feelings for those who suffered were very great: was this not because he had himself suffered? To have known what it is like to be cold and starving, even if it is in a large house in Grosvenor Square, may have helped him. In many this might simply have provoked sympathy for others in similar states. The remarkable additional fact is that he went on to do something about cold, filthy, starving children in Whitechapel, and wherever he found them.

He was by all accounts abnormally sensitive, and he was described as being without that extra skin needed to be tough in politics. But his heart drove him on, and his very clever brain and his iron will made him win against heavy odds. For he fought against many vested interests. All the greed of the capitalist and the entrepreneur was set against him. All the self-seeking of political parties opposed him. The world of glittering prizes which hated his Christian seriousness was antagonistic, and felt he was betraying his own upper class. Even radicals like Cobden and others were deeply suspicious of him for a time. Was he not mad to take them on at all, and to fight for nearly sixty years against such odds?

As we shall see, his sense of duty, of obligation to God and man (in that order), drove him on, and his belief in the rightness of his cause sustained him. The love of his wife and friends and family who shared his values bore him up and helped him to carry huge burdens. It has been said that all good politicians must be able to sit on the fence. Lloyd George, a much later reformer of a different kind, may have mocked an enemy by saying that he sat on the fence till the iron entered his soul, but he knew that every party politician had to compromise. Equally, to preserve party loyalty, fences constantly had to be mended. In that sense good fences made good neighbours in the Houses of Parliament.

Shaftesbury was not good at fences. He certainly would not sit on a fence if he could help it, even to save his soul. Every principle he held dear (and he had many high principles) prevented it. True, his sympathies and wish to do good often leapt over obstacles to join forces with anyone who acted rightly in a just cause. But his problems in compromise and co-operation also made him more bitter and lonely. There were some barriers that he erected which seem, with hindsight, to have been unnecessary.

He often attacked with what he may have thought was righteous indignation, where something more human, like pique, might have been the cause. His attacks on the Salvation Army are a case in point, and we will discuss them when considering his religious allegiances later. To well-meaning friends he certainly seemed to be acting irrationally at times, when he turned fiercely on good and proper activities simply because they did not conform exactly to his own views.

## What kind of Christian was he?

Shaftesbury said he was 'an Evangelical of the Evangelicals': but was he? I find him in many ways neither balanced nor typical. He was attracted to extreme and intolerant views. It is important to note how he came to his Christian faith, and how it developed in the way it did over the years, becoming more rigid and less balanced as it grew. Yet the faults in his faith seem a necessary part of his great work.

Professor Geoffrey Best pithily sums up a key issue – Shaftesbury's conscience:

> Lord Shaftesbury's especial claim to greatness was that he personified the conscience of his age, the early Victorian age ... He could easily have made a successful political career ... His uniqueness lay largely in his having deliberately rejected it. That rejection was made on conscientious grounds.

There is no doubt that Maria Millis, a servant and housekeeper who loved him in his childhood, taught him the elements of the Christian faith. He spoke of her in this way, and wore the gold watch she gave him to the very end of his long life. She had the same great importance as the young girl who pointed Naaman the captain of Syria towards the prophet Elisha in Israel in order to obtain healing.

Maria was from Woodstock, an evangelical parish where she had learned a warm, clear and simple faith. She had gone into service at Blenheim Palace with Anthony's mother Anne, and had moved with her to London when Anne married Lord Ashley, Anthony's father. She told Anthony Bible stories, taught him a simple prayer which he used daily throughout his life, even when his devotions began at six in the morning, as they did later. In the year before he died, he promised to write down the prayer for Edwin Hodder, but did not do so. How valuable it would have been to know what she taught, and how he used it all!

Shaftesbury often said that she was 'the best friend I ever had in this world': in an important sense it was true in that she planted the seeds of faith and knowledge in him. The faith he learned from her became a thread which guided him through the maze of his life. But she also gave him the love and affection his mother did not. For Shaftesbury there was no doubt about his answer to Cowper's question

> Can a woman's tender care
> Cease toward the child she bare?

for he had experienced such dereliction, mitigated by Maria Millis and her devoted mothering. Some would seek to see a conditioning experience at work, linking his faith to the need for love.

There is a good deal of evidence that he never had enough early loving to sustain a sense of self-worth in his later life. His diaries record a frequent return to dark and empty feelings. As we have noted earlier, the death of Maria Millis when Anthony was eight or so must have been as devastating to his emotional development as losing a mother.

We have no record of a conversion experience, but in his thirties he grew close to Edward Bickersteth, whose book *A Practical Guide to the Prophecies* points to how he influenced Shaftesbury. The second coming of Christ, the future of the Jews, the millennium and the day of judgement: these 'last things' became very important to Shaftesbury. In some ways Lord Ashley (as he then was) became identified, perhaps too much, with one wing of the evangelical movement of which Bickersteth was a leading light.

He grew in his general Christian knowledge: theology was his favourite study. The quotations we have given earlier indicate how much he was taken up with the effects of sin on man in society. He looked to reform of social evils as a step towards helping those (both children and adults) who might then be freed to live and learn more fully. Shaftesbury's ultimate longing was that those whom he had helped in their social lives should later be helped to come to know God in Christ.

Auden wrote of Yeats:

> In the deserts of the heart
> Let the healing fountain start.

Was there a healing fountain in Shaftesbury's desert? It is hard to say with any certainty. His private diaries show him to be, as he told Hodder, 'a mass of contradictions'. There is more darkness than light in the many extracts Hodder printed, more hurt and pain than there is healing and comfort.

## The fights of faith

It would appear that often the comfort and joy which Shaftesbury enjoyed was in fighting for truth and for right, against error and evil. He fought against ideas and practices he thought wrong in both Church and state.

It was a time of bitter religious conflict. He found it easier to tolerate and help Roman Catholics than what would now be called Anglo-Catholics. As noted earlier, the Oxford Movement, to which his cousin E. B. Pusey belonged, and which Shaftesbury called the Tractarians and Ritualists, was anathema to him. It is sad to see him becoming a 'party man' in religious strife, having refused to be a party man politically. Similarly Charles Kingsley, whose fight with John Henry Newman will be recalled, was not acceptable as a Christian Socialist. They might have been allies in fighting social evils, but Shaftesbury would have none of it.

When he formed the Church Pastoral Aid Society (which still flourishes in a way many of the causes he espoused do not) there were more quarrels. Gladstone and the High Church party split off to form their own version, with ordained priests. Shaftesbury was ahead of his time in wanting laymen to help in the Anglican ministry. Yet time and again his intolerance towards any view opposing his own came out very clearly.

Together with Pusey and others who accepted the Bible as God's word, he was bitterly opposed to any 'higher criticism' from what he called the 'Neologians'. Shaftesbury coined this word to describe the liberal theologians of his day: Colenso, Milman and Seeley (the author of *Ecce Homo)*. In 1852 he complained that the Tractarians were in league with liberal theologians to attack evangelical religion and weaken its influence in the Church. An acrimonious correspondence with Pusey ensued on the subject.

Shaftesbury was perceptive, and he saw the need for a united front in defence of revealed truth. He wrote of the 'March of the Intellect': he wanted men's minds to submit to the revealed truth in Scripture. But his perfectionism, rigidity and over-conscientiousness made common cause with others difficult. As he grew older he became more and more isolated. Yet the list of societies of which he was the figurehead (President or Chairman) occupies four pages of double columns of print in his first biography. It is part of the aforementioned mass of contradictions that Shaftesbury should have been in such demand, so widely loved and honoured in public, and yet be so different in private.

A prime reason for letting his diaries, which are so revealing of his personal anxiety, be used for biography was to do justice to those who worked with him. Shaftesbury said: 'I could never have done the few things I have, had I not been supported by true, zealous, earnest men, who gave me their time and their brains to help forward the different movements.' He refused to be called a leader, but he was certainly a facilitator who worked tirelessly to fight, and inspire others to fight, for the many good causes he espoused. We must consider some of them in detail.

**Fighting the trade in lunacy**

The part Shaftesbury played in improving the lot of psychiatric patients is little known. Today there are Mental Health Act Commissioners whose duties relate to the Mental Health Act (1983). In his day Shaftesbury was for fifty years Chairman of the Commissioners in Lunacy. The scene then was very different, and only by a great effort of historical imagination can we begin to grasp his achievement.

Shaftesbury wrote that 'there is nothing poetical in this duty': an understatement, since it was repulsive, and the visits to asylums were offensive to heart, eye, ear and nose. It was his sense of duty that led him to be one of the fifteen Commissioners. He was to remain in this work for fifty-seven years. He described it as the hardest of his tasks, working on behalf of 'the most helpless, if not the most afflicted portion, of the human race'.

Attempts had been made to license and inspect private houses which confined more than one lunatic: such attempts, made fifty years before Ashley began his work, were of very little use. The powers provided were not used. Quite apart from private madhouses, there was little provision for public hospitals or for pauper lunatics.

Attempts were made to draw attention to abuses at such places as the Bethlehem Hospital (Bedlam) in London, and at the York Asylum. In York in 1793 the pioneer Retreat, still a psychiatric hospital today, was started by a group of Friends. In London the Governors of Bethlehem tried to cover up its scandals.

Shaftesbury would visit an asylum on a Sunday, since the keepers sought their own amusement then and left the unhappy patients in pain and filth. He described one such inspection thus:

> When we began our visitations, one of the first rooms that we went into contained nearly a hundred and fifty patients, in every

> form of madness, a large proportion of them chained to the wall, some melancholy, some furious, but the noise and din and roar were such that we positively could not hear each other; every form of disease and every form of madness was there. I never beheld anything so horrible and so miserable.

What did he do to change it all? His almost inaudible speech seconding the motion led to Robert Gordon's two Acts of 1828: a beginning of reform. The Commissioners collected evidence slowly, and a new Act of 1845 became the most important lunacy legislation of Shaftesbury's lifetime. It required the building and proper running of county and public asylums. The pauper psychiatric patients were also better provided for, and the private madhouses better regulated.

It was difficult and demanding work: a weekly board meeting of the Commissioners took up a large part of Shaftesbury's time in preparation and carrying out decisions. The public were still liable to react to any hint of scandal. Twice there were select committees of inquiry, when on one occasion Shaftesbury had to answer over nine hundred questions during three days. He defended doctors (the small number interested in mental illness, that is) and social workers against lawyers and public interest.

It is a measure of his success in helping to improve the way patients were 'certified' as needing treatment that in 1859, of 185,000 issued, only seven certificates needed further examining, and even these were found to be good.

In the year before his death Shaftesbury sought to defend against lawyers and the Law Lords the practice of delegating responsibility to doctors for certification. There were pressure groups in Parliament who wanted to undo some of Shaftesbury's carefully planned reforms. They are generally seen as wanting to take backward steps in psychiatric care. For a time his actions succeeded in delaying the retrograde changes. Soon after his death the Act of 1890 (according to Kathleen Jones, the historian of these laws) 'was to hamper the progress of the mental health movement for nearly seventy years'.

To make further sense of Florence Nightingale's suggestion that he did all this fine work because he was in need of psychiatric help himself, we must turn to his private life once more.

**Private griefs and joys**

Shaftesbury loved taking the annual holiday at the seaside and visits to the zoo with the children and holidays abroad. He cancelled everything to make sure his children were not disappointed. They brought him much joy which he shared fully with his wife in spite of their chronic financial difficulties. These were made worse by his father's death and his inheritance of the estate in Wimborne St Giles in Dorset. This estate was in disrepair, and much as Shaftesbury loved it it remained an enormous drain on his resources, for he felt obliged to improve such things as the workmen's cottages, in accordance with his well-known reforming principles. Thus, far from improving his finances, the estate and its upkeep and improvement was a handicap to him, causing much anxiety and loss of funds.

His eldest son was a great concern to him. Anthony was idle and caused anxieties because of his capacity to get into debt: he was once arrested for debt, and his father had to borrow the £500 to set him free. He was sent to school at Rugby but had to leave. He was a great disappointment to his father. One biographer, Professor Best, says that Anthony 'may (I can find no evidence one way or the other) have shown early signs of that lack of mental balance which led him to take his own life in 1886'. Soon after inheriting the title, his son shot himself in a hansom cab.

The losses by death during his own lifetime were hard for Shaftesbury to bear. His brother died at Eton after a long boxing match where he had been given too much brandy. Shaftesbury's reaction, although he was a good boxer himself, was to become set against prize-fighting of that kind.

A favourite son, Francis, died at Harrow after a sudden illness. Another son, Maurice, developed epilepsy which led to much medical expense: he was to die while being treated in Switzerland. A daughter, Mary, developed severe asthma and died, in spite of every care, of a chest infection: Shaftesbury was shattered.

Later one of his favourite daughters, Conty, died while being treated for tuberculosis in the South of France, soon after he lost his wife Minny. Another son had to be removed from school with meningitis to be cared for at home. In spite of such tragedies, which were perhaps not unexpected in the absence of effective medical care, there was still much joy. He continued to love the estate at St Giles; one of his sisters, who was by then a wealthy widow, helped him to build two new towers for the great house.

He loved the village festivities as much as he hated the London high life. He records the vivacity he felt at the two village suppers to celebrate Harvest Home. Three ambassadors were on one occasion being entertained at St Giles on behalf of his father-in-law Lord Palmerston. They must have taken strange accounts back to their countries of the unwontedly festive seventh Earl among the tenants whose lot he had done so much to improve.

His private life of prayer, Bible study and the meditations written in his diaries and letters show a great deal of the man. He was humble and modest, and indeed often talks of his sense of failure, especially in his written prayers. He used the Bible for what he called divination: looking for a verse to guide him in making decisions. This was sometimes a dangerous practice, cutting out balanced thinking by looking for direct, immediate answers and guidance. The loving counsel of friends, had he admitted them to his private world, might have brought much wisdom, warmth and comfort which he seems to have lacked.

He was almost desperately anxious that his family and children should share the personal faith which was so important to him. Yet he did not neglect the other aspects of care for them, as his parents had done with him in his own childhood. Perhaps his grandchildren, romping around the large house and gardens in St Giles, saw more of the happy and fun-loving side of him, in a period of lonely and forsaken old age.

**Refusing high office**

Shaftesbury's political career is marked by milestones which show high offices that he declined. He also refused the first offer of the Garter, but accepted it on the second occasion. He was asked to accept the post of Chancellor of the Duchy of Lancaster more than once, to go to the Home Office, to be Lord Lieutenant of Ireland, and Secretary for Ireland.

Why did he decline high office? His argument was that he was called of God to serve the poor. Once, he was thought of as a possible leader of the Tory Party, and therefore a Prime Minister. It was certainly part of his day-dreams and of his ambition. His early hero-worship of the Duke of Wellington and his close social network of powerful friends made this an expected thing. Close relations, as Lord Palmerston was by marriage to Minny's widowed mother, would have made such steps to high office – and indeed the highest offices – natural and almost inevitable.

His piety and his very firm ideas, which became rigid and unshakeable later in life, made the compromises needed in working in a Cabinet almost impossible. His colleagues might admire him, but they would not give in to his single-minded view on the importance of the Bible and its teaching as he understood it.

An example is his view of Sunday: he was a sufficiently strict Sabbatarian to do away with both Sunday posts and the possibility of bands playing in the parks on Sunday. He only succeeded in stopping work in the Post Offices for three weeks. The anger both of the postal workers and of the users led the Government to bring back the Sunday post. When his principles about rest on the Lord's day led to his measures to close both the British Museum and the Crystal Palace on Sundays, then the poor who had regarded Shaftesbury as their champion turned against him. For two Sundays he put up barricades outside his Grosvenor Square home because he feared mob violence.

The poor did not always like the way in which *he* saw their best interests. To his credit, he believed recreation should be available at other times and lent his great weight to the campaign for a regular weekly half-day holiday for working people. 'I could not surrender the Sabbath. I could not do it,' he said. When he wrote that in his diary he was thinking of his refusal to attend Sunday dinner parties. He was consistent in his principles. His own need for rest and refreshment on Sundays had partly confirmed him in his stand.

No Cabinet could agree to such strictness, however much the general spirit of the times favoured the Sunday-best approach. We should however recall that the English Roman Catholics, unlike their Continental counterparts, agreed with him about the English Sunday.

The story of how he almost accepted Cabinet office from Palmerston sheds much light on Shaftesbury's mind. This was a second offer of the Chancellor of the Duchy of Lancaster post.

Palmerston's wife pleaded with him to accept (as her daughter Minny did too) because the Queen wanted it. An almost paranoid reaction followed: Shaftesbury wrote that what people were saying was: 'This man may be troublesome, get him into the Cabinet on terms which will excite the suspicion of his friends, and he will be neutralized for ever.'

After much family quarrelling and pressure he accepted, and was dressed and ready to go to Buckingham Palace to kiss hands on his appointment. A messenger came to say that a last-minute substitute had been found by Palmerston, and he was not to go to the Palace. Shaftesbury describes his reaction: 'It was, to my mind, as distinctly an act of special providence as when the hand of Abraham was stayed and Isaac escaped.'

**'Do not cast me away when I am old'**

Shaftesbury was seventy-one when his wife died. Minny had been ill for nearly four years and died less than three months before their favourite daughter Conty also died. The grief of losing Minny was something that remained with Shaftesbury to the end. At first he dealt with it by working, feeling that Minny would have wished it, and that her wishes must be obeyed.

We have already noted how he admired her disposition as well as her faith. When she had gone there were regrets for his hasty temper and his cantankerousness. His diary entries are moving. 'How many times have I, in my excitable spirit, said unjust and cruel things to her! What a placable spirit! What a power to forgive! And what a sublime power to forget!'

He knew how she excelled in such qualities, and as the years advanced his own unrelenting, unforgiving nature grew worse. In public, and even more in his diaries, he expressed his distress. It was at times the kind of persecutory anxiety that we meet in paranoid patients: 'I may be loved in Bethnal Green but I am despised in Belgravia.' His opinions and feelings about many colleagues and friends became more bitter.

**Illnesses grow worse**

As I see it, Shaftesbury's grief made his tendency to depression worse. The main features of many chronic depressives are severe anxiety and agitation, together with outbursts of a paranoid kind. Shaftesbury had a good deal of this mixture of symptoms, and he was very distressed. Of course he hated the absence of Minny, and the silence, 'unbroken by that sweet silver voice that always had a tune to ravish my heart'.

Though work was a solace, it was also a strain because he was always overworked. Before his last, and as it turned out brilliantly effective, public examination about the Lunacy Commissioners, he was for many months in a terrible state of anxiety. He said he was 'never so weighed down and never so continuously unwell in my life, oftentimes with sensations as though I should drop dead'.

His physical problems included tinnitus and later deafness, and severe stomach problems which suggest he had a peptic ulcer; they were almost certainly made worse by strain and stress. I find it hard to agree with those who attribute all his symptoms to his nervous nature and constitution.

His anxiety and depression did, however, have some effect on his bodily ailments, particularly since he did not look after himself well. On top of it all was his increasing loneliness in the Christian world he knew and loved.

## Losing Christian friends

Some friends were lost, inevitably, as they died. More sad was the way he lost friends by quarrelling with them on relatively minor matters. He was deeply upset at one Bible Society meeting that he chaired, that a speaker should suggest that the Gospels were more inspired than the book of Chronicles. Shaftesbury wrote he wished that 'England would read our current history in the light of the second book of Chronicles'.

Some might concede the historical value of the Old Testament passages he delighted in, and at the same time believe that the Gospels do have a different quality of writing, and also of use. He would stick to his point that it was all or nothing: 'It would be easier for me to give up revelation altogether, and reject the whole scriptures, than accept it ... on terms imposed ... by high criticism.' Again, it was the way he perceived the liberal Neologians at work, diminishing the value of the text of Scripture.

He threw himself into new schemes. He supported Plimsoll in his work to help merchant seamen with the Plimsoll line and all the safety measures that went with it. He supported an anti-vivisection movement. He argued publicly with Tait, the Archbishop of Canterbury. He protested about the Queen's giving John Brown a gold medal for his services. He led a successful protest in the Lords against Queen Victoria being titled Empress of India.

His mentor Haldane, who had followed Bickersteth, was harsher and more bigoted in his views. It is generally thought by his biographers that Haldane was a sad and bad influence. Shaftesbury seemed to become alienated from the evangelical mainstream that he had loved, and which loved and honoured him. Even Haldane and he quarrelled publicly over the relatively small matter of the second Afghan War. So good friends became defectors, and his loneliness and depression increased. There was no such thing as a smaller or less significant issue for the ageing Earl.

**His last year: in harness**

Each man's death diminished him, even though he found it hard to distinguish friends from enemies. The goodies easily became baddies, and to his credit he reckoned up in his diaries the good qualities of his enemies. An example was Pusey: 'intensely and fearfully as I differed from him ... I could not but love the man'.

There were still, in his eighty-fourth year, 'an abundance of chairs'. He presided, as usual, at the round of May annual meetings. He was also active, and made one of his best speeches about psychiatric patients in that year. That was when he resigned in protest from the Chair of Commissioners in Lunacy. When the government administration that planned changes with which he disagreed fell, he resumed his post: his expressed wish was to die in harness. He worked to the last, for he was unwell only in August and September, and he dictated letters to his daughter Victoria up to his death on 1st October 1885.

We have had little space to note the wide range of his activities. His interest in education was shown in the Ragged Schools: he said he would prefer to be their President than President of the Royal Academy. The London City Missions had been another of his great works: they were what he preferred to the Salvation Army. The quiet, steady and persistent work of mission was what he wanted to support, not revivalism.

When Moody and Sankey came to England, he was glad to help and approve, though sad not to be on their committees. For he had always welcomed every effort to bring the gospel to the unchurched people, and welcomed 'theatre meetings' and other settings for evangelism. In attacking the Salvation Army he did so because he felt they were importing an order of things not compatible with the New Testament. No doubt he also felt his own efforts were being eclipsed, and something of this comes out in his qualified support for Dr Barnardo.

The determination to go on working is shown by his visits, only two months before he died, to the Home Office to discuss new revelations about child prostitution.

No wonder then that his public, national and international fame was celebrated at Westminster Abbey at his funeral. The roads from his home in Grosvenor Square to the Abbey were lined with deputations from all the societies he had so long served. Their banners were inscribed: 'Naked and ye clothed me', 'A stranger and ye took me in'. The poorest wore some token of mourning.

Although a statue of Shaftesbury stands in the Abbey, he refused to be buried there, preferring St Giles in Dorset. In spite of all his deep unhappiness, his long life's battles had publicly been those of the happy warrior. Shaftesbury reminds us of Wordsworth's lines:

Who is the happy Warrior?
Who is he That every man in arms should wish to be? –
It is the generous Spirit, who, when brought
Among the tasks of real life, hath wrought
Upon the plan that pleased his boyish thought.

What he learned from the woman who was like a mother to him, and the needs of the paupers he saw at Harrow, had shaped his boyish ambitions. Whatever he confided to his diaries of his own deep misgivings about himself, his friends and the world, he had amply fulfilled his early ambitions.

Many felt he could have been Prime Minister, as great as Gladstone or Disraeli. However, Shaftesbury may have left much more of an imprint on society because he followed his own principles and his own conscience. Above all, his life gives the lie to the view that evangelical Christians do not see the need, or act upon, the social obligations of the gospel of Christ.

**His own self-assessment**

Six years before he died Shaftesbury issued instructions that three texts should be carved on his grave's memorial stone. By looking at each in turn, we may see something of his own estimate of himself.

'What hast thou that thou didst not receive?' (1 Cor. 4:7). I consider this to refer to his sense of stewardship for a number of things. Firstly, his aristocratic lineage and all the advantages it gave him. Even more, he felt that his wife, and the family they had together, were gifts he treasured and felt very responsible, in an awesome way, for looking after. Then all that grace brought him: his faith, his love for God and man. He saw them all as gifts.

There is another side to stewardship: perhaps he did not enjoy it all as much as he should, or as he might have done had he not inherited also a lifetime of debt and financial insecurity. The Christians around him thought more of sin and salvation than of the joy of God's creation gifts. His sense of duty was part of his stewardship of what he had received, and it helped him to do justice and walk humbly with his God.

'Let him that thinketh he standeth take heed lest he fall' (1 Cor. 10:12). This is the middle one of the three verses on his memorial tablet. Clearly he is applying this to himself, as St Paul intended. Does he mean it in the sense of the great apostle saying in another place, 'lest having preached to others I myself should be a castaway'? I think not: there is no flavour of Cowper's fear of final loss in Shaftesbury.

'By this sin fell the angels' refers to *pride,* and I think there is ample evidence that he fought against his pride, often without success. It is amazing to read, in reference to his conduct towards his father, that he may have sinned against God, but never against man. There was something about Shaftesbury that defended himself against such knowledge of how he had hurt and sinned against others. There was a natural pride and a supernatural pride; he sometimes reminds us of the old saying about pride of grace being quite a dangerous form of pride.

Perhaps his exercise of humility and modesty was a response to knowing the risks pride brought. He was aware that assurance of salvation was not the same thing as presumption. He, of all people, rejoiced with trembling.

With a father like his, it is easy to feel that God was for him something of a tyrant at times, driving him to fulfil his faith by doing good works. It seems that at times he worked in the spirit of Milton's sonnet:

All is, if I have grace to use it so,
As ever in my great task-master's eye.

Some have seen this use of the verse as a reference to falling into sin, or to some final breakdown that he may have dreaded. That may be stretching it too far. A fall from his high ideals was certainly part of what he meant to imply; perhaps a fall from grace which, in his worse moments, he may have feared.

'Surely I come quickly. Amen. Even so, come Lord Jesus' (Rev. 22:20). This last verse of the Bible reminds us of Shaftesbury's strong belief in Christ's second coming. This belief is shared by millions everywhere who recite the creeds and believe them. It is celebrated in churches in every Advent season. Shaftesbury believed it passionately as something which motivated his work, to hasten this coming. He did not have Dr Johnson's awe of it, for Johnson would weep at the *Dies Irae, Dies Illa.*

It was with longing and joy that he awaited Christ's return, for a final righting of wrongs among other things. If one lives too much in an atmosphere of apocalypse and of thoughts of the last things which go with it, the effects can be remarkable. I do not think he was like some, reading *The Times* while checking out the books of Daniel and Revelation, though in his interest in the Jews there was something of that spirit present. He was more like the group of Christians who adopted as their slogan: 'Evangelize to a finish and bring back the King.' For Shaftesbury, 'as you look forward to the day of God and speed its coming' (2 Pet. 3:12) was a daily reality for most of his last fifty years.

**Serving and suffering**

His personality and temperament seem to me to have become increasingly those of the over-sensitive person. His rigid and controlling habits may have stemmed from obsessional traits, but he did not suffer from them in the same way as Bunyan or Luther. That he was so sensitive to suffering led him directly to his long and epic struggles to relieve it. But it still caused him personal suffering.

The form that suffering took, as we have seen, was severe depression, usually expressed in his diary more than to anyone else. The anxieties – sometimes obsessive, sometimes persecutory and paranoid – were worse as he got older. He tortured himself with some of his fears, which were unwarranted.

With his powerful intellect, it was a tragedy that he believed that 'Satan rules in the intellect, God in the heart of man'. In his own way he loved the Lord with all his mind, as the first commandment says we should. But as he grew older his mental world narrowed and he seemed to lose the free exercise of his intellect in the service of truth. He was often on the defensive when he might have been a powerful advocate for the faith which he shared with many others in the many different evangelical movements he led. With an even more powerful will, he made himself work when most of us would have stopped, if only to take stock and take a breather. He did have holidays – full of fun and laughter, as was often reported by those who were there – but *work* was his watchword.

His heart was where love dominated. The wider family of those dozens of organizations and movements for whom he was the active figurehead and leader were an extended family to love, and they responded with love in full measure. It is one of the many contradictions of which he spoke when he gave his diaries to Edwin Hodder, that he seemed incapable of feeling, and realizing, how much he was loved. One of the great sadnesses of his life is that there were so many quarrels within that large Christian family.

At his best, at the height of his powers, he exercised a magnetism of love, drawing people together. Later he drove them apart only too often.

At his Westminster Abbey funeral they sang a well-known hymn of Charles Wesley. His life, so often wrong-headed, reminds one that his heart, more than that of many in his age, was 'touched by the lodestone of God's love'. The hymn that one would have wished to have been true of his work *all* his life, was marvellously true for *much* of it:

Touched by the lodestone of thy love
Let all our hearts agree;
And ever towards each other move
And ever move towards thee.

*Further Reading*

Edwin Hodder's *Life and Work of the Seventh Earl of Shaftesbury, K. G.* is easier to obtain in the one-volume popular edition (London: Cassell, 1892) than in the original three-volume edition. Hodder quotes extensively from the diaries and letters given to him by Shaftesbury.

The best modern life is Geoffrey B.A. M. Finlayson's *The Seventh Earl of Shaftesbury* (London: Eyre Methuen, 1981) – it is scholarly and readable, and the author has had access to many other documents.

Georgina Battiscombe, *Shaftesbury: A Biography of the Seventh Earl 1801–1885* (London: John Constable, 1988) is easily the best for most readers; it is full, well-researched, and keeps the reader's interest. Geoffrey F. A. Best, *Shaftesbury* (London: Batsford, 1964) is a superb short summary. J. Wesley Bready, *Lord Shaftesbury and Social Industrial Progress* (London: George Allen & Unwin, 1926) is a remarkable account, with special emphasis on the contemporary background and Shaftesbury's links with the evangelical movements before him. J. L. and B. Hammond, *Lord Shaftesbury,* fourth edition (London: Cassell, 1969) gives an excellent account of his work, but without any emphasis on his faith: it is *Hamlet* without the Prince of Denmark, but in its way is very helpful. John Pollock, *Shaftesbury: The Poor Man's Earl* (London: Hodder & Stoughton, 1986) is a sympathetic account.

There are a number of other earlier works on Shaftesbury, and his speeches were published in 1868.

# 5

## Up-hill All the Way?: Christina Rossetti (1830–1894)

My heart is like a singing bird
  Whose nest is in a watered shoot;
My heart is like an apple-tree
  Whose boughs are bent with thickset fruit;
My heart is like a rainbow shell
  That paddles in a halcyon sea;
My heart is gladder than all these
  Because my love is come to me.

Christina Rossetti, 'A Birthday' (1857)

What can I give Him
  Poor as I am?
If I were a shepherd
  I would bring a lamb,
If I were a Wise Man
  I would do my part, –
Yet what I can I give Him
  Give my heart.

Christina Rossetti, 'A Christmas Carol' (1872)

If any family makes us feel that the past is a different country, and that they do things differently there, it is the family of Rossetti. The children in the Rossetti family used to love reading Gothic romances. Theirs was, in real life, a bizarre family. Dante Gabriel, Christina's brother, was the leader of a new movement in art: the Pre-Raphaelite Brotherhood. At times his life resembles a horror story. When his wife killed herself he placed his poems in the coffin beside her face, between her cheek and hair. Then, seven years later, he had the coffin dug up to retrieve his verse.

Christina was the youngest of four children, with an elder sister, Maria, who became, late in life, an Anglican nun. Dante Gabriel and

Christina were very alike as children in that they both had fiery tempers. They were known as the 'two storms'.

Her other brother, who was a year older, William Michael, lived to edit her poems (almost a thousand of them in the 1904 edition, which was often reprinted) as well as the works of Dante Gabriel. William's work in the Excise Office – now absorbed into the Inland Revenue – somehow exemplifies his role as the balanced son who provided the common sense so much needed. It was their mother's wish that they should all be devout Christians. However, William eventually declared himself an agnostic. In spite of this difference from his sisters, it was he who prepared the family writings for publication, and who tried to hide away the family skeletons, by sealing them firmly into cupboards.

In later life, Christina stood out as the devout Christian; she would have nothing to do with the bohemian life-style of the artists who joined Dante Gabriel to form the Pre-Raphaelite Brotherhood. At first, Dante Gabriel called his work 'art-catholic', but gradually moved away from his mother and sisters both in belief and in way of life. Nevertheless Christina was honoured by the Pre-Raphaelites: Holman Hunt, in his painting 'The Light of the World' which is familiar to so many people, used Christina's face as a model to obtain the expression he wanted for his face of Christ. He and John Everett Millais were the first to join Dante Gabriel Rossetti.

Of the four who next joined the Brotherhood, James Collinson became Christina's fiancé when she was not quite eighteen. Within two years Collinson returned to the Roman Catholic faith, and Christina broke off the engagement on the grounds that he no longer shared her kind of Christian faith. She would reject a second suitor ten years later for the same reason.

**Songs for strangers and pilgrims**

Her own faith was always derived from the Bible; a whole book has recently been devoted to showing how her verse is rooted in Scripture. Indeed, Christian themes are quite obvious in the vast majority of her poems. She called one book, *Songs for Strangers and Pilgrims.* Sadly, her themes are more often about self-denial, conflict and renunciation than joy and peace in believing.

Christina is important to us, not only because she has been called the finest English woman-poet of the nineteenth century, but also because her life shows the dilemmas of the Victorian woman and, more especially, of the Christian woman of that time. As a female, she was condemned to a second-class role. The most recent biography of Christina Rossetti, by Kathleen Jones, takes its subtitle, *Learning Not To Be First,* from her poem, 'The Lowest Room', written in 1856:

Not to be first: how hard to learn
That lifelong lesson of the past;
Line graven on line and stroke on stroke,
But, thank God, learned at last.

The denial of her right to be fully herself seemed, to Christina, a clear part of her Christian duty, and that duty was for her paramount. That was why she renounced two possible husbands; they could not share, precisely, her own faith.

She considered her sister and her brothers, Dante Gabriel in particular, before herself. She placed the needs of her mother and her aunts well above her own. In fact, the importance that her mother had for her can hardly be exaggerated and is summed up in a dedicatory sonnet in which Christina writes:

Sonnets are full of love, and this my tome
    Has many sonnets: so here now shall be
    One sonnet more, a love sonnet, from me
To her whose heart is my heart's quiet home,
    To my first Love, my Mother, on whose knee
I learnt love-lore that is not troublesome;
    Whose service is my special dignity,
And she my lodestar while I go and come.

And she goes on to say:

In you not fourscore years can dim the flame
Of love, whose blessed glow transcends the laws
    Of time and change and mortal life and death.

We may legitimately wonder whether Christina's devotion to her mother prevented her from separating sufficiently, to grow, develop and live her own distinctive life. Her mother had taught her a warm and pious way of thinking and feeling. And whenever Christina read or wrote, she would try to hide, or cut out, anything that might offend a pious mind, like that of her mother.

**Times of suffering**

Christina bore much illness with fortitude. We shall try to understand what it meant to be ill for four of her late teenage years, and to be diagnosed as suffering from hysteria. Such a diagnosis usually covered a complex pattern of problems and symptoms. Today, the label would be considered dismissive; we try to understand all the factors involved and to help a suffering adolescent find solutions rather than give a pat diagnosis.

When she was thought to have tuberculosis, with symptoms, as usual, of coughing and spitting blood, she was sent off to Hastings where she slowly recovered. For many, the outcome was less favourable, even fatal, in the absence of specific treatment.

Later on, in midlife, Christina developed serious thyroid trouble. It was a time when Graves' disease (exophthalmic goitre), with a highly over-active gland, was dangerous and almost untreatable. She suffered for seven years, became very fat and developed brown, discoloured skin. These were the inevitable later effects of the subsequent low thyroid function (myxoedema). In those days, without appropriate treatment such as exists today, both high and low thyroid function carried health risks that were sometimes severe and occasionally fatal. Yet, even when she had myxoedema, Christina was able to joke about the change in her appearance: 'If only my figure would shrink somewhat! For a fat poetess is incongruous, especially when seated by the grave of buried hope!'

Her last three years were clouded by breast cancer, involving surgery at home and much pain and suffering. Her faith was tested severely, and all the temperamental problems of a morbid melancholy again came to the fore.

**Internal conflicts**

She was a child of two cultures: the Italian and the English. This added a further dimension of conflict to her life, as well as a great deal of interest and colour. Both her Italian and her English verse reflect the diversity of her heritage.

The richness of her cultural background was evident in her daily life. Her father earned little money, and the genteel poverty of the family contrasted with its wealth of talent and promise. We may honour Christina for choosing to suffer 'along with the people of God' in a way rather reminiscent of Moses, forsaking his Egyptian culture. Nevertheless we may regret that she did not explore her own potential more fully. There are certainly some expressions of anger and resentment in Christina's writings; but she seems to have considered these emotions wrong, and she sought to conquer them.

Was Germaine Greer right in saying that Christina was 'appalled by the uncontrollable violence of her own nature' and used 'piety as a metaphor for her own frustrated sexuality'? Her famous poem 'Goblin Market' is about 'forbidden fruit' and one sister rescuing another from the temptations of that fruit. The message seems to be that sexuality in the wrong context must be rejected. A great deal has been written about 'Goblin Market', a long poem that runs to seventeen pages in a current edition. The lines are short, and the language is simple and full of erotic imagery.

It is perhaps surprising that Playboy produced an editorial on the poem (complete with illustrations of their own) as an example of Victorian pornography. Christina was so prudish that not even naked fairies were allowed in the illustrations of her books. Every writer reads into the poem the interpretation that he or she wishes to bring, and it is very hard to know what Christina herself intended. There is nothing quite like 'Goblin Market' in the rest of her verse, and it is important to describe its contents, and to sample it.

Laura and Lizzie are two sisters; Laura gives in to the goblin men who offer their fruit. Laura has no money, and the goblin men ask for a lock of her hair; she sucks the fruit the goblin men offer, and returns home, only to grow worse in health as she seems to be expiring for lack of more of the delicious juices she has tasted.

When Laura is 'dwindling, seemed knocking at Death's door', Lizzie decides she must brave the dangers, and takes a penny to buy the fruit which Laura now needs. The goblins refuse, unless she joins their feast. Lizzie asks for her money back, and the goblins assault her physically, but,

Lizzie uttered not a word;

Would not open lip from lip
Lest they should cram a mouthful in:
But laughed in heart to feel the drip
Of juice that syruped all her face.

Lizzie rushes back to Laura, because the juices provide 'the fiery antidote' that Laura needs. Laura responds to Lizzie's request to

'Hug me, kiss me, suck my juices
Squeezed from goblin fruits for you,
Eat me, drink me, love me;
Laura, make much of me;
For your sake I braved the glen
And had to do with goblin merchant men.'

By doing what Lizzie asks, Laura recovers. All this is described in passages of astonishing force and passion. The moral, at the end, is:

'For there is no friend like a sister
In calm or stormy weather;
To cheer one on the tedious way
To fetch one if one goes astray,
To lift one if one totters down,
To strengthen whilst one stands.'

This moral is recounted to their children when, years later, both Laura and Lizzie are wives and mothers.

Enough may have been quoted here to show that contrasting meanings may easily be read into the poem. It evidently shows a great awareness of the appeal of the sensuous and erotic in life. This may reflect how Christina felt before she decided to reject any full expression of her own sexuality. We must bear in mind that Dante Gabriel Rossetti and some of his artist colleagues were becoming notorious for their sexual license when Christina was still a young girl.

Some see the poem as a message about the solidarity of sisterhood. It seems to well up from the writer's heart and mind, and is surely proof that Christina was fully aware of desires, erotic and otherwise, that can hurt and heal. Its 500 lines should be read. The poem can be taken, as many children have taken it, as an exciting story about girls and 'goblin men', representing the way innocence may be exploited by evil.

Whatever else it is about (and I am as uncertain of its full meaning as many others who have read it), it does seem to say something important about how both Christina and Maria renounced the permissive sexual life advocated by their brother Dante Gabriel. To them, such expression of love was forbidden because of their Christian commitment to chastity.

But while she rejects forbidden ways of sexual fulfilment, Christina's longing for love is described clearly in her poem to another woman poet, 'L.E.L.' (Laetitia Landon):

> I feel no spring, while spring is well-nigh blown
> I find no nest, while nests are in the grove:
> Woe's me for mine own heart that dwells alone,
> My heart that breaketh for a little love.
> While golden in the sun
> Rivulets rise and run,
> While lilies bud, for springtide is begun.

The last of the seven stanzas reads:

> Yet saith a saint, 'Take patience for thy scathe';
> Yet saith an angel: 'Wait, and thou shalt prove
> True best is last, true life is born of death,
> O thou, heart-broken for a little love
> Then love shall fill thy girth,
> And love make fat thy dearth,
> When new spring builds new heaven and clean new earth.'

Did Christina get it all wrong? She might have been helped to a more accepting attitude towards her own sexual needs, and might, in marriage, have found a proper fulfillment in the way her mother, whom she adored, had done. Her brothers certainly thought Christina was wrong to renounce marriage, but to her it seemed the right path for her to take.

**Naples, Tuscany and Dante**

Christina was baptized atAll Souls, Langham Place, not far from her parents' home. That home was full of the noise of four young children. The family's financial hardship was due to the father's inability to earn much as a teacher of Italian, whether from his private pupils or as Professor at King's College, London.

Christina's father was a political refugee from Naples; he accounted for half of Christina's Italian genes. Her mother was seventeen years younger and, although a Polidori from Northern Italy, she was in fact part English, her father having married an Englishwoman. It was her mother who taught Christina an evangelical Christian faith. Frances Rossetti had been a governess before her marriage at the age of twenty-four. Both Christina and her sister Maria listened to the instruction based on the Bible, *The Pilgrim's Progress* and the *Confessions of St Augustine,* and both girls grew up as devout Christians. The evangelical influence was to be overshadowed to some extent by that of John Keble, E. B. Pusey and John Henry Newman in the Oxford Movement, later called the Anglo-Catholic wing of the Church of England.

The reading in the family was not, of course, entirely religious in nature; all four children enjoyed the *Arabian Nights* as a special treat. All of them became expertly bilingual, and quickly showed precocious skills in writing. Their early games, in which they competed to produce rhymes and sonnets, taught them much skill in the writing of verse.

Gabriele Rossetti was an immigrant who had fled from Naples. He had a very exciting past. In Naples, a friendly British ship had sent two sailors to his house and they had lent him a uniform with which to escape to Malta and then to London. He had to flee because he had supported the Napoleonic King of Naples and, when the Bourbons returned to the city, his life was at risk. Gabriele was born to peasant stock in the Abruzzi – his father was a blacksmith – but a nobleman had spotted his talents and had had him educated in Naples.

Like so many single women, Christina devoted many years of her life to help care for a parent. Gabriele Rossetti became increasingly blind and, for this and other reasons, had to give up his post as a professor at King's. Later, his private pupils had to go too. His study of Dante became all-important; he once remarked that Dante had appeared to him in his study, painting his own portrait. Nursing this ailing father was one of Christina's later trials.

**Writers all**

Sometimes Christina escaped from the centre of London to visit her Polidori grandfather. The scholarship and culture of Gaetano Polidori was most congenial to her; he not only taught Italian but translated Milton into Italian. He had a small printing press in a shed in the garden, and employed a compositor from Sicily to work it. Maria, Dante Gabriel and Christina had their verses printed by the eccentric grandfather from Tuscany. At that time Christina was seventeen.

His influence was greater in her childhood because he lived in a village in Buckinghamshire, and the six-hour coach journey there transported Christina to a different world. She described her schooling in poetry as being largely 'the delightful liberty to prowl all alone about my grandfather's cottage grounds ... quite small, and on the simplest scale – but in those days to me they were vast, varied, worth exploring'.

There was a family magazine, the *Hodge Podge,* and later the *Illustrated Magazine,* to which the four children contributed. Christina did not think that she excelled, but Polidori, her grandfather, predicted that hers would be the most brilliant future. He was surely proved right, and her astonishing facility in verse is evident to anyone who reads the selections which are still easily available. Her carol, 'In the bleak mid-winter', has been called one of the most perfect poems, and of course it is a carol, set to music by Gustav Holst among others, that is sung by millions. Little do they know of the agonies out of which she learned to write so consummately well.

Her uncle, her mother's brother John, was a less happy writer. He was a doctor who travelled with Byron, and who, under his influence and that of Mary Shelley, wrote a gothic novel, *The Vampyre.* He was unstable, gambled heavily and committed suicide nine years before Christina was born. Such a sad story suggests a tendency to depression, which may also have affected Christina and other members of the family.

She grew up surrounded by Italian visitors of all kinds and classes. By that subtle learning process which occurs in extended families there is little doubt that Christina absorbed a rich and colourful literary culture, taking it for granted.

In her adolescent years something happened, hinted at by her brother William in his memoir, which changed her. Exactly what happened is something of a puzzle. Part of it seems to have been the normal process of growing up, with its crises of identity in adolescence. Her family and friends considered that she had an illness, somehow tainted with religion.

## Beginnings of illness

In her early teens Christina became unwell. The fragments of information we have make solving the jigsaw puzzle all the more tantalizing. The stormy, gifted, promising girl of twelve had been, according to her brother Dante Gabriel, 'while still a child ... poignantly melancholy whenever alone'. By nineteen, she had already apparently established a regime of giving up her own rights in life, and putting her Christian faith first. She broke off her first engagement to marry, on the grounds of James Collinson's difference in matters of faith.

During these years she was under the care of Dr Charles Hare. He diagnosed both anaemia and hysteria. She was also seen by distinguished physicians and a gynaecologist, for the Rossettis, however poor, always sought the best doctors. A friend of the family reported to her first biographer that Hare had told him that 'when she was about 16-18 she was then more or less out of her mind (suffering, in fact, from a form of insanity, I believe a kind of religious mania)'.

With hindsight we may be very suspicious of diagnoses such as 'hysteria' and 'religious mania'. It is important to try to understand Christina's situation during these years. Her sister was away from home, working as a governess. Christina, who was at home with her mother, made it clear that she did not want to take up the same career. Perhaps this course was more difficult because her mother, like her sister, had been a governess. Her father, having suddenly become almost blind, was unable to work. It was now her mother who had to advertise for pupils of her own. There must have been pressure for Christina to earn. Working as a governess was an obvious possibility for her too.

Christina states that she came to see the advantages of being an invalid; to adopt the sick role would mean being cared for at home, and it would have the added bonus of not being sent away. Perhaps ill health for her, as for her friend Dora Greenwell, was 'a little cave to run into, with many social immunities'. She was certainly left to her own devices when she recovered, and she could indulge in writing, and enjoy being what she called an 'escaped governess'. But her illnesses were not put on like those of a malingerer, they were genuine.

My view is that she did, indeed, inherit an unstable nervous make-up. She suffered markedly from mood swings in childhood and adolescence. What happened to her in her teens is a complex matter, with social and family pressures playing a part. Her Christian faith, as a result of these teenage years, emerged as the dominant element in her life. Her devotion to God became even more important than her devotion to her mother. Later she felt she had to obey the precepts of the Bible, even when this meant that the welfare of other members of her family, and their expressed wishes, came second to them.

Her flashes of joy, like shafts of sunshine after rain and clouds, are all the more remarkable because of the prevailing mood of sadness. Perhaps with more balanced Christian teaching her output and indeed her life might have been different. She might have been healthier if there had been better medical care and counselling available. Whether being more 'normal' would have enabled her to produce better poetry is quite another question.

### A rebellious teenager submits

The onset of puberty has been seen as an important factor at this time. The swings of mood induced by hormonal changes are no doubt relevant. We do not know at what age Christina cut her arm with a pair of scissors following an incident when her mother had reproved her. Such self-harm is very common in adolescents today, and does not necessarily lead to a psychiatric diagnosis. But in Victorian times it could easily have led to a diagnosis of mental illness of the kind Christina's doctors made.

Christina may well have exhibited some degree of instability, as did her brother and her uncle. She sought, partly as a refuge from the storms of adolescence, the certainty of Christian discipline and control. Some see this as repression, but 'realistic suppression' might be a better term for it. That she did not lose her sense of humour is evident in such fragments as 'On Albina', which she wrote at the age of fourteen:

> The roses lingered in her cheeks
> When fair Albina fainted;
> O gentle reader, could it be
> That fair Albina painted?

Most of her juvenilia praises the myrtle and the rose, and is preoccupied with fleeting life, death and eternity; perhaps the thoughts of youth have always been thus.

The family began to attend a church in Albany Street, whose vicar, the Rev. William Dodsworth, was a High Anglican on his way to Rome. He stressed the need for a strict piety and self-denial; Christina responded with what I see as the asceticism of adolescence. Later this hardened into something more lasting, when she 'set her face as flint', as she put it.

One of her father's bright pupils, Lady Isabella Howard, went into a decline and died at the age of eighteen. Christina, who had admired her greatly, wrote many poems about her. Such an event, together with the departure of her sister Maria, and her father's sudden loss of sight, must have increased her insecurity.

There were marked obsessional traits in Christina. These became evident in adolescence, as is commonly the case. They are well described by her brother William:

> This introduces us to what I regard as the one serious flaw in a beautiful and admirable character – she was by far overscrupulous. Scrupulosity may be a virtue: over-scrupulosity is at any rate a semi-virtue, but it has, to my thinking, the full bearings of a defect. It is more befitting for a nunnery than for London streets.... Her temperament and character, naturally warm and free, became 'a fountain sealed'.

While making due allowance for the bias, or partiality, of a brother describing his sister, I think most biographers would see these comments as accurate. Christina cannot be well understood without acknowledging that her personality became set in an obsessive compulsive mould.

The Christian faith became, for mother and daughter, more and more important. William may be right in seeing Christina as incorporating the tenets of the Oxford Movement into her own obsessional scheme of life. She was rigid too in her opposition to Rome and to what she saw as Mariolatry. It became important to her not only that her writings should carry a Christian message, but that she should live that message, as she came to know it.

**First affair and renunciation**

It seems to me, though the evidence as to how it happened is so fragmentary, that Christina's faith was already deep and fixed by the time she was seventeen. Sadly, she was shy, reserved and retiring.

It was then that James Collinson appeared and fell in love with her. Her brother William describes the relationship as 'an affair of the heart which brightened and darkened the life of Christina Rossetti ... it struck a staggering blow at her peace of mind on the very threshold of womanly life, and a blow from which she did not fully recover for years'.

The engagement was agreed after Collinson decided to leave the Roman Catholic faith for the Anglican one and, as we have already noted, it was broken off by Christina when he returned to the Roman fold. On 12 December 1848, when she had just passed her eighteenth birthday, she wrote:

When I am dead, my dearest,
    Sing no sad songs for me;
Plant thou no roses at my head,
    Nor shady cypress tree:
Be the green grass above me
    With showers and dewdrops wet:
And if thou wilt, remember,
    And if thou wilt, forget.
I shall not see the shadows,
    I shall not feel the rain;
I shall not hear the nightingale
    Sing on as if in pain:

And dreaming through the twilight
    That doth not rise or set,
Haply I may remember,
    And haply may forget.

Such words have found a place not only in anthologies, but also in the minds of many couples who have contemplated or suffered such separation. It is the authentic Christina speaking, as she was to do in many more verses. Her response, the depths stirred by her love, did not correspond exactly to the stimulus: Collinson appeared to others who knew him to be colourless and changeable.

One incident shows the intensity of her feelings, and of her physical reaction to those feelings. Soon after she broke off the engagement, she met Collinson while walking near Regent's Park; she fainted from the shock and fell to the ground.

It is said that at no time are our feelings so acute as in adolescence and early adult life. But Christina's capacity for such feeling was well preserved till her death, aged sixty-four. I think it likely that her devotion to God and Christ was already well formed before this event in her life, which was so like an earthquake for her. In the following years her decision to renounce love and sexual fulfilment hardened and, when the second man she loved, Charles Cayley, proved equally impossible for her because of his lack of Christian faith, she wrote more about her 'world of hope deferred', and how, in the words of Proverbs 14:10, 'Each heart knows its own bitterness.'

## High priestess of the Pre-Raphaelite Brotherhood

A new biography suggests that if Christina had had any kind of absorbing occupation, or a wider social life with the possibility of other relationships, the Collinson affair would have been relegated to its proper place, 'a teenage romance that had failed to mature'.

And yet she was hardly alone. Her home was like an Italian centre where, as her brother recalls, all kinds of people sought out her father: exiles, patriots, politicians, literary men, musicians, fleshy good-looking Neapolitans, keen Tuscans, emphatic Romans. More to the point, there were the artists who gathered around her brother Dante Gabriel Rossetti and formed the Pre-Raphaelite Brotherhood. This Brotherhood, of course, largely excluded her; yet she has been called the purest, most typical Pre-Raphaelite of them all.

The group wanted to get back beyond the classical art of Raphael to a nature that was loved for its own sake, for its richness and colour. That was the first declaration of their manifesto in the journal they produced, called *The Germ*. They also sought to be deliberately medieval, preferring subjects that were poignant or morbid. They attempted to bring words and pictures together, and to unite the natural with the supernatural. It was, in fact, a tall order.

William Rossetti gives a long list of people of talent and distinction who formed a part of Christina's world. Perhaps she endeavoured to remain detached from them because of her faith, and her firm resolve to obey its precepts.

We catch glimpses of Christina's role. Edmund Gosse described her as the high-priestess of Pre-Raphaelitism; and the poet Swinburne, so far removed from her in the kind of life he led, dedicated one of his volumes of verse to her, saying that she was 'the Jael who led their host to victory'. Perhaps Jael, the woman who in the book of judges lured Sisera into her tent and gave him milk to drink, and when he slept, exhausted, killed him by hammering a nail into his head, is not a happy comparison. Perhaps Swinburne saw in Christina something of Jael's steely determination.

It was partly because of their drinking, and their bohemian lives, in which sexual activity of various kinds played a large part, that Christina was only allowed to be an honorary and honourable member of the Brotherhood. The Brotherhood was also sexist and voted to exclude her because she was a woman. It seems to me that, just as she is regarded by some as a puritanical High Church woman, so she might also be called a protester, who pitted her own strict standards against the artistic licence of her brother and his friends. For instance, she pasted bits of paper over Swinburne's offending lines. If her scruples came to the fore in such a little thing, they most certainly prevented her from joining in other more riotous activities such as Swinburne sliding naked down the banisters.

Ruskin may well have been right when he said that the Pre-Raphaelites recognised only one truth in all they did, and this truth was obtained from nature and from nature only. Christina could not, in any sense, accept a philosophy that advocated a return to the noble savage, and a denial of the discipline that she had espoused. That discipline, for her, meant sexual self-denial to the point of renunciation. It has often been remarked that some of her generation cultivated an ideal of love without sex, rather in the manner of the medieval knights they so loved to paint.

Her love of nature was evident in her enjoyment of plants and animals. Dante Gabriel was eccentric enough to keep a kind of zoo or menagerie in his garden and house at one stage. Christina loved it all, and has left us sketches of the wombat, squirrels and foxes.

In some of her poems she links flowers with their symbolic meaning, at times most effectively. Her poem 'A Birthday', the first verse of which is quoted at the head of this chapter, shows the way images from nature enrich her writing:

> Raise me a dais of silk and down;
>     Hang it with vair and purple dyes;
> Carve it in doves and pomegranates,
>     And peacocks with a hundred eyes;
> Work it in gold and silver grapes,
>     In leaves and silver fleur-de-lys;
> Because the birthday of my life
>     Is come, my love is come to me.

It must be added that, even in her early writing, she stressed that everything she celebrated in the world of nature and human love was temporal. Nothing was more typical of her than to move from the transitory to the eternal, from earth to heaven, from the human to the divine. Her seven verses entitled 'The Heart Knoweth Its Own Bitterness' form a fine example. The last verse reads:

> Not in this world of hope deferred,
>     This world of perishable stuff –
> Eye hath not seen nor ear hath heard
>     Nor heart conceived that full 'enough':
> Here moans the separating sea,
> Here harvests fail, here breaks the heart:
> There God shall join and no man part,
> I full of Christ and Christ of me.

## Second love and refusal of marriage

Seven years after those lines were written, Christina met and grew to love the second man who wanted to marry her. He had been close to the family for some time, and was rather different from James Collinson. Charles Cayley was a brilliant linguist and translator of Dante, who had produced a metrical version of the Psalms. By the age of thirty-five Christina realized she had grown to love him; yet she refused to marry him, ostensibly because he was an agnostic.

Cayley seemed blind to the intensity of Christina's affection for him. She described him as 'the blindest buzzard she had known'. It seems their contact was limited to occasional games of cards with Christina and her mother. Yet her feelings for Cayley were strong, and even in her last years she spoke of him with great affection.

Why did she renounce sexual love and marriage for a second, and final, time? The reasons she gave included Cayley's poverty, but William, out of brotherly interest, and to overcome her objection, offered Christina a home for both of them, with him. There have been many Christian women who, following St Paul's precept, refused to be unequally yoked with an unbeliever. But those who have studied Christina closely believe, probably rightly, that she loved God too much to give herself to a man completely. It is impossible to tell whether there may also have been some physical revulsion on Christina's part from all that sexual love implied.

Cayley had a comic as well as an endearing side. He must have seemed very lacking in social skills when, after an awkward silence with two ladies at a social function, he eventually asked what they thought of the Gulf Stream. Perhaps it was a coded message, signalling that it was time for a little warmth to melt the cold ice. The incident surely appealed to Christina's undoubted sense of humour.

The depth of her feelings is shown in one of a sequence of fourteen sonnets. In these she imagines herself speaking as three 'unknown women' might have done, hence the title *'Monna Innominata'*. The three women are Dante's Beatrice, Petrarch's Laura and the unhappy Elizabeth Barrett Browning. The sequence is an ambitious series, well achieved. One that most concerns Cayley and her conflict deserves close reading:

Trust me, I have not earned your dear rebuke, –
  I love, as you would have me, God the most;
  Would lose not Him, but you, must one be lost,
Not with Lot's wife cast back a faithless look,
  Unready to forgo what I forsook;
  This say I, having counted up the cost,
  This, though I be the feeblest of God's host,
The sorriest sheep Christ shepherds with his crook.
Yet while I love my God the most, I deem
That I can never love you overmuch;
  I love him more, so let me love you too;
Yea, as I apprehend it, love is such
I cannot love you if I love not Him,
I cannot love Him if I love not you.

This sonnet, like the others, has been scrutinized to show its technical perfection: but really it is a cry from her long-divided heart. When poor Cayley, the scholar, bequeathed her his books upon his early death, he left her the many unsold copies in Longmans' warehouse. Did he *know* what was going on in his lover's heart? He died suddenly, leaving her also his writing desk, and in it her letters and a ring in an envelope. She ordered her letters to be destroyed, but continued to care for Cayley deeply till her death. It was an unlikely and unfulfilled romance.

Christina wrote in one of her prose works, *Time Flies*:

> We also love our own beloved without on the whole wanting them to be different. They are themselves, and this suffices. We are quite ready to like something superior, but it contents our hearts to love them.... We remain actually fond of the blameless oddities, the plain face abides as the one face we prefer.

**Her married brothers**

William Rossetti is important because of the care he took of Christina, giving her and her mother a home, as well as constant support. That he did not share her faith makes it remarkable that he should tolerate all her foibles, her extreme views, and still care for her. Christina was delighted, later in life, to be able to earn enough from her writing to repay William a little, and to leave him some money when she died. William's first love, Henrietta Rintoul, was close to Christina, but for various reasons she failed to meet William's needs, offering him, eventually, a platonic marriage, which he refused to accept.

Christina became a loving aunt when William married Lucy Madox Brown, and had three children. Lucy was the daughter of the author Ford Madox Brown and, like him, she was an artist. At the time of William's marriage Christina was aged forty-four.

Dante Gabriel had, as an artist and poet, been closer to Christina. He always wanted to read and approve anything she submitted for publication. Gabriel, the idolized leader of a new movement in art, was talented but unbalanced. His tragic marriage to Lucy Siddall, an artist who had been his model for some ten years before they married, and its lugubrious finale was mentioned earlier. Lucy's only child was stillborn, and her depression must have been accentuated by Gabriel's conduct, his drinking and his flagrant infidelities.

Gabriel's later illnesses were a mixture of serious depression and mental confusion. He attempted suicide with laudanum, following the example of his wife, but whereas she had been successful, he recovered. Later his condition was made worse by his addiction to chloral for sleep, and to alcohol. In his second serious illness he was attended by Henry Maudsley, whose benefactions later made possible the Maudsley Hospital. In Dante Gabriel's last illness, where a depressive episode was followed by a stroke, Christina moved in to the bungalow where her brother was being nursed, and helped to care for him until he died in 1881, aged fifty-five, a tragic waste of an immense talent.

### A dutiful daughter becomes ill

After Christina's second refusal of marriage it became clear that Frances Rossetti, her mother, had to be cared for; this became Christina's prime duty. As mentioned above, her closeness to her mother can hardly be overestimated, and she would never do anything to upset her mother's firm and largely evangelical views.

Like so many Christian daughters before and since, Christina was expected to live a life of self-sacrifice, and in some sense to return the care her mother had lavished on her as the youngest and most dependent child. She fulfilled her duties punctiliously. Her mother was seventy when Christina rejected Cayley's offer of marriage, and she lived on till 1886, dying at the age of eighty-six. From the time of her sister Maria's death in 1876 Christina looked after her two aunts as well.

Her writing prospered, and she was published in America with some success. Letters and visitors came for Christina as a result of her new fame. However, she continued to dress in black, and made no concession to fashion or material comfort.

A famous Max Beerbohm cartoon, often reproduced, shows her brother Dante Gabriel talking to the demurely dressed Christina, while the chairs around are draped with newly delivered Liberty fabrics which she refuses to have made up into clothes. Dante Gabriel is saying: 'What is the use, Christina, of having a heart like a singing bird and a water-shoot and all the rest of it, if you insist on getting yourself up like a pew opener?' But insist she did, for the rest of her life. She would have had great sympathy for Quaker principles of dress, and other communities like the Amish or the Huttentes. In many ways her life was as quiet as a nun's.

When she was forty-one a mysterious illness affected her which, perhaps not surprisingly, was thought to be due to her nerves. Dr William Jenner, physician to Queen Victoria, saw her; but since he was busy with the Royal Family he left her care to his deputy, who was puzzled. Her difficulty in swallowing was put down to nervous constriction. The story proceeds relentlessly and distressingly until the cause, an over-active thyroid gland, was properly diagnosed.

Because thyroid problems are so much easier to treat now, it is hard today to realize what Graves' disease, associated with popping, protuberant eyes, meant in terms of suffering in Victorian times. Christina had most of the possible symptoms. Her heart was affected, her hair fell out and she lost a lot of weight. There was also local pressure from the gland in her neck which affected her voice and risked obstructing her breathing. But no operation was possible in 1871. Doctors attended three times a day, and her life was thought to be in jeopardy.

At a time when her brother Gabriel was taking overdoses of laudanum and writing facetious letters about founding a Mutual Suicide Association, Christina was facing possible death. Even in the 1950s a thyroid crisis, with its effect on the heart and the whole body's metabolism, could still be fatal. Modern medication for thyroid disease, and safer surgery, were not available to Christina. Her convalescence was slow and complicated. Her thyroid almost certainly went through the opposite problem of not producing enough, so that, as mentioned earlier in this chapter, her weight gain was part of myxoedema or hypothyroidism.

She worried about her mind, since she could not concentrate. Low thyroid function often affects the memory, so that a person may appear demented when they simply need some extra thyroid tablets, or it can lead to depression. Christina had severe symptoms of both kinds. Later, she had angina, which sometimes follows myxoedema. It shows how much Charles Cayley still meant to her that he was the only person outside the family whom she would see when her appearance was so disfigured by her thyroid problems.

In 1876 her sister Maria died and, six years later in 1882, she lost Dante Gabriel, followed in 1886 by the final blow, her mother's death. She had been devoted to all three out of love and a sense of duty. Her grief must have added to the other reasons, physical and spiritual, for her depression.

In the years from 1870 to her death in 1894 she produced seven prose works, most of them published by the Society for the Promotion of Christian Knowledge. These met the needs of a predominantly Christian readership. One was *The Face of the Deep,* a devotional commentary on the Book of Revelation. Such writing may make us feel that John Bunyan was right to worry about those who 'meddled with the Apocalypse', and yet the work of 550 pages makes a fascinating contribution to commentaries on the last book of the Bible. As she goes through the book she explains only a little, but her approach is mainly to turn the verses into short prayers. She also frequently inserts her poems into the commentary, adding to its worth, and showing a side of her work that mattered greatly to her and to her many readers.

Her later years were sad; she told William of her obsessions, her fears of hell and of judgement. She wrote to him, asking the agnostic William to 'pray for me that I may not, after having (in a sense) preached to others, be myself a castaway'. In a lesser way she was like Cowper in sharing such fears.

**Learning from Christina**

What we learn from Christina Rossetti's life and work depends on what we ourselves bring to our reading of, or about her. Anyone may enjoy her songs, the lyrical verse that sadly stopped some time in middle age. I have tried to quote sufficient to show just how splendidly she wrote; her technique satisfies the mind, and the feelings that she expresses often pierce straight to the heart.

But there is much more than bitter-sweet singing. Over much of her writing there seems to hang a censor's notice saying: 'For Christians Only'. The material comes straight from the Bible and her limited Christian experience. But she is not sectarian; she liked to meet with Dissenters, as if her spirituality crossed the boundaries of both denomination and tradition.

She did not follow an antique drum, or fight battles of long ago. In her Christian writing she has a directness that marks her out as special. Her love of God, her devotion to truth as she saw it in Scripture, and her anxious scrupulosity about obeying Christ as well as loving him, are all of a piece, a seamless robe. However, she used her religion to avoid much that might have enriched her life. I think she was not taught properly about faith, nor was she ever in an environment that could help her to move on from confession and absolution to some better, fuller Christian life.

It is as if, like Gerard Manley Hopkins, who so admired her verse, she remained trapped in a world Luther and Bunyan both knew but from which they moved on – a world in which fear and uncertainty predominated. The certain knowledge of God's love, the full assurance of faith, and the undying pledges of being accepted in the Beloved were often inaccessible to her. In her fifties and sixties she lived in terror of hell. Not all of this was due to the depression from which she suffered from time to time. Some of it may have been due to inadequate Christian teaching.

I think she had not been taught properly to feel the truth of such words as those of Jesus that no man can snatch the sheep out of his Father's hand. She saw herself as a silly sheep, and feared she might not make it to the eternal fold. A Puritan treatise on assurance of salvation called *Heaven on Earth* would have been foreign to her. Heaven, like sexual fulfilment, was beyond her grasp, and no foretaste of it, no spiritual ecstasy or any special savouring of grace was allowed. She could never have sung, with A. M. Toplady:

> More happy, but not more secure,
> The glorified spirits in heaven.

Her family situation also hampered her in some respects. The youngest of four, she became the dutiful daughter. Her elderly father, so much older and so different from her mother, did not help. It is surprising that her father, always alienated from the Roman Church, published before his death a set of Italian verses called *Arpa Evangelica.* Would that he had shared such singing with his daughters.

She saw it as her duty to be submissive, as we have described. Such submissiveness has blighted the lives of many Christian daughters, and a few sons too. We should learn that to impose additional conflict and divided loyalty in the name of God is sometimes unwarranted, and may cause havoc.

It is no wonder that Christina wrote, in the famous poem from which the title of this chapter is taken:

> Does the road wind up-hill all the way?
> Yes, to the very end.
> Will the day's journey take the whole long day?
> From morn to night, my friend.

In my work hardly a month goes by without a case in some way similar to Christina's crossing my path. So often parents, or brothers and sisters, impose a view, in God's name, on a submissive soul who should, instead, be encouraged to grow and learn, and develop her (or his) own identity. It can be, and in Christina's case it was, a travesty of normal Christian development. She rejected the role of governess, and the constraints of her family on her time may have caused an inevitable delay in her finding her role as a writer and poet.

F. L. Lucas, in her book *Ten Victorian Poets,* says much that deserves to be read and reread. She quotes Sir Walter Raleigh as saying: 'The only thing Christina makes me want to do is cry, not lecture.' When we look at the pictures of Christina we see the attractiveness of her face diminish over time, partly because of the ravages of thyroid disease. Lucas sees past the face to her self. She says that, unlike Jael, Christina hammered the nails into her own flesh; Hopkins did it literally, Christina metaphorically. Lucas adds:

> Christina knew few things, but she knew them well; and one of them was her own mind ... like other women poets she shared the fact that they have escaped being educated out of their senses ... she was no great creator of characters. But she had one ... Goodness, grace and courage were hers. For lack of a little more feather-pated gaiety her life became a thing grim to contemplate. But poetry is a thing of isolated moods: there it mattered less than in life that she wanted gaiety, seeing that she had genius. Thanks to it she still stands first among English poetesses.

**Grace unlocking genius**

We should heed the Irish poet P. J. Kavanagh, who wrote of Christina recently: 'She should be shown to the young in schools because she would teach them to "hear" other poems. Her range is narrow but deep, and echoes, like a well.' Her brother called her a 'fountain sealed', because she was so rigid and so unyielding in her Christian principles when others about her were becoming famous for their rejection of grace and of its demands upon their lives. However, I think we can see ways in which Christina's experience of grace unlocked her talent, and enabled her writing to flow.

It is as if her creative talent, unable to find fulfilment in marriage and child-bearing, was sublimated into her writing. Originally, sublimation referred simply to the chemical process (of heating and then cooling) whereby a substance is distilled into a purer form. The word has come to mean a way of transmuting impulses – such as sexual drives – into activities of a higher order. This, I think, is what happened to Christina Rossetti. Whether such a severe degree of self-denial and sublimation was necessary to distil her rare creativity is another question.

Her themes were narrow in focus. Perhaps she felt like Jane Austen, who wrote of herself in 1816: 'The little bit (two inches wide) of ivory on which I work with so fine a brush as produces little effect after much labour.' Jane Austen has many admirers who read her work avidly, and Christina has received similar appreciation, which has been increasing in recent years.

She and her brothers and sister practised the writing of sonnets and other verse in childhood. This early experience enabled her to sharpen to a fine edge her God-given skill, and she became a poet who strove for, and often achieved, perfection of form. Her faith gave her the subject matter to which she often returned. She came to feel that she had a special way of conveying a Christian message in both her verse and her prose writings.

Because her life involved so much suffering and self-denial, her writing contains the great themes which have inspired all Christian art and deeply religious writing. We cannot wish her different, in her life or her writing, without taking away the very honesty that makes her so special. For those who desire to hear, and who listen carefully, there is much in Christina Rossetti that calls to us, as it were, from 'deep to deep'. And even those of us who hear her almost casually, as at Christmas, or while leafing through an anthology of verse, cannot fail to notice how uniquely her genius expresses her experience of God's grace.

In her lesser-known carol 'Christmastide', with its first line 'Love came down at Christmas', she summed up what mattered most to her:

> Love shall be our token,
>     Love be yours and love be mine,
> Love to God and all men,
>     Love for plea and gift and sign.

*Further Reading*

C. H. Sissons' *Christina Rossetti: Selected Poems* (Manchester: Carcanet Press, 1984*)* is the best selection and the most easily available.

A recent biography, Kathleen Jones, *Learning Not To Be First: The Life of Christina Rossetti* (Oxford: OUP, 1992), is most helpful. Georgina Battiscombe, *Christina Rossetti: A Divided Life* (London: John Constable, 1981) is excellent. *The Poetical Works of Christina Georgina Rossetti* (London: Macmillan, *1928)* contains nearly all her verse, and a memoir by her brother William Michael Rossetti.

As ever, the sumptuous studies come from North America. R. W. Crump's edition of *The Complete Poems of Christina Rossetti* (Baton Rouge, LA: Louisiana State University Press, 1979 and 1986) comprises four large volumes, and is now the standard text. Of the many American studies, I would select two in particular: David A. Kent (ed.), *The Achievement of Christina Rossetti* (Ithaca, NY: Cornell University Press, 1987) is full of interest; Edna Kotin Charles (ed.), *Christina Rossetti: Critical Perspectives 1862–1982* (Cranbury, NJ/London: Associated University Presses, 1985*)* is a splendid summary of how views have changed over the years, and includes many Freudian, Jungian and feminist readings. F. L. Lucas, *Ten Victorian Poets* (Cambridge: CUP, 1940) is very perceptive and helpful.

A maverick among biographies is Lona Mosk Packer's *Christina Rossetti* (Cambridge: CUP, 1963). Alone, and perversely, she believes an artist called William Bell Scott was a lover and an important explanation of much of Christina's verse. The idea, set in an otherwise excellent book, has been firmly discredited.

Frances Thomas, *Christina Rossetti* (London: Self-Publishing Association, 17 St Paul's Place, London N1 2QF, 1992*)* is the fullest life, written with access to new sources.

# 6

# Take my Life: Frances Ridley Havergal (1836–1879)

It is good to read poetry; it is better to write poetry; but best of all is to live poetry.

(*Rupert Brooke, in a letter)*

Best to say I am a maid of all work in the household of God.

(*Frances Ridley Havergal's reply to an American request for an autobiography*)

What about self denial? ... Consecration does not supersede this, but tranfigures it. Literally, a consecrated life is and must be a denial of self. But all the effort and pain of it is changed into very delight.

(*Frances Ridley Havergal* in *Kept for the Master's Use)*

O fill me with Thy fullness, Lord,
Until my very heart o'erflow
In kindling thought and glowing word,
Thy love to tell, Thy praise to show

*F R H*

The name of Frances Ridley Havergal (or simply her initials, F R H) became widely known in the reign of Queen Victoria, not only in the churches of Victorian Britain but throughout the world. In America she became loved and admired for her Christian writings and especially for her hymns. Even today, we sing some of her hymns regularly in many of our churches – hymns such as

Take my life and let it be
Consecrated, Lord, to Thee

and many more. She also wrote robust and rousing hymns, which many of us do not associate with her name. We should try and give her the honour which is her due, which she never sought in her own brief lifetime: her achievements and her peculiar genius should be celebrated, for what she did with her special gifts, and because (as she might say) for the grace of the Giver. Her short life had much sadness and frailty but also much fulfilment. She declined offers of marriage and found the loneliness that followed these decisions very painful.

Her extended family valued her: as a much-loved aunt she looked after the children of two of her older sisters as a kind of governess to them.

She was one of the heroines of one of the Christian renewal movements of her time, which became centred on the Keswick convention and Mildmay, as well as many of the 'holiness' movements in North America. Yet she said emphatically that her discovery of the teaching and experience of consecration came to her directly, and not through any meeting, organization or convention. I believe it was because she lived her message that it became so effective, and not simply because she read about the Christian life or wrote about it.

**The youngest daughter's unexpected fame**

She was a Shropshire lass, who spent most of her life near the river Severn, and not far from Worcester where her father became a Canon, and minister in one of the Worcester churches, after having been a country rector for many years. She was his unexpected sixth child, with three older sisters and two older brothers. She was educated at first at home: this was in a home where her father taught his own pupils, to eke out his stipend of £29 a year. She became quite an intellectual, a blue stocking. Because of long stays in Germany, she was fluent in German. From the days of her early schooling she was fluent in French. Her father, her brother and her nephew aged twelve all encouraged her, – almost as a matter of course – to learn to read New Testament Greek and some Hebrew. More than any of her achievements, the love of music which she inherited from her father led to her writing hymns and poetry. Her second name of Ridley inspired a poem in praise of the Reformation Bishop Ridley, but she was in fact named after one of her father's friends and ex-pupil William Ridley, her godfather.

She became a 'sweet singer of Israel' and sang her own hymns so well that she became a popular choice by many Christians who were keen to have her help in their work of outreach and mission. Though shy and reserved by nature, she entered that world of popular music and became one of its leaders. She became aware of her hold on the Christian readers of her day, and in some of her letters the word *'hit'* occurs, showing that she was glad to be 'in the ratings' as they might be described today. Her humour leads her to ask a friend if she is right to question her own wish to write yet another book, and to ask whether it is simply the last big cheque which is persuading her to write again. The temptations of being a best seller were real ones: my own copy of her little book *Kept for the Master's Use* was one which is noted as bringing that book's print run to a total of 248,000 copies: in total it sold far more.

She wrote some twenty five books, some large and substantial, some small and easily put in a pocket. By any standard (though her Victorian elegance would have made her dislike the phrase) she was 'top of the pops' in her day and her popularity continued for decades after she died, tragically young, at the age of forty-three years. The large volumes of poetry, including the long and difficult *Moonlight Sonata* were still in use at my own home. When I was trying, at the beginning of World War II in 1940, to find suitable verses to memorize and to recite at the children's festivals I became familiar with the Havergal style, some of its problems and also its positive aspects.

Her writings circulated in her day in *millions*, and after her death a number of her books were translated into French, German, Swedish and Russian. Her hymns remain popular in Welsh versions. When her sister Maria put together a memoir in her book *Memorials of Frances Ridley Havergal* the sales figures of that book alone over the next few years came to a quarter of a million copies. We will try to describe the quality of her work, while also acknowledging the quantity in which it was sold and read.

## The Havergal Family

Her father was no ordinary country vicar. William Henry Havergal graduated from Oxford in the year after the battle of Waterloo. His fame rests on the same special musical gifts that Frances was to inherit. Havergal's *Old Church Psalmody* (1847) is said to be the father of most modern collections of hymn tunes: and his own name was attached to many of the most popular ones. When Frances was born her oldest sister Miriam was nineteen, Maria (to whom in later life she was very close) was fifteen, and Ellen was thirteen. Both her older brothers became well known Anglican ministers: when she was born her brother Henry was sixteen and Frank was six. It is not surprising that Fan or Fanny as she was called should become her father's favourite daughter.

Her father called her 'Little Quicksilver' perhaps because of her mercurial temperament. She was seen to be a very fast learner, and seemed to the family and friends to be precociously bright and intelligent. While her father led the regular family prayers, she would be the one to insist on sitting on his knee while he read the Bible. She had a life-long feeling of a special relationship with her father, and may have repaid some of her debt to him in editing his hymn book after his death.

Her mother, too, adored her gifted child. Mother was a kind of governess to the young children. Frances started scribbling hymns when she was seven years old, perhaps as a reward for the attention she was given. When she was aged nine, she began writing letters in rhyme rather than prose to her brothers who were at Oxford University. All in all, it began as an idyllic childhood. But her mother died when Frances was twelve, after an illness that had been long and painful. Though her mother is spoken of as full of a tenderness towards Fanny, she was also able to say to her: 'Fanny, pray to God to prepare you for all he is preparing for you'. Thirty years later Frances recalled it, and said it had been 'a life-prayer' with her. It may seem to parents of our own day to be a rather heavy burden to lay on a girl of eleven, trying to cope with what seemed an inevitable loss of her mother. But these were Victorian days, and it must have seemed both natural and inevitable for a pious mother to speak in that way to a dutiful daughter.

We know that to lose a parent at that age is a peculiarly severe source of grief, issuing often in depressive illness in later life. Frances certainly grieved bitterly. Recalling how she felt after more than a year of grieving her mother's death, she wrote: '... life began to seem such a little thing to me, ... what was there in it to care for? Things happened which tended very strongly to confirm these sad thoughts.... As the beautiful spring came on there was a mist of melancholy over the very flowers; they opened, well, what matter? they would fade again, and so would everything'.

What help the young teenager had, who can guess? Perhaps grief and bereavement were not given the care and concern that we now think they deserve. But the next year seems to have been one of recovery, for she was sent, at fourteen, to a boarding school in London.

**Her Education and First Steps in Faith**

Frances went to the same remarkable school in Belmont, near Campden Hill, London to which her three sisters had been sent earlier: her sister Maria has left us a clear account of it. It was a fashionable establishment accepting girls from aristocratic families of many nations living in London, and also popular with professional families. The 60-80 girls were required to talk French as a general rule. They were allowed, if walking as a school group in Kensington Gardens, to speak English. The teaching was said to be of a high order. Both the Italian master and the dancing master were well known as those who had also taught the Princess Victoria.

The central figure was the headmistress, Mrs Teed: she had been converted to an evangelical faith which she was very keen that the girls should share. Mrs Teed taught at morning and evening prayers and at a Bible class once a week. She also taught from the Anglican Prayer book. While the content of the teaching was almost certainly little different from what her father had taught Frances for years, there was a difference in the very marked level of feelings which Mrs Teed hoped that her pupils might share. Some accounts suggest that the school experienced something like a small religious revival. Frances arrived in the school's last year, before it was to be closed. The fact that it was her own final year seemed to lend an urgency to Mrs Teed's ministry. Since her conversion, the well paid dancing master who earned £600 a year – an enormous sum in the 1830s – was dismissed, since she wanted to concentrate on the Christian aspects of education. A Christian magazine of the time praised Miss Teed for not 'preparing pupils for scenes of worldly gaiety and dissipation'.

Frances loved the company of the other girls, and seems to have discovered her role as confidante and something of a counsellor which was to be so important later. The strong feelings associated with the 'revival' atmosphere left her cold. But one special friend, Elizabeth Clay, had a conversion experience which led in due course to missionary service in India, an outcome Frances envied and for which she praised Elizabeth. As is the way of a same-sex boarding school there was one girl called Diana for whom she had 'a perfectly idolatrous affection' – as Frances described it – 'an affection such as, until that time, I had never given to any one'. Diana had a conversion experience too, which she longed for Frances to have also: she did not share any such thing, and though she learned much from Diana she describes herself as being, at that time, 'more disheartened than ever'.

The school closed after Frances had been there for one term. Perhaps the most important consequence was that one of the teachers, Caroline Cooke, later became her stepmother. Miss Cooke would visit Frances' sister Miriam at Oakhampton. While Frances was also visiting there Miss Cooke was in fact able to help her to take the first steps to commit herself to faith in Christ. It was soon after this experience that she learned that Miss Cooke was to be her father's second wife: she was twenty years younger than her father, and one can only guess what conflicts this new development caused Frances to suffer, even then. Later the step-mother's spite was to be experienced at its full venom.

There was another brief period of schooling at Powick, near Worcester, where the atmosphere was less pressurised and she began to shine as a pupil. But an attack of erysipelas (a much more dangerous streptococcal skin infection in those days) meant a long illness and a stay at home. Her eyes were affected for a time, but she was then sent off to the coast of North Wales to recover properly. She wrote letters to her friends from Llandudno describing the fun of sea bathing and mountain walks. She preferred above all to take solitary, slightly dangerous mountain walks where she would, in such wild places, take out her little New Testament and read and pray.

### The German Connection

The next school was entirely unexpected and came about because of her father's growing problems with his eyes. It was decided that he had to go to Germany to be treated by a well-known Prussian eye specialist. Frances accompanied her father and stepmother and they settled for some time in Dusseldorf: here, in 1853 at the age of sixteen years she entered a typical Prussian girls' school or Gymnasium. Although she was only at this school for a term, when the examination results were announced she was astonished to hear what all the masters had agreed: 'Frances Havergal: *Numero Einz*'. She was top of the class.

It seemed greatly to her credit that, in a German state school, she had been able in a first term to achieve such distinction. Of the hundred or so girls, a number had been spiteful and unpleasant to her – partly no doubt because she was a foreigner who was excelling. She attributed the spite to the difference in religion, which may, perhaps, have been a secondary matter.

The next six months were a joy to her, because she was moved to the home of a German pastor to study with him and share the family life. It was in a village on the Rhine called Obercassel, near Bonn: Frances was happy to be in the country and within sight of the famous mountains, the Drachenfels. She describes her contented life: 'I like my quarters amazingly and am very happy. I get up at five o'clock, breakfast at seven; then I study for four hours. Of course my books are nearly all German, and I write abstracts; I give one hour to French literature.... The German language is very easy to me.... It is most absurd now when I begin to speak in English; I cannot get to think in it....'

This pastor's home was a formative experience for her in learning both a new language and so much of its literature. There was a nearby family of Count zur Lippe where she had been a welcome visitor: this aristocratic family lived simply, giving half their income away. She was to return to the pastor's home four years later in the summer months and again in the winter of 1865 when she became godmother to one of the children. She visited them again on the way to Switzerland in 1869. I think there is evidence that she was able to learn something of the 'Higher Life' movement during her time with this pastor's family, and in mixing with these devoted German Christians.

It was while she was in Germany that she saw a painting: 'a

picture of our Saviour in the study of a German Divine' with the motto 'I did this for Thee! What has thou done for Me?' and she wrote six verses, of which the first and the last read:

I gave My life for thee,
My precious blood I shed,
That thou might'st ransomed be,
And quickened from the dead
I gave My life for thee;
What hast thou given for Me?

Oh, let thy life be given,
Thy years for Me be spent,
World-fetters all be riven,
And joy with suffering blent.
I gave Myself for thee:
Give thou thyself to Me!

This simple, unadorned directness of style was to be typical of her poems and hymns at their best. There was always an appeal for a believing response, and for action.

**Cinderella and her stepmother**

At seventeen Frances returned to live in a room in a rented house in Worcester where her father lived now with her stepmother Caroline. There is a good deal of evidence that Caroline was envious of Frances and made things hard for her. Later, when she joined them in a house in Leamington after her father's retirement Caroline was to forbid visitors who came for help and counsel to Frances, because of the wear on the carpet on the stairs leading to her attic room there. More painful was the fact that Caroline, for many years later on, would not let Frances' name or initials be used in publications on which she worked for her father. These pressures were endured by Frances, but at her father's death after a sudden stroke in 1870 she wrote a poem with the title 'Our Father' which reflected her distress with such lines as

A home to me it cannot be
Without my father's face.

Unlike Cinderella, Frances was to be helped by her two married sisters who were able to cheer and help Frances by asking her to teach their children. For Frances, this governess role was fulfilling, as we shall see.

Throughout the period from her return from Germany at the age of seventeen to her father's death when she was aged thirty-four, the underlying conflict with her stepmother was a sad fact of her life. But her education continued in spite of all the conflicts caused by the fact that Caroline and Frances both cared so deeply about Mr Havergal. There was an underlying element of competing to love and serve him. Both women grieved after his death in markedly different ways, and it appears that Caroline had a severely morbid grief reaction where the hostility she felt after her bereavement was focused on Frances, who felt deeply hurt by it.

At seventeen she little realized how distressing such aspects would be, and was excited as she prepared for her confirmation in Worcester Cathedral. She took this most seriously, as she did her further education. Her father helped her to learn and enjoy New Testament Greek, and her twelve-year old nephew, as mentioned earlier, began to teach her the rudiments of Hebrew (later to be augmented in Ireland by a Hebrew scholar there). She was a very keen pupil and began to commit large tracts of the Bible to her memory in English, and she learnt a few portions in Hebrew from Isaiah and Genesis. It has been pointed out by one author that for Frances this was a real form of 'learning by heart' rather than rote learning. Her feelings were engaged, as well as her formidable intellectual powers.

Her confirmation service was recorded by her in detail, and she was very moved when Bishop Pepys prayed, with his hands placed on her head: 'Defend, O Lord, this Thy child with Thy heavenly grace, that she may continue Thine for ever, and daily increase in Thy Holy Spirit more and more, until she come unto Thy everlasting kingdom'. That day, aged seventeen, she wrote a poem *In The Cathedral 17 July 1854* which reflects her feelings and beliefs after an experience which was for her, so meaningful:

'Thine for Ever.'
Oh! 'Thine for ever.' what a blessed thing
To be for ever His who died for me!

My Saviour, all my life Thy praise I'll sing,
Nor cease my song throughout eternity.

It foreshadows what were to become her most cherished beliefs, and some of the themes for which, because of her gifts of later and fuller expression, many others were to grasp the facts of Christian faith better through her more developed writing and her songs, hymns and verse.

**Irish Interludes**

Her sister Ellen met and married a widower called Giles Shaw whose two children lived in Cheltenham with their grandmother: this was the link with John, Giles' son, that brought her to learn Hebrew. Shaw lived some twelve miles from Dublin where he owned a flax and corn mill on the banks of the Liffey. While staying with her married sister there she became involved in helping in the local Protestant school, met a friend who was a Hebrew Scholar, and was introduced to the Irish Society's work. Giles Shaw shared with Frances and her father a deep desire to spread better knowledge of the Bible in Ireland.

Frances became a keen supporter of the Irish Society and was soon organising collections to support its work on her return to Worcester. It was part of what she had learned from her father in his support for missionary work, which he supported from the Protestant and Evangelical perspectives which were unquestioned at the time. Unlike her sister Maria it was not easy for Frances to be a partisan Protestant. She liked the fact that the Irish Society sought to bring Irish Bibles and the gospel to places where there was no religious influence in parts of Ireland. It was different from the more sectarian work of the Irish Church Missions. It stirred up again her wish to be a missionary somewhere, as her old school friend had found it possible to be when she went to India, a vocation she had so much envied her for enjoying.

But it was not to be, and a trip to Ireland to see more of the work had to be abandoned: but Frances was by now active in Worcester in her father's parish work of visiting and teaching, work which she shared with her sister Maria and her stepmother Caroline. It was a full life, but she was also continuing a habit of disciplined reading. I was surprised to note that she read the works of the great Puritan divine Thomas Goodwin as they were being reprinted: a hard task for anyone, but perhaps it shows the studious habits her father and family taught her.

No one who read so widely and so deeply would easily become a glib versifier. She was also beginning to write more, and in 1860 her first poems were published by a magazine. She was delighted, but used her first cheque to buy her father a silk cassock, sewing inside it a message saying this was 'the first fruits of my pen'.

**Teaching her sisters' children**

It was not only her sister Ellen in Ireland that provided some relief from the burdens of work in a new parish to which Canon Havergal had moved from Worcester to a small parish of Shareshill near Wolverhampton. Her oldest sister Miriam had four children and she decided to ask Frances to come and live with them and help to teach the four children. For the next seven years (1860–67) Miriam's large home at Oakhampton was her base, though she felt deeply about not having a home of her own. She had the special care of two of Miriam's daughters and was deeply upset when one of these died at the age of fifteen, when Frances had just left.

She was a very good but demanding teacher, and the four children when together would give her a very hard time. But she enjoyed the experience of being a governess, and her time of hard work was relieved by holidays in Wales, Scotland and Germany.

Sometimes she wrote of her failures to interest the children in religion. She wrote of their 'peculiar and malignant naughtiness': any parent who has struggled with children who do not wish to obey or co-operate may recall this feeling. But on the whole they loved aunt Fanny, and easily lured her away from study to the outdoors and the games which she loved to play with them.

These years of teaching her sister's children provided some relief from the pressures of her father's new home with her step-mother. She still visited her father at Christmas and New Year but she was beginning to grow and develop as an independent person. Her inner world was often one of sadness, conflict and uncertainty while she looked for guidance on what course her future life should take.

Her visits to her brother Frank and his family at Hereford helped her in this time. Frank was by that time Vicar-Choral at Hereford Cathedral. At Oxford he had been influenced into becoming an avowed Anglo-Catholic and his father was sad about it, but Frances had spirited discussions with Frank who was known as both saintly and amiable. Frank welcomed her work in his parish, doing her usual teaching and parish work in spite of her fiery Protestantism. Frank's five children loved her and she was a great influence on their development and their Christian work: the eldest of the five children was referred to by the Bishop of Hereford as the best curate in the diocese. A memorial bell was added to Frank's parish church in Frances Havergal's memory after her death, in a token of thanks for her work in the parish.

Her Irish links changed happily for Frances when Ellen and her husband Giles Shaw moved from Ireland (because of the troubles) to a large country house near Bewdley called Winterdyne: here she was again a welcome visitor, and the warmth of Winterdyne is reflected in some of her verse and her stories for children.

> And silvery Severn swiftly flows
> With an extra sparkle and glitter and shine
> Under the woods at Winterdyne

Again there were four children aged between six and ten, and again she served as their governess in 1868, finding these children easier than Miriam's had been at Oakhampton. She wrote that 'I got fonder than ever of the children and they of me too – I quite enjoyed teaching them, and they were so loving and docile it was all pleasure'.

She may have needed this store of pleasurable memories when her new home became a room at the top of the house, after her father's retirement – aged seventy-five – to Leamington, where he continued to preach in local parish churches. It will be recalled that her step-mother put a stop to the many visitors who came to Frances for spiritual help, because of the wear on the stair carpet. This was as nothing to the sudden death of her father after a stroke at Easter 1870. Her father had delighted in seeing Frances' first book of poems, *The Ministry of Song*, published the year before, and now he was gone. Frances was able to 'flash up and talk and laugh when spoken to.... But God knows how intensely I miss him, and how desolate and fatherless I do feel....' All the changing scenes of life in this decade gave her experience of teaching, of parish work and evangelization which was to stand her in good stead in the remaining hectic nine years of her life.

**Solace in Work with New Men**

Two men were to look to Frances Havergal for help, and both became very important in her life and service, making up to some extent for the loss of her father. The first was the Rev. C. B. Snepp, vicar of Perry Barr near Birmingham, and the other the Rev. John Tinson Wrenford, vicar of St Paul's Newport. Mr Snepp was the first to write to Frances after her father's death asking for her help in producing a new hymnbook *Songs of Grace and Glory*. She was delighted and soon Mr Snepp – some fifteen years older than Frances – was visiting her at Leamington and she was visiting his family at Perry Barr. This work led to her joining in some of Mr Snepp's parish missions, and enjoying the family's companionship on Swiss Alpine holidays. Her work with the full music edition of *Songs of Grace and Glory* was important: their differences about accepting some hymns led to some amusing arguments. Frances was as much a Calvinist in her faith as Mr Snepp, but she was more tolerant of good hymn-writers who might have not been as orthodox as Mr Snepp wished. For Snepp, even opening *Hymns Ancient and Modern* was to betray his faith: Frances sought to persuade him that one hymn including the phrase 'Son of Mary' must be included since Mr Spurgeon had included it! Their considerable work was finished with a good deal of satisfaction in the joint enterprise. Mr Snepp would sometimes ask Frances to write on a particular topic, but she would say that a hymn had to be 'given' to her – she could not simply sit down and write one. There are a number of such hymns such as that for Ascension Day written in 1871 (based on Ephesians 4:8, 'He ascended up on high') for which she composed one of the hymn tunes that is still sung, *Hermas*:

Golden harps are sounding, Angel voices ring,

Pearly gates are opened – Opened for the King;
Christ, the King of Glory, Jesus, King of love
Is gone up in triumph To his throne above.
All His work is ended, Joyfully we sing,
Jesus hath ascended! Glory to our King!

Mr Snepp was a welcome relief from the problems which she encountered in preparing her father's work for publication in a new form called *Havergal's Psalmody* (to include his previous book on psalmody, his work on a 100 psalms and hymn tunes, and some new unpublished material). Frances did all the work for the new book, but her step-mother wrote the introduction and insisted on keeping the name of Frances out of the book: it was a petty, painful and sad experience. As already mentioned, it was an aspect of her step-mother's morbid grief reaction after the death of her father.

Further problems were to follow: when Frances became ill with her first attack of typhoid fever with complications, her step-mother nursed her devotedly as she had nursed her father: their relationship seemed to improve. In only two years time Caroline herself became ill and Frances had to nurse her through a long and painful terminal illness. She was helped by the coming of her sister Maria to the home in Leamington, and by professional nurses. Mrs Havergal died in 1878: Frances was to be buried in the same spot just over a year later.

Her friendship with Mr Wrenford was because of his involvement in one of the 'holiness movements' and a small pamphlet he had written called *All for Jesus*. This led to visits to Newport and to sharing parish work there. It became part of her burgeoning work – for the YWCA and associated movements and for many missions in England.

Other famous names appear in her life: Robert Pearsall Smith, who was so impressed with her hymns. He was the one who made them known in the Keswick Convention with his colleague Dr James Mountain in *Hymns of Consecration and Faith*. Hannah Pearsall Smith whose book *The Christian's Secret of a Happy Life* was a popular exposition of 'consecration' teaching, continued actively in Christian work after her husband's breakdown and disappearance from the scene.

Frances was now known in the London scene by her publishers and admirers, and yet what made for her lasting fame was to happen unexpectedly, on Advent Sunday 1873, while she was staying at her sister Ellen's home at Winterdyne.

**The Experience and The Meaning**

A modern writer says that it is possible 'to have the experience and to miss the meaning': it is important to take careful note of what Frances says about her experience on Advent Sunday. This is how she described her experience, and something of what it meant to her, to her sister Maria:

> '... I first saw clearly the blessedness of true consecration. I saw it as a flash of electric light, and what you see you can never unsee. There must be full surrender before there can be full blessedness. God admits you by the one into the other. He himself showed me this most clearly. You know how singularly I have been withheld from attending all conventions and conferences; man's teaching has, consequently, had but little to do with it. First I was shown that "the blood of Jesus Christ His Son cleanseth us from all sin", and then it was made plain to me that He who had thus cleansed me had power to keep me clean; so I just utterly yielded myself to Him, and utterly trusted Him to keep me.'

To her this was an experience that was a divine gift, coming direct from God to her soul and spirit. Was it, perhaps, an experience of assurance of salvation in a sense which she had never felt before? Was it for her an experience of the words in Ephesians 1:13 about the 'sealing of the spirit'? Some have sought to describe it as a variety of religious experience she shares with Roman Catholic believers like Theresa of Avila or Blaise Pascal. I certainly believe it was a mystical experience without any of the emotional pressures of a large or small meeting – or indeed anyone else present. It was in the category of the Apostle Paul's 'Christ-mysticism'.

A few months after this a biographer tells us of a letter to Mr Snepp in which she writes:

> 'Oh it was so sweet, so glorious to see something of that, the being His very own, the serving Him and pleasing Him, the being utterly at His disposal, and with Him, and in Him, and all for Him, on and on through ages and ages of eternity. My whole Heart said, 'Whom have I in heaven but Thee? and there is none on earth that I desire beside Thee!'

*The Oxford Book of Mystical Verse* reprints parts of one of Havergal's long poems from her book 'Under His Shadow', reminiscent of Henry Vaughan's 'deep but dazzling darkness':

> They say there is a hollow, safe and still,
> A point of coolness and repose
> Within the centre of a flame, where life might dwell
> Unharmed and unconsumed, as in a luminous shell,
> Which the bright walls of fire enclose
> In breachless splendour, barrier that no foes
> Could pass at will
> So, in the centre of these thoughts of God,
> Cyclones of power, consuming glory-fire –
> As we fall o'erawed
> Upon our faces, and are lifted higher
> By his great gentleness, and carried nigher
> Than unredeemed angels till we stand
> Even in the hollow of His hand.
> Nay more! we lean upon His breast –
> *There*, there we find a point of perfect rest
> And glorious safety. There we see
> His thoughts to usward, thoughts of peace
> That stoop in tenderest love; that still increase
> With increase of our need; that never change,
> That never fail, or falter, or forget.

Such a long fragment gives some sense of how deeply she thought about the meaning of her experience and expressed it in her own poetic style. Perhaps her other plainer descriptions may help us more. Her new life in Christ was summed up in four phrases: *surrender, continual cleansing, absolute trust and implicit obedience.* Better still, her little book *Kept for the Master's Use* gives her own clear explanation of her famous hymn *Take my Life.* 'Consecration is not so much a step as a course; not so much an act as a position to which a course of action inseparably belongs.... What we want now is ... to fulfil that course.'

She shared the joy and peace in believing with the many people who had found the same sort of experience in Keswick, in holiness meetings and in what has been called 'the more temperate climate of Mildmay'. In some sense her hymns and books became one of the clearest and sweetest voices of that renewal movement.

**Answering her Critics**

Some have suggested that only if you are a maiden aunt with a sufficient private income can you live the sort of life Frances Ridley Havergal then lived: it is not for a busy mother with children and a demanding husband. Perhaps so: but many quite ordinary folk who had none of Frances' gifts of expression in verse, hymns and music knew something of this same experience. For she believed, with George Herbert, that 'a servant with this clause, makes drudgery divine'.

Psychologists, especially those of the school of Freud, would say that sexual frustration had a lot to do with it. They would go on to say that the gross, impure demands of sexual instincts were transformed and purified by a process of *sublimation* into her love for God. They might speak further, with explanations about her excessive love of her father and the early loss of her mother. So, they might say, she looked for the perfect father and the perfect love, and this was inevitably channelled into religion. Of course there is something in all that sort of explanation but not enough to account for it all, by any means.

Frances was quite explicit in recognizing some of the Christian truths which the unbelieving critic may try to see as skeletons in her closet. She wrote to her friend Elizabeth Clay of 'the restfulness of recognizing the Lord Jesus as the heavenly Bridegroom – the Husband – meeting all the special woman's need of one to bow to and to love and obey – submitting, acquiescing, and obeying with great gladness, because with great love'. Modern feminists, and many men, may find such views hard to accept, but it was part of her faith. She could write to another friend to 'Ask the Lord, if it is not His will you should marry, to make you perfectly content, and then to take away all the wish out of your heart, so that you may be "free to serve" with your whole mind undistracted by it.'

She really came to live the simple language of her hymn *Take My Life*, which asks God to use all the elements of her life for himself. She was sometimes teased about the couplet, '*Take my silver and my gold, Not a mite would I withhold*', and felt it would be good if she sent fifty pieces of jewellery to the Church Missionary Society. She was delighted to learn that they had realised the sum of £50, almost twice her father's stipend for a year. But it was all done with good humour and common sense. She said that the fact that just because Scripture said that 'The King's daughter was all glorious within', she must not be *outwardly* a fright to those who looked at her.

The couplet, '*Take my will and make it Thine, It shall be no longer mine*' has also been criticized on other grounds, by comparing it with the words of Edwin Hatch's famous hymn, '*Breathe on me Breath of God*'. Hatch, it will be recalled, says rather:

> 'Until with Thee I will one will,
> To do and to endure'.

Perhaps it reflects the difference between the mystic who wishes to be taken up into union with God and to lose himself, and the more balanced Christian view that we do not lose our own personalities. Hatch reminds us that God works in us to will and to do, and we have then to 'work out our own salvation', rather than accepting the catchphrase 'let go and let God'. It is not the surrender of the will, but the wish to live in obedience to God's will, that matters.

Behind Havergal's simple teaching which could be so easily understood by her readers was a wealth of Christian understanding based on Scripture and her extremely thorough training and education in Christian theology and belief. In that respect she was very different from many of the evangelists of her time, and indeed many of the leaders of the holiness movements. Seldom can so learned and professionally skilled a woman have worn all her gifts so lightly and with such grace.

**The Swiss Connection**

She lived in the days when Thomas Cook and Henry Lunn – both fine Christian men – were seeking to pioneer holiday excursions in a new way, that has linked their names with the holiday industry to our day. One of the new destinations was Switzerland and in particular the English came to love the Alps and the whole Swiss experience. For Frances her fluent French and German made her time spent in Swiss holidays much easier. She had five long vacations and loved the mountain climbing.

Her experiences in the mountains grew increasingly important to her. She became something of a nature poet, a very important source of balance in her thinking: for to her God was as much her Creator as her Redeemer. It is so easy for Christians in her mould to think only of salvation: she did not do this. She said, jokingly no doubt, that the psalmist David must have seen Snowdonia to write as he did about the mountains. She wrote one poem about the Alps where she adopted George Herbert's convention of having the words printed to look like a mountain: a harmless 'conceit' of Herbert's type with *Easter Wings* printed to look like wings.

She was glad to throw off her staid Victorian decorum on her Swiss holidays, a process which had been foreshadowed by her early holidays in Llandudno when she would disappear into the wilder mountains nearby.

When she saw Mont Blanc she wrote: 'Mountains, real ones, are more to me than any other created thing' – she loved Mont Blanc, and the Jungfrau and the Matterhorn. She was a good mountaineer: her guide said she went like a chamois. She felt so much better after the 'atmospheric sal volatile' of the mountains. She writes of the delicious freedom and sense of leisure of those days, the renewing of youth, and the storming of the mountains with alpenstocks, scrambling and leaping, laughing and racing 'as if we were, not girls again, but downright boys'.

With her desire to excel she went up with a guide from Chamonix to Les Grands Mulets. She could not quite understand the excitement on her return with Mr Snepp and the two guides, until she realized that they knew it was the first ascent of the season, and that it was also the first ascent by a lady. There were cannonades in celebration, and Frances pleased the local newspaper editor by agreeing to write an article for his *Journal de Geneve.*

She could not help allegorizing all her experiences with her guides, as she did so much of the Old Testament in her books, to find reflections of Christ and types of 'Our Glorious Guide'.

It all enriched her beliefs and experience. It was perhaps inevitable that she should mix her holiday fun and pleasure with some Christian service and she would join in with French or German speaking Swiss with no sense of any sectarian divide, and sometimes evangelize.

Between 1869 and 1876 she had five long vacations in the Alps, lasting six to eight weeks, and usually accompanied by relatives or friends like the Snepp family or Elizabeth Clay her schoolfriend whose work in India with the Zenana Missionary Society she had so much envied.

Each time, except in 1874 when she returned with typhoid fever to endure a period of pain and suffering, she was always invigorated and ready for new challenges

**The sweet singer of Israel**

Frances Ridley Havergal has been described as a sweet singer: for our day and age, is she too sweet? It may be that the Victorians had a sweet tooth for dainties. When we feel that there is too much sugar present in some of her verse and stories for children, we must allow that sentiment was highly regarded by the Victorians, more perhaps than passion and emotion. If we compare Havergal with Ira D. Sankey, the singer and composer whom we associate with D. L. Moody the American evangelist, we may perhaps feel kinder towards her. *The Sacred Songs and Solos* of Sankey and Moody were stable diet for believers and for evangelists of that age. But the sentiment of Sankey is much more gushing and sentimental than Havergal's hymns. If one searches for them, there is something in Havergal also of the type of expression we find in '*Where is your wandering boy tonight*?' or the old favourite '*Softly and tenderly Jesus is calling*'. Such songs had their place, perhaps an honoured place, at one time. But we may think of the metaphor that too much sugar rots your teeth, and it spoils the taste for many. It seems certain when one studies the pattern of Christian living in the late Victorian time and later, that a diet of unmixed Sankey and Moody hymns led to a kind of spiritual anaemia. It is fortunate that Havergal was similar to other hymn-writers like Wesley and Watts in sticking closely to the language of Scripture, and in writing in plain language which made for easy singing and understanding.

In spite of the differences between her and Ira D. Sankey, it was an important event for her when Sankey and his wife visited Swansea to see Frances Havergal in the nearby Mumbles. Sankey had prayed publicly for her when she first suffered from typhoid fever in 1874, and their stay near the last home made for Frances by her sister Maria was a happy one. Sankey said he would take some of Frances' new music back with him to America.

The fact that she had a good voice as well as exceptional musical ability led her to be asked to take a leading role as a singer at many services and in many mission settings in places like Bewdley, Liverpool and many others. Her work was most commonly with women and girls, but she found that it could be equally effective with boys. She would sometimes give the story behind a hymn before singing it, and there is an account of more than one hostile listener won over by her method and her manner, so that the content of her message reached home, and led to faith in Christ. That was always her aim and purpose, and she sought to keep everything else subordinate to the purpose of winning others for her Master, and persuading her Christian listeners to come to a deeper and richer experience of God by giving themselves more completely to Christ and Christian service.

One has to think separately of her musical gifts, and of her abilities to write. She could and did write hymn tunes, but she never achieved her father's success in composing hymn tunes. Her father had won the Gresham prize for his musical work, and his name is still honoured among musicians who know their debt to him in church hymnody. Frances went to see two musical authorities: Professor Hiller, of the musical academy of Cologne, who gave an opinion on her abilities in composition. He may have damned her with faint praise: she 'bore the stamp of talent not of genius', he said. Since her question to him had been as to whether music should be her life work, she must have been discouraged.

The other musician, who gave her singing lessons, was Signor

Randegger in London: he said her voice was that of a mezzo-soprano: he said she had 'talent, taste, feeling and brains'.

One of her biographers says that she 'reveals depths of spiritual depression alternating with periods of happiness, the former tending to be associated with times of ill-health and the latter with physical well-being...'. Although the *Autobiography* concentrates more on 'the dark night of the soul' that she was going through, it would be wrong to give the impression that this was her whole experience. It was a time of social and sexual frustration for her, though she was also aware of successes and feared pride would come from her 'desire to have a name'. That she was beginning to be well known even then is reflected in the fact that her father, Canon Havergal, writing to her brother Frank in 1866 says: 'she has won more laurels in Germany than I care for her to wear'. She wrote to her sister Maria that what she really desired was 'to be a soul-winner', and it was to this that she had increasingly dedicated her life.

**God's University of Grief**

One of her biographers speaks movingly of Frances Ridley Havergal having been a graduate of God's University of Grief. We have seen earlier in this book how, like C. S. Lewis and William Cowper, she had lost her mother before she reached puberty, and had many other griefs to do with her father and her step-mother. She had many years of her twenties and thirties when she was depressed, and this was sometimes so clearly linked to her physical frailty that one may easily forget the possibility of mood swings in one so afflicted with grief in earlier life. The child who was called quicksilver because of her mercurial temperament doubtless also showed such quick changes of mood and sensitivity of spirit later in her life.

Her last years were to be affected by the fact that she picked up an infection on her way home from a Swiss trip, which proved to be typhoid fever. In those days there were no inoculations against typhoid and paratyphoid, and the enteric fevers were often fatal.

Her first illness with typhoid fever ended in recovery after a lot of pain, when she was cared for by her step-mother in Leamington and at Winterdyne, her sister's home. During the illness Frances found that she had lost the fear of death which had dogged her since childhood.

In April 1875 she had been very ill for four months and was told she could not work for another six months. She found it amazingly possible not simply to submit to the suffering but to rejoice in it. Yet she was sad that 'the whole gift of verse is taken from me' for about a year. Yet in 1874 she had been able to write one of her most loved hymns, '*Like a river glorious is God's perfect peace*'.

Many have thought that her memory of the river Severn, which had been near to a number of the places where she had lived, and which could be seen from her sister's splendid home at Winterdyne, was mixed with her allusion to Isaiah 48:18.

During the period of convalescence she went with her sister Maria to the Mumbles, near Swansea and stayed in Park Villa, Caswell Bay. After her step-mother's death in May 1878, the home at Leamington was broken up with all its attendant anxieties, and Maria and Frances made a home in the Mumbles, within sight of the Gower Peninsula, which was to become Britain's first National Park. It was not easy to dispose of the contents of her father's home, and she spent some months staying with members of the family before arriving (with thirty-two packages) in their new home. There, according to Maria, the expression Frances often used was 'What emancipation!'.

Soon she was back at her routine, up at seven, at work after breakfast answering her many letters and writing. 1879 seemed a year full of promise: she visited London where her delighted publishers went over plans for her new books and new songs to be brought out. Yet another proposal of marriage was made to Frances, and declined by her. She describes enthusiastically how 'teetotal work has taken up me' – the temperance movement was seeking to provide an alternative life-style to fight the great problems of alcoholism. She found to her surprise that she was gifted in work with boys, and records one day when she recruited twenty-five boys to sign the pledge, joining the village 'Temperance Regiment'. She seemed unstoppable in her efforts: even the man painting outside her study window had to be helped, because though he was perched on his high ladder he was asking her how he might realize his wish to be 'out and out on the Lord's side'.

Visitors came: not only Ira D. Sankey and his wife, but her old friend Elizabeth from the Punjab, and her friend and colleague

Baroness Helga von Cramm from Switzerland. And new departures were planned, with a visit to Ireland due on 4 June to visit remote mission stations there.

But it was not to be: in late May a feverish attack returned, and a doctor diagnosed peritonitis due to a return of her typhoid fever. Her family came, since it was obvious she was now dying. She asked her brother Frank to give her Communion at her bedside, and wrote: 'It is not the performance of the rite, *no safety in that*; but it is obedience to his command and as a remembrance of His dying love'. She had two sisters and her brother to comfort and help her, and although often in great pain she still spoke and sang with the utmost clarity. She said 'I am lost in amazement' ... 'There hath not failed one word of all His good promises' and sang snatches of her favourite hymns. Even allowing for her sister Maria's self-admitted tendency to exaggerate, and the Victorian fondness for death bed scenes, it is hard not to be moved by her death at forty-two years of age. As a friend of her parents had prophesied, 'That child will die singing' and so she did.

**Lasting Lessons**

Miss Havergal was a teacher most of her life, in different ways: what lessons would she like us to learn from her short, uncertain life? She was very aware of her gifts and what her family and her genetic inheritance and her upbringing had given her. In fact she was always hard on herself, in the spirit of that word: 'from him to whom much has been given, much will be required'. Even though she said she did not believe in sinless perfection, she was still, quite certainly, a perfectionist by temperament. Her standards were forbiddingly high, and even on the glaciers and by-ways of the Swiss Alps she had to excel. May we then learn the dangers of being so self-punitive in the search for the perfect, and say with Voltaire that 'the best is the enemy of the good'? How I wish that she might have said to her sister Maria 'What emancipation!' much *earlier* in her life: but the beliefs underlying women's liberation and feminism were not for her, and the main lesson from her personality to me is the value of real commitment and true consecration.

I think her hymn '*Take my Life*' may have frightened many away. It seems so full of absolutes, and leaves so little room for manoeuvre.

For her, it was not something that she achieved, but something she was given by God. The messages of the hymns, she felt, were directly from Him. Of course, she valued all the 'means of grace' also – her Bible, her prayers, her Book of Common Prayer, the Anglican services which had been so much of her life from childhood.

Is another lesson not to be afraid of her Christian mysticism, since it was always hedged about with the certainties of the Christian revelation and teaching based on Scripture? Her devotion as 'maid of all work' has not been adequately described in this sketch. She took on almost everything she was asked to do in the work of mission, evangelizing, singing and speaking. She wrote for many periodicals as well as for her publishers, and it is good that there were rewards in sales and in revenue. But again, she did what she did for Christ, and her wish to be obedient to Him above all, was always evident. Perhaps she did take on too much and her health may have suffered partly because of that: we can never be sure about such things.

All her work of mission, of visiting and teaching took place within the context of the Church of England. The Anglican parish system, when led by devoted, learned and godly ministers, was much used by God and blessed with fruit. She commented that many criticized the Anglicans: 'Every fungus on the brave old tree of the Church of England is spied and described, but rarely does any one take the trouble to tell of its fruit'. Of a mission in thirty Birmingham parishes she wrote: 'The results, while showing God's sovereignty in sending His Spirit as and where He would, were such as to call for deep thankfulness and in some parishes the blessing was Pentecostal indeed.' She loved her God as Creator as well as her Redeemer, and though she could write three long poems in praise of Bach, Handel and Mendlessohn, it was her more direct and simple hymns that have lasted and which may still be found in many of our hymnbooks. She was herself amazed that this was the case. I wonder what she would have said if she could know that when a new Bishop was consecrated in the Anglican Cathedral of Cairo in 1974 he chose an Arabic translation of *Take My Life* for use in the service. In our modern arguments about the place of words and music in our Christian worship, what might she have said? I am not competent to speak of music, but I note that she felt both words and music were God's gifts and to be used with the utmost care and discipline. Her passages in which she describes the sheer joy of joining in the choruses of Handel's *Messiah* reflect her deep pleasure in her own voice and in music itself. Perhaps she would have lessons for those of us responsible for hymns and spiritual songs nowadays. But what she shows most clearly is her life-commitment: she lived in the spirit of what she wrote – and men, women and children could see that transparently in her life.

The challenges both of her earnestness in faith and her fun in the enjoyment of God's creation remain part of her peculiar gifts to us today. Another prolific hymn-writer of a generation before hers was a learned and godly person called Reginald Heber. He was ten years younger than her father and famous for many hymns like 'From Greenland's icy mountains, From India's coral strand'. His career ended as Bishop of Calcutta. Some of Heber's words fitly commemorate not only Frances Ridley Havergal, but the large numbers whom she helped to bring to Christ:

A noble army, men and boys,
The matron and the maid
Around the Saviour's throne rejoice
In robes of light array'd
They climbed the steep ascent to heaven
Through peril, toil and pain,
Oh God to us may grace be given
To follow in their train.

*Further Reading*

Janet Grierson *Frances Ridley Havergal: Worcestershire Hymnwriter* 1979 The Havergal Society 38 New Road Bromsgrove B60 2JJ

T. H. Darlow: *Frances Ridley Havergal: A Saint of God* (London: Nisbet 1927)

Frances Ridley Havergal: *Poetical works* 2 Vols (London: 1884)

*Life Mosaic* 1887 (includes *The Ministry of Song* and *Under the Surface* in one bound volume) with paintings by B. von Cramm

*Kept for the Master's Use.* (London: Nisbet)

*The Royal Invitation*

Boxed set of *Ministry of Song, Under the Surface* and *Under*

*His Shadow Nisbet, London 1882 and many other booklets*
Maria V. G. Havergal. *Letters of Frances Ridley Havergal*
*Memorials of Frances Ridley Havergal 1880*
J. Julian. *Dictionary of Hymnology* (London: 1907)

# 7

# Immortal Diamond: Gerard Manley Hopkins (1844–1889)

What would the world be, once bereft
Of wet and of wildness? Let them be left,
O let them be left, wildness and wet;
Long live the weeds and the wilderness yet.

The world is charged with the grandeur of God.
It will flame out, like shining from shook foil.

Gerard Manley Hopkins

Earth's crammed with heaven
And every common bush afire with God;
But only he who sees, takes off his shoes
The rest sit round it and pluck blackberries.

Elizabeth Barrett Browning

Why should we pay attention to a Jesuit poet who died just over a hundred years ago? For some he is a green Gerard: a prophet and priest for ecologists, who cared deeply for the environment and what Victorian Britain was doing to harm it. For others he is a great poet born out of his time, who used language to show truths that were clear to him, but not to his contemporaries. Even his friends rather despised him.

His Christian faith permeated his whole life. Two aspects of his faith are particularly striking. The first is his passionate belief that we and nature around us exist to praise and give glory to God – a common enough Christian belief, but few have held it or lived it with the intensity of Hopkins. The second is that, as a Christian of great ability, he suffered deeply because of his intense nature, and found God in the face of much rejection and depression. This is more than enough reason for many, who suffer likewise, to read and know Hopkins.

His writings throw a brilliant and clear light on the vicissitudes of mental suffering:

O, the mind, mind has mountains; cliffs of fall
Frightful, sheer, no-man-fathomed. Hold them cheap
May who ne'er hung there.

Most of those who read him love his fine nature poetry, as in 'God's Grandeur' or 'Pied Beauty'. But he was not a nature poet as others might be. His view of nature was deeply Christian. How many ecologists who love nature can follow him when he writes of a bluebell: 'I know the beauty of our Lord by it'? This was not just whimsy or a manner of speaking; he meant it.

His best poem (as he himself called it) is about a falcon, 'The Windhover'; it is dedicated 'To Christ our Lord' in the subtitle. It is clear that when he wrote he wished to explore, in the bird's flight, the reflection of the glory of Christ.

His faith explains and gives fuller meaning to his poetry. A Jesuit writer put it well: our liberal views today cannot easily allow us to see that Hopkins' faith was 'vitally dogmatic, historical and institutional'. By this his Jesuit admirer did not mean that he was constrained by the dogma of his time, but rather that the faith, to Hopkins and to his Church, was always the same.

He does not meet with antipathy today. On the contrary he is enormously popular. His verse was not published till long after his death; since then it has been reproduced in many editions and has sold well for decades. There is now even a video available of his life and work for those who prefer that medium.

If anyone, during his Christian life, 'cried out of the depths', Hopkins did. He brought treasures out of his own personal darkness. His writings shed a marvellous light on our ordinary world for those who are willing to let it shine. He has a quality like that of Henry Vaughan, who could say almost casually that 'he saw eternity the other night'. It was little wonder that W. H. Auden referred to him as 'A Knight of the Infinite'.

**'Ah Nature, framed in fault'**

Hopkins was the eldest of nine children, born in Stratford, Essex, in 1844. He was educated at what was later called Highgate School.

The headmaster was cruel and punitive. At school it was natural for him to read his Bible in the dormitory, and he did this in spite of ridicule. He fought for fair play at school. He won a poetry prize, and one of the masters (afterwards Canon R. W. Dixon) was to become a friend in later life who loved and valued his poetry when few others did.

He won an exhibition to Balliol College, Oxford. There he was at first happy, but he wrote of the 'long success of sin' at that time. No one else who knew him at that time thought him vicious. Perhaps he felt sinful in much the same way as Charles and John Wesley might have done in their Oxford days. When Wesley wrote 'vile and full of sin I am', he was referring not to his conduct but to his *sense* of sin. Hopkins – like the young Wesleys – might have seemed a bit of a prig if judged by outward appearance, but his sense of moral failure was acute.

The seeds of later conflicts were sown at Oxford. He had been brought up in a pious, moderately High Anglican home. At Oxford he came under two very different influences, one Christian and ascetic, and the other aesthetic and liberal. E. B. Pusey and other leaders of the Oxford Movement encouraged fasting and a higher degree of ritual in worship than he was used to at home and school. Benjamin Jowett, who was admired for his learning, sent Hopkins to Walter Pater as tutor. To judge from early essays he might easily have become an aesthete and dilettante if Pater and other similar dons had won his allegiance.

Other close friends found themselves caught up in conflicts which led to tensions and unhappiness. Three of those whom Hopkins knew well during his Oxford days later took their own lives. But the first two years at Oxford were full of pleasure in his work and social life. Then, in his third year, he became convinced that he should become a Roman Catholic. A year later he entered the Jesuit order for nine years of training.

He wrote: 'I have never wavered in my vocation, but I have not lived up to it. I destroyed the verse I had written when I entered the Society and meant to write no more.' He called this the destruction of the innocents. We may be glad that there were other copies of his early writing and that these survived. His later writing, much of it at the behest of his superiors in the Society of Jesus, is bound up with his mature faith, and also his recurrent depression.

**'No worst, there is none'**

How depressed was Hopkins, and why? In 1885 he wrote:

> The melancholy I have all my life been subject to has become of late years not indeed more intense but rather more distributed, constant and crippling. One, the lightest but a very inconvenient form of it, is daily anxiety about work to be done, which makes me break off or never finish all that lies outside that work. It is useless to write more on this: when I am at my worst though my judgement is never affected, *my state is much like madness.*

When he says 'all my life', is this an expression of a rather gloomy frame of mind in which everything appeared dark, seen through 'blue-tinted' glasses? His attitude to himself was usually harsh and severe and, by his own high standards, he was bound to be 'an unprofitable servant'. He was, in other words, an obsessive compulsive personality.

From adolescence onwards he had been very anxious. All who knew him said how conscientious he was. He needed to be in complete control of his life and to succeed in all tasks to his own high standards. Thus it was hard for him to be bound by a vow of obedience to his superiors. Also, sadly, the Jesuits sent him to places and positions which were not congenial to him. His gifts were not suited to his abilities and temperament: in fact, many would say he was a born Franciscan who had strayed into the Jesuit order.

He often became seriously depressed. In the face of many depressive trials he had a Christian answer to suffering:

> Why? That my chaff might fly; my grain lie, sheer and clear.

Knowing that this was his aim did not make it any easier for him to bear his suffering. Often he felt 'pitched past pitch of grief'.

Hopkins also had many enthusiasms, which he describes well. His bursts of activity were intense, and his happiness was sometimes ecstatic. Whether this meant he was elated and ill in the way that manic-depressive patients are when in the manic phase, it is hard to tell. My view is that his mood swings were often within the normal range for his personality type. I think he was of a cyclothymic as well as an obsessional temperament. That is to say, his up-and-down swings of mood were part of his intense response to the world around him. As a poet, an artist and a man of finely tuned spirituality, he felt very keenly. This applied to the good things in his life, as well as to the bad.

**Was it inherited?**

Gerard's parents were both devout and cultured. He was the eldest of their nine children. No one else in his family seems to have suffered from depression. His father did not himself experience any great loss, but was by profession a loss adjuster, in marine insurance. Two of Hopkins' longest poems were about shipwrecks, which may reflect an early interest in his father's world. His father wrote verse too, published in two volumes which are as unknown as his son's have become world famous. The Hopkins Society honours the son but not the father. His father had an intense curiosity about anything and everything, a characteristic we find also in Gerard Manley Hopkins.

His mother was the daughter of a surgeon who trained with the poet John Keats at Guy's Hospital. Her interests were wide in artistic and scientific fields. She was a remarkably cultured woman, and very devout in her Christian life as an Anglican. Her son's conversion to Rome grieved her greatly. He wrote to her warmly and lovingly, the last letter being sent a month before his death, aged forty-four.

His mother lived to the age of ninety-eight. In her extreme old age she received the first published volume of her son's verse. It had been slowly and carefully edited by an old friend, Robert Bridges (then Poet Laureate), and it was dedicated to her. She died thirty years after her son.

Two brothers became artists and lived to old age. A sister became an Anglican nun. While his temperament owed much to his parents and family, Hopkins does not seem to have inherited a predisposition to depression. Yet the influences of his family had a great deal to do with the kind of life he led.

He was a very English person, rejoicing in the good things of British imperialism. In a letter to his mother he says that he warms to the Welsh and that he considers himself half-Welsh, but he does not explain why. We can only speculate that he was referring to a possible Welsh origin for one of his parents, or that the happy times he had spent in Wales made him look upon it as his adopted country. We will examine in some detail not only the Welsh influence, but also the Scots and the later, and dire, Irish influence upon Hopkins.

**The Dunce: 'A Mercy from God'**

The Scots connection began in 1872 when he was four years into his training as a priest. While studying in the library at Stonyhurst he fell upon a thirteenth century book. It was the work of the philosopher and theologian Duns Scotus. Its effect on Hopkins was remarkable: 'I was flush with a new stroke of enthusiasm. It may come to nothing or it may be a mercy from God,' he wrote.

The influence of Duns Scotus on his life and thought was considerable. For Duns Scotus believed that every person, and every thing, possessed a special quality of being. He had complex theories of knowledge, about how we know and see things. Earlier Scotists were so sectarian that they were called 'Dunces', opposed to other forms of knowledge. Hopkins was never such a Dunce, however; he experienced Duns Scotus as a kindred spirit and made him his hero. To see why Hopkins valued Duns Scotus one poem will suffice. It begins:

> As kingfishers catch fire, dragonflies draw flame

and goes on to say:

> Each mortal thing does one thing and the same:
> Deals out that being indoors each one dwells;
> Selves – goes itself, *myself* it speaks and spells;
> Crying *What I do* is *me: for that I came.*

Hopkins had long wrestled with attempts to explain the essential nature of things. A tree, a leaf, a cloudscape or a pattern made by frost: he spoke of its 'inscape'. It was his way of describing an interior landscape. There is no denying that his language became obscure and convoluted at times. 'Instress' was a favourite word too, leading a witty modern author to comment on it as 'Hopkinstress' .

We need not imitate his complexities to see his point. Applied to human beings it fits in with his view that God has made each person uniquely different. At a time when his own religious order was trying to put its stamp on him, Hopkins related strongly to the need to preserve each person's unique qualities.

He said that whenever he saw something done well, his instinct was to turn away from it and do otherwise. It may now be a commonplace to allow a person to 'do his own thing'; but for Hopkins this was a sacred duty. I think he was right: being caught up in the imitation of a chosen hero or following the crowd can be very harmful to the individual and can arrest his development both spiritually and in ordinary life.

In a later poem, 'Duns Scotus's Oxford', Hopkins celebrates the fact that as a poet and a person Scotus provided a Christian basis and gave permission, as it were, for being different. Thus he praises Scotus

> who of all men most sways my spirits to peace;
> Of realty the rarest-veined unraveller; a not
> Rivalled insight, be rival Italy or Greece.

**'This world of Wales'**

Hopkins spent three happy years in training at St Beuno's near the cathedral city of Llanelwy (St Asaph). His love of Wales went as far back as his student trips there, when he wrote some lovely verses such as:

> Who long for rest, who look for pleasure
> Away from counter, court or school
> O where live well your lease of leisure
> But here at, here at Penmaen Pool?

It is a far cry from sprung rhythm, 'instress' and his later style. His time in Wales played its part in changing his language. He learned Welsh (and wrote verse in *cynghanedd),* and made exciting discoveries of this technique which included alliteration, chiming of consonants and internal vowel rhymes, as well as devices such as *sangiad* (word jumping) and *dyfalu* (listing of metaphorical titles). He could not long pretend that he had learned Welsh simply to convert the natives.

He had found the tools he was first to use in tightly-worded forms. They suited his temperament and his wish to express truths and insights tellingly. Using his new-found techniques, he burst forth in one of his greatest poems, 'The Wreck of the Deutschland':

> Thou mastering me
> God! giver of breath and bread;
> World's strand, sway of the sea;
> Lord of living and dead;
> Thou hast bound bones and veins in me, fastened my flesh
> And after it almost unmade, what with dread,
> Thy doing: and dost thou touch me afresh?
> Over again I feel thy finger and find thee.

There are thirty-five such stanzas. I confess it took me many years to bring myself to read them properly. The poem contains the phrase 'an ark for the listener', and certainly one feels the need for an ark, to be safe among the floods of images that Hopkins produces. One needs, almost, to read the poem aloud with attention and perhaps devotion. The Jesuit periodical *The Month* refused to print it; having initially accepted it, they said they dare not use it. It was this rejection, Hopkins thought, which led to his first depression.

He had hoped for peace, but instead he began to suffer nervous and physical symptoms which dogged him to his death. The facts surrounding the poem are important. *The Times* reported the shipwreck, with dramatic accounts of how five exiled nuns died on the *Deutschland.* It was his superior who had told Hopkins to write a poem about the shipwreck. He had felt released from his vow of silence. He knew the poem was good: the best part of himself had gone into it. He was deeply ashamed of his apparent failure before his friends in the Society of Jesus, for which he had given up all. It was a deep hurt, made worse by the low opinion Bridges had of the poem.

**His editor: Robert Bridges**

Robert Bridges was a key figure in the life of Hopkins because he was such a good friend to him and because he kept, transcribed and published Hopkins' verse (twenty-nine years later). It is a long story, but the fact remains that if Bridges had not been Poet Laureate, Oxford would not have published Hopkins. The two men were close at Oxford, where Bridges at first intended to enter the Church, but actually became a doctor and afterwards an established poet. He called himself a fastidious freethinker. But he was an Anglican and he wrote hymns and edited the *Yattendon Hymnal.*

When Bridges also attacked Hopkins' remarkable poem (calling it 'a great dragon which lay at the gate' of his verse 'forbidding entry') he felt doubly rejected. In fact Bridges, who wrote six volumes of verse, is less read now and has been completely eclipsed by Hopkins. But in North Wales, at that time, all that Hopkins knew was how bitter it was to fail. Another long poem, 'The Loss of the Eurydice', was also refused by the Jesuit journal. This had a predictable effect on his spirits. Hopkins wrote: 'I have done little and shall do less ... the impulse to write is wanting, for I have no thought of publishing.'

The grounds for criticism were obscurity, poor grammar and syntax: on one level Bridges was right. Behind it lay a love for Hopkins, but a hatred of the Jesuits and the Roman Catholic faith. The real failure was that Hopkins' gift and genius were not recognized by Bridges. Hopkins mulled over his rejections; and it must have been the case with him, as in Proverbs 14:10, that his 'heart knew its own bitterness'.

We are of course grateful that Bridges patiently stored so much of what Hopkins wrote. But how regrettable it is that Hopkins had no inkling of his posthumous fame. During his lifetime he showed his verses to only eleven people. Indeed he feared that being published might be worse than being silent; he did not want to be 'heard unheeded'. Yet he felt the pain of having to 'hoard unheard'. It was not good for his morale, and the problems he experienced at the age of thirty kept returning to trouble him.

**'To seem the stranger'**

Although Hopkins was a stranger in Wales, he came to love it. He wrote some of his best verse there, and was not always unhappy. There were many lighter moments, and he became liked as a wit and practical joker. The students took time off for fishing, and at the evening meal they compared their catches. On one such occasion Hopkins was asked what he had caught. He burst out with, 'I caught this morning morning's minion' – the famous first line of his great poem 'The Windhover'. Perhaps it was his response to being teased, or it may have been in keeping with the humour of a closed institution such as St Beuno's.

He tried to convince the Welsh scholar Sir John Rhys that the basic forms of Welsh metre reflected an aspect of Celtic character. How much a fly on the wall in Rhyl might have learned! I think this little vignette illustrates Hopkins' enthusiasm for following an idea through to a logical conclusion.

Hopkins' 'third remove', to Dublin, was a disaster; he was Professor of Classics there for the last four years of his life. He was as unhappy in Dublin as his hero John Henry Newman. Hopkins hated the infighting of academic life. He also hated terrorism and the way some churchmen seemed to sanction it in Dublin.

However, all was not black; he said he could 'kind love both give and get' in Ireland. Though feeling a stranger, he much enjoyed such pastimes as playing and composing music with the professor of music. He took up Egyptology with zest. He would play practical jokes: he once stopped to ask a ploughman to show him how to plough a crooked furrow. He took his work seriously and, as chief examiner, marked three hundred papers, six times a year. It might have driven anyone to a frenzy of despair. He (being scrupulously fair) devised a system of half and quarter marks, but often failed to add them up correctly.

There were periods of despair, and during these he wrote six sonnets which, he said, 'were wrung from him almost unbidden'. They describe his feelings with terrible, crystal clarity. What has been called his idiom of despair is stripped to bone and sinew. We will study these sonnets below.

He died in Dublin, aged forty-four, of typhoid fever which caused peritonitis. It seems likely that he had lost the will to live. His Irish friends cared for him devotedly. The illness was long and gave his parents time to be with him, and he was able to tell them how happy he was at the last.

**'The authentic cadence': 'what I do is me'**

What was Hopkins like? He was short, with a head that seemed too large for his body, and large hooded eyes. A fellow trainee wrote: 'All that met him knew him as a refined and cultured scholar, literary, musical, artistic and above all original. And he was loved by all who knew him as a man of tender, self-devoted, sympathetic character, oversensitive and delicate, perhaps, to face without much suffering the rough work of the world.' He had a playful and sometimes outrageous sense of humour. He was aware of a compulsive originality.

His Victorian reticence hides much. Some thought him homosexual, but all agree he was chaste. The only evidence is of the customary passionate friends at school and college. Robert Bernard Martin, his most recent biographer, believes he fell in love with a young man called Digby Dolben, who did not return his affection. He chose a closed bachelor existence, where the vows and the monastic rule limited his life.

When he writes of marriage he does so with a warm concern for its happiness and integrity. To his friend Bridges he wrote of his 'spooniness and delight' in married couples. But for himself he chose a rigid ascetic path, full of 'habits of perfection' and involving frustration of his own nature, not simply sexually, but as an artist and creative mind. He had mixed feelings about being published; who has not? He would at times refuse to co-operate with friends who wanted to see his poems in print.

He took his vows very seriously, and the vow of obedience even more so than poverty and chastity. I can think of no one who could have helped him (as Staupitz helped Luther) to discover the true comfort that was available in his religion, but which he was missing. No one seems to have shown genuine respect for his talent, let alone nurture and care for the whole man, blessed though he was with such a remarkable poetic gift. No one helped him to be happier than he was; perhaps his sense of isolation was self-fulfilling.

Hopkins must always have been a difficult man to help: he was obsessional and rigid in his perfectionism. He was like those sensitive people who wear a carapace, hiding their vulnerability behind a hard shell, for self-protection. Much as he loved his friends, like Bridges and Dixon, and his family too, it was to God that he had directed and gathered up all his love as far as he could.

I think this is an essential clue to knowing Hopkins, and he gives it to us in a sonnet, written during his last year at Oxford:

Let me be to Thee as the circling bird,
Or bat with tender and air-crisping wings
That shapes in half-light his departing rings,
From both of whom a changeless note is heard.
I have found my music in a common word,
Trying each pleasurable throat that sings
And every praised sequence of sweet strings,
And know infallibly which I preferred.
The authentic cadence was discovered late
Which ends those only strains that I approve,
And other science all gone out of date
And minor sweetness scarce made mention of
I have found the dominant of my range and state –
Love, O my God, to call Thee Love and Love.

To respond to God's love was his duty and pleasure. When he felt free to respond, his verse and his letters ring with praise or with quietly meditative passages on the love and glory of God. There are also poems which celebrate that love as reflected in human love. But by the same token, he was sometimes unable to respond to God or to his love; instead he felt deserted and miserable. Then he produced telling descriptions of the depression that many of us feel at times, but cannot so well express.

**'My winter world': 'time's eunuch'**

Hopkins often writes of himself as a failure. He sees himself dwelling in a cold and desolate winter world. If he could have known what an enormous readership he would have, long after his death, he might have felt very differently. His paraphrase of Jeremiah which begins

Thou art indeed just, Lord

describes how he felt:

... birds build – but not I build; no, but strain,
Time's eunuch, and not breed one work that wakes.
Mine, O thou lord of life, send my roots rain.

His sense of failure reflects his impossibly high standards. As with the young Martin Luther, the life that Hopkins led as a trainee Jesuit priest, with its strict adherence to the rules, coupled with his severity with himself, fostered his anxiety and his obsessional traits. These grew out of all proportion. Such obsessive anxiety leads easily to depression.

As we read his early verses we note a kind of soft asceticism of adolescence, as in 'The Habit of Perfection':

Elected Silence, sing to me
And beat upon my whorled ear,
Pipe me to pastures still and be
The music that I care to hear.

In its own way the poem is a brilliant statement of his belief that each of the senses has to be denied in order to achieve perfect holiness: but it has a luscious, sensuous quality that makes the giving up seem almost too easy, like the nun in *Heaven-Haven* who says,

And I have asked to be
  Where no storms come,
Where the green swell is in the havens dumb,
  And out of the swing of the sea.

He exchanged this approach – that of a novice – for a hard, harsh and sometimes brutal ascetism. Who can tell what might have happened if he had chosen an academic career, like Ronald Knox; or a gentler contemplative order? We may recall that Duns Scotus, his great hero, was a Franciscan. He was ill-assorted with St Thomas and St Ignatius Loyola, the patron and founder respectively of the Jesuit order.

There were many real failures in his life. He failed as an artist, a musician and a composer. He failed as a professor in Dublin. Of his artistic failure he wrote: 'You know I once wanted to be a painter. But even if I could, I would not, I think, now, for the fact is that the higher and more attractive part of an art put a strain on the passions which I should think it unsafe to encounter.' It reminds us of the sonnet which begins:

> To what serves mortal beauty – dangerous; does set dancing
> blood –

and its ending:

> Merely meet it; own,
> Home at heart, heaven's sweet gift; then leave, let that alone.
> Yea, wish that though, wish all, God's better beauty, grace.

He failed to pass his theology examinations at St Beuno's. We need not make too much of this, since he was not well. He was in a very gifted class, and his marks were not high enough to justify a fourth year's study. I think it may also have been due to the old problem of a difference of opinion with the examiners. Hopkins was loyal to Duns Scotus, and his views were not shared by his examiners.

It was decided to send him to teach in a school in Chesterfield. There 'my muse turned utterly sullen in the Sheffield smoke-ridden air'. He spent time in several deprived parishes in Liverpool and Glasgow. The slums made him say he felt 'in a manner a Communist'. But he became aware that he did not have the common touch. He failed, both in teaching and preaching, to win some success because of his poor skills in communicating.

He went, via another spell at Stonyhurst, to Mayfair's famous Farm Street Church. Here he was away from the unpromising pupils and the slums. Again he failed as a preacher. In an address to women, he chose as his sermon theme, the Church. He described her as a cow with seven udders which were the seven sacraments. The Victorian ladies were not amused; they complained, and the visiting priest was given a dressing down for his lack of taste.

It reminds us of an earlier catastrophic failure as a preacher while training in Wales. On that occasion he chose as his sermon theme the feeding of the five thousand, and he compared the sea of Galilee to the Clwyd valley, saying that the sea was shaped like a man's left ear, with the Jordan river entering at the upper rim and going out by the lobe. With the precise use of images which Jesuits were taught to use as their founder commended, Hopkins went on relentlessly, placing the towns near Galilee in relation to the 'ear'. Long before he was half-way through, his fellow students collapsed in hysterical laughter and Hopkins had to stop. He was not a gifted preacher.

**Fame: 'the true and appointed air of genius'**

Hopkins suffered from the failure to find fame during his lifetime, and from the lack of acceptance and appreciation for his style of verse. Both these disappointments affected him deeply.

The perfecting of his poems – the 'lettering', as he called it was a joy; it was fun for him. He describes it in sexual imagery:

> England whose honour O all my heart woos, wife
> To my creating thought.

And again in the last sonnet dedicated to R. B. (Bridges), which is ripe with images of conception and gestation:

> The fine delight that fathers thought; the strong
> Spur, live and lancing like the blowpipe flame,
> Breathes once and, quenched faster than it came,
> Leaves yet the mind a mother of immortal song.

A writer on Hopkins has recently said that the shock and power of his verse is orgasmic. It might be truer to say that in his creative effort he expressed his whole person. Other forms of creativity were sublimated and diverted into verse, and that was why the failure to be accepted hurt so much.

Hopkins said that 'fame, the being known, though one of the most dangerous things to man, is nevertheless the true and appointed air, element and setting of genius and its works'. He despised the fame awarded by 'a random, reckless, incompetent and unjust judge, the public, the multitude'. He also thought that the want of fame did artists much harm.

I consider that for many years he suffered from a kind of spiritual anoxia, or lack of oxygen, which a proper recognition would have put right. His peers and his proper public could not (or would not) give him the attention and warm regard which were his due. He needed love, in the sense of an 'unquestioning affection' (as his latest biographer puts it). To survive happily, he wanted constant encouragement and admiration, and these were not available to him.

Strangely, he minded less about his failure as a naturalist. Grigson calls his absorption with nature a passionate science. He wrote of it mainly in his private journal. The poems in the anthologies do less than justice to this aspect of Hopkins. Once, after the epic eruption of Krakatoa, Hopkins' careful observations of sunsets and cloudscapes were published in the prestigious journal *Nature*. Such recognition came only once in a blue moon.

Many misjudged his intelligence, and even at times thought him somewhat simple. When he was in the garden one winter morning at Stonyhurst, closely observing a pattern of frost on the flagstones, the gardener became concerned. One of the superiors told the gardener that they were privileged to watch a learned scholar at work. The gardener's response was to say: 'That Mr 'Opkins is a natural.'

**His spiritual conflicts**

Over and above all this there were times of even deeper suffering 'with this tormented mind tormenting yet'. There were crises and recoveries, afflictions that many Christians have been through.

Sometimes he experienced an intense darkness, which others have called the dark night of the soul. At such times he felt desolate and perhaps bereft of inspiration: 'Mine, O Thou Lord of life, send my roots rain,' he cries. In an early verse he writes that his prayers must meet a brazen heaven. He expresses this movingly, thus:

I wake and feel the fell of dark, not day.
What hours, O what black hours we have spent
This night! what sights you, heart, saw; ways you went!
And more must, in yet longer light's delay.
With witness I speak this. But where I say
Hours I mean years, mean life. And my lament
Is cries countless, cries like dead letters sent
To dearest him that lives alas! away. I am gall,
I am heartburn. God's most deep decree
Bitter would have me taste: my taste was me;
Bones built in me, flesh filled, blood brimmed the curse.

Selfyeast of spirit a dull dough sours. I see
The lost are like this, and their scourge to be
As I am mine, their sweating selves; but worse.

Death seems preferable to this. But Hopkins must have considered and rejected suicide, for he writes:

Can something, hope, wish day come, not choose not to be.

Did he have depressive delusions? Probably not, but his reference to 'the lost are like this' suggests to me depression, with a hint of damnation.

The other 'Sonnets of Desolation', as they have been called, give the full picture of his misery. They include the five poems beginning with the lines:

No worst, there is none. Pitched past pitch of grief,
Not, I'll not, carrion comfort, Despair, not feast on thee;
My own heart let me more have pity on; let
Patience, hard thing! the hard thing but to pray,
To seem the stranger lies my lot, my life.

Such sonnets contrast with happier ones of praise and glory. But even in Hopkins' most unhappy verses not all is gloom, for he accepts conflict as part of the spiritual life. His phrase 'wrestling with (my God!) my God' echoes the Genesis account of Jacob's struggles, which is also the theme of Charles Wesley's great hymn 'Come, O thou Traveller unknown'.

While his conflicts may never have been fully resolved, Hopkins derived some peace and respite through patience. This he ascribes to the grace of God, who

    more and more distils
Delicious kindness.

Peace is said to be a wild wood-dove that visits intermittently, leaving a fragmentary quiet: 'That piecemeal peace is poor peace.' He described, long before his dark Dublin days, how God does this:

And so he does leave Patience exquisite
That plumes to peace thereafter.

'Rare patience' is God's way of bending our rebellious wills to himself; it is a 'natural heart's ivy which masks our ruins of wrecked past purpose'. Another image is of patience filling our 'crisp combs' with honey. This refers back to the medieval idea of the believer as a busy bee – busied with the means of grace, the habitual activity of daily devotional life.

**'Leave comfort root-room'**

It must be said that Hopkins allowed little space for comfort. In his work it is there, but fleetingly, as when he sees God's smile behind the world, an unforeseen and unexpected smile that 'lights a lovely mile'. One of the Sonnets of Desolation needs to be read in full to see this:

My own heart let me more have pity on; let
Me live to my sad self hereafter kind,
Charitable; not live this tormented mind
With this tormented mind tormenting yet.
I cast for comfort ...I can no more get
By groping round my comfortless, than blind
Eyes in their dark can day or thirst can find
Thirst's all-in-all in all a world of wet.

Soul, self-, come poor Jackself, I do advise
You jaded, let be; call off thoughts awhile
Elsewhere; leave comfort root-room; let joy size
At God knows when to God knows what; whose smile
's not wrung, see you; unforeseen times rather – as skies
Between pie mountains – lights a lovely mile.

Almost inevitably, our minds turn back to such kindred spirits as Martin Luther, William Cowper and George Herbert. They knew a good deal about Christian certainties as well as sadness and despair. The faith that burns and glows in Luther was at best a slowly burning ember in Hopkins. His only reference to Luther is as 'the beast from the wild wood': just as the Papal Bull spoke of him when it ordered his destruction, beginning with the words: 'A wild boar hath entered thy vineyard, O Lord'. Luther was a person to be sought out and destroyed. But in fact he might have taught Hopkins much for his comfort.

Hopkins once turned to John Henry Newman for advice, and was told: 'Don't call the Jesuit discipline hard, it will bring you to heaven.' Perhaps in being hard on himself, Hopkins, like Cardinal Newman, was reacting against a teaching about faith which seemed to him too easy; a kind of cheap grace. Any reader, coming from some of our other Christian writers to Hopkins, is bound to miss the sense that grace is something God *gives*, freely and lovingly, although at great cost to himself. No discipline, however harsh, can *earn* God's mercy or forgiveness.

We may easily forget that physical discipline, including the inflicting of pain on oneself while kneeling, was common in Hopkins' day. It is not surprising if we turn away with abhorrence from such institutionalized masochism. Yet, though the language and accents in Hopkins are not always ours, I feel the true heart of Christian faith is there. It may be obscured, it may sometimes be distorted by his own feelings or false perceptions. But he is a Christian believer, and his faith is clear even when he enjoys little of the comfort that he could have had. We might wish that his roots had gone down to more sustaining waters in Christian teaching.

Hopkins has been described by one reader as producing 'a terrible crystal'. The most beautiful form of crystal is no doubt the diamond, and it is well known that diamonds are simply carbon which has been exposed to intense heat and pressure over a very long period of time. In Westminster Abbey, in Poets' Corner, the stone that bears the name Gerard Manley Hopkins and his dates has the two words: 'Immortal Diamond'. These are the words that end the difficult poem 'That Nature is a Heraclitean Fire and of the Comfort of the Resurrection'. In this poem the Professor of Classics plays with many platonic arguments in the first fifteen lines. Then Hopkins' Christian voice takes over:

Enough! the Resurrection

A heart's-clarion! Away grief's gasping, joyless days,
dejection.

And with the last four lines this remarkable man of God points to his own hope of finally overcoming his fears:

In a flash, at a trumpet crash,
I am all at once what Christ is, since he was what I am, and
This Jack, joke, poor potsherd, patch, matchwood, immortal
diamond
Is immortal diamond.

**'God's better beauty, Grace'**

The most lasting impression Hopkins leaves for us is his concern that grace should be an expression of a 'better beauty'. This is brought out in two ways. He suggests, firstly, that in giving up the enjoyment of natural beauty we may find something even more fulfilling; and, secondly, that grace, when lived out in daily life, makes all our 'goings graces'.

Take the second point first: it is well expressed in the poem beginning 'As kingfishers catch fire'-

I say more: the just man justices;
Keeps grace: that keeps all his goings graces;
Acts in God's eye what in God's eye he is –
Christ – for Christ plays in ten thousand places,
Lovely in limbs, and lovely in eyes not his
To the Father through the features of men's faces.

Does Hopkins go too far in this? He states here a truth not often so daringly expressed, for he would certainly have agreed that the Word was made flesh once and for all in Christ. Yet, he says, grace should make us behave graciously, as being forgiven should make us more forgiving, and being justified should make us more just in our dealings. We must not forget his Red Letter to Bridges, in which he says the conditions in his parish made him feel, in a manner of speaking, a communist. But his most daring insight was to see grace in the lives of men and women as if they themselves expressed the new life of

Christ in which the Father delights.

Hopkins reminds us forcefully that grace must affect our lives if our experience of it is to prove genuine and not feigned. The same might be said of his wish for chastity of mind, a state which seems often to be disregarded by modern Christians. Hopkins expresses an iron resolve to 'cut off a hand' or 'pluck out an eye' if it offends, which is of course simply a part of the teaching of our Lord in the Sermon on the Mount.

Perhaps most remarkably, he retains a Christian sensitivity to the beauty of nature and to the value of nature's wildness. It is only the mind illumined by grace that can see and enjoy properly the grandeur of God in his world. It is no wonder that ecologists want to protect nature from being more 'seared with trade; bleared, smeared with toil'. In one of his well-known poems, 'God's Grandeur', Hopkins sees the fallen or *bent* world cared for by God as a mother cares for her child. Perhaps he is thinking also of Jesus' lament over Jerusalem, 'how often I have longed to gather your children together, as a hen gathers her chicks under her wings':

> And, for all this, nature is never spent;
> There lives the dearest freshness deep down things;
> And though the last lights off the black West went
> Oh, morning, at the brown brink eastwards, springs –
> Because the Holy Ghost over the bent
> World broods with warm breast and with ah! bright wings.

Hopkins may often have received a cold shoulder, where he might have rightly expected warmth, but many poems and letters attest to his experience of God as a secure refuge and fortress (as he is portrayed in the Psalms). While he enjoyed little softness or comfort in his life, he most certainly knew what it was to take shelter with the Lord, and could himself have said, 'I sing in the shadow of your wings' (Ps. 91:4; 63:7).

*Further Reading*

Many editions of Hopkins are available. The best selection is Catherine Phillips, *Gerard Manley Hopkins,* Oxford Authors (Oxford: OUP, 1986); she has also edited *Gerard Manley Hopkins: Selected Letters*

(Oxford: OUP, 1990).

Gerald Roberts, *Gerard Manley Hopkins: Selected Prose* (Oxford: OUP, 1980) is excellent. W. H. Gardner (ed.), *Poems and Prose of Gerard Manley Hopkins,* in Penguin Classics, has been reprinted thirty times since 1953. W. H. Gardner and N. H. MacKenzie (ed.), *Poems of Gerard Manley Hopkins,* fourth edition (Oxford: OUP, 1967) is also available. Walford Davies (ed.), *Gerard Manley Hopkins: The Major Poems,* Everyman Classics (London: Dent, 1979) has the best introduction I know. Charles Williams edited a second edition (Oxford, 1930).

A life of Hopkins still in print is Paddy Kitchen, *Gerard Manley Hopkins: A Life* (London: Hamish Hamilton, 1978). Also of interest is Eleanor Ruggles, *GMH: A Life* (London: John Lane/Bodley Head, 1947).

*GMH Portrait of a Poet* comprises a short life and selection of his verse and letters, and a video written and performed by Peter Gale (The Picture Publishing Company, 108 Clarendon Road, London W11 2HR) is a successful and interesting departure.

Erudite studies abound, e.g. Robert Boyle, *Metaphor in Hopkins* (Chapel Hill, NC: University of North Carolina Press, 1960). M. Bottrall (ed.), *Gerard Manley Hopkins: Poems,* in the Casebook series (London: Macmillan, 1975), gives a good selection of such studies.

A facsimile edition of Hopkins' poems is promised by Oxford University Press.

The recent biography by Robert Bernard Martin, *Gerard Manley Hopkins: A Very Private Life* (London: HarperCollins, 1991), is distinguished from previous lives because the author was given access to many sources previously undisclosed by the Jesuit order.

Norman White, *Hopkins: A Literary Biography* (Oxford: Clarendon Press, 1992) is the fullest account of his life and works.

# 8

# Fighting Ritual Child Abuse: Amy Carmichael (1867–1951)

Hast Thou no scar?
No hidden scar on foot, or side, or hand?
I hear thee sung as mighty in the land,
I hear them hail thy bright, ascendant star,
Hast thou no scar?

Hast Thou no wound?
Yet I was wounded by the archers, spent,
Leaned Me against a tree to die; and rent
By ravening beasts that compassed Me, I swooned:
Hast *thou* no wound?

No wound? No scar?
Yet, as the Master shall the servant be,
And pierced are the feet that follow Me;
But thine are whole: can he have followed far
Who has nor wound nor scar?

Amy Carmichael, *Gold Cord*

How entered, by what secret stair
I know not, knowing only He was there.

T. E. Brown

O Love, thou lightenest all my ways,
Within, without, below, above,
Flow through the minutes of my days,
The sum of all my life be love.

Amy Carmichael

I never knew Amy Carmichael, but I felt I had met her in 1951 when I bought and read her largest book, *Gold Cord: The Story of a*

*Fellowship.* It is an account of the founding of the Dohnavur Fellowship in South India. She drew around her a family that set up their work in a decrepit missionary compound near a jungle village called Dohnavur. Their aim was to serve the local people by bearing witness to Christ. Amy, soon to be called Amma (after the Tamil word for mother, *Ammai),* was the undisputed head of the family and the fellowship for nearly fifty years.

She was a writer of distinction. She had a genius for expressing the mystical Christian insight while telling a story of triumph or disaster, and she knew how to appeal for the prayers of her readers. She wrote thirty-five books; and sales of the British editions have exceeded half a million. Amy was distressed when her books were called 'popular', perhaps because she was an elitist; she was glad of the twelve Braille editions for the blind, and of the translations into fifteen languages. At least eleven of her books are still easily available.

To take up her story now is like entering a time warp. The sepia photographs, Amy's own scattered poems throughout *Gold Cord,* and the frequent quotations from great Christian mystics and missionaries of the past are as enchanting as ever. They seem to belong to another era; yet, on reflection, their contents are right up to date. For Amy and her friends soon found themselves dealing with girls who were the victims of ritual sexual abuse, or 'temple prostitution' as it was then called (it was not made illegal until 1970). They were summoned to help with the temple babies, born as a result of the prostitution. The first three brought to Dohnavur were dead within a year.

Amy hated many things about the India of the Raj as she found it, and in a sense she went native. Today it would be more acceptable for a Western woman working in India to wear native dress; in 1900 it was not so common. She did not wish to be a colonialist, taking Western culture to the East. We live in a time when Eastern religions have become a part of our Western thinking; Zen, yoga and its meditation techniques and the trek to India and Nepal preoccupy so many in the affluent West. It was not so in Amy's day.

Amy was very aware of the spiritual world and was by any standard a Christian mystic. She believed in the strength of silent prayer and in relying on the power and love of Christ. She knew that these were greater than any of the alien sounds and destructive powers with which she met, head on, in her long life in the India that she loved.

**Seeking the real Amy**

Amy says, in parenthesis about herself, that 'a breakdown in Japan led to India'. Dates and extended factual descriptions are not easy to find in *Gold Cord;* to Amy, the eternal is more important than the temporal. We learn that the first temple child came to Dohnavur in 1901; but many chapters may be read, with great profit, without a single date being given. In one sense it does not matter: but sometimes facts recorded about time and place are in themselves meaningful and enrich our understanding. Not every incident needs to be spiritualized.

The facts, when we have them, speak for themselves – very loudly and effectively – without being shut away in a special locket of secret meaning to which only Dohnavur has the key. Amy wrote an early book called *Things as They Are.* She wrote it in the spirit of the famous editor who said facts were sacred, but comment was free. It is a surprise that, in her later books, one has to search for the facts, which are often overlaid with the interpretation of later years; an interpretation that may or may not be correct.

The biographies by Bishop Frank Houghton and Elizabeth Elliot are a great help, yet both writers are brought down at times by what one might call a 'Dohnavur virus'. By this I mean that critical appraisal and careful assessment are exchanged for a kind of hero-worship which is not very helpful. 'Dear children, keep yourselves from idols,' those final words in John's first letter would have been close to Amy's heart. But many of us like to fashion our role models, and those whom we admire, into idols of one kind or another.

Surely Amy, whose poem 'Hast Thou no scar?' heads this chapter, would be glad of an accurate, detailed sketching of how her scars came about, and of how she soldiered on in spite of the hurts. That is the overwhelming impression from all her early writing: a transparent honesty, a determination to tell the truth about what it is like to be a worker for God, sometimes (like Ruth) sick for home amid 'the fields of alien corn'.

Later on, as she grew older, while prayers for healing were still made at Dohnavur, she became sicker and her pain and suffering increased. During her last twenty years, to the end of her long life, she ruled Dohnavur very firmly from the bedroom to which she was confined. At times she seems to have been an autocrat; yet Dohnavur started as a kind of group home for her 'family'. It became 'the Family' with a capital 'F', and Elizabeth Elliot recounts how it was a family with some unusually rigid beliefs. For instance, it was out of the question for any American to work in Dohnavur. Amy's human faults and foibles seem both comic and tragic if we look at her story without rose-coloured spectacles.

'Better a thousand times effective peculiarity than ineffective ordinariness'; these words, written of D. M. Thornton of the China Inland Mission, were clearly part of Amy Carmichael's belief too. From whatever angle we focus our attention on her, our predominant impression is that God's grace enabled her to overcome many difficulties, from within and without, in her own life and in the life of the Fellowship:

No purer joy can be
Than to be one in Thee;
Bound by one golden cord
Of love to our dear Lord.

Albert Schweitzer took his three doctorates (in music, medicine and theology) to the Belgian Congo where he worked to repay the white man's debt to the black man. In his endeavour he was a million miles away from the vision of Amy Carmichael: for hers was no quest for the historical Jesus. On the contrary, she had found the living Christ and she wanted to make him known. The name of Dohnavur deserves to be as well remembered as that of Lambarene, where Schweitzer built his hospital.

Dohnavur exposed a traffic in child sexual abuse in India, and Amy did something about it. We in the West have learned in recent years of the extent of child sexual abuse among ourselves, and we have no reason to be complacent. In my view only a tight-knit caring community like Dohnavur can deal with the feelings and pressures that child abuse can generate.

## Celtic origins

A brass Celtic cross lay on her bedside table. Amy Carmichael was able to finger it, in the years when she could not get up unaided, and to remind herself of its inscription, *IHS*. The initials may have signified for Amy, as they did for Emperor Constantine *In hoc signo vinces,* 'In this sign conquer'. If so, these words held a very different meaning for her than for him. Whereas the emperor thought they were to do with his military conquests, Amy's idea of 'soldiering' – a favourite word – was to suffer hardship in the service of Christ, and to fight a spiritual battle against evil.

This interpretation of the initials *IHS* is given by her recent biographer Elizabeth Elliot. While it may be right, another, older version, associates them with the Latin words *Iesu Hominum Salvator,* 'Jesus, Saviour of Mankind' (a kind of shorthand for the name, Jesus). It was certainly this belief, that Christ died for all, that Amy wanted to share with those who had never heard of Christ. It was proper that this cross of hers had a Celtic form, since her origins were in Scotland, by way of the coast of Northern Ireland and Belfast. These origins provided a powerful base from which her special mission could take shape and find fulfilment.

The Carmichael family was of Covenanting stock in Ayrshire, Scotland. The first Carmichael settled in Ireland in 1705. There were two flour mills leased by the Carmichael family, who were known as good employers and fine Christians. They were part of a Presbyterian group which had left the Church of Scotland in a secession based partly on doctrine and partly on patronage rights. Her father and uncle were able to give £500 for the building of a schoolhouse: an index both of their wealth at that time and of their generosity.

Amy's mother was the daughter of a doctor in Portaferry. On her mother's side she was a Dalziel, which, in old Scots, means 'I dare'. This became the family motto. Amy was proud that she was descended on her father's side from those brave Christians called Covenanters, and on her mother's side from the Royalists who persecuted them. There was something catholic and unifying about her spirit in later life which she liked to attribute to this union of opposites.

In 1859 there were remarkable manifestations of God's Spirit and grace at work in many parts of the Western world. Perhaps most important for Amy, the minister who was warmly supported by her father had known something of this religious revival in Belfast. Her mother, too, had found release from a formal and cold religion and had discovered a more joyful faith in the wake of 1859. Her father, marrying when he was thirty-seven, found Catherine Jane Filson a splendid helpmeet in creating a warm and solid home, where discipline was firm, and love and fun were mixed with a very strict Christian commitment, as seen in family prayers, Sunday observance, and a desire to win souls for Christ.

**Delights and disasters**

Amy was the oldest of eight children, born in December 1867, and grew up in a large house in Millisle, a small village in County Down on the rocky north coast of Ireland. She recalls her childhood as an extremely happy one, when she was the undisputed leader of the children, her three sisters and four brothers. From the nursery window they could see the sea and the rock, Ailsa Craig, which provided a focus for them to watch the sea's changing activity. Their father taught them to swim in the sea, and Amy loved to ride her horse, galloping along the sands, as she was later to do on her early holidays in India, in the days before the fifty-three years without leave or furlough.

A family magazine called *Scraps* was started, to which all the children contributed. Amy was the editor and wrote under the pen name 'Nobody'. Later, her letters to friends about her missionary work were called 'Scrappies'; it seems she retained a lifelong wish to hide under the style of being nobody. She detested being photographed, but loved to have fine illustrations in her books. Visitors who were skilled in the craft prepared these pictures, but they were refused permission to include her likeness.

All this foreshadowed the way in which her personality developed: it is part of the contradictions of her temperament that she nearly always insisted that she was right and that all must agree with what had been 'shown' to her to be the right course, and yet at the same time she was in many ways self-effacing.

Her early life included lessons in prayer: she prayed for blue eyes and was sad to find, the next day, that they were still brown. Thus she learned that 'No' was sometimes the answer! She was sent to a boarding-school in Harrogate when she was twelve, but had to leave after three years because her father's income had been drastically cut. The flour business, which had moved to Belfast from Millisle, was suffering from competition from American imports. Moreover, her father had lent money to a friend, who lost it all.

These financial disasters took her back to Belfast, but not before her conversion at a CSSM mission in Harrogate. She felt that, as a child, she had nestled in God's love as she had sat on her mother's knee and enjoyed the comfort of her arms about her. At sixteen, she made her own commitment, and described this as the Good Shepherd having drawn her into his fold. She wrote:

> Afterwards when I began to understand more of what all this meant I found words which satisfied me. I do not know who wrote them:
>
> Upon a life I did not live,
> Upon a death I did not die,
> Another's life, Another's death,
> I stake my whole eternity.

It was the beginning of a long spiritual pilgrimage in which the reality of her sense of Christ's presence grew as the years passed. But the delights of her home and family were equally real, and her father's decision to take her to London to see the sights gave her much pleasure. Soon after this, when she was eighteen, her father died at the age of fifty-four, of double pneumonia. The last words Amy read to her father were from John Milton:

> All is best, though oft we doubt
> What the unsearchable dispose
> Of Highest Wisdom brings about,
> And ever best found in the close.

She must have grieved over such a severe, sudden loss. But she showed little evidence of mourning, and recalled Milton's words often and wrote of them many years later. She had to be an additional mother, a role which often falls to eldest daughters. And, at eighteen, she threw herself into helping others; in particular the mill-girls and others in the slums of Belfast.

**Keswick and the dear old man**

A year and a half later she met a man who took on the role of a new father, Mr Robert Wilson, was to 'adopt' her and have her as a replacement for the daughter he had lost when she was Amy's age. They met in Glasgow in 1886, at a convention run on Keswick lines of which Mr Wilson was the chairman.

When Amy heard the Keswick message about holiness and 'the Higher Christian Life', she felt it was vital for her to respond with a further, fuller commitment of herself to Christ. As for many others who made a clear and simple decision in the Keswick of those days, there were far-reaching results. Little did she know then that she was to be the first missionary supported both financially and in other ways by the Keswick Mission Committee.

The fact that she had a special relationship with the chairman of the Keswick Convention had a further importance in Amy's life. Robert Wilson owned coalmines in Cumberland and lived at Broughton Grange in the Lake District. He was a Quaker, but was involved with other groups apart from the Society of Friends. He worked with both a Baptist and an Anglican church near his home.

He went to Belfast to chair a Keswick-style convention, and while there met Amy's aunts and her mother. When he visited them, he read a verse from Frances Ridley Havergal which for him, and for Amy, crystallised the Keswick experience:

Master, how shall I bless Thy name
  For love so great to me!
For sweet enablings of Thy grace,
  So sovereign, yet so free,
That taught me to obey Thy word,
  And cast my care on Thee?

Many had profited from the Keswick teaching of that time, but few would have guessed that Amy would write of the Keswick chairman, Mr Wilson: 'At last in 1890 he asked my mother to let me stay with him for the greater part of the year as his own daughter ... certain great lessons not yet learned had to be learned, and Broughton Grange was the appointed school.' Wilson had lost his wife in the year that Amy's father had died. He lived with his two sons in the large house, and longed for the company and comfort he had lost.

It was an unusual decision, and many might have questioned the wisdom of a young woman of twenty-four sharing the life of a man of sixty. Profound emotional complications might seem inevitable, however correct and morally blameless the relationship. It led to a remarkable amount of learning. But eventually Amy reached the unexpected decision to leave him and to give up the position which had placed her at the centre of evangelical life and activity.

When she decided, after two years, that she was called to missionary work, it caused much pain to the 'Dear Old Man'. She was in some ways a personal assistant to a senior leader in the Christian world of that time. She was living at the hub of much important activity of which Keswick was only a part. He was distressed, as were his two sons, who by then had learned to love the attractive interloper.

**Decisions for life**

Wilson was the only man inAmy's life, and her relationship with him was more intimate than that with her father. Robert Wilson had a very special place in her heart. Elizabeth Elliot, with her special knowledge of Amy and her colleagues at Dohnavur, maintains that Amy knew nothing about sex, and preferred not to know. She chose a single life, and made celibacy a special rule for many workers in Dohnavur. While in the Lakes, living as Mr Wilson's daughter and absorbing his unusual version of the Keswick teaching, there was time to think, to learn, and to come to decisions which would affect her whole life.

It was Wilson who chose the slogan, still used at Keswick: 'All One In Christ Jesus'. Few at the Convention can have been such well-taught Quakers, with such catholic loyalties to anyone who loved their Lord, as Mr Wilson. It seems likely that Amy learned, in the Quaker meetings, much about the role of silence, and of responding to the Spirit's promptings. Mr Wilson financed her missionary work in the 'faith' missions where she chose to work, and gave her much more than the money she used so frugally. His spiritual legacy bore fruit in the barren soil of South India. While with Robert Wilson, Amy learned, as she wrote,

> to drop labels and to think only of the true invisible Church, to which all who truly love the Lord belong ... what would labels matter? ... I grew to value the quietness of the Friends' way of worship, and also to care very much for the beauty of the Church of England ways.

She must also have built up, at the same time, a love of her heavenly Father who, she felt, demanded many sacrifices from her: the most searing, in some ways, must have been the denial of sexual fulfilment.

During her time with Mr Wilson, Amy's health was recovering from overwork in Belfast and later in Manchester. Her mother had moved to Manchester to help her with her work there. Mrs Carmichael had been able to do this because two sons had gone to America, and the other two to Canada and South Africa. Amy had insisted on living in a room of her own, sharing the poverty of the girls who worked in the factories and lived in the slums. She was trying to help, and win them for Christ. She had been asked to go to Manchester precisely because her work of a similar kind in Belfast had been so successful.

Amy had been spending part of her week with her mother and two sisters, and the rest in her filthy, rented room. As usual, she worked too hard and her health suffered. Her visits to Mr Wilson at Broughton Grange, with her family, were partly to help recover her health. It was due to illness that she finally gave up Manchester and moved to the Lakes to spend two years living with the Dear Old Man. Overwork, illness and change of vocation are recurring themes in her life.

### The call and the rejection

Amy had at first thought that she was to stay with Robert Wilson as his personal assistant until he died. But she became increasingly convinced that it was her duty to be a missionary: on a snowy evening in January 1892 she heard the call to work abroad, and she expected to sail somewhere before the end of that year. Her destination was uncertain. Wilson was devastated when she told him of her calling; his two sons were bitter about it, and the Keswick leaders made remarks that cut her to the quick.

She thought of going to Ceylon, and then considered China. Dr Hudson Taylor of the China Inland Mission comforted Robert Wilson at the Keswick Convention. Her mother gave Amy her full support and understanding. Mr Wilson came to accept that she should apply to the CIM, and insisted that she sign herself Amy Wilson Carmichael, to show that he gave his approval, as to an adopted daughter. Her outfit for China was bought and packed.

The CIM doctor examined Amy and refused to pass her as fit for China. It is indicative of the note of high drama on which Mr Wilson lived that he should say: 'He has given me back my Isaac. Praise Him!' Amy, in the guise of Isaac, was allowed to get down from the altar, as Bishop Houghton puts it. But only for a year. She felt very sure she was to work abroad, and she had hopes that she might begin her work with the Rev. Barclay F. Buxton, in Japan.

Amy sailed with other CIM missionaries to Shanghai, and there found a letter from Mr Buxton to say she was welcome to join his work on the west coast of Japan. She arrived in Japan in May 1893, where she worked extremely hard, with some limited and some lasting success. When, fourteen years after her departure, Barclay Buxton's nephew visited a village where about fourteen people had embraced the Christian faith as a result of Amy's work, he found them firmly rooted in the faith.

Within a year she wrote to her mother to say she was leaving Japan to rest in Shanghai with CIM friends in order to recuperate from her breakdown. She suffered from 'Japanese Head' and from neuralgia; she had a collapse, blamed partly on the loss of her umbrella which was meant to shield her from the sun. She felt like a reject; doctors advised a long rest, but the details are not disclosed.

**Recall and recharge**

From Shanghai, Amy felt called to Ceylon and went there to work for a short time. While in Ceylon she heard that the DOM (the affectionate initials by which Mr Wilson, the 'Dear Old Man' was known to Amy's family) was ill after a stroke. She sailed for England, and travelled overland from Brindisi to Rome, Paris and Calais to save time. She reached Broughton Grange before Christmas 1884. Her father-in-God, Mr Wilson, recovered; and she was able to rest and recharge her batteries. She also put together her first book, *From Sunrise Land.*

Amy soon felt that she was called to a new charge: to work in India. A friend from Bangalore wrote to say that the climate in that part of South India was delightful and healthy. She applied to the Church of England Zenana Missionary Society. In spite of the fact that she said no doctor would pass her to work in a tropical country, she was accepted, with strong support from Keswick leaders. Soon after his seventieth birthday, Mr Wilson again said goodbye to his lovely adopted daughter. He was never to see her again, though he pleaded with her to visit him again. He died in 1905, having to the end supported his Amy with finance and with much prayer.

With little fuss Amy left for India in 1895. She stayed there till her death in 1951. During all that time she never took leave at home. As Bishop Frank Houghton wrote, her half-century of service began 'so quietly, almost casually'. Amy Carmichael did not believe anything was casual, and gradually, over the next seven years, she began to realize what a charge she had been given. Her own views became very much at odds with those of other missionaries, and at one time there was a committee to try and obtain Amy's recall to England. She became convinced, and no friend or enemy could ever shake her conviction, that Dohnavur was her calling, and that every detail of the work as she had planned it had received divine sanction.

**Preparation for a family**

At first Amy worked alongside a mission hospital, and came to know the missionaries in Bangalore. Gradually she found herself learning Tamil, and then met Thomas Walker, the famous missionary leader of Tinnevelly. She came to admire and love Walker and his wife; they in turn helped her to learn the language, to acclimatize and to think in the Tamil way. Amy was delighted when she passed her language exams. Walker noted her despair at the attitudes of the colonial English, what she called the 'foreignising tendency'. He and his wife and friends encouraged and supported Amy and taught her many things essential for her survival.

Walker was then freed from his high administrative job in the Church Missionary Society to do what he wanted, which was to work in the villages as an itinerant evangelist. Amy joined him, and with a bullock cart and a tent sent from England they gradually formed a band of Indian and English workers. Amy continued to work with this group until, in 1901, she stumbled on the facts about ritual sexual abuse which 'caused a new thing to begin and I was rooted for life'.

The first event that led to Dohnavur was the arrival of Preena, a girl of seven who had been devoted by her widowed mother to the service of the temple gods. She had escaped and returned home to her mother, but the temple women had found her, branded her hands with hot irons, and spoke of her being prepared for marriage to the god. She escaped again, and was brought to Amy's bungalow while the latter was drinking her early morning tea on the verandah. Again, in such a casual way, her life's work became clear to her: it was to seek and wherever possible to save girls from ritual sexual prostitution.

Later, babies were brought from the temples and were cared for; then boys came from the temples too. That side of the work was built up, and a hospital was erected. A community of the most unusual kind was slowly formed. Amy was a kind of Teresa of Avila, matching the Spanish reformer in her zeal, in her devotion to Christ and to her charges, and also in the intense and contradictory elements of her dominating temperament.

Having apparently refused several proposals of marriage and set her face like flint towards an ideal of complete chastity, of celibacy for herself and (if possible) for her colleagues, she developed a large family of Indian, and some English, fellow workers. Above all, the children and babies who were saved from the temple service, with all its squalor, grew up as her own children; she was Ammai, the mother.

**What Amy did in Dohnavur**

Amy Carmichael would rebuke us for suggesting that she did anything. She would say that any achievement in Dohnavur was due to God's grace: it was his love in action. We may accept that, and also appreciate that Amy's qualities of mind and spirit were the instruments used in creating the Fellowship.

Dohnavur had begun as one of the Villages of Refuge in that part of South India. It had been founded by a German missionary in 1824, and named after Count Dohna, whose money had been given to build it; hence its name meant the village of Dohna. It was out of the way, and its remoteness was a protection against the persecution which had created a need for Christian refuges. The bitterness of Hindus and Muslims towards converts to Christianity had in no way abated.

The Dohnavur Fellowship was not registered as a trust till 1927, and then only for the purpose of legally holding land and buildings. Its story is told as a romance in *Gold Cord;* it is a moving account which has to be related in full, since the details of growth and development are all so remarkable. The themes concern the role of faith – for no settled finances were ever available – and the triumph of character over adversity.

First, the reason for settling in Dohnavur was that the decrepit buildings could be adapted to house the band of workers who now began to care for both girls and babies on a day-to-day basis. The usual work, of witnessing in the villages, gradually had to be abandoned. Once begun, the new work had a life of its own, and Amma, as she was now known, began to plan to build according to 'the Pattern shown in the Mount'. She expressed herself in that way, alluding to Moses without thought of pride or of identifying herself with such a great leader. It became her manner, her style, to seek God's guidance, and to receive it, usually in the form of an inner voice, or sometimes a vision. Then would come the certainty as to what should be done. The Family might be asked their views, but no one would successfully disagree with Amma.

Later on, workers who did disagree were usually asked to leave, and considered unsuitable. Failure of any kind was not tolerated. In 1916 Amma formed the 'Sisters of the Common Life', modelled on Gerard Grote's Brotherhood of the Common Life in Holland. It was her *order,* as strict as any monastic order, for the elite women in Dohnavur who were willing to sign a 'confession of love'. The way she describes it all is typical of the old Amy in her new guise. She states first that 'The Cross is the attraction'. She wrote dictums such as, *'My Vow*: Whatsoever Thou sayest unto me, by Thy grace I will do it', and *'My Motto* – Love to live: Live to love'.

In *Gold Cord* Amy recounts in some detail how between 1916 and the time of writing (1932), between twenty and thirty girls signed the confession. She does not say, as is made clear elsewhere by Elizabeth Elliot, that to marry was to forfeit one's membership of the sisterhood. It was as near as could be to a religious order, with vows of poverty, chastity and obedience, and undoubtedly Amma functioned as the mother superior.

**Amma's achievement**

Amy Carmichael built a community that began as a group of persons who loved the Lord and sought to share suffering in the service of others, and in particular of the children who had been deprived of love and given or sold for religious and sexual prostitution. That alone justifies our regard for her and our special gratitude, respect and affection. But, under God, she did far more: the work widened to include more medical work, and more rescue work of various kinds. Above all, Dohnavur came to stand for a special kind of spirituality.

It is in her gift for expressing her devotion to Christ and to his service that Amy Carmichael's name lives on. She took the best of a certain type of Keswick teaching – very different from that of the last few decades – and infused it with a blend of many Christian traditions and ways of thinking which she had derived, in the first place, from her links with Robert Wilson. For her, 'the Higher Christian Life' became a question of finding, to use well-worn phrases from childhood arithmetic, not the lowest common denominator but rather the highest common factor. I have spoken to some distinguished Christians who were alarmed at the books found in her bedroom when she died. But Amy makes no secret of them in her account in Gold Cord:

> Our meetings were mainly in English. Except our Bible and the *Pilgrim's Progress*, there were no books in Tamil ... Rolle and Suso and Tersteegen ... Bishop Moule and Josephine Butler of our own time, and Thomas à Kempis, pupil of Grote and Brother of the Common Life, Samuel Rutherford and Pere Didon, brothers

> in spirit though divided by the letter of the law, and the brave and burning souls of every age, these had left torches.

Her books contain many judicious quotations from Christian mystics of all times, and of course the Bible has the special place she always believed it should have. At Dohnavur, the verbal inspiration of Scripture was a firmly held belief. However, the way Scripture was interpreted owed almost everything to her own special blend of mysticism and practicality and, we have to admit, to some prejudice also.

**The fall: twenty years of illness**

As previously mentioned, Amy Carmichael was an invalid for the last twenty years of her life. In 1931 she was visiting a newly built house to inspect the work and, in the twilight, went into the shed that was to serve as an earth closet. The coolies had dug the hole inside the door instead of at the back of the shed. Amy fell, broke her leg, dislocated an ankle and twisted her spine. She was driven by lorry to Dr Howard Somervell, forty-six miles away. The broken bones were set by him, but we can only guess at the quality of care available in 1931 in a remote country area. Her suffering was intense, and only partly remedied. Much prayer for Amma's healing was offered up, but the answer seemed to be 'No'.

Amma was in pain, of varying severity, for much of her life after this accident. She wondered, as did her friends, whether there was a curse on the house involving some demonic forces. Amma and her friends always looked for such explanations when faced with the incompetence or failure of workers, and perhaps they were more enlightened than those who accepted a simpler set of explanations.

Dohnavur's mother led the work from her bedroom for the rest of her life, becoming increasingly in need of close and careful nursing. The community had separated from its Anglican links: from 1925 onwards it was quite independent, and in 1927 it had become officially registered as a Fellowship. To lose an active leader so soon after these events was a blow, but the Fellowship survived and flourished, in spite of Amma's invalid state.

She wrote of the 'crashing disappointments' of the last twenty years. Indian women, whom she had valued greatly, died, and Amma's hopes for them as future leaders perished with them. Her cherished

English fellow workers were a great support, but the blows, such as the death of Godfrey Webb-Peploe, were hard to endure.

When his brother, Dr Murray Webb-Peploe, decided to leave Dohnavur (where he ran the hospital) to join his wife, Amma was intransigent. Murray's mother agreed that he should return to his wife and their twin children in England. Mr W. H.Aldis, home director of the China Inland Mission and chairman of the Keswick Convention, wrote to urge that he should do so. To Amma this was betrayal, for commitment to Dohnavur Fellowship was for life. Elizabeth Elliot summarizes her attitude thus: 'If God had shown her one thing, would He show the rest another thing? There is no instance on record of Amy's accepting another's guidance after she believed she had been given clear guidance in a matter.'

The work went on, with some changes as the children grew in age and in numbers. Then in 1948 Amma fell on her way to the bathroom and was afterwards confined totally to bed till her death in 1951. She was buried in God's Garden, a graveyard with no headstones, in Dohnavur, where she belonged. The only memorial is her name, in its formal style *Ammai*, inscribed on a bird-bath. But the whole saga of the Dohnavur Fellowship, and the volumes she left, are memorials that remain, for thousands, as a challenge and an inspiration.

## Disentangling the gold cord

The most lovely cords can become entangled. Is it possible to disentangle Amy Carmichael's personality? She herself said, 'I am a cross between a potato and a vegetable marrow.' She was a saint whose Irish temper could make her 'lay on like a fishwife'.

There were perhaps three major strands in her temperament which, together, made her the peculiar genius that she was. The first is her perfectionism; the second her ability to turn every crisis into a drama; and the third her mystical devotion to her Lord and Master. Her wide reading, her use of the language of Scripture and of the later saints in whose work she was steeped, helped her to express these traits in writing that was gifted and memorable.

Her colleagues thought her a saint, and only admitted that she must have been a sinner because we all are: they 'never saw it'. But these were the colleagues who stayed in Dohnavur; the ones who disagreed left, rejected or under a cloud. Stephen Neill, later the brilliant Bishop ofTinnevelly, worked there with his parents, both of whom were doctors. He describes her oracular mystique, her sense of power, the punishments used in Dohnavur. He was dismissed, and his parents had left earlier after six months' work. Amy's response to differences of opinion, and to friction of any kind, was to be rid of the irritant.

By her perfectionism I mean that her obsessive-compulsive personality took the form of a rigid devotion to discipline. By any standard, to work without leave for fifty years qualifies her as a compulsive worker, indeed as addicted to work, a workaholic. Her counsels in such books as *If*, were counsels of perfection. She wanted to be surrounded by people who accepted her standards, which were high and in some instances absolute. The only way she could deal with disagreement was to reject the offender. Instead of seeing disagreement as a difference of opinion, often of minor importance, it would be elevated into a crisis, and spiritual (even demonic) influences would be invoked as the cause.

In that part of the nineteenth century in which she grew up, many doctors would have called her love of crisis and drama hysterical, just as Christina Rossetti was labelled hysterical. Now we are more sophisticated. However, the old label concealed some important personality traits, which quite often did, and still do, contribute to illness. It has been said that the hysterical person will make any situation into a stage on which to act out his or her personal drama. There was, it seems to me, much of that tendency in Amy Carmichael. It led sometimes to her 'good to be spoken of as evil', and with some justification. Autocracy and tyranny remain evil, no matter how much they are wrapped up by Amy, in her writings, with enigmatic references to a 'pattern' which she alone had been shown, and which in her view others should never change, or even question.

**Mystic and mother superior**

As to her special kind of spirituality or Christian mysticism, a whole book, not a sketch, would be required to do it justice. The devoted following among her readers bears witness to her ability to express something rare: a perception of spiritual realities. She was a poet who wrote some superb verse, including some which was meant only for the family at Dohnavur to sing. The oracular element, where she is able to encapsulate a thought in a sentence, is evident in her little book *If*. Each statement was printed in heavy, bold type, with one to each page to make meditation easier. Thus:

> **If I fear to hold another to the highest because it is so much easier to avoid doing so, then I know nothing of Calvary love.**

Such statements are not for quick reading or browsing, but must be taken slowly, well diluted, as in homeopathic remedies. It is easy to suffer a surfeit of strong words.

Amy Carmichael believed strongly in her visions; she would *see* a situation and feel that it was God who had shown it to her. She would *hear* a word, usually a verse from the Bible, and feel it was God speaking directly to her. I think it is fair to say that she felt she probably belonged to an uncommon band of Christians who lived on a higher plane of spirituality.

Members of any 'Order', living in a closed community, are likely to create their own special tier of believers: they may not at first think they belong to the *top* tier, but gradually arrogance and spiritual pride sets in, and corrupts. 'Lilies that fester smell far worse than weeds.' The workers at Dohnavur called themselves 'Sisters of the Common Life', but they were *uncommonly* aloof in their standards, and quick to reject those who differed from Amy's, or Amma's, inspired view on any matter, large or small.

It is interesting that she does not quote Teresa of Avila, whose idiosyncrasies she mirrors on a smaller scale. The German mystics who influenced Luther for a time continued to guide her thinking. It is a pity that she and her Family became so isolated from other Christians, with whom they might have shared a great deal.

It seems to me sad, for instance, that after her accident she should have minded so much that she could not sleep on the floor, as she had been accustomed, but had to have a bed. And when her illness became worse, after her second fall, it was hard for her to pray while lying on her back. She then wrote that she 'seemed to see Him, as He was for a few immeasurable minutes, not upright but laid flat on His Cross'. She shared with Gerard Manley Hopkins a need to suffer, but never took note of his message, to 'leave comfort root-room'.

However unbalanced, harsh and petty Amy Carmichael may at times have been, there remained much solid gold, of lasting worth, in her achievement. Despising as she did the gods and goddesses that decorated a myriad Indian temples, she would not have wished us to turn her into a goddess, an idol or an icon.

She took the command in the Gospels to 'be perfect' with the utmost seriousness. A passage that she frequently cites is that of St Paul about building with gold, silver and costly stones, and not with wood, hay or straw: 'his work will be shown for what it is, because the Day will bring it to light' (1 Cor. 3:13). Her ambition, however imperfectly fulfilled, may serve for each of us – that 'the sum of all my life be love'.

*Further Reading*

Elizabeth Elliot, *Amy Carmichael: Her Life and Legacy* (London: Marc Europe, 1988) is a most helpful account. Frank Houghton, *Amy Carmichael of Dohnavur: The Story of a Lover and Her Beloved* (London: Hodder & Stoughton, 1953; London: SPCK, 1985) covers similar ground, with less assessment and more of Amy Carmichael's own words. Stuart and Brenda Blanch have edited an anthology, *Learning of God: Readings from Amy Carmichael* (London: Triangle/SPCK, 1985).

Some of Amy Carmichael's books are: *Gold Cord: The Story of a Fellowship* (London: SPCK, 1935); *Candles in the Dark* (London: Triangle/SPCK, 1981); *Edges of His Ways* (London: SPCK, 1981); *God's Missionary; Gold By Moonlight* (London: SPCK, 1973); *If, His Thoughts Said ... His Father Said* (London: Triangle/SPCK, 1987); *Mimosa* (London: SPCK); *Whispers of His Power* (London: Triangle/SPCK, 1982); *Towards Jerusalem,* (verse) (London: SPCK; CLC). Most of the above titles have been republished by Christian Literature Crusade in the United Kingdom.

# 9

# The House That Jack Built: C. S. Lewis (1898–1963)

> Joy (in my sense) ... might almost equally well be called a particular kind of unhappiness or grief. But then it is a kind we want. I doubt whether anyone who has tasted it would ever, if both were in his power, exchange it for all the pleasures in the world.
>
> C. S. Lewis, *Surprised by Joy* (1955)

> ... for me, reason is the natural organ of truth; but imagination is the organ of meaning. Imagination, producing new metaphors or revivifying old, is not the cause of truth, but its condition.
>
> C. S. Lewis, 1939

> Look for yourself, and you will find in the long run only hatred, loneliness, despair, rage, ruin and decay. But look for Christ and you will find Him, and with Him everything else thrown in.
>
> C. S. Lewis, *Mere Christianity* (1952)

C. S. Lewis was a don at Oxford for nearly thirty years, and in 1954 became Professor of English at Cambridge University, a post he held until his death in 1963. In his inaugural lecture in Cambridge, he described himself as a dinosaur belonging to a bygone age. It was the kind of ironic remark he loved to make: he knew that he had already left his mark as a writer about Christian faith – perhaps more clearly than any other modern writer.

His influence was to grow, and continue, as he used his mind in the service of the faith. His imaginative gifts, evident in his science fiction and his children's books, *The Chronicles of Narnia,* enabled him to reach millions. Yet his other works, which explain and defend the beliefs that became so dear to him, also continue to sell.

The personality that C. S. Lewis showed to the world was not always the one we have since come to know. He hid many hurts behind a social façade of the busy, successful bachelor. He grew up in Belfast, and Ulster Protestantism formed his early background. At the age of four Lewis announced to his family that his name was 'Jacksie'. His father continued to call him 'Jacks', and his friends always called him 'Jack'. But it was by his two initials, standing for Clive Staples, that the public knew him.

His father's incapacity to understand Jack was as much a part of the hurt as losing his mother when he was nine. He has written of the move from Belfast to 'Belsen', as he called his school: there, more harm was done to a growing boy.

I do not want to put Lewis on the psychoanalyst's couch or even on the sort of psychiatrist's chair that seeks to explain *away* what mattered most in his life. But I will seek to show how understanding and insight, obtained mainly from his own writings, can help us to enjoy Lewis in a fuller and deeper way. Like the other heroes discussed earlier, Lewis suffered much and achieved more than many. His experience of grace was central to his achievement.

His fame depends not on his many academic writings, though they are still read and appreciated. It was because this young don became a Christian and found, almost by accident, that he had a marvellous gift for writing about the Christian faith in clear, robust and simple words that he became famous throughout the world.

When Lewis first became well known there were many who claimed, like the editor at the Oxford University Press, that *'The Allegory of Love* and *Preface to Paradise Lost* had brought Lewis to the heights, but the theological books were just one long decline and fall'. Most of us would consider this an unwise and premature judgement, and it has now been proved quite wrong.

**Early suffering**

I believe that Lewis' desperately unhappy later childhood, after his mother's death, had many repercussions. His mother died of cancer when young Jack Lewis was nine years old and his brother Warnie was thirteen. Nearly fifty years later he was to marry a woman who was dying of cancer, and who had two boys aged nine and ten. C. S. Lewis' father, Albert, loved Jack and Warnie, but he was hard and unfeeling in his handling of them, and decisions about their education were taken without any regard for young Jack's emotional needs. The fact that Lewis saw himself as a physical replica of his father made it all the more difficult for him to accept Albert. Although he described his father as having a streak of genius in him, they were never able to get on together.

In his book on his early life called *Surprised by Joy,* Lewis has described his schooling, the ghastly separations from all he loved in Belfast for the horrors of English boarding schools in the period 1908–12. It is no wonder that his sexual development was at first impaired, and that he seems to have been, for some years, something of a 'lover of the whip', as he wrote to a friend. We should not forget the sad consequences of corporal punishment, and that Lewis had one headmaster who flogged indiscriminately.

Yet his very defects, such as his bullying (which may have been his way of defending a very sensitive and hurt part of himself), helped him fit into the world of young dons in the Oxford to which he returned in 1919, after being wounded in the First World War. Going off to the War with another Irishman, Paddy Moore, each gave the other a firm promise that, if either one of them died, the other would look after the surviving soldier's parent.

**Defects and design**

Lewis' peculiar personal suffering and his own defects of personality seem to have played a large part in his life and in the production of many of his books. An outstanding example of this is his small book A *Grief Observed,* which he wrote following his wife's death. This book, and the narrative behind it, gave rise to the play *Shadowlands,* which ran with great success in the theatre and introduced many to C. S. Lewis for the first time. The story of his late marriage and his wife's death was also shown on millions of television screens, and was a successful film.

There are other examples, as we shall see, of books and articles which Lewis wrote that not only hit the target at which he aimed but, as it were, scored a bull's eye. He loved Greek myths; would he have applied the story of the Greek archer Philoctetes to himself? The wounded Philoctetes never failed to hit his mark, whether in battle or in competition, so long as his wound continued to suppurate.

But as soon as the smelly sore healed, his ability as an archer left him. It returned only when his malady broke out again.

Was it just a myth? Did the myth become fact in Lewis' life, so that the hurts and wounds that afflicted him, early and late, led to his achievements? It is worth spending some time and effort to find out. Jack Lewis grew to be not only a giantkiller, but something of a giant himself, and I think the secret of his strength is once again in his weakness. Or, as Lewis himself would be too modest to say, like the apostle Paul he found that God's grace was sufficient for him, and that his strength was made perfect in weakness.

**Surveying the edifice**

To describe and assess the 'house' that Jack built is a large task. In the pages that follow, I try to confine myself to what C. S. Lewis himself said, to the words of his brother Warnie, and to other first-hand sources such as Lewis' letters to close friends like Arthur Greeves in Belfast. In examining what others have said about him I have aimed to give as accurate an account of his mind and personality as possible. What he built, his achievements, arose from his character and the extreme hard work he put into all that he attempted.

Like so many, I owe a great deal to his writings: but I deplore the C. S. Lewis *cult*, with its in-fighting and unbalanced views. Lewis always seemed to attract both liking and loathing in equal parts. He himself seems to have cared little about whether he was liked as a person, and some arguments about him resemble battles over the bones of saints in the Middle Ages. He was no plaster saint, and he should not be treated as if he were an infallible oracle.

Inevitably we must separate out different aspects of Lewis' life and examine them topic by topic. My aim is to build up a series of views, showing his many-sided talents, his failures and his successes.

**Foundations: heredity**

How much did Lewis owe to his inheritance? He was an Ulsterman, born and bred in Belfast of Protestant stock. He knew his grandfather on his father's side, who was living with them in the year his mother died (in fact he died in the same year). It was this grandfather, Richard, who emigrated from Cheshire to Ireland with his wife, Martha Gee from Liverpool. Richard, as part of his adult education, wrote many essays which were distinctly theological. He had left behind, in Cheshire, a large family; his own father, Joseph (Lewis' great grandfather), was a Methodist minister who turned farmer in order to feed his eight children. Joseph's father before him had been a farmer, in Flintshire, just over the border in Wales.

'I'm more Welsh than anything,' he once said to his friend George Sayer, 'and for more than anything else in my ancestry I'm grateful that on my father's side I'm descended from a practical Welsh farmer. To that link with the soil I owe whatever measure of physical energy and stability I have. Without it I should have turned into a hopeless neurotic.'

Lewis' father, Albert, was grandfather Richard's sixth child. He was born in Cork, but from 1868 onwards the family was resident in Belfast. Because of his father's success in his new boiler-making business in Belfast, Albert obtained a better education than his elders. In particular his teacher W. T. Kirkpatrick helped him immensely. After being articled in Dublin, Albert qualified as a solicitor and thereafter worked successfully in his own practice in Belfast.

Lewis' mother, Flora, was one of four children from a neighbouring home in Belfast. Her father, Thomas Hamilton, was the local rector and was bitterly anti-Roman Catholic. He had taken a First in theology at Trinity College, Dublin, and after ten years of travel and chaplaincies had married a clever and aristocratic woman, Mary Warren, whose culture and eccentricity both showed in the rectory's management. Flora was a brilliant student of mathematics and logic at Queen's College, Belfast. On his mother's side Lewis' lineage included an Irish bishop, and the Warrens' ancestry could be traced to the Normans.

When Lewis was seven his parents moved to a new house – 'Little Lea' – on the edge of the Belfast suburbs, giving easy access for him and his brother to County Down, which they grew to love. His brother calls the new house the worst designed he ever saw. Lewis says of it: 'I am the product of long corridors, empty sunlit rooms, upstair indoor silences, attics explored in solitude, distant noises of gurgling cisterns and pipes, and the noise of wind under the tiles.' And it was a house full of books.

**Foundations: upbringing**

As we read of the first nine years of Lewis' life in Belfast we see them through his eyes, and those of his brother Warnie, as a paradise that was lost when their mother died in 1908, when Jack was some two months short of his tenth birthday. He was fortunate in his brother, and they were

> two frightened urchins huddled for warmth in a bleak world ... With my mother's death all settled happiness, all that was tranquil and reliable, disappeared from my life. There was to be much fun, many pleasures, many stabs of joy; but no more of the old security. It was sea and islands now; the great continent had sunk like Atlantis.

He was a bright, precocious child, who enjoyed the world that opened to him as a middle-class boy at the beginning of the century. He had a nurse who was 'nothing but kindness, gaiety and good sense ... as nearly as a human being can be, simply good'. She told him the old fairy tales of Ireland. A governess who joined the household later seems to have had little influence. His mother taught him French and Latin. His one holiday abroad was with his mother in France, near Dieppe.

Two servants became enemies, and he and Warnie were confederates in a world of their own, *contra mundum.* The boys could not understand father's intense talk of politics with his friends: they came to think it was the only kind of adult conversation possible. It was animated by Protestant concerns for what the British government should do in the face of Catholic threats.

When Warnie built a toy garden in a biscuit tin, Jack was captivated, and claims it gave him a greater sense of longing than the green hills of Castlereagh which they could see from the nursery windows. He devoured all available books, and the newly published Beatrix Potter gave him special pleasure: one of hers, *Squirrel Nutkin*, he returned to often. It was the idea of autumn in that tale which again and again awoke in young Lewis the intense desire that he describes in *Surprised by Joy.*

As a child Lewis created a world of animal characters. Recently these stories have been collected into book form under the title *Boxen,* complete with the author's drawings. They give some insight into his early love of animal characters who wear human clothes and talk. Later, poetry gave him an unexpected (now celebrated) moment. In Longfellow's *Saga of King Olaf* he read:

> I heard a voice that cried,
> Balder the beautiful
> Is dead, is dead ...

With these words, he had his most piercing experience of joy, which he sharply distinguishes from Happiness or Pleasure: 'it might almost equally well be called a particular kind of unhappiness or grief. But then it is a kind we want. I doubt whether anyone who has tasted it would ever, if both were in his power, exchange it for all the pleasures in the world.'

These are strong words, and have given rise to much speculation, some of which we will consider when we come to his discovery of George MacDonald's *Phantastes* some ten years later. Concerning the above experience of joy, Lewis remarks: 'I cannot be absolutely sure whether the things I have just been speaking of happened before or after the great loss which befell our family.'

It would help us to know if he is speaking of a time *after* his mother's death. His words might suggest that he was looking back to a lost paradise. The surgeon's fiery scalpels which had operated on his mother's cancer in the home had for ever barred re-entry into that lost Eden. It might explain in part the painful longing that was such a vital part of his grief. Indeed, I think a kind of nostalgia coloured his whole life. Hard work and high achievement did much to assuage his grief, but his dread of emotions almost certainly dates back to his mother's death. Later we will see how, in the *Narnia* books, he writes about 'the healing of harms' in the ultimate sense.

A boy who lived nearby, Arthur Greeves, was to share many emotions that Lewis could not confide to others. He wrote regularly to Greeves – often weekly – and these letters have helped to trace his emotional development which was hidden under a carefully cultivated shell, as a lobster or a crab might use its carapace to protect its sensitive nervous system.

**Foundations: education**

His father was distracted with sorrow after his wife's death and, after much consultation with others, young Jack was sent to an English school in Hertfordshire. The headmaster there delighted in physical punishment, and his school was 'at once brutalizing and intellectually stupefying'. A boy's father brought a case against the headmaster in the High Court, and the school continued to worsen till it was closed in 1910. That Lewis was not exaggerating may be confirmed by other reports about the school, and the fact that the headmaster was certified insane when the school closed.

A short spell in a school in Belfast was followed by a decision to send Jack to the city of Malvern; Warnie was already at Malvern College, and Jack was sent for two years to a small preparatory school nearby called Cherbourg. He was happier there and began to make strides before obtaining a scholarship to join Warnie at the College. There, by contrast, his unhappiness was intense.

His father gradually came to a decision to send Jack to stay at the home of his own old schoolmaster, William T. Kirkpatrick (referred to as 'The Great Knock'). Having settled in Great Bookham, Surrey, after his retirement in 1912, Kirkpatrick had begun taking pupils privately and had helped Warnie to get into Sandhurst. It was here that Lewis arrived in September 1914, for two years of intense study which may have had more influence on his mind than any other period of his schooling.

His teacher's method was to give him a Greek or Latin text and tell him to get on with it, with the help of a lexicon, till he could read as well and as rapidly as the teacher himself. Lewis was soon able to do the same in French, German and Italian. Instead of Lewis being persecuted at Malvern for his idiosyncrasies, Kirkpatrick helped him to develop fast and furiously; but it was a lopsided, predominantly intellectual growth. The emphasis was heavily on logic and dialectic: every remark was challenged and had to be justified. Lewis says that a few years later his teacher would have been called a Logical Positivist.

In December 1916 Lewis arrived in Oxford, where he sat and passed a scholarship examination and was accepted for University College. He had one more examination to pass in March, and in April

1917 he took up his studies at the College; only twelve men were there, since Flanders and France had claimed the rest as fatalities in the Great War. Lewis volunteered (for Irishmen were not obliged to enlist), and was both a student and a trainee officer. In June he was moved to Keble College, which was then a barracks. His new room had to be shared with Edward (Paddy) Moore, who introduced him to his mother, Janie Moore. She was to dominate his life for the next thirty-three years.

**Shaking the foundations**

More than once, Lewis attempts to understand what is going on in those parts of our selves of which we are not fully aware. This may in part be a reflection of the huge and long-lasting effects that two people had on his own development: George MacDonald ('my master') and Mrs Janie Moore. Mrs Moore (or Minto as she was often called) had a complex role in his life for over thirty years. We might say that both these figures irrupted in his life and shook Lewis to his foundations. MacDonald became important in 1916, Mrs Moore in 1918. Both had a profound effect on his mind and heart.

Many Lewis admirers were surprised when he published his *George MacDonald Anthology*. He was displaying a secret passion which had started when he bought a copy of MacDonald's *Phantastes: A Faerie Romance* at a station bookstall. The book seems to have been the account of MacDonald's search for a perfect woman, doubtless related to his own mother's death when he was eight years old. A favourite quotation of MacDonald's is from 'Novalis': 'Our life is no dream, but it ought to become one and perhaps will.'

As a result of reading a book by someone who had been through a similar experience, Lewis gained access to all the feelings he had bottled up and put away after losing his mother. The book seems to have had little to do with MacDonald's theology, but rather with the description of a journey which he takes in the person of his hero 'Anodos' (meaning 'No Way'). Lewis wrote later:

> But in another sense all was changed. I did not yet know (and I was long in learning) the name of the new quality, the bright shadow that rested on the travels of Anodos. I do now. It was Holiness. For the first time the songs of the sirens sounded like

> the voice of my mother or my nurse ... That night my imagination was in a certain sense, baptized; the rest of me, not unnaturally, took longer. I had not the faintest notion what I had let myself in for by buying *Phantastes* ... the whole book had about it a sort of cool, morning innocence, and also, quite unmistakably, a certain quality of Death, *good* Death. What it actually did to me was to convert, even to baptize (that was where the Death came in) my imagination.

In a manner of speaking, what Lewis received through MacDonald was the gift of freedom to 'fancy' and to exercise his great imaginative talents. It was a sense of release, similar to that which Bunyan gained in prison in Bedford and which set free his genius for writing in the new style of *The Pilgrim's Progress.*

Lewis and Mrs Moore had come together as a result of the soldiers' pact made with Paddy Moore, which C. S. Lewis honoured. It was learned in September 1918 that Paddy had been killed. Janie, his mother, wrote to Lewis' father:

> I just lived my life for my son and it is hard to go on now ... Of the five boys who came out to us so often at Oxford, Jack is the only one left ... Jack has been so good to me ... He possesses for a boy of his age such a wonderful power of understanding and sympathy. He is not at all fit yet and we can only hope will remain so for a long time.

The role of Mrs Moore is a profoundly complex one in his life, beginning with his return from France as a wounded soldier in 1917. The relationship later came to involve much love and affection and, on his part, a kind of devotion which held Lewis in bondage to her. He wrote in *Surprised by Joy*: '... one huge and complex episode will be omitted. I have no choice about this reticence. All I can or need say is that my earlier hostility to the emotions was very fully and variously avenged.' We must bear in mind Lewis' other comment:

> When I came first to the University I was as nearly without a moral conscience as a boy could be. Some faint distaste for cruelty and meanness about money was my utmost reach – of chastity, truthfulness, and self-sacrifice I thought as a baboon thinks of classical music.

Now that the diaries Lewis kept during the 1920s have been published (entitled *All My Road Before Me),* his devoted friend and editor Walter Hooper admits the peculiar qualities of the relationship. Hooper writes: 'This combination of means and opportunity invites, though it does not demand, the conclusion that Janie King Moore and C. S. Lewis were lovers.' We can only leave the subject as a question to which there are no definite answers, even though Lewis' diaries for this period contain many references to Mrs Moore.

What is remarkable is how the young ex-soldier cared for a woman old enough to be his mother, and lived for over two decades in grinding poverty, made worse by his financial commitment to helping Mrs Moore and her daughter Maureen.

**'If I should die'**

Brief as his war experience was, it had other large effects on Lewis. It led to a worsening of his relationship with his father, who would not respond to his letters and telegrams trying to arrange what might well have been a last meeting with his beloved Jacks. His father feared the break in his own routine, and the U-boats in the Irish Channel. In the mean time Lewis spent all his leave with Paddy Moore's family.

He spent his first Christmas in the trenches, and describes them in ways that suggest he was content – 'a man can sleep quite snugly and braziers for warmth and cooking' – and he had books to read. In 1919 a friend asked him how on earth he managed in the army. Lewis replied that he loathed it and was very much frightened in France, 'but I never sank so low as to pray'.

He was away with trench fever before returning to the battle in April 1917. He surprised himself by taking sixty Germans prisoner. During a German offensive his sergeant was killed and the shrapnel of the shell that destroyed his sergeant also wounded Lewis; he fell and thought that he too was dying. By May 1917 he was in hospital in London. In due course he was discharged. Twenty years later a piece of the shrapnel had to be removed from his chest, and he was left with a bladder weakness for life, which got worse in his last years.

There was another, later casualty: Lewis the poet. Hitherto he had believed himself primarily a poet, and was delighted when a volume of his verse was published in 1919. Although one poem, 'Death in Battle', had been published in John Galsworthy's journal *Reveille,* there was no enthusiasm for it. His next volume of verse *(Dymer)* seems to have received a similarly tame reception, and Lewis' hopes of being a fine poet finally died. He continued to write verse: some of the best appearing in *The Pilgrim's Regress.*

**Return to Oxford: *Lebensraum***

His return to Oxford soon marked Lewis out as a brilliant, hardworking student who was to get a Triple First. Inexorably the young undergraduate collected a First in Mods, a First in Greats and then the Chancellor's English Essay Prize. Yet, in 1922, the brilliant young ex-soldier was not able to find employment in the University.

His father agreed to continue his allowance, since there was hope of a Fellowship. The Master of University College advised him to stay a further year and take a degree in English Literature, which Lewis did and enjoyed hugely. In due course he obtained a First, for a third time, as was expected of him. His love of the authors he read was mixed with a kind of fear that the best of them – John Donne, George Herbert, Thomas Browne – were Christians. He made many friends who were Christians. In retrospect, the move from philosophy to English was crucial.

Yet no university post appeared until, in 1925, he was elected to a Fellowship in English at Magdalen, and he moved into his rooms in the New Buildings set in the lovely Addison's Walk. He had found his place in the University, and he was to grace it for nearly thirty years until he moved to a chair at Cambridge.

During this nerve-racking time there had been bigger worries: where to live with Mrs Moore and her daughter Maureen. They moved from one set of rented rooms to another on nine separate occasions before settling for some six years in Headington. He was not to find a proper home with Mrs Moore and Maureen until Warnie joined them. In 1930, all three adults put together enough mortgage money to buy The Kilns at Shotover Hill, Oxford. This house, with its garden and grounds covering eight acres, was to be C. S. Lewis' home till he died.

He lived a difficult life as a bachelor don, and he looked after Mrs Moore, and did many chores for her, day in and day out. In College his time was divided between his diligently given tutorials, his lectures, and his administrative duties as a Fellow. He attended to his duties in exemplary fashion. He also spent much energy on keeping his life in separate, rigid compartments. College life was hermetically sealed from Mrs Moore, as she was from the College. His friends knew nothing of his emotional turmoil. Hardly anyone knew about his struggle over belief in God, so well documented in *Surprised by Joy.* His first conversion, in 1929, was simply to acceptance of God as God, and had little to do with any specifically Christian way.

A few months later he visited his father for the last time, finding him ill with cancer. Four days after he returned to Oxford his father died, on 25 September 1929. Lewis was to bemoan for many years the abominable way he had treated his father: 'no sin in my whole life now seems to be so serious' he was to say in 1954.

**Becoming a Christian**

It is hard to unravel the way in which Lewis became a Christian, as opposed to a believer in God. He began to read Christian books and, in the New Testament, studied the Gospel of John and (in 1931) St Paul's Epistle to the Romans, 'the first Pauline epistle I have ever seriously read through'. He did not get on well with so-called devotional books, but found doctrinal books helpful.

He wrote later that many 'would find that the heart sings unbidden while they work their way through a tough bit of theology'. In 1931 he also opened his mind to Greeves as follows:

> What has been holding me back (at any rate for the last year or so) has not been so much a difficulty in believing as a difficulty in knowing what the doctrine *meant: you* can't believe a thing while you are ignorant *of what* the thing is. My puzzle was the whole doctrine of Redemption: in what sense the life and death of Christ 'saved' or 'opened salvation to' the world. I could see how miraculous salvation might be necessary ... What I couldn't see was how the life and death of Someone Else (whoever he was) 2,000 years ago could help us here and now – except in so

> far as his example helped us. And the example business, tho' true and important, is not Christianity: right in the centre of Christianity, in the Gospels and St Paul, you keep on getting something quite different and very mysterious expressed in those phrases I have so often ridiculed ('propitiation' – 'sacrifice' – 'the blood of the Lamb') – expressions wh. I cd. only interpret in senses that seemed to me either silly or shocking.

It was his friends at the Inklings (see p.284) who provided him with the missing link. J. R. R. Tolkien (the author of *The Hobbit* and *The Lord of the Rings)* and Hugo Dyson – both Christians of a Catholic persuasion – helped him most at that time. They showed him that he could accept myths of dying and reviving gods in pagan stories; in fact he was moved by such accounts provided he met them anywhere except in the Gospels. The same letter to Greeves in 1931 goes on:

> Now the story of Christ is simply a true myth: a myth working on us in the same way as others, but with this tremendous difference that *it really happened:* and one must be content to accept it in the same way, remembering that it is God's myth where the others are men's myths ... Christianity is God expressing Himself through what we call 'real things'.

Lewis then asks: 'Does this amount to a belief in Christianity?'

It was at any rate a beginning. There used to be many stories about people being led away from faith in Christ by comparative religion and the writings of such as J. G. Frazer in *The Golden Bough.* It seems probable that Lewis took his first steps to Christ and his cross along the unlikely route of the myths he knew so well. One thing must be added: Lewis quickly found for himself how important moral obedience was, and this began with his own acceptance of the words of our Lord in John 7:17, 'If anyone chooses to do God's will, he will find out whether my teaching comes from God or whether I speak on my own.' A heavy emphasis on avoiding new sins, and expunging old sins that he might have committed (pride especially), crops up frequently in his writings.

**Puritania: the Ulsterior motive**

A clue to understanding what Lewis was going through is provided by what Tolkien called the 'Ulsterior motive'. Lewis was weighed down by excess baggage from Ulster days: forms of false Puritanism, better called a Victorian religious hypocrisy (so very different from the buoyant, healthy Puritanism of John Bunyan's religion at its best). In a letter to Greeves dated 6 December 1931, Lewis tells him he now sees how much Puritanism counts in the Greeves make-up, and as he goes on to describe Ulster Puritanism it is as if he is describing something from which he himself has suffered:

> ... if you ever feel that the *whole spirit and system* in which you were brought up was after all right and good then you may be quite sure that that feeling is a mistake ... My reasons for this are 1. That the system denied pleasure to others as well as to the votaries themselves: whatever the merits of self-denial, this is unpardonable interference. 2. It inconsistently kept some worldly pleasures, and always selected the worst ones – gluttony, avarice etc. 3. It was ignorant. It could give no 'reason for the faith that was in it'. Your relations have been found very ill grounded in the Bible itself.... 4. 'By their fruits ye shall know them'. Have they the *marks* of peace, love, wisdom and humility on their faces or in their conversation? Really, you need not *bother* about that kind of Puritanism. It is simply the form which the *memory* of Christianity takes just before it finally dies away altogether, in a commercial community: just as extreme emotional ritualism is the form it takes on just before it dies in a fashionable community.

This is a key passage. It explains part of Lewis' book *The Pilgrim's Regress,* which he wrote (completing the first draft in two weeks) while staying with Greeves in Belfast in 1932, less than a year after he wrote this letter. The pilgrim, called 'John' in Lewis' account, sets out from a country called 'Puritania', and much fun is made of the practices of the people in that version of the Ulster of his earlier life.

**Spiritual development**

The Ulster factor is easily forgotten when considering a man who seems so much the complete Oxford don or Cambridge professor. Lewis told one enquirer who asked about his personal religion that he was a Protestant. His decision to avail himself of the help of regular confession came, he said, from the exhortation in the Prayer Book. The Communion service suggests that a Christian can seek 'ghostly counsel and advice ... if he cannot quiet his own conscience ... by opening his grief ... that he may receive the benefit of absolution'. This became Lewis' regular practice for the rest of his life. As an Ulsterman, with his built-in fear of Popish practices, his first confession was, he said, like going through a wall of fire. From this time on, his spiritual director was very important to Lewis, though we hear little about him.

I wonder if his dislike of hymns and organ music resulted in part from his experience of poor quality hymns and music during his early life? Perhaps he never obtained the key to enter and enjoy that treasury of Christian spirituality and teaching that is contained in hymns fired in the crucible of profound experiences of grace. If not, it is a thousand pities: such hymns have given many the 'stab of joy' of which Lewis spoke in another connection.

Perhaps a man whose great ambition was to be a fine poet could not tolerate the rather different discipline of the hymn-writer. In turning away from hymns, he was more than half-blind to those sources that gave Christians a liturgy far finer than the richest mass or requiem. To have lived without enjoying Wesley and Watts, and their fellow hymn-writers, is like having a prolonged vitamin deficiency. Ulster and Puritania, like public-school religion, has a lot to answer for in explaining Lewis' emotional and spiritual life.

### Going to the devil

The book that made Lewis famous enough to appear on the cover of the American news magazine *Time* was *The Screwtape Letters.* The letters were originally written for a weekly church news-magazine called *The Guardian,* now no longer published. In such an unlikely setting thirty-one weekly letters appeared. The £62 that Lewis earned went, in accord with his wishes, to a fund for widows of clergymen. It was his decision to give all monies made from his religious writings to charity, for, as he explained: 'I felt that God had been so gracious in having me that the least I could do was give back all the money made in His service.'

Where did Screwtape come from? Lewis said he traced the idea to a book of letters called *Confessions of a Well-Meaning Woman,* written by Stephen McKenna. The heroine-authoress in this story was a catty hypocrite bent on destroying the lives of those she wrote about; she did it in a humorous style by turning black into white and white into black. Perhaps Lewis' clear definitions of good and evil owed something to Ulster too. For his description of temptation, on the other hand, he says he looked mainly into his own heart.

In writing to his brother Warren in 1940, Lewis describes how the idea for Screwtape came to him:

> I was struck by an idea for a book which I think might be both useful and entertaining. It would be called 'As one Devil to another' and would consist of letters from an elderly retired devil to a young devil who has just started work on his first 'patient'. The idea would be to give all the psychology of temptation from the *other* point of view.

**Screwtape: fact and fiction**

The story is simple: a young man becomes a Christian, has a difficult mother and smart sceptical friends; he does the customary things like reading an enjoyable book, falling in love, meeting his loved one's Christian parents, and getting killed (like so many) in the Blitz of 1940. Imperceptibly, almost innocently, he finds his way to the devil. Lewis said that the effort of speaking through Screwtape almost smothered him and gave him spiritual cramp, as he twisted his mind to see things from a diabolical point of view. In spite of all this, he succeeded brilliantly.

But did he believe it all? Lewis said it was not part of his creed, but it was one of his opinions. He was not a dualist, believing in a power opposite to God. In what sense, then, did the devil exist for him? He wrote:

> I believe in angels and I believe some of them, by the abuse of their free will, have become enemies to God and, as a corollary, to us. These we may call devils. They do not differ in nature from good angels, but their nature is depraved. Devil is the opposite of angel as Bad Man is the opposite of Good Man. Satan, the leader or dictator of devils, is not the opposite of God but of Michael.

He added that in his view this agreed 'with the plain sense of Scripture, the tradition of Christendom, and the beliefs of most men at most times. And it conflicts with nothing that any of the sciences has shown to be true.'

He also stated that both to disbelieve in devils and to have an excessive and unhealthy interest in them (as is surely evident now in the decades following his death, with films like *The Exorcist)* are equal and opposite errors. *The Screwtape Letters* contained a good deal of humour, and a great deal of plain Christian teaching – not least about the ordinary facts of spiritual life, such as: 'Murder is no better than cards if cards can do the trick. Indeed the safest road to Hell is the gradual one – the gentle slope, soft underfoot, without sudden turnings, without milestones, without signposts.'

**Scholar and popular writer**

Although, externally, Lewis managed to keep his life at Oxford in watertight compartments, it was not long before his faith and his new inner life affected all aspects of his work. There was cross-fertilization between his scholarship and his popular writings, whatever is said to the contrary. We cannot fail to see a close link between his *Preface to Paradise Lost* and *The Screwtape Letters* and *The Problem of Pain.*

Charles Williams probably helped Lewis to bridge the gap. Williams was a scholar without formal education who worked for Oxford University Press. He and Lewis were acquainted with each other's writings before they met. The outbreak of the Second World War brought Williams to Oxford, and soon afterwards he joined the Inklings.

Williams inspired Lewis in a number of ways: his book *The Place of the Lion,* and his series of supernatural thrillers, opened Lewis' mind to possibilities which were to be realized in future books like *The Chronicles of Narnia.* Williams, Lewis felt, had also understood Milton. Lewis arranged for Williams to lecture in Oxford on Milton's *Comus,* and later recalled how remarkable it was to see the Oxford students 'who filled the benches listening first with incredulity, then with toleration, and finally with delight, to something so strange and new in their experience as the praise of chastity'.

On the subject of Milton, Lewis came to believe that the critics who said we must 'disentangle from theological rubbish the permanent and human interest' were quite wrong about the great Puritan poet. Lewis, now a Christian, warned that 'some (by no means all) of the things the atheist reader must "try to feel as if he believed", I actually, in cold prose, do believe. But for the student of Milton my Christianity is an advantage.' This is particularly true when Lewis explores the biblical teaching on Satan, the fall of man, and man's sexuality before and after the fall. These are themes which lent a lot of substance to his writing in *The Screwtape Letters.*

In a similar way, his book *The Problem of Pain* owes a lot to his scholarly studies. Here, as in his work on Milton, Lewis is dealing with God's power and goodness, man's fall and wickedness, and with heaven and hell. His style is racy, his idiom modern, and at the same time he explains some of the great truths of Christian thought and examines the subject of human and animal pain. He takes the old teaching about being made perfect through suffering, and applies categories like tribulation and affliction to the modern world of 1940.

*The Problem of Pain* faces facts which, sadly, many of us as Christians find very hard to face. Often we think (quite wrongly, in my view) that all pain and hurt should be healed and done away with, as if by magic, in this earthly life. Lewis could not be aware when he wrote the book how much pain he was to suffer in the future, and how he would be known to millions (through *Shadowlands)* for surviving it.

### The Inklings: 'We band of brothers'

Lewis found great succour in weekly meetings of the Inklings: usually on Tuesdays at lunch-time in a pub called the Eagle and Child, and on Thursday nights in Lewis' rooms in Magdalen College. The group would read parts of any work in progress, and discuss and debate (anything and everything) till late at night.

J. R. R. Tolkien was probably the most important member of the Inklings. He had a special feeling for Lewis since he had, in some degree, been instrumental in bringing him to the Christian faith. Tolkien's chapters, to be published later as *The Hobbit,* were read to the group, and so was *The Lord of the Rings*. Did any of them guess that these books would bring Tolkien such fame and fortune and be translated into many languages? Tolkien, like Lewis, was a most remarkable professor of English, but it is for this private world of fantasy which he is remembered. The Tolkien cult in America chose a leading figure from his *Ring* series and had a slogan: 'Gandalf for President'. Such widespread popularity is an unusual achievement for an Oxford don.

Tolkien was later to say that being a cult figure in one's lifetime was not pleasant, and had made him feel small and inadequate. He added that the nose of even the most modest idol cannot remain untickled by the sweet smell of incense. As Lewis increased in fame, Tolkien referred to him as 'Everyman's Theologian'. Over the years the fans of both Lewis and Tolkien were to increase in numbers and in fervour, being counted in millions.

**Brother Warnie**

Other 'Inklings' played important parts: Lewis' brother Warnie was one. Major Warren Lewis attended the Inklings regularly, after being evacuated from Dunkirk in 1940 and then put on the reserve in Oxford. Warnie continued to be close to his brother: they were confederates first and last. Lewis loved Warnie and, in spite of Warnie's relapses during forty years of alcoholism, often requiring hospitalization, he never faltered in his affectionate care. Warnie outlived Jack by ten years, and was buried in the same grave as his brother in Headington parish church.

Warren writes with pride of his own literary achievement in writing seven books about French history. He notes in 1972: 'Since I began writing in 1953 my earnings come to a total of £9,766.10. Not so bad for a complete amateur who was over fifty-eight when he turned author!' His diaries are full of artless, pungent comment. Warren writes in 1967: 'I often wonder at the mystery of heredity. He and I, born of the same parents, he so brilliant, I so much the reverse. How and why?'

The coming of Charles Williams, with his reputation as a novelist, historian and poet, changed the character of the Inklings, partly because of Williams' friendship with Lewis. Williams' was a talent of rare and disturbing quality, and deserves much more notice than this brief sketch can give. When he died suddenly in 1945, Lewis wrote to a lady:

> I also have become much acquainted with grief now through the death of my great friend Charles Williams, my friend of friends, the comforter of our little set, the most angelic man ... I can't put it into words. One seems at moments to be living in a new world. Lots, lots of pain, but not a particle of depression or resentment ...

Hugo Dyson, who was also important in helping Lewis to find his faith, was a frequent visitor to the Inklings, as were Lewis' doctor Dr R. E. Havard, Nevill Coghill, John Wain and Gervase Mathew. Sometimes Lord David Cecil would be present. The usual number was six.

Owen Barfield was an Inkling and a friend of special importance to Lewis. At the time of writing, Barfield is the sole survivor. He became a solicitor in London, and was therefore not often present. But his friendship with Lewis was deep and vital; Barfield became his literary executor. Barfield's own faith, owing a lot to Rudolf Steiner and his teachings, was an important bond between them.

**Fun and games**

The Inklings were not merely writers forming a seminal literary group. They also had some riotous fun. Referring to them, Lewis said: 'No sound delights me more than male laughter.' It has been fairly remarked that sometimes things went beyond a joke, as when they decided to put up a candidate for Professor of Poetry who was manifestly not as worthy as either Lord David Cecil or Sir Edmund Chambers (a literary scholar and retired civil servant).

Lewis fought successfully for the election of Adam Fox, chaplain at Magdalen, and even arranged transport for those Oxford MAs who supported Fox. It is a discreditable side of both Lewis and the Inklings. Tolkien boasted that they had defeated a Knight and a Noble Lord.

Oxford dons were not amused about Lewis' role in this affair, and it is probably right to conclude that this silly incident had an adverse effect on Lewis' Oxford career; he may have deserved a chair, but he was never given one. C. Day Lewis beat him in a later election for the Chair of Poetry. The Oxford authorities may have agreed with the editor quoted earlier, who disliked Lewis' popularity, and perhaps also his Christian associations.

Envy and jealousy are powerful and destructive emotions: perhaps there was a naive element, appropriate to the authors of *The Hobbit* and *the Narnia Chronicles*, which disdained such simple motivators in men of lesser stature than themselves.

**Broadcasting: *Mere Christianity***

Looking with hindsight at C. S. Lewis' three series of talks given on the BBC, it is evident that one could not then have predicted that they would become the popular volume *Mere Christianity.*

In his reply to the Director of Religious Broadcasting at the BBC, Lewis had said that he thought that

> the New Testament, by preaching repentance and forgiveness, always assumes an audience who already believe in the Law of Nature and know they have disobeyed it. In modern England we cannot at present assume this ... The first step is to create, or recover, the sense of guilt. Hence if I give a series of talks I should mention Christianity only at the end, and would prefer not to unmask my battery till then.

The first series of talks, about right and wrong, and about what Christians believe, was followed by a series called *Christian Behaviour.* Lewis dealt with the cardinal virtues, but then homed in on social and sexual morality and Christian marriage. He talked of forgiveness, of pride as the greatest sin of all, and of charity, hope and faith.

A third series of talks, *Beyond Personality,* which purported to describe the basics of the doctrine of the Trinity, did not dwell long on that subject. Lewis asked questions such as whether Christianity is hard or easy, and whether it is about nice people or new men. The whole series was admirably adapted for easy listening and reading, so that very difficult ideas might be grasped. It is all suffused with a practical concern to help, and not to put off, the seeker after truth.

**Sex and C. S. Lewis**

It is important to stress how totally Lewis accepted, in these talks, the ideal of chastity, and a high standard of Christian marriage. 'Either marriage, with complete faithfulness to your partner, or total abstinence.' He makes no bones about the difficulties and the problems that are thereby raised for modern folk. He also adds that 'a cold, self-righteous prig who goes regularly to church may be far nearer to hell than a prostitute. But, of course, it is better to be neither.' This reminds us of our Lord, telling the priggish religious Pharisees of his day that the harlots and the tax-gatherers would enter the kingdom of heaven before them.

In the preface to the three collected talks (*Mere Christianity* – using the word 'mere' to mean 'essential' or basic Christianity, agreed by all), Lewis writes: 'When a man who accepts the Christian doctrine lives unworthily of it, it is much clearer to say he is a bad Christian than to say he is not a Christian.'

There will be critics who will want to condemn Lewis for not disentangling himself, after his conversion, from his relationship with Mrs Janie Moore. Lewis was thirty-three and Mrs Moore was fifty-eight. There are strong hints that, whatever his relationship with Mrs Moore was before his conversion, there were changes in the relationship after Lewis became a Christian. She was angry with Lewis and his brother for their new Christian practices, such as going to Communion. He cared for her till she died at seventy-eight.

In his talks Lewis also said a good deal about psychoanalysis, and a little about sexual deviations. He freely admits his own sado-masochistic tendencies in his letter to Greeves, his Belfast boyhood friend. But tendencies do not always lead to practices. It is implied that he derived some perverse pleasure from serving Mrs Moore's domestic needs so that he was, she said, 'as good as an extra maid'. Perhaps, in some degree Lewis sought suffering, humiliation or degradation in this strange relationship.

A description that Lewis gives Greeves about a visit to a performance of Flecker's play *Hassan* in Oxford in 1931 is evidence of Lewis' disturbed sexuality. Hassan faints on stage after being compelled to witness the torture of the lovers. Lewis writes: 'Warnie went out half way through. I felt quite sick but thought it almost a duty for one afflicted in my way to remain, saying to myself "Oh you like cruelty do you? Well now stew in it!"' When Lewis describes Flecker as being too morbid and licking his lips and gloating, one inevitably wonders whether the same tendency to enjoy pain in relation to love and sex formed a part of what Lewis called his own 'affliction'.

There are no clear and definite answers to the questions about Lewis' sexuality, and we cannot dispute his own words, or those of Mrs Moore. We have already seen how Walter Hooper, in his preface to Lewis' diaries, described the position. What happened during Lewis' slow development in his pre-Christian days is clouded in doubt. He asked his friend Greeves to cut out some personal references from his letters; what these contained we may never know.

We do know, however, that there was for Lewis a late flowering of happiness. When he was over sixty, he recalled his brief marriage. He wrote in *A Grief Observed* (using the pseudonym N. W. Clerk for himself and 'H' for his wife Joy):

> For those few years H. and I feasted on love; every mode of it – solemn and merry, romantic and realistic, sometimes as dramatic as a thunderstorm, sometimes as comfortable and unemphatic as putting on your soft slippers. No cranny of heart or body remained unsatisfied.

It is as if, a few years before he died, he was to have a foretaste of the 'healing of harms'.

**Lewis and science-fiction**

We might ask what made Lewis write his science-fiction trilogy and propel himself into space with a novel about Mars *(Out of the Silent Planet)* and Venus *(Perelandra* or *Voyage to Venus)* and *That Hideous Strength?* He implied, like Bunyan, that: 'I did it mine own self to gratify.' Lewis had been fascinated by science-fiction writing and the possibilities of time-travel, and he began to feel that these might represent a vehicle for expressing Christian views of man, and for injecting some disturbing and unacceptable teaching into a modern medium. He derived real pleasure from using science-fiction for his own purposes.

His idea was to combine the expression of Christian truth with myths of intergalactic travel. Thus he wrote about unfallen worlds, and the fall of man. No doubt some who have taken up a lurid-looking paperback edition of *Out of the Silent Planet,* expecting to find a space-travel story, have been surprised, like the young friend of Dorothy L. Sayers who exclaimed: 'Why, this is a story about Christianity. Maleldil is Christ, and the Eldila are the angels.'

The trilogy about space-travel was for Lewis another kind of testing of his strong belief that the imagination is a truth-bearing faculty. Begun in 1938, the trilogy ended in 1945 with *That Hideous Strength: A Modern Fairy-Tale for Grown-Ups.* The author wrote that this third book was about a triple conflict: 'Grace against Nature and Nature against Anti-Nature (modern industrialism, scientism and totalitarian politics).' Lewis created an organization called N.I.C.E. (the National Institute of Co-ordinated Experiments) for this book. The book, with echoes of the tower of Babel, devil worship, the battle between good and evil, and set in what appeared to be the kind of college politics he hated, was a remarkable achievement.

**Demolished in debate**

It would be wrong to see Lewis as enjoying uninterrupted success at Oxford; in one sense, that city was once again to deserve to be called the home of lost causes. There was a painful failure, perhaps related to the faults in his personality which we noted earlier.

Lewis had been trained in logic and philosophy during his years with Kirkpatrick in preparation for entry to Oxford. It was inevitable that these subjects formed a key part of his character armour, in which he trusted. His position as President of the Socratic Club at Oxford was no doubt in part due to his love of philosophy, and Lewis made a pugnacious use of his dialectical ability in defence of Christianity. It was therefore a shock for him, when he had a pitched battle in the Socratic Club with a woman who was both a committed Christian and a formidable philosopher, and he lost. The woman in question was Elizabeth Anscombe, later to be Professor of Philosophy at Cambridge.

Miss Anscombe had written a criticism of the third chapter of Lewis' book *Miracles,* attacking his view that naturalism, as opposed to supernaturalism, was self-refuting. She presented her paper as an attack at a meeting in Oxford in 1948. Lewis was shown up as a deficient thinker, as many thought him to be, in an area that he had chosen to write about. He was out-gunned as the President while arguing on familiar ground, in the presence of friends. One of Lewis' most brilliant pupils, the theatre critic Kenneth Tynan, had said that if any book could have converted him to the Christian faith *Miracles* would have done so.

After the encounter with Anscombe, Lewis told a future biographer, George Sayer, that 'his argument for the existence of God had been demolished'. It was little comfort for him to hear Hugo Dyson comment: 'Very well – now you have lost everything and come to the foot of the Cross.' Yet Dyson was trying to convey an important insight and message to Lewis.

Lewis was aware of the spiritual dangers of his work, and summed up the deeper issues touched off by the Anscombe encounter in a poem called 'The Apologist's Evening Prayer':

From all my lame defeats and oh! much more
From all the victories that I seemed to score;
From cleverness shot forth on Thy behalf
At which, while angels weep, the audience laugh;
From all my proofs of Thy divinity,
Thou, who wouldst give no sign, deliver me.

Thoughts are but coins. Let me not trust, instead
Of Thee, their thin-worn image of Thy head.
From all my thoughts, even from my thoughts of Thee,
O thou fair Silence, fall, and set me free.
Lord of the narrow gate and the needle's eye,
Take from me all my trumpery lest I die.

**Rebuilding: writing from the heart**

Oxford had witnessed an important failure. The blow to Lewis, who had such faith in his own logic and dialectic abilities, was a heavy one. Perhaps it was a necessary learning experience for someone who had paid so much heed to his head, and so little to his heart. It may have led him to use the philosopher's stone less often as a bludgeon. It would appear that the defeat in the small Socratic Club was far more hurtful than being twice passed over for a professor's chair (a Merton chair which Tolkien had long coveted for his friend Lewis, and also the Poetry chair).

As with any failure that brings good results, or any hurtful encounter that heals, the consequences were far-reaching. They seem to have included his decision to write more from the heart, and to return to the imaginative world, as he was to do in *The Chronicles of Narnia.*

Was this return to a different writing style a regression to childhood? There are those who say that in many important ways Lewis never grew up. His bullying and his boorishness, his refusal to see that meekness and gentleness are Christian virtues which might endear him to his fellow dons at Oxford, were some of his many blind spots. Yet these were certainly defects that he might have attended to and, by attending to them, he might have grown in grace, and achieved a desirable natural development. There was to be much suffering before his character and behaviour changed.

One statement reads like his own apology for a life-style that became, eventually, second nature to him. In *Theology* in March 1940 he wrote an article called 'Christianity and Culture', which Green and Hooper summarize thus:

> (1) The safest and shortest way towards salvation is devotion to the person of Christ. (a) Most men glorify God by doing to his glory things which, though not *per se* acts of glorification, become so by being offered to him. (3) Though culture in itself will save no man, it sometimes has a distinct part to play in bringing souls to Christ – is sometimes a road *into* Jerusalem, and sometimes *out.* (4) People such as himself, who are not fit for any other kind of work, are justified in making their living by teaching and writing.

He was to write much to help expound his faith and to describe the most painful and rewarding experiences of his life. He did not, of course, cease to be an intellectually gifted scholar. He seems in his later books to have written 'with head and heart together' as Bunyan said we should read. These years became a time of harvest, showing the benefits of his vast reading, his tenacious memory and his clarity of expression.

**Through the wardrobe: to Narnia**

Above all it was *The Chronicles of Narnia* that made Lewis' genius known to many who cared nothing for his cherished Christian beliefs. To some extent the figure of Aslan (the Turkish word for lion) was his way of saying something about Christ to a pagan, alienated post-Christian world. Lewis seems to have worked from pictures which would suddenly appear in his mind, such as a queen on a sledge, or a faun. Much of his best writing gains its special power from this strong visual imagination. He said that when he was writing about Narnia

> suddenly Aslan came bounding into it. I think I had been having a good many dreams about lions about that time. Apart from that, I don't know where the Lion came from or why He came. But once He was there He pulled the whole story together, and soon He pulled the other six Narnian stories in after Him.

Lewis had begun his first Narnia story some years before his bad experience at the Socratic Club in 1948, but it was only then that he returned to the book which emerged in 1949 as *The Lion, the Witch and the Wardrobe.* For millions of readers and viewers of the television adaptations, the extension of Lewis' work which became *The Chronicles of Narnia* may appear to dwarf the rest of the edifice of his achievement. But this is only what appears from a distance, and solely from certain perspectives.

When he began to read chapters to the Inklings, Tolkien was frankly mocking: 'It really won't do you know! I mean to say: "Nymphs and their Ways, The Love-Life of a Faun". Doesn't he know what he's talking about?' Hugo Dyson had been saying how fed up he was with yet another elf in Tolkien's stories. But Lewis went on, finding in Roger Lancelyn Green a friendly critic and reader. Green pointed out the echoes from other children's books: Lewis must have read a story by E. Nesbit which came out when he was ten, with its magic world and the station called *Bigwardrobeinspareroom.* Lewis only remembered it when prompted to do so by Green.

The real wardrobe where Lewis first played was in the Little End Room in the family home in Belfast. There, he and Warnie would retreat from the adults arguing in the house, to play and give free rein to their imagination. He returns to a more complicated form of play when the children in *The Lion, the Witch and the Wardrobe* push their way through the fur coats and enter the magical world of Narnia, where it is always winter and never Christmas in that first story. In his creative work Lewis used many devices, symbols and pictures that he recalled from his study of myths and legends, as well as the children's books he had read.

Twenty-five years after completing them, the Narnia books were the bestsellers of the Penguin Puffin paperback series. They still sell and sell, and generations of parents pass on their childhood secrets about Narnia to their own children. It is hard to think why Tolkien had profound reservations – was it envy? There were many other criticisms: the cruelty Lewis shows (which is surely present in all fairy stories) was disliked by some. Others disliked the Christianity they sniffed out in Narnia.

David Holbrook, in his book *The Skeleton in the Wardrobe,* mounts an attack, based on his own Freudian beliefs, upon Lewis. To reply to his attacks would take many pages. Holbrook is a literary critic who has written some eighteen books on education and criticism from a psychoanalytic viewpoint. I think that psychologists and psychiatrists have moved away from Freud and the assumptions so often taken for granted by Freudians.

More importantly, Holbrook attacks Lewis as much for his Christian faith as because he dislikes Lewis' fantasies. In my view, to reduce much of Lewis to 'paranoid-schizoid fantasy' does little to help us to value properly the achievement of the Narnia books. Of course there are pictures of good and evil, love and hate. The presence of these contrasts, and the conflict between them, cannot be wholly explained in terms of the loss of his mother and its consequences. Lewis, says Holbrook, 'clings closely to the insistence that the Christian myth is the only one that is true'. So much we may agree with; and we may add that Lewis had a profound knowledge of other myths also.

**Deeper magic from the dawn of time**

Lewis said in 1948: 'People won't write the books I want, so I have to do it for myself: no rot about "self-expression".' And yet Narnia is not about the inside of a magical wardrobe, it is a magical story about the things that had, for so many years, lived inside the mind of C. S. Lewis. In the strange interior world in which he grew up, the pull of Northern magic featured large. The 'stab of joy' had led to, and was in some way consummated in, his discovery of Wagner's version of the *Ring of the Niebelung.* He had found in many other legends, like the Greek ones, the material on which his mind had fed. His Christian beliefs were the source of his faith and trust in the 'deeper magic' which appears in Narnia when Aslan, the Christ-figure, operates against the machinations of evil magic.

But we must not venture too far along this road of explanation, for Lewis himself said:

> Some people seem to think that I began by asking myself how I could say something about Christianity to children; then fixed on the fairy tale as an instrument; then collected information about child psychology and decided what age-group I'd write for; then drew up a list of basic Christian truths and hammered out 'allegories' to embody them. This is all pure moonshine. I couldn't write in that way at all. Everything began with image....

So much for those who misinterpret Lewis when he writes fairy stories, myths or romances. One cannot convey – certainly not to children – what one does not have. They see through the humbug better than adults. It seems that Lewis conveys some sense of awe and wonder, perhaps even of the holy, 'the numinous', of which he writes elsewhere. This sense of the magical was so strong in him for so long that he could make children share it.

The place of the lion had been created in his life by the advent, indeed the invasion, of God's grace. While Francis Thompson could describe the Hound of Heaven and his pursuit of him in the person of Christ, Lewis uses the figure of 'The Great Angler' for God, saying he did not know that the hook was in his mouth, and that he was soon to be caught in the net, even while he spoke grandly of seeking God.

Long before Narnia was conceived, Lewis had written in *The Problem of Pain* an unusual chapter on animal pain, which ends with a meditation on lions and lionhood:

> I think the lion, when he has ceased to be dangerous, will still be awful; indeed, that we shall then first see that of which the present fangs and claws are a clumsy, and satanically perverted, imitation. There will still be something like the shaking of a golden mane: and often the good Duke will say, 'Let him roar again.'

Whatever else may be said about Lewis as a writer of children's stories, his seven Narnia books have placed him among the immortals. That is due not to the books' sales, but to their enduring quality; and that surely relates in turn to the honesty with which Lewis spoke his mind in them – using both his intellect and his imagination.

**New beginnings**

His literary success with the Narnia books may well have helped Lewis financially, and the money was needed to pay for Mrs Moore's care in an Oxford nursing home. Having shown some signs of senile decay, the last two or three years were to show a rapid worsening, until she died in 1951. There was, for Lewis, great relief.

His brother Warnie had suffered from further alcoholic episodes at this time and incurred more costs until he was admitted to the Warneford hospital. Warnie recovered, as he always did, but the band of brothers called the Inklings began to peter out and die.

Lewis' Oxford career was also coming to an end, with something of a bang, in the form of his volume in the *Oxford History of English Literature* (*OHEL,* as he always called it). And Cambridge beckoned, with a newly created chair of English which he took up in 1954. Lewis wrote of it:

> I'm on the eve of a great adventure ... I'm already half frightened of what I have done; but twenty-nine years of pupils' essays is enough, bless 'em ... I shall be at Oxford in the Vac. and on weekends in the term. My address will be Magdalen*e*, so I remain under the same patroness ... I have exchanged the impenitent for the penitent Magdalen.

Lewis found Cambridge to be like the Oxford of his youth, and he enjoyed it hugely, loving the country-town atmosphere of Cambridge and the fact that no car-maker had polluted it. It was a kind of re-entry to the joys of scholarship without the burdens of tutorial or administrative chores. He was fifty-six when he gave his inaugural lecture, a remarkable time for a new beginning in anyone's life.

His entrance on the Cambridge stage is eclipsed in the story of his life by the appearance at this time of a small American woman, Mrs Joy Gresham, later known as Joy Davidman, whom he was to marry in 1956.

## Marriage: gain and loss

W. H. Lewis, the brother who had known and shared Jack's life under the despotism of Mrs Moore ('an autocracy that developed into a stifling tyranny, as I experienced myself during the years of my inclusion within this incomprehensible menage') may be the person best able to help us to a clear and unsentimental view of Lewis' marriage. He writes:

> Meanwhile he had met the woman who was to bring him so much happiness in love and marriage. Joy Davidman was American by birth and Jewish by race. She and her husband, William Lindsay Gresham, were avid admirers of Jack's work and became Christians partly under his influence. She met Jack for the first time in 1953 ... By 1955 she was on close terms with Jack.
>
> For Jack the attraction was at first undoubtedly intellectual. Joy was the only woman whom he had met (although as his letters show, he had known with great affection many able women) who had a brain which matched his own in suppleness, in width of interest, in analytical grasp, and above all in humour and sense of fun ... A woman of great charity, she had an unbounded contempt for the sentimental.

## Joy's early life

Joy Davidman had been precociously able as a child in New York; her parents were Jews from Eastern Europe who settled in the Bronx. They were both teachers, were comfortably off and were able to take holidays all over America, even in the Depression. Born in 1915, Joy had a brother four years younger with whom she got on well. Her father had turned away from Judaism and become a socialist.

He brought home IQ tests from school and was disappointed when her brother Howard's result was 147, a very high figure; and delighted that Joy's IQ was above that measurable on the scale. By eight, Joy had read H. G. Wells and declared herself an atheist who intended to be a writer. Howard, having been told by his father he would come to nothing, became a doctor and later a psychiatrist.

After Hunter College, Joy became a communist and very publicly supported a cause which in the late 1930s was a dangerous activity. She went to Hollywood as a trainee scriptwriter, but failed to please M-G-M with her scripts; she disliked the place and left. However, she did become a writer, her stories and poems were published, and she joined the staff of the communist journal *New Masses.* At a party function she met a Spanish Civil War veteran, Bill Gresham, whom she married in 1942. She claimed that what Spain had done to make her husband lose his communist enthusiasm, childbirth did for her.

Bill was six years older, and made a living by singing folk music. Alcohol and tuberculosis had contributed to ending his first marriage, and a serious suicide attempt led to years of Freudian analysis. Within two years Joy had two sons and moved to a house twenty miles north of New York City in an attempt to get her husband away from a woman with whom he was having an affair. But Bill had further drinking problems and a serious nervous breakdown.

## She meets C. S. Lewis

While her husband was in hospital, Joy became desperate, and had a remarkable religious conversion: she found herself suddenly praying to God although she had not previously believed: 'I was the world's most surprised atheist ... God came in and I changed. I have been turning into a different person since that half minute.' At first Joy turned to the Jewish faith that her father had rejected. But she was dissatisfied, and began to read Francis Thompson, whose poem 'The Hound of Heaven' she suddenly understood as a parable of her own life. Then she read C. S. Lewis, and the New Testament. By 1948 she was attending church and became what she had dreaded becoming – a Jewish apostate who embraced the Christian faith.

When she wrote about her new faith in the *New York Post,* her brother Howard broke his connection with her entirely, and never saw her again. Her parents too were sad at what they took to be mental disturbance. Her foes were those of her own household, and soon her husband was also an enemy. Bill drank more, and his infidelities became a string of affairs and one night stands.

Having met Chad Walsh, a minister who had written of *C. S. Lewis, Apostle to the Skeptics,* Joy, with great trepidation, wrote to Lewis in 1950. Letters were exchanged, and a debate began between Joy Davidman and Lewis. She espoused his views on marriage and divorce and tried to mend her marriage. Bill stopped drinking but still seemed far from well and his infidelities continued. In 1952 she decided to cross the Atlantic to see Lewis.

On the ship to Liverpool Joy completed her book on the Ten Commandments, *Smoke on the Mountain.* She found a flat in Belsize Park, London, and eventually visited The Kilns in Oxford, where Warnie and Jack enjoyed having the two small boys. The boys were delighted to be given the typescript of the Narnia story *The Horse and His Boy* to read. Later, the book was dedicated to them. In 1953 Joy heard that the divorce for which Bill had filed (on grounds of desertion and incompatibility) had come through, and that he had married her cousin Renee, as expected.

In 1954 Joy's parents visited her in London, and Lewis had tea with them in the Piccadilly hotel, and later invited them to Magdalen for lunch. A year later Joy and her two sons moved to Oxford. The house in Headington had been found by Lewis, and he paid the rent. Soon they were seeing each other daily, and by 1955 there was no doubt that the love that Joy had long felt for Lewis was being returned. Joy wrote to a friend that 'the most wonderful ecstasy came from just holding hands and walking on the heather'. How precisely one thing led to another is a puzzle, but Lewis felt he had to abide by the Church's ruling against marrying a divorced woman.

**Shared joys, shared pain**

Early in 1956 the Home Office refused to renew Joy's permit to stay in England. Lewis could not face losing her or the two boys, David and Douglas Gresham, whom he cared for deeply, and he did not want them to go back to Bill's custody.

On 23 April 1956 Lewis and Joy married in the registry office at Oxford; Lewis pretended that it was a pure formality, to keep Joy in England. Later, he failed to persuade the Bishop of Oxford to give permission for their marriage in the Church of England. The reason for the refusal was that Joy had been divorced. Then, suddenly, there was a blow that no one expected. After Joy fell and broke her leg there was an emergency admission to hospital. Pains put down to fibrositis in June were abruptly found to be due to bone cancer resulting from a malignant breast tumour.

Everything was now changed, and Lewis announced his marriage in *The Times*. At forty-two years of age, Joy was in hospital dying of cancer. To make things easier, the breast lump was removed. Her ovaries were removed too, and the femur was operated on. Lewis prayed that he might take on her bone pain, and later he felt that his osteoporosis was somehow linked to this prayer. He thought of it as a sort of 'substitution' such as his friend Charles Williams loved to write about. Lewis still wanted his marriage to be recognized by the Church, but the Bishop refused to bless it.

Lewis turned to the Rev. Peter W. Bide, who agreed to pray for recovery by laying hands on Joy, and to perform a bedside marriage ceremony. In due course radiotherapy was given for the cancer. Joy began to improve, and Lewis wrote to a friend: 'My wife's condition has improved, if not miraculously (but who knows?) at any rate wonderfully.' In January 1958 the doctors told them that Joy's cancer had been arrested and that the bones now seemed normal. Until October 1959 she was well. Then they learned that the bone cancer had reappeared. Yet they were able to enjoy holidays in Greece, as they had done earlier in Wales.

In May 1960 Joy's right breast was removed, and in July 1960 she died, after much pain. The joy that they had shared was part of the deeper healing process that occurred in the sexual life of C. S. Lewis. And the richness of their life together was reflected in his writings, which owed much to this period of great happiness in marriage. There was also a sense of fulfilment in having two young sons with him in The Kilns.

**Love and C. S. Lewis**

It was during the years with Joy – when, as he put it, they feasted on their love together – that Lewis prepared the radio talks that led to his book *The Four Loves*. In some ways this book is a summing up of the loves that had been important in his life.

In part the book looks back to the strong bonds of affection with his brother and with the key figures in the Inklings whose friendship Lewis had enjoyed for so many years. Perhaps in so doing, the book highlights his failings. He says: 'I can trace the pre-history of friendship only in the male line.' Few feminists, and nowadays not many men, would agree with that. Lewis was a misogynist, said his friends. He loved not only male company but men's coarse humour; and he would not tell his favourite bawdy stories if women were present.

At worst, this is the Lewis of the 'Beer and Beowulf' nights at College. His rough behaviour may have been modified after his conversion, but it was perhaps never fully abandoned. His friend Roger Lancelyn Green, in saying Lewis was the most converted man he had met, may have been thinking of other, more important, aspects of Lewis' life. There were weaker brethren who were upset by his heavy cigarette smoking (sixty a day) and his pipe, and the beer and other drinking. One such was Dr Bob Jones Jr., who visited Lewis at Oxford from Bob Jones College in the USA. Speaking for the 'Bible Belt' folk who had taken Lewis to their heart, he said: 'That man smokes a pipe, and that man drinks liquor – but I *do* believe he is a Christian!'

Lewis may have been insensitive to the scruples of some, but he was also exceptionally conscientious in counselling those who wrote to him for advice and help, and this was another side of his personality. His many letters to those in need, whether financial, spiritual or physical, bear clear witness to the kind and caring side of his nature.

It may now seem incredible to us that in the United States the Episcopal Radio TV Foundation decided to ban Lewis' *Four Talks on Love,* recorded at their request, because the talks were so frank as to be, in their view, pornographic. He was told: 'The trouble, Professor Lewis, is that you have several times brought sex into your talks on Eros.' He turned the talks into the book which appeared in 1960 and was called, by Martin d'Arcy, a minor classic. Some may still find parts of it objectionable.

*The Four Loves* deals first with need-love and gift-love. After describing affection and friendship Lewis writes about Eros and charity. Under Eros, there is a subheading dealing with what used to be called Venus – i.e., genital expressions of love. Lewis explains that God can transform all types of natural love into a part of divine love. Any love, however, can turn into a daemon if it is worshipped and treated as a god, he states elsewhere.

One recalls the description of sexuality in another of his books, *The Great Divorce.* A man's ghost carries a little red lizard on his shoulder, and this animal constantly whispers in his ear and dominates him. When he finally allows it to be killed, the lizard does not in fact die, but is transformed into a great stallion, silvery white with a mane of gold, on which the man rides away. Thus a mean and brutal lust is transformed into a true love that is enjoyed as the man rides on and controls his passion.

Charity is the last of the four loves. With charity, God's grace is at work making his gift-love real, first as we experience it ourselves and then as we offer it to others. Need-love, through grace, becomes a 'full, childlike and delighted acceptance of our Need, a joy in total dependence'. The third aspect of charity, which Lewis calls a supernatural Appreciative Love, turns us 'from the rivulets to the Fountain, from the creatures He has made lovable to Love Himself ... because we shall find them all in Him'.

He wrote of love with his customary skill and intelligence; but perhaps also with the knowledge that he was going to lose the love – his wife Joy – which had mattered most to him.

**Who then devised the torment? – Love**

We may recall that his great friend, Tolkien, said of Lewis' book on prayer that it was not about prayer, but about Jack praying, and that Jack's books were always about himself. The comment reflects an interesting contrast in style and personalities. Tolkien creates a world that is detached and dense, quite separate from his feelings and his personal life. Lewis, even when he rewrites a myth like that of Cupid and Psyche in *Till We Have Faces,* could well be drawing a portrait of himself in the narrator Orual.

Many consider *A Grief Observed* – a short book of only sixty pages that Lewis wrote to describe his reactions to Joy's death – his best. In his account of his own grief Lewis lays bare his heart, and his feelings about God. It is here that he expresses his fear that God may, after all, be a 'cosmic sadist'. This remark has led Richard Harries, a later and more sympathetic Bishop of Oxford, to comment that there may have been some inherent weakness in Lewis' belief in God. I am reminded of T. S. Eliot. The latter's poems used to be condemned by Lewis in the Inklings, and, on one occasion, Lewis' closing comment was, 'It's all bilge, of course.' Yet Lewis shared a good deal with Eliot, and some lines in the *Four Quartets* especially find echoes in Lewis.

Perhaps Lewis disliked what he saw as Eliot's New England Puritanism. Eliot had a more formal life-style – Virginia Woolf described him as wearing four-piece suits – and this was very different from Lewis. Yet they both shared a deep seriousness, which is especially apparent in their attitude to what might be called the goodness and severity of God. While the language of Lewis and Eliot is of course more modern than Bunyan's, for them, as for Bunyan, grace included the realities of heaven and hell.

Lewis' book on heaven and hell, *The Great Divorce,* describes the awful pain and grief that can be involved in personal relationships. In this book, his master, George MacDonald, guides him around the borderlands of heaven and explains to Lewis the eternal conflict between good and evil, and how everyone has to make choices, since 'you cannot take a little of Hell in your pocket with you, to Heaven'.

Perhaps Lewis would have liked to be a modern John Milton, expounding, as only a great poet can, the Christian vision to the modern reader. But then how many would have read such verse? Although, strictly speaking, he was a relative failure as a poet, Lewis' poetic gifts illuminate all he writes, and millions who might never have read a long poem have enjoyed his children's stories, his fantasies and his other, more plainly Christian writings, into which he channelled his great gifts.

## The weight of glory

I know of no other place where Lewis so well expressed the hope that grace might perfect the work that God begins in the human heart, as in one of the very few sermons that he gave, 'The Weight of Glory':

> The promises of Scripture may very roughly be reduced to five heads. It is promised, firstly, that we shall be with Christ; secondly, that we shall be like Him; thirdly, with an enormous wealth of imagery, that we shall have 'glory'; fourthly, that we shall, in some sense, be fed and feasted or entertained; and finally, that we shall have some sort of official position in the universe – ruling cities, judging angels, being pillars of God's temple ...
>
> ... Apparently, then, our lifelong nostalgia, our longing to be reunited with something in the universe from which we now feel cut off, to be on the inside of some door which we have always seen from the outside, is no mere neurotic fancy, but the truest index of our real situation. And to be at last summoned inside would be both glory and honour beyond all our merits and also the healing of that old ache ... At present we are on the outside of the world, the wrong side of the door .
>
> ... But all the leaves of the New Testament are rustling with the rumour that it will not always be so. Some day, God willing, we shall get in. When human souls have become as perfect in voluntary obedience as the inanimate creation is in its lifeless obedience, then we will put on its glory, or rather the greater glory of which nature is only the first sketch . . .
>
> Then the new earth and sky, the same yet not the same as these, will rise in us as we have risen in Christ. And once again, after who knows what aeons of silence and the dark, the birds will sing out and the waters flow, and lights and shadows move across the hills and the faces of our friends laugh upon us with amazed recognition.
>
> Guesses, of course, only guesses. If they are not true, something better will be. For we know that we shall be made like Him, for we shall see Him as He is.

Erik Routley, who sat in the crowded church in Oxford when this sermon was first delivered, has left his account:

> Here ... you felt ten times more so when listening, was a man who had been laid hold of by Christ and who enjoyed it ... the way he used words as precision tools, the effortless rhythm of

> the sentences, the scholarship made friendly, the sternness made beautiful ... That's poetry in the service of the Gospel.

**Last years: illnesses**

The last three years of Lewis' life were plagued by illness. His weak heart – and he had at least one heart attack – often made him breathless. With typical self-mockery he said that he gasped 'like a new-caught fish which no one has the kindness to knock on the head'. His old friend Dr Havard seems to have made something of a mess of the prostate problems which developed – at least that was the opinion of a later Cambridge doctor, when the Heath Robinson-like contraption for draining the bladder was found. Lewis laughed at his occasional accident because of this crude apparatus. It is likely that periodic mental confusion during his last years was due to a mixture of kidney trouble and heart failure, rather like Martin Luther's illness.

Lewis continued to commute between Oxford and Cambridge, and to write and read. His friendship with Tolkien had long cooled, which Lewis regretted, saying in a sad note to 'dear Tollers' that 'The public – little dreaming how much you dislike my work, bless you! – regard us as a sort of firm and would only laugh at what would seem to them mutual back-scratching.' Despite such estrangements, there were many close friends who supported and cared for him. New ones, like Walter Hooper, who came over from the University of Kentucky, were happy to serve Lewis and to guard and cherish his legacies with a fierce loyalty.

Lewis died on Friday 22 November 1963, a date which many will recall as the day that President John F. Kennedy was assassinated. The vast publicity surrounding Jack Kennedy may have eclipsed the news of Jack Lewis' death. Lewis had long since lost the fear of death that had dogged him for so long: he said, in many different ways, how he longed to reach the land towards which he was headed. One colleague, who visited him a short time before he died, said that never was a man better prepared. A poem written by Lewis in 1949, entitled simply 'Epitaph', is quoted by his close and oldest surviving friend, Owen Barfield:

> Here lies the whole world after one
> Peculiar mode; a buried sun,

Stars and immensities of sky
And cities here discarded lie.
The prince who owned them, having gone,
Left them as things not needed on
His journey; yet with hope that he,
Purged by aeonian poverty
In lenten lands, hereafter can
Resume the robes he wore as man.

Barfield wrote of this poem recently: 'I am in the habit of thinking of those lines as Lewis's own epitaph.'

**Secret strengths**

Where did the secret of C. S. Lewis' strength lie, and why do his writings still have such power and provide so much succour today? Three elements stand out. First, the qualities of mind with which he was endowed – gifts of God's common grace. Second, the fact that, in his young adult life, until his conversion, he knew for himself the difficulties of believing in God and Christ. Third, and above all, he took the faith he found in his thirties very seriously and began a life of devotion and private prayer which sustained him till his death.

His mind was as strong in imaginative power as it was in reasoning ability. We may recall how he said that 'living almost entirely in my imagination' was a feature of his childhood; he constructed the animal world of Boxen at that time, before his mother's death. His profound wish to be a poet was partly because of the free rein poetry would give to his imagination, coupled with the discipline that it would impose.

His education, and the years with Kirkpatrick in particular, allowed his reasoning powers to become exceptionally strong. At Oxford his switch to English from philosophy was in some ways accidental, but he applied himself to his new field of literature with splendid results. What he had learned by careful study enabled him to write, lecture and debate with a special clarity and force. He was aware of the clash between reason and imagination, and his wish was to reconcile them:

Oh who will reconcile in me both maid and mother,
Who make in me a concord of the depth and height?

Who make imagination's dim exploring touch
Ever report the same as intellectual sight?
Then could I truly say, and not deceive,
Then wholly say, that I BELIEVE

Strength and speed were both highly developed features of Lewis' intelligence, and he brought them to the service of Christ's gospel. In a rejoinder to Professor Norman Pittenger he said, 'most of my books are evangelistic'.

His second source of strength, his close acquaintance with the unbeliever, was gained in the trenches in France in the First World War, and during his revolt against the false Puritanism of Ulster. Among the young surviving soldiers who returned to Oxford after that War, he shared, and lived in, the atmosphere of despair and irreligion. He read all the writers who, in different ways, gave reasons for having nothing to do with God, Church or Gospel. They are the writers he describes so well in *The Pilgrim's Regress.*

When he came to believe in God, and then in Christ, he wanted to point others to the way that he had found. Had he not had such a close contact with those whom he was trying to reach, his power to communicate successfully with them would have been much less.

**Lewis' life of prayer**

The third source of Lewis' strength was prayer. He wrote a book on prayer in the last year of his life, having set it aside nine years earlier as a book he could not finish. He was shy of speaking of the role of prayer in his life. His friends have written about its importance for him. Lewis set aside a specific time; an hour or an hour and a half daily was spent in prayer. His worn Prayer Book, complete with jottings of his meditations on grace on the endpapers, shows how he valued the College prayers in the morning and his diligent Sunday attendances at the parish church.

Private prayer was even more important to him – not so much at night (he advised strongly against leaving such an important thing till bedtime), but in the morning or in the early evening. In a quiet, slow-moving train, as on his journeys from Oxford to Cambridge, Lewis would pray. He believed in intercession and petition in prayer.

Of course he experienced times of dryness, 'like posting letters to a non-existent address', and he learned that suffering strengthened the power of prayer. Those who think of him mainly as a dry-as-dust intellectual may learn from his stress on prayer. He described some aspects of it thus:

> Prayer in the sense of asking for things is a small part of it; confession and penitence are its threshold, adoration its sanctuary, the presence and vision of God its bread and wine. In it God shows Himself to us. That He answers prayer is a corollary – not necessarily the most important one – from the revelation. What He does is learned from what He is.

Lewis never learned to drive a car, and Clifford Morris was his regular driver. Mr Morris was a devout Christian, accustomed to extempore prayer in groups. Lewis and he would often, in his later years, spend considerable time together in prayer. In some ways the sense of duty, the moral sense, was very well developed in Lewis: by applying it to the duties of his devotional life he found (and shared) a deep source of spiritual power.

### The pointing finger

Lewis shrank from the cult of admirers that began to form around him and his writings. What Tolkien had said about his own reaction to being idolized, Lewis felt even more strongly. He had said in 1934 how much he disliked 'the personal heresy' in criticism, that is, the idea that there must be an intimate connection between the author's life and the work he produces. The author, he wrote, 'is not a man who asks me to look at him. He is a man who says "look at that" and points; the more I follow the pointing of his finger the less I can possibly see of him.' Thus the author's private and personal experience is transformed into one that is 'public, common, impersonal, objective'.

Later he said of his autobiography: 'The story is, I fear, suffocatingly subjective; the kind of thing I have never written before and shall probably never write again.' Did he feel that he had fallen from grace in writing about himself, or was he saying that, within limits, it was proper for an author to consider his own inner life as well as external things?

My view is that his mind and his life gave a special form and colour to how he pointed to the things that mattered most to him. But the truth was out there: the myth had become fact, the Word had become flesh, eternity had been encapsulated in time; and heaven and hell had been revealed by the coming, the teaching, and the life, death and resurrection of Christ.

In the most important of senses, Lewis chose to make his finger point towards Christ. In this way his religious function was to be like that of John the Baptist, who said 'Look! The Lamb of God who takes away the sin of the world.' Lewis chose the figure of the Lion, and used him convincingly. Whether it is the Lamb slain before the foundation of the world or the Lion of the tribe of Judah that is used as a symbol, it is salvation-history that we are asked to consider. And just as the book of Revelation writes of the wrath of the Lamb, so Lewis has upset some readers by his descriptions of *The Last Battle* and his views on the ultimate reality.

When I relate the lost happiness of Lewis' childhood to his interest in Milton's great epic, *Paradise Lost,* this should not be interpreted as detracting in any way from the objective value of the beliefs that Lewis came to hold.

He was able to write so convincingly of God, Christ, heaven and hell because he had himself followed the directives of others in his search for the reality of grace. And he used all his powers – reason, imagination, humour and warm personal concern – to convey the message to others and to say 'Look!' in a way that would lead millions to consider the Christian message in a new and fresh way.

**'Why this waste?'**

C. S. Lewis gave a great deal of his time and energy to writing on Christian themes and to writing letters to those who sought his counsel. No doubt some would consider that all this was a waste, and that he should also have kept his fortune instead of giving so much of his earnings to the needy. He might have gained greater fame as a scholar, collected more academic distinctions, and accepted political awards (such as the CBE which he was offered).

He refused the awards of a Prime Minister in order that he should not be identified with any political stance, since he feared that this might prejudice readers whom he wanted to reach. He detested the idea of being perceived as belonging to any 'Inner Ring': the clubbable Lewis cultivated solitude rather than paying the price for joining an 'in' group.

So devoted was Lewis to his work that he never read a newspaper, listened to the radio or watched television. He said that if anything important happened someone was sure to talk about it. For most of his adult life it was part of his strategy to redeem the time. He used it all to good purpose, and would care little if we called him a workaholic. He loved writing: his studies became a labour of love for Lewis; the motive for all the hard work became the love of Christ.

Lewis, in whimsical fashion, regarded himself at both Magdalen College, Oxford, and Magdalene College, Cambridge, as under the patronage of Mary Magdalene. It was of her devoted offering to Christ, it will be recalled, that the question was asked 'Why this waste?'

For Mary is traditionally identified, with little evidence, with the woman recorded in all four Gospels as having anointed the feet of Christ with expensive perfume. The version of Luke the physician (Luke 7:36-50) is perhaps the most helpful. The woman of the city, who was a sinner, gets into the house of Simon the Pharisee and, with her alabaster flask of ointment, anoints the feet of Christ. Lewis brought his own precious flask of ointment – his vast learning, of which he was indeed proud. He used this learning, like his patroness Mary, for Christ. It might surely be said of Lewis that, like her, 'his sins which were many were forgiven, for he loved much'. Many a Simon, many Pharisees and disciples in Oxford, said that it was a waste, but it seems clear to me that Lewis gave his learning to Christ's service out of love, because so much had been forgiven him. It was his experience of grace, in other words, that made him do it.

J. R. R. Tolkien, though less close to Lewis in his last ten years, spoke for many friends when he wrote: 'we owed each a great debt to the other, and that tie, with the deep affection that it begot, remained. He was a great man of whom the cold-blooded official obituaries have only scraped the surface.'

The impressive edifice that Lewis has left us, and that is still being explored by many readers and writers, has many separate, disparate rooms. It may, like the nursery-rhyme house that Jack built, be lopsided and contain some unusual ideas. Yet, in his best work as a Christian writer, Lewis sought to share and convey his understanding of the one and only true myth: the Word made flesh. His Christian writing has about it the quality of an offering of thanks to God for the grace he has shown in Christ. As in the Narnia books, his wish is to share his own hope in the Word made flesh. He seeks to increase our capacity to pursue our own way, 'further up and further in', into that world, that universe, of grace.

*Further Reading*

Much of C. S. Lewis' output is still readily available in paperback from Collins Fount. His autobiography is *Surprised by Joy: The Shape of My Early Life* (London: Collins Fount, 1977).

*Biographies*

A. N. Wilson, *C. S. Lewis: A Biography* (London: Collins, 1990); George Sayer, *Jack: C. S. Lewis and His Times* (London: Macmillan, 1988); Roger Lancelyn Green and Walter Hooper, *C. S. Lewis: A Biography* (London: Collins, 1974); William Griffin, *C. S. Lewis: The Authentic Voice* (Tring: Lion, 1988).

*Letters and Diaries*

Walter Hooper (ed.), *All My Road Before Me: The Diary of C. S. Lewis 1922–27* (London: HarperCollins, 1991); Clyde Kilby and M. L. Mead (ed.), *Brothers and Friends: Diaries of Major W. H. Lewis* (New York: Ballantine Books, 1982); W. H. Lewis (ed.), *Letters of C. S. Lewis* (London: Geoffrey Bles, 1966); Walter Hooper (ed.), *They Stand Together: The Letters of C. S. Lewis to Arthur Greeves (1914–1963)* (London: Collins, 1979); C. S. Lewis, *Letters to an American Lady,* ed. Clyde S. Kilby (London: Hodder & Stoughton, 1967).

*Other books*

James T. Como (ed.), *C. S. Lewis at the Breakfast Table and Other Reminiscences* (London: Collins, 1980); Brian Sibley, *Shadowlands: The Story of C. S. Lewis and Joy Davidman* (London: Hodder &

Stoughton, 1985); P. J. Schakel and C. A. Huttar (ed.), *Word and Story in C. S. Lewis* (Columbia, MS: University of Missouri Press, 1991); Clyde S. Kilby, *The Christian World of C. S. Lewis* (Grand Rapids, MI: Win B. Eerdmans, 1965); David Holbrook, *The Skeleton in the Wardrobe: C. S. Lewis's Fantasies: A Phenomenological Study* (Cranbury, NJ/London: Associated University Presses, 1991); Lyle W. Dorsett, *And God Came In: The Extraordinary Story of Joy Davidman* (New York: Macmillan, 1983); Humphrey Carpenter, *The Inklings* (London: George Allen & Unwin, 1978); Chad Walsh, *The Literary Legacy of C. S. Lewis* (London: Sheldon Press, 1979); Gareth Knight, *The Magical World of the Inklings* (London: Element Books, 1990); Michael H. Macdonald and Andrew A. Tadie (ed.), *G. K. Chesterton and C. S. Lewis: The Riddle of Joy* (Grand Rapids, MI: Wm B. Eerdmans; London: Collins, 1989).

# 10

## Stresses of Success?: J. B. Phillips (1906–1982)

> If you can cope with Triumph and Disaster
> And treat those two Impostors just the same
> ... you'll be a man, my son.
>
> Rudyard Kipling

> The translator is a traitor.
>
> Italian proverb

J. B. Phillips might have lived and died a publicly successful parson and parish priest, except for the fact that he had a special genius for translating and communicating. In his autobiography *The Price of Success* he gives a clear record of what it was like to suffer from recurrent depression. The study of his personality, his first breakdown very early in his career, and his subsequent suffering, may help us to understand the nature of anxiety and depression.

It was not only his early failures, but also his amazing achievements which throw light upon his personality and his illness. His success as a translator of the New Testament, and his writings about it, led to ten million of his books being sold. His *Letters to Young Churches* alone had sold over a million copies ten years after it was published.

His translation was eventually overtaken by the Good News Bible, and later by others such as the Living Bible and the New International Bible. When sales of his own translation began to fall, after the huge initial success, Phillips felt his work was no longer publicised as it should have been. It may have been part of his feeling of rejection at times, but the roots of his sense of failure, felt even at his most conspicuously successful times, went deeper than anything to do with new versions.

**Early influences**

Phillips attributes many of his problems to his father, who had come to London from Plymouth at the age of fourteen. His father, having lost his home life when his own father (a Plymouth police officer of fairly high rank) died, worked in the Post Office while teaching himself accountancy and living in poverty in a bed-sit. Phillips' father joined the Civil Service and worked his way up the ranks of the ministries of health and labour.

The picture he paints of his father is of an extremely meticulous, ambitious and hard-driven obsessional man. His main concerns were living within his means, dread of a bank overdraft and a recurring theme of 'We can't afford it'. Their poverty meant that there was no money for sweets, except the large jar bought in the Civil Service stores, from which a few sweets were doled out to Jack and his brother and sister from time to time.

With promotion they were able to move from Barnes to East Sheen, not far away in London's suburbs, where a maid was acquired and life became less poverty-stricken. Phillips recalls the relief of having a maid to help his mother who was already ill with cancer. His mother is recalled as remarkable in many respects, such as getting a job at the beginning of the century, when women who went out to work, as she did in the Post Office, were a rarity. More important for her children's development is that she is described by Phillips as 'not being the motherly type at all ... and rarely showed any warm affection or indeed emotion of any kind'. Though Phillips describes his childhood as happy and his world at that time as relatively peaceful and secure, it is evident that seeds were being sown which produced fruit of lasting bitterness for him.

His parents were genuinely loving to each other, but the picture that emerges from Phillips' account is of poor parenting, dominated by his rigid and anxious father, whose obsessional personality traits he inherited in full measure. In addition, he must have learned the value of being a perfectionist while living in such a home.

**Education**

His older sister Dorothy (who became a missionary in India) and his younger brother Ken (who was to become a missionary in China, and later a rural dean in Woking, where he died of multiple sclerosis) do not seem to have suffered in the way Phillips did. His father was very keen on the best education for his children, and they all went to university in spite of their relative and by then genteel poverty.

After dameschools Phillips was sent to a bad preparatory school which he recalls with disgust. 'It was run by a peculiarly nasty little Welshman who ... was not only ignorant but a sadist. He is the only man I have ever met who positively drooled over causing pain to others.' He was happy to escape to Emmanuel School in Wandsworth as a day pupil: he was bright but not exceptional. The fact that the air raids of the First World War were regularly interrupting London school life did not help. Many of the best teachers were away at the War.

From school he went to Emmanuel College, Cambridge: he failed to get a scholarship, and relied on his father's support. The first year caused him much financial misery and embarrassment. He only obtained a third class honours in Classics, and read for the English Tripos, with F. R. Leavis as his helpful tutor. His last year at Cambridge was happier. After university he taught at Sherborne preparatory school for a year before deciding to train for the Christian ministry at Ridley Hall, the most evangelical college he knew.

Before we resume his story we must return to his religious development. No one would have guessed from anything that had happened hitherto that J. B. Phillips would be world famous as a translator of the New Testament into modern English. It may well seem, on later examination, that the limits – perhaps we could even call it a strait jacket – imposed on his emotional development may have led him indirectly to his real life's work.

### Losing mother and losing faith

His mother had suffered from cancer for some ten years before her death in 1921, when young Jack Phillips was fifteen. He became, as he thought, a confirmed atheist: 'I gave up my religious faith utterly, for what use was prayer and talk of the love of God when I returned daily to this horrible caricature of the sprightly, witty mother I had known and loved?'

He describes graphically how his father had tried to nurse his mother as soon as he came home in the evenings. She lost her hair, 'her body had shrunken to a tortured lump of flesh, and the pain was very great'. After her death his father was grief-stricken and absent, leaving his three children to Rhoda, a treasured domestic helper. Worse followed: his stepmother arrived in the form of his father's wartime secretary, and she was a 'fault-finding ... terrifying kill joy'. Since his younger brother had gone to boarding-school and his sister to London University to study, Jack was left alone to bear the brunt of having, from the age of fifteen, no real home. He recalls:

> I had to put up with more than my share of my stepmother's rudeness and frigidity. I can remember once saying casually, 'Well, I think I'll go up to my room now.' Back came the freezing reply, 'It's not your room, John' (she insisted on calling me this though everyone else called me Jack), 'it is the room I allow you to use.' This was wounding enough, but we found out that little by little all our childhood treasures disappeared, including anything that could remind us of our mother.

He turned to playing with building a radio, and wrote twice for a wireless magazine to make a little money. But though he had a flair for radio and similar things, to receive communications from outside the home was no real help. He needed, but did not have, loving support during a time of tortured adolescent loneliness.

It is no wonder that he describes himself as a very late developer, and immature in his emotional responses. The wonder is that his nervous system stood up to early adult life in the way it did. Home was where the hurt was; he felt it deeply, and he was glad to leave it for Cambridge University.

### Finding faith and a vocation

At Cambridge he came to know many Christians through CICCU, the evangelical organization which he felt followed a narrow way but produced some very fine and attractive people. For the first time he heard fervent and persuasive preaching, but felt he had no 'conversion' experience. He joined the Christian Union, but with reservations that persisted. He describes his visit to the Keswick Convention of 1925:

> The hymn singing was moving, the prayers were offered with

> touching sincerity, and the speakers spoke with what seemed to me great power. I cannot honestly say that I took in much from them, but it was almost literally Heaven to find oneself, with the girl I felt I so deeply loved, among so many people who, despite their funny little taboos, were plainly devoted to Jesus Christ. I was enormously exhilarated and felt that I really must, decisively, throw in my lot with those lovable devoted people.

An important link was formed when (together with his brother and sister) he became a regular guest at the home of an evangelical clergyman whom he calls Father Trout. At this second home, only a few miles from his father's new house in Woldingham, Surrey, Phillips found a haven where there was love, affection, friendship, laughter and gaiety. He recalls the Sunday night talks where 'Trout' made the letters of the New Testament come alive for the young Phillips, a fact he recalled later when he started his translations of these letters.

He chooses the pseudonym of 'Father Trout' because, although the Protestant clergyman hidden behind it would not have liked the title, it was, for young Phillips, a way of thinking of his new friend's paternal and patriarchal attitude. In other words Phillips enjoyed having found a new, real spiritual *father,* who helped him to grow and develop. While at Cambridge Phillips received fifty pounds a year from him. Trout eventually spoke of ordination for Phillips, and must have guided him to Ridley Hall, Cambridge. While there, Phillips describes himself as 'a determined fundamentalist ... nothing would penetrate my rigid theology'.

**First breakdown**

Phillips tells us he took the simpler of two ordination courses and was ordained deacon in London's dockland, and accepted his first curacy at St John's Penge, not far from Crystal Palace in South London. A bare two miles from this was a Lutheran church where the young Dietrich Bonhoeffer was to minister in the same decade, before his return to Nazi Germany and martyrdom. Phillips nearly died in Penge for different reasons.

He found the work extremely difficult, partly because of his shy temperament, and because he rightly felt that he had been ill-prepared for it. He found the poverty around him distressing, and followed a rigid pattern he had formed in his own mind, without showing any ability to adapt himself to his changing situation.

He fell ill with abdominal pain, and but for his sister's insistence on a second opinion he might have died. The second doctor rightly diagnosed appendicitis with peritonitis, and after operating on him the surgeon said he did not expect the patient to last the night. Phillips describes a near-death experience, and dreams which were presumably part of a severe toxic and confused state. He felt he had nearly died, and on being turned back by a dream figure in white, he burst into tears. He woke to find the night nurse assuring him he would live.

In those pre-antibiotic days of fairly primitive surgery in a cottage hospital, his health must have suffered badly. There followed a severe depressive illness. The symptoms of this had started during the previous autumn of 1933, and he had been told to take a long break in Eastbourne. He had only just returned to Penge when the infected appendix and peritonitis overwhelmed him.

His Eastbourne friends directed him to his first and best psychiatrist, Dr Leonard Browne, a distinguished Jungian who had helped to found London's Tavistock Clinic (which remains a first-class centre for training in psychoanalysis and psychotherapy). He benefited from treatment from Dr Browne, and recovered sufficiently to accept an offer of work as editorial secretary to the Pathfinder Press, where he worked hard for a year and learned a good deal about editing, writing and typesetting. It was a strenuous form of occupational therapy, and he was pleased to accept an offer of a curacy in St Margaret's, Lee, in south-east London.

**Marriage and the Second World War**

Phillips describes with amusement his discovery that Gilly, his new rector in Lee, was passing off published sermons as his own, and how he persuaded him that some acknowledgment to the original authors was due. After a year living with his employer, Phillips took a bed-sitter in a guest house, where he met and married Vera Jones.

It is hard to believe, looking at the photographs of the young J. B. Phillips, that this tall, dark and handsome man was as innocent and ignorant of women as he describes himself to have been at that time.

It is easy to forget that such inexperience was common: Leonard Browne had helped greatly in guiding him to see the links between love and sex, but he was still slow to learn. His shyness, and memories of previous unhappy experiences in matters of the heart at which he only hints, were fairly crippling.

Vera agreed to marry the curate who was earning only seven pounds a week, not knowing that war would be declared six months after their wedding or that their church in Lee would be destroyed by bombing.

Phillips had been made priest in charge at the nearby Church of the Good Shepherd, and was happy there. In 1941 he began to translate the letters of the New Testament. This was started after finding out that the young people who attended his youth club on Sunday evenings in Lee just could not understand the language of the Authorised Version. It was for them that he began to translate the letters of Paul, and Phillips was delighted that the young people were enthusiastic because they could now make sense of the inspired words.

Vera could not have guessed that the curate she married would soon be conceiving and producing a book which would change their world totally. That was her husband's secret story of the War, leading – after difficulties which are well worth recounting – to the publication of *Letters to Young Churches* in 1947.

Vera had two miscarriages before having their first and only child. A daughter, Jennifer, was born in May 1946, a little more than a year after the family had moved to Redhill. Being vicar of St John's, Redhill, was the setting of Phillips' work for the next ten years. It was the beginning of an intensely fertile period, when the fruits of his labours were scattered world-wide. But his success as a writer and translator was to be dogged by failures in his health, and much suffering: what has been called personal barrenness with ministerial fruitfulness.

**Success story**

We must go back to Phillips' reading of rough translations to the groups of young people who met on Sunday evenings in Lee, South London. Having read and admired C. S. Lewis' books, Phillips sent a copy of his translation of Colossians to Lewis. He received a prompt and encouraging reply: Lewis hoped he would carry out his plan of doing all the epistles. He set aside a morning, once a week, for translation, and what was started in 1943 was finished in 1946.

Any new author may expect what happened to Phillips: 'I sent it round to several publishers, all of whom sent it back, firmly and politely, with a rejection slip. Then, armed with a letter from C. S. Lewis, I sent it to his publisher, Geoffrey Bles.' Bles eventually agreed to publish, with C. S. Lewis' suggested title *Letters to Young Churches,* and a foreword from Lewis. In the first year it sold about 1,300 copies, but a year later it was selling that number each week.

I often wonder what the readers of publishing firms say when they learn about the best-seller that got away. So often, as in the case of Frederick Forsyth and many others, as much as in J. B. Phillips' case, a promising talent is neither spotted nor encouraged. It was the large sales in the USA which determined Phillips to go on with other works of translation, just as much as the favourable reviews in most papers in Britain. Why, then, was success on an undreamed-of scale followed by such depression in his case?

**Illness and personality problems**

The first answer is to say firmly that it was not a case of success spoiling J. B. Phillips. *The Price of Success,* the title of his own account, unfinished before his death, is in that sense ill chosen. For as we have seen from his own account, the first depressive illness was during his first years as a curate, when little or no success could have been predicted from his track record.

It is vital to bear two things in mind as we follow the next thirty-five years of growing fame and blessing on his work. Leonard Browne was right in saying there were two aspects to the problem: Phillips' personality and his illness. In the last forty years or so we have learned a great deal about obsessive-compulsive personalities and about those who suffer from affective disorders (with their peculiar mixture of misery, panic anxiety and sheer mental pain). Anyone who wants to review the scientific evidence should consult a volume such as *Fears, Phobias and Rituals* by Professor Isaac Marks. What light can such knowledge shed on such people as J. B. Phillips?

We have already seen how he inherited his personality from his obsessional father, and quite possibly from his unmotherly mother too. His upbringing did nothing to make these inherited traits and characteristics any easier to bear: rather the contrary. Does personality change with the years? I think not, for it may be defined as that collection of attributes in a human being which enables us to predict how he will react to any new situation.

When there was any new change in his life Phillips found it an excessive strain, as obsessionals almost invariably do. It made him much more subject to obsessive anxiety, to panic attacks and to depression. This is shown in the last fifty years of his life, from 1932 to 1982.

Might his personality problems have been helped more effectively? I certainly think so: Dr Browne was a well-trained analyst, and indeed a friend of Jung. But psychotherapy cannot be done effectively in a matter of weeks or even months. Not even a man like Browne, who happened to be Christian and was uniquely able to help Phillips on many counts, could succeed by simply writing letters to him, as he did. He would have needed to see Phillips once a week for some years to help him move towards effective solutions to his problems. In a sense Phillips was just as scrupulous in his perfectionism as the young monk Martin Luther. But Luther had a spiritual director in the form of Staupitz. I cannot find anyone that Phillips had to fill that role. In some ways he seems to have been a loner, somewhat distant from those who might have been able to help him.

It is fair to note that Phillips repeatedly refers to his own poor state of physical health and strength. Had he been blessed with a more robust constitution, the story might have been different. His first depression followed a serious physical illness that nearly killed him, and great care should have been taken to prevent overstrain. To allow him in one year to book three hundred speaking engagements was surely the height of folly: no wonder his doctor in Plymouth said Phillips was 'scooped out'.

The nature of his affective disorder is hard to determine without many more facts. He writes of some long periods in his life when he was aware of great energy and when he was able to work very hard and finish work before the deadlines were due. Details are lacking, but no doctor can read these parts of his life and letters without wondering whether Phillips suffered at times from the opposite of depression, that is elation and overactivity. It may be that he simply rose to the demands of the occasion, and that he did not have a bipolar affective disorder (or manic-depressive illness as it used to be called). He certainly has put all readers in his debt by his clear description of his recurrent depressive disorders.

**Mental pain**

*The Price of Success* has a chapter entitled 'Light at the End of Tunnel'. In it Phillips describes how, while signing copies of his book *Four Prophets* in Salisbury, he was seized by irrational panic and phobic anxiety. His wife drove him home. He felt he was as bad as at his first breakdown in 1932. His faith seemed to have deserted him emotionally: that is, belief was still there but none of the comforting feelings that usually went with his faith.

He went into hospital, and his psychiatrist asked him to write down his description of how he felt: the section headed 'Mental Pain' refers to four aspects of his depression. The first was what he called diminution of the personality, an erosion to the point of fearing final destruction of himself, not of death, but of ceasing to be anything. The second was a sense of alienation, of everything being out of joint; words and music were discordant, and money seemed to have no value. The third was of self–condemnation, with cruel savagery exposing everything that had been done as useless and worthless. The fourth was what he calls agony by comparison. This reminds us of William Cowper's famous hymn 'Where is the blessedness I knew'. Phillips found the comparison of present misery with previous joy caused a feeling of the excruciating difference: this added to the pain. I think he is here describing the same feelings that John Keats describes in his poem 'In a Drear-nighted December':

> But were there ever any
> Writhed not at passed joy?
> To know the change and feel it,
> When there is none to heal it
> Nor numbed sense to steel it,
> Was never said in rhyme.

Phillips, writing near the end of his life, sees these as four emotional torments, which when they come together daunt the bravest. Happily he speaks also of the process of recovery. He makes much of the help to be found in sharing the darkness with others who have been through it. His wife's book, *The Wounded Healer* (written with Dr Edwin Robertson, who had been such a close and valued friend), contains letters which help us to see how such diverse people as Dr Frank Lake, Dr Leslie Weatherhead and Harry Williams helped Phillips by sharing their knowledge and experience.

I find it sad that he was not helped by medication. Nowadays such non-psychiatric forms of treatment as the use of beta-blockers may alleviate the anxiety by stopping the excessive effects of adrenalin on the body: they do this without sedation and without any risk of dependence. By the same token, there are nowadays many forms of antidepressants which might have helped someone who suffered as much as Phillips.

Above all, the modern emphasis on cognitive therapy and on behaviour therapy might have helped him. Since Phillips was so interested in the way his mind worked, and so willing to learn, it would almost certainly have helped him to receive the type of treatment which is based on learning theory, and on knowing how to cope with both anxious and depressive thoughts and feelings. There is, however, no evidence that he had any of these modern benefits.

Sensible psychologists and others conducting such therapy are often applying beliefs which have been known in different forms from ancient times. It is of some importance to note that cognitive therapy is very similar to the advice given to believers in the letters of the apostles Paul, Peter, James and John, which were the very stuff of Phillips' *Letters to Young Churches*. Here are some examples of his renderings:

> Don't worry over anything whatever; tell God every detail of your needs in earnest and thankful prayer, and the peace of God, which transcends human understanding, will keep constant guard over your hearts and minds as they rest in Christ Jesus. (Phil. 4:6-7).

> Love contains no fear – indeed fully-developed love expels every

> particle of fear, for fear always contains some of the torture of feeling guilty. This means that the man who lives in fear has not yet had his love perfected. (1 John 4:18)

Many such examples might be multiplied. Phillips must often have felt that his own intense anxiety, guilt-feelings and depression appeared to contradict the faith about which he wrote so well. In one sense, I believe that the man who (because of some biochemical problem in his brain and constitution) feels ill with depression has as little to blame himself for as a diabetic who feels ill.

We must not, however, over-simplify the complexities of depressive illness. Phillips might have had more biochemical help today; and many other kinds of treatment are now offered for chronic or recurrent depression. Even so, good people still suffer.

We may think, rightly, that the knowledge that Phillips had might have been better applied to his own case. But was it not ever thus? The physician who is an expert on the theory of therapeutics cannot always apply it to himself and find healing.

**Attacks and achievements**

J. B. Phillips became something of a guru to many: he was a regular and faithful letter-writer and helped a large number of people. His achievements were solid and lasting: particularly his eventual translation of the whole of the New Testament, and also of four Old Testament prophets. Such books as *Ring of Truth* helped many who had been troubled by attacks on the Christian faith. It was good that the Archbishop of Canterbury should give him a Lambeth DD and that Exeter University should have given him a DLitt. How the pupil who had struggled at school and at Cambridge must have been glad to have these tokens of recognition of what he had done!

But there were many attacks. Many disliked his tampering with 'scripture', although it seems that, for some, all they really minded was that the King James Version was being replaced. One letter may be taken as typical:

> Will you be kind enough to tell us who gave you the authority to violate and trifle with the Sacred Word of GOD. There is only one translation of the Bible and that is the Authorized Version;

> the King James Version, and any other copies are Sacrilege and an insult to simple humble folk such as myself....
> PS I regret that I am not a member of any church but I do like to hear the reading of the Bible.

Eventually he prepared a formal letter for such objectors.

Phillips was often attacked, but the letters of thanks and praise more than made up for those crying sacrilege.

**The translator's art**

Phillips says that translating the New Testament was like working as 'an electrician re-wiring an ancient house without being able to turn the mains off'. Phillips compels admiration for his willingness to proceed with his solitary task, unaided by any committee of scholars.

I am reminded of that earlier scholar, William Tyndale, much of whose single-handed work went into the Authorized Version. It is worth comparing Tyndale(i) with Phillips(ii), giving the 1534 translation before that of 1947. The first quotation is of Romans 8:31, the second of 2 Corinthians 4:16-18.

> (i) What shall we then say unto these things? If God be on our side: who can be against us? which spared not his own son, but gave him for us all: how shall he not with him give us all things also?
>
> (ii) In face of all this, what is there left to say? If God is for us, who can be against us? He who did not shield his own Son but gave him up for us all – can we not trust such a God to give us, with him, everything else that we can need?
>
> (i) Wherefore we are not wearied, but though our outward man perish, yet the inward man is renewed day by day. For our exceeding tribulation, which is momentary and light, prepareth an exceeding and eternal weight of glory unto us, while we look not on the things which are seen, but on the things which are not seen. For the things which are seen, are tempora!: but things which are not seen, are eternal.
>
> (ii) This is the reason why we never collapse. The outward man does indeed suffer wear and tear, but every day the inward man receives fresh strength. These little troubles (which are really so

> transitory) are winning for us a permanent and glorious reward out of all proportion to our pain. For we are looking all the time not at the visible things but at the invisible. The visible things are transitory: it is the invisible things that are really permanent.

The differences are obvious, yet probably worth touching on. Many felt angry with Phillips because, as he said, he believed the work of a translator was 'to convey the meaning of one language into the meaning and sense of another'. He tried to reproduce in today's hearers and readers the same emotions as were produced by the original documents so long ago.

Perhaps we need men for all seasons as translators. Sir Thomas More considered Tyndale a traitor, and played his part in the beastly business of finding him and having him kidnapped, strangled and burned near Brussels in 1536. What Phillips suffered was mild in comparison: he told his critics that every translator was also an interpreter. There will always be some who consider the Italian proverb true, that the translator is a traitor.

Translating the Gospels was dangerous work for E. V. Rieu, who found himself, at the end, turned into a Christian believer. One poet has put it vividly, saying that Rieu, who was translating the word, found that the Word had translated him. In relation to Phillips, the work he had done led him to publish his *Ring of Truth* to describe how he had been affected, and confirmed in his Christian faith, by translating.

**Convincing success stories**

Two examples of the best sort of success are very impressive. A seventy-seven year old Japanese businessman had been reading *Letters to Young Churches* in the train while commuting to Tokyo. He wrote to Phillips: 'for the first time I understood what Christianity was all about, and my whole life was transformed'.

A headmaster wrote from New Zealand, telling how a young man sentenced to a reformatory school for a term ended up in solitary confinement. He took the *Letters* as one of his chosen books, saying afterwards that 'old things have passed away, all things have become new'.

Phillips comments: 'How can anyone deny the power of God

speaking without human intermediary through his inspired writings?' For twenty years a flood of thousands of such letters came to him, and similar messages still continued to reach him till the end of his life.

Dr Leonard Browne had told the young curate that he was trying to reach a performance of 130 percent even then. There was something about the challenge to translate the New Testament that met this need to excel. As Phillips put it himself, he felt it met his need 'to be so wonderful as to be beyond all criticism'. The volume of universal praise confirmed for a long time his belief in his success, but nagging doubts seeped back into his mind. As to some attacks, they came, he felt, from people who held the same fundamentalist views as he had done at Cambridge. This may not always have been true, but it was Phillips' way of defending himself against even legitimate criticism. He freely admitted that he had left behind him the rigid and limited views of his Cambridge student days.

**A witness to the truth**

Phillips says that he wrote his book, *Ring of Truth: A Translator's Testimony* partly because he was sure of God, and of the basic integrity of the documents he had translated. He wrote in 1967, and found a welcome from many who loved and appreciated *Ring of Truth* because it helped them at a time when scholars were attacking the Christian faith. Phillips puts it bluntly:

> Few people have had such a close contact with the New Testament as I have ... I do not care a rap what the 'avant-garde' scholars say; I do very much care what God says and does. I have therefore felt compelled to write this book. It is my testimony to the historicity and reliability of the New Testament.

As a student at Ridley Hall, Phillips had chosen to avoid the subjects of church history, the growing pattern of worship, and the development of theology. He chose to live for much of his life within a very narrow focus, an area in which he could both control and excel. For a perfectionist both these features are vital. He insisted that he was a communicator and not a scholar, and he was right.

**The spreading influence**

The fact that in 1955 he moved to Swanage may have removed Phillips from ordinary parish duties. But quite soon the world was his parish, in a bigger sense than John Wesley meant when he coined that phrase. His name became well known throughout the English-speaking world, and some of his writings were translated into Asian and other European languages. His lectures and broadcasts also prompted letters from many people seeking help and counsel. Phillips was generous in his response, and some of his letters are collected in the volume called *The Wounded Healer.*

It is a remarkable fact that those who have themselves suffered from depression can often help fellow sufferers better than the tough, muscular folk who have never felt a twinge of doubt or anxiety. Phillips' books, such as *Making Men Whole,* met a real need. He met with criticism because he was willing to speak out about what he saw as the excesses of some modern evangelicalism. This was in spite of the fact that 'he was an evangelical and frequently conducted Missions', as his editors, his wife and Dr Robertson, put it. They point out that Phillips' letters show that 'ultimately he triumphed, retaining his faith and his sense of humour. As soon as someone turned to him in need, he forgot his own distress and gave help at once.'

He founded a charitable organization for Christian communication, and the profits from his writings went into that to help the cause he believed in so deeply. Many gifts and grants were made from this trust to help those who needed finances in their Christian work. In spite of his chronic ill-health, his work continued to the very end of his life, and the autobiography he was writing when he died helped many to understand how a very successful Christian leader may yet suffer from much depression and anxiety.

**A child of light walking in darkness**

An extract from one of his letters shows how Phillips viewed things in perspective:

> These periods of spiritual dryness which every saint has known are the very times when your need of God is greatest. To worship him may or may not bring back the lost 'feeling', but your contact with God in prayer and praise will strengthen you spiritually

> whether you feel it or not ... Times of spiritual apathy are the very times when we can do most to prove our love for God, and I have no doubt we bring most joy to his heart when we defy our feelings and act in spite of them.

Phillips came to accept his nervous pain as an illness, and in spite of it he was able to go on working most of the time and to produce many works on which we have been unable to touch in this brief sketch. At the end of his autobiography he wrote:

> All the recoveries that I have known have a pattern of ebb and flow. But if the real inward self is committed to God the direction is onward and upward however battered we feel at times.
>
> As far as I am concerned my affliction, which lasted on and off for a long time, was rarely so bad that I could not work at all. But I had to change my own attitude towards what I was trying to do. I had done enough rushing about speaking, preaching and lecturing, and I must give more time to reflection on what I believed and proclaimed.

No autobiography, no amount of reading Phillips' books, can accurately reflect his inner life and his state of mind. His suffering continued from time to time, and his anxious, depressed temperament may not have changed very much before his death in 1982. Yet he had endured much, and succeeded beyond his expectations. He must have reflected often on the contrast between the ideal and the actual in the lives of Christian believers. It seems to me that he always held on to the ideal, the counsels of perfection, as in his own translation of Philippians 4:11-13:

> Nor do I mean that I have been in actual need, for I have learned to be content, whatever the circumstances may be. I know now how to live when things are difficult and I know how to live when things are prosperous. In general and in particular I have learned the secret of facing either poverty or plenty. I am ready for anything through the strength of the one who lives within me.

*Further Reading*

J. B. Phillips, *The Price of Success: An Autobiography* (London: Hodder & Stoughton, 1984). Vera Phillips and Edwin Robertson, *J. B. Phillips: The Wounded Healer* (Grand Rapids, MI: Win B. Eerdmans; London: Triangle/SPCK, 1984).

Phillips' translations are all contained in *The New Testament in Modern English, revised edition* (London: Collins, 1972), and *Four Prophets: Amos, Hosea, First Isaiah, Micah. A Modern Translation From the Hebrew* (London: Collins, 1967).

Others of Phillips' writings are: *Your God is Too Small* (London: Epworth, 1952); *Plain Christianity and Other Broadcast Talks* (London: Epworth Press, 1957); *Ring of Truth: A Translator's Testimony* (London: Hodder & Stoughton, 1967); *New Testament Christianity* (London: Hodder & Stoughton, 1956); *Making Men Whole* (London: Collins, 1955); *A Man Called Jesus: The Gospel Story in 26 Short Plays* (London: Collins Fount, 1978). There is also an anthology: Denis Duncan (ed.), *Through the Year with* J. *B. Phillips* (London: Hodder & Stoughton, 1974; Evesham: Arthur James, 1983).

# 11

# Physician, Preacher and Politician: Dr D. Martyn Lloyd-Jones (1899–1981)

Mr Lely, I desire you would use all your skill to paint my picture freely like me, and not flatter me at all; but remark all these roughnesses, pimples, warts and everything as you see me, otherwise I will never pay a farthing for it.

(*Oliver Cromwell (1599–1658) quoted in Horace Walpole, Anecdotes of Painting in England)*

You can always tell a Barts man, but you can't tell him much.

(*An old saying)*

Type of the wise, who soar but never roam
True to his kindred points of heaven and home.

(*William Wordsworth: Ode to a skylark)*

The greatest expository preacher in Europe.

(*Emil Brunner, visiting Westminster Chapel in 1949)*

## A Tale of Two Princes

In August 2000 the National Library ofWales had decided to mount two exhibitions in its magnificent building overlooking the town of Aberystwyth and facing the broad sweep of Cardigan Bay beyond the town, its churches and university. The first and larger one was to commemorate Owain Glyndwr (1354–1416), the last of the Welsh Princes whose last parliament had met at the nearby town of Machynlleth.

The second exhibition was dedicated to the life and work of Dr D. Martyn Lloyd-Jones. It seemed natural to me to think of him as one of the last of *the princes of the pulpit.* Hundreds had been to see the Lloyd-Jones exhibition daily, who knew and cared little about Owain Glyndwr. In that August month the numbers had been much augmented by the fact that for two weeks Aberystwyth hosted the annual conferences of the Evangelical Movement of Wales. Many visited the English conference, which attracted large numbers from far afield. The other conference, conducted in the Welsh language, also drew many to the seaside town. To a large degree those Christians owed an enormous debt to the man whose birth in 1899 was the occasion of the National Library of Wales bringing together the books, letters, photographs and videos which made up an impressive collection of reminders of a man who had been a famous son of Wales. He never forgot his roots, and never ceased to speak his native language at home with his wife, and often preached in Welsh as well as English throughout his life.

I have learned a good deal since the time, now over fifty years ago, when I fell under his spell like so many others. I sometimes think he was made up of equal parts of the wizard Merlin on the one hand, and of a Welsh prince of the pulpit on the other. Much power derived from both aspects of his temperament. One of the things that friends who are scholars in the field of learning about the courts of the Welsh princes have taught me is that the local bard was there not only to praise his Prince, but also to appraise him. In his songs the bard was given a licence to criticize the local prince and sometimes describe the humorous aspect of the court, as might the court jester or the wise fool in Shakespeare's plays. I hope some such licence may be granted to me, who am neither bard nor portrait painter, but someone who remembers the glory days and the lasting influences of a prophetic teacher and preacher.

Inevitably during my psychiatric training at The Institute of Psychiatry in 1969 and since then I have wondered about how what I learned about psychology and personality might help to understand Dr Lloyd-Jones better. As in the other sketches I have sought to stick to facts and avoid speculation: the addresses which include much about Dr Lloyd-Jones himself provide ample material without the need to speculate, and his actions sometimes spoke louder than his words. I will try to offer an account of his achievements, and of some of the events that caused pain to those many admirers who loved him, but had to disagree with him.

**A Wealth of Documentation**

There are many records of his preaching, and his sermons have been published in book form. The total number of books is now eighty and still counting with further posthumous publications likely. Many of these are listed at the end of this chapter under *Further Reading.* His life was celebrated in a monumental two-volume study by Iain Murray. The first volume published in 1982 was called *The First Forty Years.* The second volume *The Fight of Faith* at 830 pages was even larger and covered the more controversial years until his death in March 1981. A selection of his letters was published in 1998 and there are a number of his papers and addresses that shed detailed light on his life. His sermons continue to be published in book form: a volume on Romans chapter 12 has just appeared and continues to take the form that the doctor prescribed: almost verbatim transcripts of the spoken word. This decision on the author's part has meant effectively that there is no attempt to make the written text more accessible to readers who found his style difficult to follow. In London the Christian Station *Premier Radio* currently (2001) broadcasts his taped sermons regularly. In 1999 a book in Welsh appeared, called *The Doctor's Voice*, with a selection of his Welsh talks, sermons and interviews.

Other books have attempted an assessment: one was called *Chosen By God* and is a kind of composite portrait. Others have chosen a theme such as *The Baptism of the Spirit in Dr Martyn Lloyd-Jones' Teaching* by Michael Eaton: he includes an assessment of the many tapes preached on charismatic themes. He found that the tapes and the edited book text show some remarkable differences – suggesting as it does an adaptation of the preacher's words to make an acceptable paperback as in *Joy Unspeakable* and *Prove All Things*. These last two books published by Kingsway in the 1980s were well suited to meet the interest that the renewal movement had generated, and his grandson as editor challenges readers to decide whether his grandfather was a charismatic.

In addition to all the many published sources available, I write from a close personal knowledge of Dr Lloyd-Jones, and from a Welsh background: I was brought up also in South West Wales, in Carmarthenshire. As a medical student at Barts, his old hospital, I was like many, a student member of the church at Westminster Chapel between 1947 and 1953. I continue to value his writings, and to revere his memory. I was fortunate to contribute to the Puritan Conference in 1953 which was founded with Dr J. I. Packer, and I was privileged to speak at his massive memorial service in 1981 when his old chapel was once again filled to overflow with some three thousand people. My wife and I were happy to have him as our guest when he preached in North Wales. It was a privilege to be at his funeral in the small village of Newcastle Emlyn, in South West Wales, where he and his wife are buried.

**Beginnings**

His fame lay in his genius as a preacher whose prophetic gifts had helped to change the Christian scene for good, in his lifetime and beyond it. His ministry has been worldwide through his published works. Yet his beginnings give little hint of his future fame and genius. Born in Cardiff, he was brought up first in rural Llangeitho in central Cardiganshire where his father had a general store. He then lived in London and went to Marylebone Grammar School before becoming, at sixteen years of age, a medical student at Barts (as St Bartholomew's Hospital was always known). I wonder if anyone at Barts would have predicted his peculiar genius or his future worldwide fame. Many friends and colleagues recognized his great gifts.

I am glad of an opportunity to celebrate his genius and to tell his story. I first heard him preach when I was a sixth-former, and I had heard nothing like it. His oratory and the eloquent way he held the attention of a large congregation in a crowded church could not fail to make a deep impression. I did not then know that I was to be a student at Barts myself from 1947 to 1953 and to be a student member of the church at Westminster Chapel, London. Like many others of all kinds of religious background and of none, the Sunday experience was formative and deeply influential. Many of us also went to a Friday evening session which was then a forum where any topic relevant to the Christian life and the Christian scene might be debated. Dr Lloyd-Jones was in the chair like a one-man Brains Trust, guiding, provoking and teaching by a method which, he said, he had learned at the feet of Thomas Horder (later Lord Horder), a physician who had recognized his abilities, and appointed him as his chief assistant physician at Barts, and in his Harley Street practice.

It was part of their great kindness that Dr Lloyd-Jones and his wife welcomed me and many others to their London home in Ealing, and offered much other practical and spiritual help, guidance and nurture. Inevitably, or so it seemed, one came to respect and idolize the man who was known usually as 'The Doctor'. Such was his personality, his power and influence that we were given to much excessive adulation. We not only thought like him but talked and gestured like him. It was a process of adolescent identification which may now be easily understood and forgiven.

As young hero-worshippers we were sometimes called *martinets*. This was not only a pun, but also may have been a reflection of our somewhat bigoted dogmatism as much as our poor imitations of our hero. I now feel that any young painter who had been trained in the school of an artist like Raphael would have been proud that his style might reflect something he had learnt from his master. It did not occur to me then, as it does now, that envy of great men is found in Christian circles as easily as elsewhere, and that tact and tolerance were wholly absent from our youthful repertoire.

It was once said of Dr Lloyd-Jones that 'no leader should be judged by, or held responsible for, all his followers'.As he has said to me and to others in published interviews about the problem of influence, idolization and imitation, his wish was that those whom he taught to think, should then learn to think for themselves. It was a long time before I and many of my generation who experienced the teaching of Dr Lloyd-Jones could take some steps in the direction of independence of thought. It was hard for many of us who knew and loved a great teacher and preacher of genius to move on from slavish imitation to a more critical appreciation of the man and his genius.

This chapter is a brief and biased sketch: it is not a full length portrait. I feel sure its subject – a great admirer of Oliver Cromwell – would echo what Cromwell is said to have told the artist Sir Peter Lely about being painted warts and all. Those whom we idolize in adolescence often have feet of clay which we are unwilling to notice. When I wrote an eulogy for a Welsh Christian publication on Dr Lloyd-Jones, at the time of his retirement from his church at

Westminster in 1968, he wrote to me saying that he appreciated what had been written, but that I had 'chosen an unworthy subject'. My editor had called it a panegyric, and it was full of praise, with no critical assessment. I would like in this chapter to see my subject steadily and see him whole in as far as I can.

**Plucked from the Burning**

The young John Wesley was saved from a burning Epworth Rectory when he was aged six and sometimes said of himself that he was a 'brand plucked from the burning'. It has been said that Wesley's sense of a personal destiny derived in part from that early experience. A similar sense of destiny pervaded Dr Lloyd-Jones and his thinking. Indeed, both John Wesley and the young Martyn were to grow up to be men who were short in height but great in stature. It might be argued that the two men were to have similar problems about their attitudes to the churches where they were reared and where they began their respective ministries.

In January 1910, the young Martyn was in the bedroom of the home in Llangeitho when a fire broke out. The previous day many farmers had been in his father's shop paying their bills and it was thought that the butt ends of their cigarettes had ignited some of the inflammable materials in the shop below. He was only saved by the quick action of his father, who threw him out of the bedroom window to the arms of three men standing below in their nightshirts. The house burned down, but his brother Vincent and father were also saved, while his mother and elder brother were away. It was 'a singular providence': for a ten year old boy, it must have been a formative experience.

It is worth recalling some of the facts about Llangeitho: a remarkable village largely because of the fact that Daniel Rowland, the eighteenth century Anglican curate, had ministered there. Rowland was one of the greatest of the early Methodist leaders. He was said to spend a good deal of his time in his early ministry preaching about the law: that is, he sought to produce a sense of need in his listeners, by teaching the demands of the law of God, before offering them the grace and mercy of God in Christ. There is little doubt that the large statue of Rowland which dominated the village impressed itself on the young Martyn. In his broadcast recollections for Radio Wales, Dr Lloyd-Jones said that the local churches seemed to have a singular absence of any of Rowland's gospel in 1911: they seemed formal and spiritually dead. He tells us that *'Ichabod'* was written over it all: the glory had departed.

His interests were not at all bookish until a year later: his life had been one of play and enjoying the life of a home where the shopkeeper was a centre of village life. There were enjoyable holidays with his uncle on the farm near Newcastle Emlyn where horses were bred and kept. His uncle, at Llwyncadfor, was famous for his stud and his prize winning horses: one of them was sold to the King of Egypt for a fantastic sum. He retained a lifelong love of horses.

In June 1913, the 'Sasiwn' – the Annual Association of the Calvinistic Methodist Church of Wales – visited the little village: they wished to celebrate the two hundredth anniversary of Daniel Rowland's birth. It was the first time that the young Martyn was able to hear visiting preachers of national fame, addressing huge crowds in the open air. He was 'entranced ... not only by their eloquent preaching but by their magnificent personalities' It opened his eyes to what had been missing in the church in the village which was well attended but lacking in any stimulus or sense of a full Christian life. The young Martyn began a life-long interest in the eighteenth century Methodist Fathers. I heard him say, with much feeling, as he quoted a famous novelist 'When I wish to escape, I fly to the eighteenth century'.

When he left the village school for Tregaron, a cold, damp market town where he attended the County School, it meant leaving his home from Monday morning till Friday evening and staying near the school. He wrote with feeling of the intense grief and longing he felt when he was away from the home in Llangeitho. He hated leaving his parents and two brothers. To make things worse he suffered in the winter months from chilblains, and the unrelieved pain simply made his sense of miserable grief worse. After three years at Tregaron he was a pupil in Marylebone Grammar School in London: but he owed a great deal of his intellectual awakening to the splendid teaching he received in the Welsh county school.

The loss of the burnt-out home could not, he felt, be made good by being in the new house that was built. The sense of home had been lost, he recounted later. And there were his father's difficulties in business to contend with also. Martyn had been told something about these in 1911 by an uncle, but the bankruptcy his father announced in January 1914 was still a great shock to the whole family. His father had been to Canada but had returned without finding any suitable work there.

**'I was never an adolescent'**

When Dr Lloyd-Jones made this remark about himself, one ponders why. Was it that a blight was cast over his early years by the failures in his father's business? Very few Barts medical students would have had to help with their father's milk round before going on to the prestigious and class-ridden hospital that boasted of its history, tradition and excellence. Such was the case: the young Martyn had trudged the streets around Westminster looking for a suitable London base for his father to set up a new business. He has described it all vividly. There was real hardship in those days, and little time to play, or to be an ordinary adolescent. The Great War of 1914–18 had also cast dark clouds over critical years in his development.

His older brother Harold had died unexpectedly in the influenza epidemic of 1918: Harold was aged twenty, and had been invalided out of the army with a heart condition. To lose an older brother was a deep and lasting hurt. Sixty years later, when Dr Lloyd-Jones was talking to an eldest daughter who had lost a sister, he told her simply: 'You never get over it'. To my mind the grief that he felt as a schoolboy who was a 'weekly boarder' away from home was a severe kind of nostalgia. But his grief had also been made worse by the bitterness of his father's loss of his business, and his bankruptcy and attempted emigration to Canada. I talked it over with him in his sixties, before I had learned in later psychiatric training about the importance of the losses he had been through in producing a lasting acquaintance with grief. I believe that what he endured in his adolescence had a profound effect on the young Martyn, and made him very aware of the power of grief and depression to influence a person's life.

By the age of eighteen he was the superintendent of a Sunday School in the Welsh Calvinistic Methodist Church in Charing Cross

Road. One cannot possibly overestimate that church in his development as a thinker and a debater. Though the family home was quite near to the Westminster Chapel (which he was later to fill with grateful worshippers under his own Christian ministry), his choice of a Welsh-speaking church as a young man seemed inevitable. '*Charing Cross*' as the church has always been known, is now long since closed. But at the time young Martyn went there he and his two brothers would have found themselves at one of the key centres of Welsh cultural life among the large and busy community of Welsh exiles in London.

To run its Sunday School was to enter a world of intense debate and learning. It is hard to explain how exciting a Sunday afternoon could be when men from the settings of their distinguished London careers would study some part of the Bible and end up fiercely debating its meaning and its application. There was nothing here of 'gentle Jesus meek and mild' but rather a combative and intense study of the teaching of Scripture, and the sparks would often fly as 'diamond cut diamond'. Dr Lloyd-Jones has said how three people with their powerful minds and debating skills taught him to think clearly and methodically. Especially was this true in philosophical and theological matters. He named three people: his future father-in-law Dr Tom Phillips, who was a successful ophthalmic surgeon was his class master. Did he guess then how Martyn was to figure later in the extended family? The second man he mentions was his younger brother Vincent who later became a barrister and a QC and was knighted. The third was Dr David Phillips, a theologian from Bala, where a Calvinist Methodist College had exercised an important role for many years.

I think it was at *Charing Cross*, and in the setting of that busy church, that the young Martyn learned to be combative and skilful in debate. It was a skill which, because of the speed of his intelligence and the power of his intellect, was to make Dr Lloyd-Jones many enemies as well as life-long friends in the fight of faith. He was viewed as arrogant, which perhaps he could be, but always with good reason and in later life his faith led to a gallant attempt to be humble as well. This may well have proved more difficult as his successes increased and his fame grew.

If we jump to 1925, the courage and skill in debate that he had learned, led to his speaking to the Literary and Debating Society of the Charing Cross church on *The Tragedy of Modern Wales*. It was an attack which was so blistering that it led to columns of reporting in the Welsh newspapers, and to being accused of 'wild and indiscriminate abuse of his fellow-countrymen'. A Welsh banker was moved to reply to him in the letter columns of a newspaper. In many respects this was, with hindsight, something like the bomb that Karl Barth was said to have dropped in the playground of the theologians with his famous *Letter to the Romans*. But the full explosions Dr Lloyd-Jones was to produce and their effects were not to be felt for a few more years, and we must return to his progress at Barts, and his rocketing to fame as the chief assistant of Sir Thomas Horder.

**The Barts Man: learning to play skittles**

I got into trouble at his memorial service in 1981, with one of the other speakers who had been close to Dr Lloyd-Jones. In front of over 3,000 who attended, we as speakers had been given eight minutes each to speak in his memory. The theme given to me was to speak about 'the Doctor as a doctor'. I spoke of his being a doctor till the day he died, for which I was rebuked: I really doubt if the one rebuking me understood what I was saying, since Dr Lloyd-Jones often spoke of himself as a medical man, and said how important it was for a doctor to retain his mystique. Far from being sorry for what I said (later printed in a little volume called *Chosen by God*), I think one cannot say enough about the ten years or so he spent at Barts Hospital.

At first he was simply a diligent medical student. Sometimes, if he had been up very early to help his father at the dairy in Westminster, he would seem sleepy and inattentive. But he was not long into his clinical work before he caught the eye of Dr Thomas Horder. On one occasion there was a disagreement: the young student's diagnosis was based on his claim to feel an enlarged spleen in a patient's abdomen, which the eminent Dr Horder's examination did not confirm. A few days later the Lloyd-Jones diagnosis was proved correct, and Horder took further note of him.

He quickly qualified as a doctor and in his London MB he achieved distinction in medicine. Even before these results were known, Horder had chosen him as his junior house physician. This began a close association which lasted from 1921 to 1927 at Barts. He went on to obtain his higher medical degree in London (the 'membership' – MRCP – of the Royal College of Physicians). His name was soon a byword for brilliance, hard work and humanity towards his patients. I knew senior staff who still recalled him – thirty years after he left Barts – with much admiration and affection. To be chosen as Chief Assistant to Sir Thomas Horder – soon to be Lord Horder – was a mark of special merit. It meant helping Horder in his Harley Street practice and having his own room there. Later his research work on a cardiac condition earned him his London University degree of M D, which in Britain is a much coveted mark of excellence in research. Whenever, in his later life, he was offered an honorary doctorate, he is said to have declined because he was satisfied with having a doctorate from London University. More important perhaps was his rejection of honours as part of his belief that academic honours and preferment might easily be corrupting.

He learned far more than medicine from Horder: he cherished the way he had taught him to think. Horder had given him his own copy of Jeavons' *The Principles of Science: a Treatise on Logic and Scientific Method (1893)*. Lloyd-Jones describes Horder thus:

> He was a thorough diagnostician and after he had collected his facts, he would reason until he reached his diagnosis. His method was to work from first principles, never jumping to conclusions. Having gathered all the data on a patient he would then set up all possible explanations for his illness like a group of skittles. These he proceeded to 'knock down' one by one, as objections were applied to them, until there was only one left.

This method was taught at the bedside and in case-conferences. Dr Lloyd-Jones, who was later to describe preaching as 'logic on fire', used a similar method. Often his approach to a biblical text was to offer, first, a series of explanations of it which did not help, before giving his own inevitably correct exposition or 'diagnosis'. This he would apply with the utmost rigour, and at times with great spiritual power, as we shall describe later.

But by 1925 the young Dr Lloyd-Jones was beginning to feel certain that his real calling in life was not to continue as a physician, but to become a preacher: it is important, in seeing his peculiar strength and certainty of vocation, to try to see how this came about. While he was working with the many poor patients who came to Barts Hospital, and also getting to know Horder's richer clientele, he had learned much of lasting value. But he was also beginning to learn more about his own heart, and beginning to experience the grace which eventually led to his becoming a minister of the gospel, which he was to serve with such distinctive genius.

**Crisis and commitment**

We may learn a good deal about how the crises of 1925 to 1927 were resolved, but we are not told much about Dr Lloyd-Jones' inner spiritual experience. He was quite reticent about how precisely his faith developed. We are allowed to deduce from what he does tell us that there was a gradual realization that his earlier professions of faith had been quite honest but had not, as he came to see, been evidence of genuine Christian belief and experience. It was taken for granted, he tells us, that all those sitting in Christian pews in the churches where he had been such an active member, were believers. Yet he came to see that the preachers he heard had not reached his conscience, that his sense of sin had been very deficient, and that he had not really sensed his need of forgiveness and regeneration.

Reticent as he is about his deepest experiences at this time, Dr Lloyd-Jones describes them in the words of the Roman Catholic poet Francis Thompson in his famous poem *The Hound of Heaven*. Thompson will be recalled as a medical student who had started taking heroin from his father's surgery, and had dropped out of training. He was found on the Thames embankment sleeping rough, and saved and nurtured by Wilfred Meynell and his family. The point of the *Hound of Heaven* is that God's pursuit of man is described in magnificent verse, beginning with the words

> I fled Him down the nights and down the days;
> I fled him down the arches of the years;
> I fled Him down the labyrinthine ways
> Of my own mind; and in the midst of tears
> I hid from him....

He was to quote these words again in his last Welsh sermon in 1980, the year before he died.

He came to know that he had been 'found of God' and by Easter 1925 he was describing experiences in the small study he shared with his brother Vincent of being overwhelmed with seeing 'the love of God expressed in the death of Christ'. In his little room at Barts next to the post-mortem room, where some of his research was being done, he sometimes had a new realization and insight into the new life that had come to him, in a deep and moving way. Such hints describe more than a conversion experience, and must have been part of a deep work of God's grace in his heart, mind and life.

His life was now that of a committed believer, and he soon began to feel that his future was to be that of a preacher of the gospel, which he had now experienced for himself for the first time as a personal reality. In 1925 he visited Aberystwyth to see the Principal of the Theological College there. He had begun to study New Testament Greek, and had found a local tutor. His conviction that he should forsake medicine for preaching was linked to a sense of being able to do something special for Wales in his new role as preacher and leader.

But after deciding to leave medicine he was assailed with doubts, and decided he must remain a doctor. He writes: 'I went through a great crisis and decided I would not do it. I made a solemn decision to go on with medicine'. But the conflict over the matter continued: 'It was a great struggle and I literally lost over twenty pounds in weight'. It is hard to be sure how the struggle was resolved. On the one hand, he says that Horder as his great mentor introduced him to others at the top of the medical profession: 'He would take me now and again to medical dinners ... and I used to hear the mutterings, the criticisms, and the jealousies. It sickened me'. On the other hand, he found many of Horder's patients were in need of more than medical help. He became distressed at the sight of patients who were ill and who recovered, only to go back to their old way of life. He realized he 'wanted to heal their souls ... I saw I was helping these men to sin'.

He mentions how apparently trivial experiences led him back to a certainty about his conviction that he should preach. An old friend asked him to go to a theatre in Leicester Square with his new bride, and Dr Lloyd-Jones went, and as he came out to the square a Salvation Army band was playing hymns. 'When I heard this band and the hymns, I said, " These are my people, these are the people I belong to, and I'm going to belong to them".' He describes it like a scene from Wagner's *Tannhauser* in a vivid metaphor – the pull of the world as against the attraction of the chorus of the pilgrims, producing intolerable conflicts.

He decided to offer himself as a minister to a part of the Welsh Calvinistic Methodist Church known as the Forward Movement, its home mission sector. The Welsh name for it is *Y Symudiad Ymosodol:* this means, literally, 'the aggressive movement'. He was accepted, and thoughts of where he might minister resulted in an offer to go to Newport, in Gwent. There he found the church too comfortable by far: he had told his fiancée that he wanted '*a raw place*' and when he received an invitation from a church at Sandfields, Aberavon he felt it was the right place for him. It was first necessary for the presbytery in London to accept his call as a genuine vocation, and this they did in the autumn of 1926.

During this period of conflict since 1925 the young doctor had become well known because of his speaking engagements. With hindsight some of the subjects on which he spoke are worthy of note: *Puritanism* was one such address. He explained to his audience that he only knew Bunyan's *Pilgrim's Progress*, and a little about George Fox the Quaker leader and about Richard Baxter, another famous Puritan. He said he had come not to talk *about* Puritanism, but to talk Puritanism. He urged his listeners to look for the best description of Puritanism in the letters of St Paul. He said Christianity was not to be found without 'the Baptism of the Holy Spirit'. In this lecture in 1926 to his local church at Charing Cross he dwelt on the Puritan virtues of soberness and restraint, and one paragraph is particularly clear as a foreshadowing of what he believed later:

'But God does not always appear to the Puritan as the Hound of Heaven. There is another mood, there are occasions when God is love, when God is a gentle Father taking an occasional walk in his garden – the earth on which we dwell. During these days nothing can equal the ecstasy of the Puritan.' He deplored the fact that plain living and high thinking were no more, and asked his audience when they would return to Puritanism. By June 1926 he felt, as he was to say much later: 'It was God's hand that laid hold of me, and drew me out, and separated me to this work.'

**Marriage and Ministry**

The conflicts of the period from 1925 had not only been spiritual. He had also been very concerned about finding the person who was to be his wife. Bethan Phillips was someone whom he had known for nine years, as a remarkably attractive woman, a medical student who was a member of the church they both attended at Charing Cross. Her father was an ophthalmic surgeon in London who came from the same village of Newcastle Emlyn in West Wales that Dr Lloyd-Jones knew so well. Bethan's grandfather was well known as a Methodist preacher and leader: Evan Phillips, one of whose distinctions was his short sermons: he only preached for twenty minutes. Evan Phillips in his life had spanned two remarkable religious revivals, that of 1859 and 1904. His son Thomas Phillips had not only succeeded remarkably as an eye surgeon, but was also the father of two children (Bethan and Ieuan) who were to have key roles in the church.

Ieuan was to be head of the home mission described above as the Forward Movement, and Bethan was to serve from 1927 to her husband's death as a key factor in his stability and success. Ieuan Phillips was already a friend of Dr Lloyd-Jones before his sister Bethan responded to Martyn's approach and agreed to marry him. It was not until after their marriage that she first heard her young husband preach. It was a remarkable decision of the young newly qualified Dr Bethan Phillips to give up her medical career to work with her husband in a 'raw place' as he had described what he sought and found at Aberavon. As a helpmeet she was a tower of strength through a marriage of exceptional quality: she must have known what might be involved in a move from Barts Hospital and Harley Street to a small church in a poor industrial area, during a period of depression in industry following the General Strike of 1926. It offered little money to live on, and much uphill struggle. Bethan Lloyd-Jones has written her own account of their time in Aberavon, near Port Talbot in South

Wales, in *Memories of Sandfields 1927–1938*. She describes how she first needed to come to know her own faith, and then entered into the spiritual battles involved in establishing the new ministry which she and her husband shared in the small but growing church.

After their marriage in January 1927 and their honeymoon in Torquay, they were able to arrive in something of a rush at Aberavon for a welcome meeting on 4 February 1927. The Calvinistic Methodist Church had its Association meetings in London in 1927. Dr Lloyd-Jones was ordained at Whitefield's Tabernacle in Tottenham Court Road. By a happy coincidence the young ordinand was able to preach from what was a memorial pulpit to Whitefield, giving the same message about the need for Christ to enter and bring a new life – a message very different from that of the other two distinguished speakers. A clear picture of the setting he worked in (The Forward Movement) is given in a recent book called *Grace, Grit and Gumption* by Geraint Fielder: compared to well known evangelists like Seth Joshua and his brother, this young doctor was a very different type of recruit to the home mission scene.

After his ordination Dr Lloyd-Jones had to slip away quickly, since his wife after a difficult delivery had given birth to their first child Elizabeth, described as the 'ordination baby'. The family life begun in such an unusual setting was to prove a happy and sustaining one for Dr and Mrs Lloyd-Jones. Their two daughters Elizabeth and Ann were to prove a great joy. As they grew up and in their own later lives his daughters were devoted to everything that was part of their father's ministry. As this ministry grew, and with it his fame in Wales, in London and abroad the family was vital as a centre of peace and support during what became, frequently, a stormy passage. He followed his daughters' careers at Oxford University and later with a proud and anxious concern for them, and they returned a loyal affection for him.

Each daughter had three children: their nurture was an important concern and joy for Dr Lloyd-Jones. Elizabeth and her husband Sir Fred Catherwood provided a great deal of help to Dr and Mrs Lloyd-Jones especially in their later years. In London they moved to a new house where Ann lived in a separate flat and looked after them. His daughters have had a great part also in the production of the many books published before and after Dr Lloyd-Jones' death in 1981. Elizabeth has been in the forefront of the important work of publishing many of Dr Lloyd-Jones' sermons since his death, as has her son Christopher. His wife lived to the age of 90 dying some eight years after her husband, having continued to share a house with her daughter Ann who did so much to care for her there. In the long partnership that Dr and Mrs Lloyd-Jones enjoyed, the fight of faith had been as important as all the many family joys and sorrows.

**Still a doctor?**

While at Aberavon Dr Lloyd-Jones had continued to see patients who came to him. It was an important fact in 1927 that, twenty years before the British National Health Service was founded in 1948, a distinguished physician was available who did not see a patient in order to charge a fee but rather as a Christian duty. Dr Lloyd-Jones' work in this area attracted some criticism but most of this was due to envy rather than genuine concern for medical ethics. At times it was fraught with problems when, as still happens today, needy Christians seek medical help from a Christian physician without a proper regard for the courtesies of letting the family doctor know fully what they are about. It may have added greatly to Dr Lloyd-Jones' burdens, but did not distract him from his main duties as a young pastor and preacher.

He described with some amusement how he sat behind two women in a bus, unrecognized, and heard one woman saying to the other: 'Oh yes, I have heard that the doctors are doing badly in Harley Street just now, so no doubt he was glad to get away and take up this work'! The local and national press were in their own way equally mixed up in their presentation of the events. They wanted to stress the romantic side, but had little grasp of what the young doctor and his wife were facing. Sometimes one feels even the Christian writers of recent years are not much better informed as to the facts: the biographers of David Watson succeed in saying that 'the great Dr Lloyd-Jones was a surgeon who had left his career in middle age to join the Congregational ministry', thus making three major mistakes in one sentence.

Dr Lloyd-Jones often returned to medical themes in his addresses and sometimes in his sermons. He believed strongly, as has been said, in the mystique of being a doctor. In reading some sermons – such as the ones on spiritual depression, one may see him actually changing roles briefly and speaking with medical authority as much as that of a preacher. It might be argued that this was at times unwise of him, but perhaps inevitable.

He kept up his reading and the medical journals were used, he said, as light reading on a Saturday night quite often. He was interested not only in mainstream medicine and followed the many changes in it, but also in complementary and alternative medicine. He could speak for over an hour extempore in the ministers' fraternal in answer to a question on acupuncture. He had a special association in later life with homoeopathy and one of its famous practitioners Dr Margaret Blackie.

**Give attention to reading**

Some inevitably asked the question that is put in John's Gospel (7:15, Authorized Version): 'How has this man letters, having never learned?' There were those who felt he should have gone through the customary channels of theological training college. We have already noted how Dr Lloyd-Jones, in 1925, had begun to learn Greek.

During those first 'hidden years' in Aberavon very serious study was part of the daily programme, and was continued in the holidays. His daughter Elizabeth recently described on the radio how she was supervised on a beach by her father, who would be sitting propped against a wall and reading a large new book by Emil Brunner, but if interrupted he would come with her and admire her sandcastles as any doting father would. Dr Lloyd-Jones described how someone had drawn his attention to the works of Jonathan Edwards, and with what joy he discovered the heavy two volume set in a second-hand book shop for five shillings, and patiently worked his way through them. When he was criticised for not preaching enough about the cross of Christ he bought the best books on the doctrine of the atonement and sought to correct the deficits in his preaching. He continued to read a phenomenal amount – and with an omnivorous appetite, although he read slowly. He also kept a spiritual journal which was on show at the centenary exhibition: my doubts as I tried to read his notoriously difficult handwriting was that anyone trying to transcribe it as 'a journey of the soul' would have a very hard task.

He confessed later in life that he had become, at times, very keen on explaining the Christian faith to an unbelieving world and possibly too interested in apologetics. But *evangelism* was his main concern and in these early years in a small church built to reach the unchurched poor, there were remarkable successes. One of the striking things was that the church secretary, who had been a very enthusiastic Labour politician locally, became entirely devoted to Christian work after his conversion under Dr Lloyd-Jones' ministry.

Dr Lloyd-Jones was ordained in the Calvinistic Methodist Church (sometimes known as The Presbyterian Church of Wales – the largest church in Wales which was, in effect its religious establishment). Fifty years later, he replied to the warm congratulations that he received from this church, saying he was very proud to have been one of its ministers. This must be borne in mind when some try to assert that Dr Lloyd-Jones was always a separatist, rather than a minister in what came to be called 'a mixed church'. His knowledge of church history became detailed and profound. His appetite for biography seemed insatiable: 'show me the lineaments of the man', he used to say. But he read everything he could get hold of that was relevant to his work, and much that simply gave him a proper grasp of the modern scene as it changed.

As an example of the breadth of his study, I once heard him begin a talk to the church meeting at Westminster Chapel, which was announced as a talk on the subject of 'Baptism'. He began ironically and wittily by inviting anyone who felt they had the answers to all the problems of understanding the teaching on baptism to come to the platform to take his place. Dr Lloyd-Jones explained that he had read every new account of the teaching on baptism that had appeared since his ordination, and he was still not quite sure what the right answers were to all the problems. But his talk was, as ever, well informed and authoritative, and I remember he favoured adult baptism by sprinkling.

Because he read so widely he was often able to quote from recent writings on a subject in order to show what he saw as the bankruptcy of human knowledge without God's revelation. He would use such knowledge – and his remarkable memory for what he had read –

simply as a means to go further and enable him to persuade his listeners to follow him in seeing the Christian answers to modern problems. His aim was to gain a hearing for a modern application of the Christian gospel, and to give the glory for all this to God. It was an example of the consecration of his intellect, abilities and strengths of personality, to the ministry and vocation which he had long felt was his true destiny.

**What kind of Preaching?**

One of Dr Lloyd-Jones' dictums about preaching generally was that it should be 'logic on fire, eloquent reason'. A comment made on his early preaching in Wales in 1927 was that 'it showed there was no incompatibility between a first rate intellect and evangelism'.

Some, who should know better, regarded him as a typical Welsh preacher. To this his answer is clearly written: 'I am not and never have been, a typical Welsh preacher. I felt that in preaching the first thing that you had to do was to demonstrate to the people that what you were going to do was very relevant and urgently important ... I started with the man whom I wanted to listen, the patient. It was a medical approach really – here is a patient, a person in trouble, an ignorant man who has been to the quacks, and so I deal with all that in the introduction. I wanted to get to the listener and then come to my exposition'. As he put it to me in discussions with him, he believed that he should always connect with his listeners. 'Only connect', in fact, might have been his slogan.

But his mature style was much more than a series of negatives. He did refuse to use the traditional three points of explaining a text, and he would never use alliterative headings. He abhorred the old Welsh notion of *hwyl,* interesting though that was as a phenomenon: the preacher would chant (some students of *hwyl* said rather like a Gregorian chant in some cases) in what seemed to be a state of dissociated consciousness. Instead of all that traditional approach Dr Lloyd-Jones believed preaching was to appeal to the mind, and through the mind to the heart and the will. As an evangelist he upset many Christians in the early part of his career because he refused to make the 'appeal' so much cherished by some evangelists in their technique. Lloyd-Jones believed the truth must do its convicting and converting work, and avoided what some traditions of evangelism refer to as the 'altar call'. This fixed decision was to bring him into conflict, later, with the early days of Billy Graham and his approach to mass evangelism then.

He would explain that sometimes he might feel a text or a theme was something *given* – but he would then have to prepare himself and his sermon by working hard on the data, to prepare the subject matter for delivery. He would state equally clearly that he would look to God and his Holy Spirit for the power and unction to accompany his efforts – which was sometimes given during the proclamation of the sermon. He claimed no special prophetic inspiration, but hoped and prayed for this particular blessing of 'the divine unction'. At its highest form, he would equate that with what his Welsh eighteenth century hero Howell Harris described when he wrote in his journal that 'The Lord came down'. Harris was an Anglican who was refused ordination, and became an exhorter, a specially gifted preacher: many remarkable men in eighteenth century history became Christians through the preaching of Harris.

Dr Lloyd-Jones used no studied tricks of rhetoric. He was a natural orator and his style made him sound as if he was speaking, almost extempore, to the needs of his hearers. But there was hard work behind it, an art that concealed both his art and his personality as the preacher. Asked why he wore a black Geneva gown in his pulpit, he replied that it was partly to hide the minister and to help the worshippers to focus on the content of the service, and the truth of the message. Because it was his aim to be a messenger, and his message was the truth as he found it in the Bible. He aimed to apply and explain what he found as God's word to his listeners. The common people heard him gladly, and a whole variety of people who passed through his congregations found themselves arrested by the truth and its effect on their hearts, minds and lives.

I think he brought the microscope back into preaching: by this I mean that he did not skate over passages with a kind of travelogue, but looked intently at the words of the text in order to extract and apply its message. He taught passionately that without finding and explaining and pressing home the biblical message which you had yourself found in the text you were not doing justice to your task as a preacher. The deep seriousness and passionate intensity was what reached the listener's mind and heart. It is not always captured on the written page. I was kindly given copies of the written versions in the form of five volumes of his sermons on The First Epistle of John. What I missed there was precisely 'the roll, the rise, the carol, the creation' that the poet Gerard Manley Hopkins (had he heard it) would surely have recognized in the great creative act that is true expository preaching.

**From Wales back to Westminster**

In 1938, after eleven fruitful years in Aberavon, and travelling as a preacher to many parts of the United Kingdom and North America, Dr Lloyd-Jones let his church know that he was leaving. He said he was exhausted, and uncertain about his future. At first, it seemed likely that he would be asked to go to the college in Bala in 1938 as its new Principal. But many Methodist ministers in North Wales regarded him as a fundamentalist to be rejected for such a role. The way was soon to open to join Dr G. Campbell Morgan as an assistant minister in Westminster Chapel. He started there for an initial six months period in September 1938. He was to stay there until 1968.

At Westminster Chapel he was to find a spiritual base vital to his new period of ministry, which was to become very important in the Christian world. He became, in many ways, its foremost Evangelical leader for some years. There were many initial problems because of the fact that the Second World War had been declared in September 1939. But soon it was clear that a new voice, a new force was present in London. His firm basis for his work was his preaching Sunday by Sunday. He sought to teach Christians in the mornings, and to preach an evangelistic sermon on Sunday evenings. The forties and fifties were to see him at the height of his God-given powers.

Dr J. I. Packer has described Dr Lloyd-Jones in the pulpit thus: 'But his preaching always took the form of an argument, biblical, evangelical, doctrinal and spiritual ... when he came to the awesome thing that he had to declare at that point about our glorious, self-vindicating God, the Doctor would let loose the thunder and lightning with a spiritual impact that was simply stunning. I have never known anyone whose speech communicated such a sense of the reality of

God as did the Doctor in those occasional moments of emphasis and doxology. Most of the time, however, it was clear, steady analysis, reflection, correction and instruction....'

As one who was there, I agree with this description. From 1947 to 1953 it was a new experience for me to hear week by week the explaining and teaching of the content of the Bible, verse by verse. He was preaching on Paul's letter to the Philippians when I first heard him at Westminster Chapel. But I remember well the Sunday mornings for two years on The First Epistle of John, and two years of preaching on *The Sermon on the Mount*. There were many other series of evening sermons, aimed more at non-believers visiting the church, but these might be equally arresting to believers who thought themselves familiar with the old truths of the Gospel.

In London he became active in many ways: as a statesman of the Evangelical world he worked closely with Dr Douglas Johnson (the founder of IVF – now known as the Universities and Colleges Christian Fellowship or UCCF). He worked to found and prosper the Evangelical Library of Mr Geoffrey Williams. Two young Christians, Raymond Johnson (later of 'Festival of Light' fame) and a young Oxford man called Jim Packer asked him for support in starting what became the annual Puritan Conference. Numbers of other Christian organizations claimed him as their speaker, chairman or Vice-President. Later IFES (the International Fellowship of Evangelical Students) benefited from his wise leadership. The preacher with an apostolic and prophetic stamp became an important Christian leader of enormous power and influence. In many ways he became a politician, as we shall see, and some of his political actions within the evangelical world led to great distress for many who could not follow his later call for secession ('to come out and come in'). We will try to follow him in his complex series of roles.

## DJ, IVF and IFES

Dr Lloyd-Jones hated acronyms and would often poke fun at them. Nevertheless, he refers to Dr Douglas Johnson in one of his letters to his friend of many years, the well-known Anglican scholar Philip E. Hughes (dated 2 March 1942) as DJ 'in some ways the most important person in evangelical circles in these days'. Since DJ is an acronym used by Dr Lloyd-Jones, and was the way in which Dr Johnson was universally known, I shall use it also. I met DJ in 1946: he was another man who had trained as a doctor, as well as in philosophy, and had given it all up in 1924 to work with what became the IVF (Inter-Varsity Fellowship). He was to serve it for forty years and was then General Secretary of the Christian Medical Fellowship for ten years. He met and worked with all kinds of Christians who belonged to different parts of the evangelical establishment. His work with Dr Lloyd-Jones was very important as soon as London became his base: indeed their association developed and spread, to be worldwide. DJ had described his close work with DMLl-J as a kind of attraction of opposites: different cultural backgrounds – he very English, DMLl-J very Welsh. Their initial experience in education showed a stark contrast, even though their medical training was similar. Each came from a church background where there was also a contrast – reflecting the centuries old distinction between chapel and church, between the gathered church and the parish church. Yet they achieved much together, and I have letters from DJ describing the ups and downs of their relationship.

I was told by Dr Lloyd-Jones in a published interview on his views that many blamed him for being too influential in the IVF and related circles. Indeed I heard it said that DJ was 'in the Doctor's pocket': but to personalize it thus may not be the whole truth. DJ tried hard to persuade Dr Lloyd-Jones to get more professional help in preparing his sermons for the press: a letter of his pleads for this, but his suggestion fell on deaf ears since it was characteristic of the preacher that he wanted to maintain complete control of his output and his material.

In frequent and regular advice, guidance and hard work together with DJ, Dr Lloyd-Jones would serve as chairman and President of IVF and later of theInternational Fellowship of Evangelical Students (IFES). It is hard to overestimate the power and influence of Dr Lloyd-Jones in the evangelical world largely because of this work undertaken in the period before, during and after World War II. He and DJ were active in the Theological Students' Fellowship (TSF) where topics were discussed under Dr Lloyd-Jones' expert chairmanship. My friends in that fellowship used to tell me that he *was* the TSF, so marked was his dominant leadership of it.

His work in starting the preparations for Tyndale House in Cambridge was another important and fruitful field. DJ, in his history of IVF, *Contending for the Faith,* describes the meeting in St Luke's Vicarage Hampstead in 1938 to form a Biblical Research Committee. This led to a conference at Oxford in 1941, when, in spite of the War and its gloom, bright prospects for what eventually became Tyndale House in Cambridge were foreseen. Lloyd-Jones gave one of the original talks and was full of wise advice in the planning and execution of this great project.

In other Christian circles, the name of Lloyd-Jones was anathema: for example, the *Church's Council of Healing*, where one leader told me only Dr Lloyd-Jones prevented the healing movement from sweeping the church. That leader died long before Dr Lloyd-Jones changed his position and viewpoint, from his early agreement with Professor B. B. Warfield's views on healing to an acceptance of healing gifts. He was later seen by many charismatic leaders as lending support to the 'gifts of healings' which were so much part of the renewal movement. But all those later developments were some decades away from his early ministry in London.

Another movement with which he would not co-operate was the *Keswick Convention*, which was central to many evangelical churches in the thirties and forties, with teaching on the Christian Life which led to phrases like 'the second blessing' to describe an experience of sanctification offered then, as part of the Keswick Convention package. Dr Lloyd-Jones had read the history of Keswick as described by B. B. Warfield and others: he saw it as derived from the Higher Life movement, in turn owing much to the Wesleys' views on sinless perfection. He wanted a much more active view of the Christian life as described in a watershed, defining address on *Christ Our Sanctification* published by the IVF press. This was a clear and effective counterblast to Keswick teaching current at that time, in the forties.

For decades now there has been a sea change in Keswick teaching, and it does not follow the strict lines that it used to do. It may well be that the speakers who have made Keswick count in the last few decades have owed much to Dr Lloyd-Jones' work for a return to a more balanced Biblical teaching. But much friction was caused by the fact that Dr Lloyd-Jones was opposed to views such as those which used slogans like 'let go and let God', and advocated a passive view of holiness in contrast to the robust fighting tradition (against the world, the flesh and the devil) which was part of the older views on Christian living.

**Books, the Library and The Banner**

In some ways Dr Lloyd-Jones had one aim, stated often: a return to the Bible as the inspired Word of God, and as a result to a more Biblical practice in personal and church life. But a very clear subsidiary aim was to get more people to read the Christian classics. He made many successful efforts to persuade publishers to reprint key books: John Calvin's *Institutes of the Christian Religion* was one of these. There were many others, and when the Banner of Truth was formed it was its aim to republish evangelical (or at least Calvinistic) literature. Sometimes Dr Lloyd-Jones was rumoured to disagree with 'The Banner': the example that sticks in my mind was when a decision was taken to reprint Bishop J. C. Ryle's *Christian Leaders of the Eighteenth Century* without the chapters on John Wesley. As I heard the story, Dr Lloyd-Jones predicted to the committee that the Banner would be a laughing stock, for leaving out Wesley, simply because they disagreed with Wesley's Arminian, as opposed to Calvinistic theology. But all in all The Banner of Truth Trust had his support and published most of his many books such as the series on Romans, Ephesians and on the Puritans. They were also to publish his biography, letters and many related books, and continue to do so, with the latest *Romans* volume on chapter 12, published recently.

He was also a key player in establishing the Evangelical Library in central London. Geoffrey Williams had gathered the Library together and when the two men met, a partnership grew up. All the old library stock was moved to a site near Baker Street, close to the Welsh Chapel in Chiltern Street, where it still is. New books were constantly added. One unhappy mistake in an advertisement referred to the Library as containing any book a Christian might need, both 'out of print and out of date', when of course what they sought to offer was both *up-to-date* works and those which were out of print.

The Library continues to be an important and effective agency, with a large section called 'The Dr Martyn Lloyd-Jones Room'.

A series of Evangelical Library annual lectures were started and was to prove very successful. I recall my flat mate returning from Dr Lloyd-Jones' lecture on Isaac Watts in 1948, full of enthusiasm after he had listened, entranced, for over an hour to a talk on Watts and his hymns, and hymnody in worship. There were many such occasions, when the speaker seemed to open the door to a world of knowledge and experience to which any Christian, whatever his denominational loyalties, could enter in and make his own. It was a period of ministry which appealed to so many: Roman Catholic and Protestant, Pentecostal or Plymouth Brethren, Methodist or Anglican – all his listeners could derive lasting benefit from his vast learning and enthusiasm.

Students might be glimpsed in many Christian bookshops seeking out books to increase their knowledge because of some seed sown, or interest stirred, by this teaching in the school of faith. We learned that Dr Lloyd-Jones was recalling us to a more biblical faith long before the work of Barth and Brunner had led to the huge revival in Reformation studies. New works on John Calvin and Martin Luther and others were to become more freely available. As we shall see, the man who said, while still a young doctor, how much he thought the Baptism of the Spirit was a vital part of Christian experience, was to have a chance to apply his teaching to the later charismatic movement, many of whose leaders like Terry Virgo and Michael Harper described him as a most helpful guide and friend to them.

**Time Warps and Idiosyncrasies**

Dr Lloyd-Jones was not at all interested in changing his appearance or modifying his habits of dress: anyone who saw him in the 1950s might have thought he had walked straight in from the 1920s or earlier. Whereas later leaders in Christian churches sought to be more obviously accessible in terms of dress and manner, and loved to be called by their Christian names, Dr Lloyd-Jones was far removed from 'that whole approach' as he might have called it. He continued to dress in dark suits, wear stiff white collars, and wear the type of boots he had always worn. If dress is part of body language, he was to seem forever a child of the 1920s.

It was a curious paradox that someone who followed modern developments with the eye of a keen observer of the fashions and foibles of human nature, should seem to live in a time warp of his own. As one puzzles over such an endearing series of traits and characteristics, one may think of it as being his own care for his personal identity – not in a vain or aggrandizing way, but simply that he took pleasure in being himself and not seeking to ape any other fashion or custom. Others who liked to think of themselves as admirers of Dr Lloyd-Jones would jump on any Christian bandwagon, and sometimes on two, going in opposite directions.

He would be years ahead of many colleagues in spotting a trend in theology or politics, and his savagely witty comments would often puncture a bubble reputation. Yet the doctor himself would seem to want to be 'unchanged, unchanging' in how he looked and how he presented himself and his message. He made up his own mind even when others would think his conclusions wrong: I remember being surprised when he told me that he did not believe Shakespeare had written the work attributed to him, but that he espoused other views. This was interesting from a man who barely tolerated Textual Criticism of Scripture, let alone Higher Criticism.

His smaller and often-changing enthusiasms were well known, whether about diet and health, food in particular forms, or how often one should take baths without affecting the skin's health. He would remark how important it was not to dilute the gastric juices at a meal. All this, if his advice and foibles were accepted, would have made for followers full of peculiar beliefs and practices. Like many doctors, he seemed at times to be a confirmed hypochondriac, while at other times his friends wondered how he could work with such cavalier disregard for his own health, and were not surprised when he would become ill with exhaustion.

It was part of his character as a preacher that he abhorred what are sometimes called topical sermons. Yet he believed that the eternal truths should be applied, with almost clinical and surgical accuracy, to the needs of his listeners in their time and place. Unlike some of his followers who shared his love of the Puritans, he did not speak in seventeenth century diction. He would have liked the later witticism saying that the Westminster Conference, as the Puritan Conference became after the enforced departure of Dr J. I. Packer, was 'to prepare the twentieth century Christian minister for whatever the seventeenth century could throw at him'. But of that, more later. There were many remarkable aspects of both his temperament and character which I will try to describe in the light of his enormous and lasting achievements

**Spiritual Depression**

In 1954 Dr Lloyd-Jones preached a series of sermons under the general heading of *Spiritual Depression: its Causes and Cure.* Two sermons (according to the Westminster Record) were preached in May 1953. Some of the sermons were based on Psalms 42 and 43. It is clear that the book's author intended it to be about spiritual depression and not about clinical depression which any person (including those who are Christians) may suffer. These were later published in book form and proved one of the most successful of all the books of sermons in terms of sales and reprints over many years since 1965. Apart from the usual edition and reprints, 'Operation Mobilisation' was able to distribute 300,000 copies. The book, its theme and Dr Lloyd-Jones' treatment of the subject of depression demand special consideration, both because so many believe it to be of great value, and because others have grave doubts about the book, as I do. It must have affected many Christians and influenced attitudes towards those who are depressed. I have seen hundreds of Christians professionally in the last seven years who have suffered grievously from depression and related symptoms: unhappily some of the themes of this book have added to their guilt and their difficulties in accepting expert help.

It is possible that the title *Spiritual Depression* is wholly inappropriate: the subject, in actual fact, is about keeping fit in a spiritual sense. It is about what makes for healthy Christian living. Why then have a number of people that I have known well found it so upsetting when they were suffering from depression? Partly it is the repeated assertion of Dr Lloyd-Jones that a miserable Christian is a contradiction in terms. This plays into the guilt which many feel when they are ill with depression – good people, whether Christian or not, who blame themselves for their own suffering. How can we explain this?

Before 1954, when the series of sermons on depression was completed, no effective antidepressant had been on the market, though some progress was made towards that in 1954. Later, in 1955–6 when new forms of medication were available freely, I know how concerned Dr Lloyd-Jones was to know which kinds of antidepressants were most effective, because he asked me about them a good deal when I was beginning my medical career, and talked to other doctors in a similar way. He wanted to know enough to be able to advise those who asked his opinion.

If the sermons are read carefully it is, of course, clear that temperamental and illness factors are allowed for and seen as separate from spiritual depression, to some extent. I am sure that Dr Lloyd-Jones believed in the effective medical treatment of clinical depression in Christians. He would thank me for treating such patients whom he knew to be under my care. It was also a fact that when such a patient might telephone Dr Lloyd-Jones he would be told that the illness was a Satanic attack. Were both views correct? Perhaps so, since it can be argued that all illness is ultimately due to sin, Satan and the Fall. But was that what Dr Lloyd-Jones meant the patient to understand by his remarking that it was an attack of the Enemy? I do not know: but it left the patient, too, in some confusion, wondering if spiritual rather that medical treatment was the more appropriate course. The confusion is sad in someone who valued clarity almost above everything in such matters. Even he seemed at times to speak with a forked tongue, and to say rather different things by way of explanation in the same matter to two people, who would compare notes and wonder what he really meant. Some believe that this is characteristic of Celts, and it is a subject explored by Dr Lloyd-Jones in a Welsh lecture on *Religion and National Characteristics* first published in 1943.

I do not have the space here to consider whether he should have made more clear the distinction between treatable *clinical depression* and something else which he might call *spiritual depression.* Dr Lloyd-Jones never allowed any serious change during the revision of what the spoken word had been – as his daughter Elizabeth said in a lecture on his books, any editorial cuts were simply met with the answer: 'Put it back in'. It was almost as if he believed in verbal inspiration of his own words: I know he did not believe this, but rather may have given that impression because of the fact that he believed the preached word was different in kind and should not be modified substantially to make it easier to read.

Had the author been willing to have changes made for the sake of updating – as in the case of antidepressants – then I believe *Spiritual Depression* would have been a much more useful book. Dr Lloyd-Jones was, I recall, very keen on learning about Prof. H. J. Eysenck and behaviour therapy. I believe, had he followed the development of cognitive behavioural therapy, Dr Lloyd-Jones might also have found that a much more fitting treatment of depression, and similar to the New Testament approach.

Another question arises: how much had Dr Lloyd-Jones himself suffered from depression? My guess is that he had known the problem well in his own life. But he chose not to discuss it, even though he writes in the very first sermon on *Spiritual Depression* about Charles Haddon Spurgeon. He attributes his depression to the gout from which Spurgeon suffered – 'the gouty condition which finally killed him'. It is at this point that he adds that a depressive condition was frequently largely physical in those who came to him for advice. Perhaps later he advised them to have physical treatment as well as spiritual help. In a footnote about one illness Iain Murray mentions that his hero Dr Lloyd-Jones suffered from gout too. But whereas Spurgeon was happy to speak of his failings (as in his lecture on 'the minister's fits' of anxiety or sadness) Dr Lloyd-Jones was much more reticent about any mood changes or depression he might have suffered. I was surprised on one occasion at an IVF conference when Dr Lloyd-Jones was 51 years of age to hear him saying how important it was to know about the realities of the *male menopause* – but he did this without any direct personal reference.

## Counsellor and Psychologist

An important part of Dr Lloyd-Jones' gifts were those of psychological understanding in the ministry of counselling. He was someone who cared greatly about the welfare of those who came for help. Many hours were spent in listening and in offering spiritual counsel, especially to those who were themselves ministers of the

Gospel. He has often been called a pastor's pastor. There is an old question as to 'who cares for the carers', and one answer was that he saw clearly the special needs of those who were shepherds of Christ's flock. He was very shrewd in seeing what the problem was – both of personality and illness – and would co-operate with other specialists and put those in need of special help in touch with a proper surgeon or psychiatrist. He was much respected by the colleagues whom he would ask to help in this way. But some eminent Christian psychiatrists felt he did not support properly their attempts to be good Christians and good doctors: he belonged, after all, to a generation which knew little about modern clinical psychiatry.

He also had definite views of his own about some inadequate forms of Christian counselling. He wrote in a very clear way about the dangers he saw, in a lecture he gave on *The Doctor as Counsellor*: 'The point is that we must be very careful not to foist our opinions on others. The counsellor is not a dictator, he is simply there to give help. While he may give his views, and with care, put them quite strongly if asked, yet all that is put to the patient must be in a spirit of real sympathy, love and understanding. As counsellors we must never be in a position to imagine ourselves as "the conscience" of another! We are there to share with those who consult us experience, knowledge, wisdom and suggestions concerning the way of cure. There are, unfortunately, Christians who feel it their duty to impose their own legalistic views on others. Our business, however, is to persuade, never to force. We must always be careful to avoid condemnation – especially in the case of a sick or agitated person. If the plain truth of the situation comes home to the patient that is one thing; but it is not our place to condemn.'

How I wish all Christian counsellors might listen to, and profit from such advice.

But Dr Lloyd-Jones made another very valuable contribution in answering some of the arguments of Dr William Sargant, then a famous psychiatrist at St Thomas' Hospital London who wrote a best seller *Battle for the Mind* (1957). The lecture Dr Lloyd-Jones gave was printed as a booklet called *Conversions: Psychological and Spiritual* and was reprinted in a book of addresses called *Knowing the Times* (published in 1989 by Banner of Truth). Sargant sought to explain all conversions and revivals in terms of Pavlov and his dogs – conditioning and other notions of Pavlov's. He saw Wesley as a 'brainwasher' like so many other religious cult leaders that Sargant studied. While Lloyd-Jones wanted to correct the mistakes Sargant made, he also used his lecture to point out how modern evangelists must avoid pressures which simply produce psychological results. His aim was to return evangelists to a preaching of the truth and a reliance on God's Spirit to make the truth real to the hearers. The lecture is of lasting worth, and it is typical that Sargant wrote to him in friendly terms and shared an admiration for Lloyd-Jones' approach and his critique. For Dr Lloyd-Jones was defending the very mainstream tradition of preaching against all popular distortions, and against subtle corruptions into what might then be called brainwashing. By implication, a leader of Billy Graham's stature was not exempt from the criticisms in Sargant's work, and the older Dr Graham went a long way to avoid undue emotional pressures in his later work as an evangelist.

**The End of a Ministry: The Lost Leader**

Dr Lloyd-Jones continued his powerful and effective ministry based at Westminster Chapel, but supplemented with many visits, during the week, to speak at churches in Wales and other parts of Britain. He often went abroad in connection with IFES meetings as well as preaching in North America and elsewhere in the world. He had also sought to help a number of organizations to understand better what his message was: one thinks of his patient attendance at committees such as that of the British Council of Churches for many years. He made every attempt to join in co–operating with like-minded believers in other churches. Then, in 1966 came the astonishing address which he gave to the Evangelical Alliance at a meeting chaired by Dr John Stott. This has been widely discussed and many views have been expressed about it. Effectively, he called for evangelicals to come out of 'mixed denominations' and to come into a closer church fellowship of evangelical believers. John Stott immediately dissociated himself from this view publicly: he said Scripture and history was against it. Dr Stott wanted to make clear that 'the remnant' was inside the church, not outside it. Dr Stott remained a warm, loving personal friend of Dr Lloyd Jones to his death in 1981, and visited him regularly.

The results were that a series of small earthquakes shook the evangelical Christian world. But one wonders how much Dr Lloyd-Jones' health had to do with some of the decisions taken by him around this time. For, on 7 March 1968 he was admitted to the Royal Homoeopathic Hospital in London for major surgery and found to have cancer of the colon. It was a serious matter, and he had been unwell for some time with abdominal symptoms: after all, acute intestinal obstruction such as he suffered does not develop until a growth is well established. His recovery was slow and painful. He decided to resign from Westminster Chapel and devote his time to publishing his sermons, and to travelling and speaking more extensively. Some six months after the operation, after a difficult convalescence, he began to preach again. His wider ministry, after resigning from Westminster Chapel, soon became more evident. Thus in 1969 he was able to spend a longer time in the United States and gave sixteen lectures at the Westminster Seminary on *Preaching and Preachers*, later published. There was, between April and September 1969, a rich and varied ministry in the United States on this last of his many trips there. He was also able to meet many old friends, play golf (after a fashion) and enjoy much needed recreation as well as working on manuscripts of his sermons for publication.

In London, a central problem that led to sad and painful decisions were those concerning church union: Dr Lloyd-Jones had made his opposition to ecumenical approaches very clear.

Dr J. I. Packer had differed from him. Packer was joint author of a book called *Growing into Union: Proposals for Forming a United Church in England* where the other authors were either Anglo-Catholic (Professor E. L. Mascall and Bishop G. D. Leonard) or evangelical (Colin O. Buchanan).

Dr Lloyd-Jones wrote to Dr Packer to say there would be no Puritan Conference at Westminster Chapel in December 1970. It was effectively rather like being sent a Papal Bull, even though it did not excommunicate Packer. Thankfully Packer survived what many of us still feel was very scurvy treatment by Dr Lloyd-Jones and his like-minded colleagues. Quickly it became known that Dr Packer was now, for them, *persona non grata*, and he was cold shouldered and rejected by people with whom he had worked closely. For instance, Packer's book *Knowing God* which has helped millions who have bought and read it was actually first published in *The Evangelical Magazine*. This magazine now cut him off totally.

The Puritan Conference to which Packer had given so much of his time and energy for nearly twenty years, was restarted as The Westminster Conference in December 1971. The Westminster Fraternal, which had met monthly for many years with great profit, was reconstituted to exclude all Anglicans and others who did not recognise the need for secession and separation from mixed denominations. There was a marked hardening of attitudes which meant that all who could not follow Dr Lloyd-Jones in his leadership of those who looked for an independent, seceded evangelical church were now without the leader whom they had loved and respected for so long. I felt, as I feel sure did many others, something of Browning's sadness about Wordsworth in *The Lost Leader*:

> We that had loved him so, followed him, honoured him,
> Lived in his mild and magnificent eye,
> Learned his great language, caught his clear accents,
> Made him our pattern to live and to die!

It may seem excessive, but for many of us the choice of Dr Lloyd-Jones to speak of 'a small remnant' of which he was to be seen by his followers as the infallible leader meant a great loss, with something about it of Browning's haunting phrase: 'Never glad confident morning again'. It is easy for a group that sees itself as 'the remnant' – in the Biblical sense – who have not bowed the knee to ecumenism to become something of a ghetto, thinking of other Christians who do not share their views as beyond the pale.

His authorized biographer Iain Murray has rewritten the history of this time under the title of *Evangelicalism Divided*. For me it makes sad reading, since Murray's agendas are evident, and he wishes to justify everything that Dr Lloyd-Jones did as right, and infallibly correct. Many who loved and honoured him thought he was not always right, and believe that his treatment of Dr J. I. Packer was shabby in the extreme. But Murray is keen to show how right Dr Lloyd-Jones was in being reserved about his support for Dr Billy Graham and his methods of evangelism, as well as being right in everything else, of course. Those whose ministry has so evidently been blessed, such as that of Dr John Stott and Dr Packer and many others who did not follow Dr Lloyd-Jones to 'come out and come in' in 1967, come under Murray's heavy lash of criticism. Perhaps in the light of earlier Christian infighting – let us say between the Wesleys and their Calvinistic friends in the eighteenth century – his criticisms of Packer and Stott are mild. But it gives substance to the ironic comment 'see how these Christians love one another'.

Murray is less interested in the divisions which the charismatic movement of renewal were to produce, but these divisions are probably more important than many others, since some thought that Dr Lloyd-Jones became a charismatic teacher. Others (remembering his earlier teaching) point out his many criticisms of the excesses of that movement. How one wishes for an *unauthorized* biography which would take a fresh look at how the evangelical world was divided by the events of 1966 and the years following. Mao Tse-Tung in China was asked what he thought were the results of the French Revolution, and replied that it was too early to tell. We too may, perhaps, feel the same about the *putsch* which ousted Packer and others who did not share the required beliefs about separation and a pure church. Packer said in one of two characteristically warm and generous papers celebrating the achievements of Dr Lloyd-Jones that he was content to say: 'Was either of us right? History will judge, and to history I remit the matter'.

**The Charismatic Doctor**

Westminster Chapel was a place of order and sobriety in its services in the fifties. Whether there was a time of great spiritual power or not, – and the minister would point out that such a question was best left to God's initiative and sovereignty – things were always done 'decently and in order'. When I visited the chapel long after his death and heard a music group singing 'Happy birthday to you' in celebration of the minister's birthday, I assumed the good Doctor would have been rather surprised. Yet he might not, having been prepared for any such aberration by his long and varied experience.

In the mid 1930s Dr Lloyd-Jones visited a small village in South

Wales where the charismatic flames of the Welsh Revival of 1904 were kept burning, however feebly. I was told by my father (one of the keepers of that flame) that Dr Lloyd-Jones had said to him: 'You have a joy here which we do not have in Aberavon'. This was, after all, the young doctor who had spoken of the 'ecstasy of the Puritan' in 1926, even before he entered the ministry. The 'joy unspeakable' was important to his thinking about the Christian life from the beginning to the end of his life. In his last years he spoke much about 'the sealing of the Spirit'.

He was very concerned about the shallowness of much of our modern Christian experience. In a number of meetings (I think in every one that I attended) we would hear Dr Lloyd-Jones speaking very clearly at the Puritan Conferences of the danger of an intellectual, dry-as-dust theology without the warmth and depth of New Testament faith. I felt strongly that many speakers I listened to were in the tradition of the 'dry dissenters' as some early nonconformists were known. When I was an elder in a church in North Wales in the sixties one still heard fellow Methodists referring to some of their colleagues as dry dissenters. I have heard it said with conviction by those close to him that Dr Lloyd-Jones welcomed the renewal movement because it looked for more depth of spiritual life than many of his followers seemed interested in: for some of them head knowledge was enough, and they rather despised mere experiences.

David Watson is described by his biographers as having been 'authenticated' by Dr Lloyd-Jones, who is reported to have said to Watson and his colleagues that in his view they had received the Baptism of the Spirit. Anglicans and others who followed such leaders as David Watson and Michael Harper believed, in those early days, that the renewal movement and the experiencing of the gifts of the spirit heralded a profound religious revival. Perhaps in one sense it did, since the changes which resulted from that movement have had a profound effect. Yet Dr Lloyd-Jones had preached and taught much about praying for revival, and he looked for something much more evidently the work of God's sovereign spirit. He looked for a revival which exalted Christ and glorified God, by an outpouring of the Holy Spirit. What he saw rather was a movement leading to a concern for phenomena and spiritual gifts such as tongues and healings.

There were many sermons preached on the topics raised by the charismatic movement, only some of which are printed in the two books mentioned *Joy Unspeakable* and *Prove All Things: The Sovereign Work of the Spirit.* The author seeks to point out how we must not shut out any experience, since unbelief may lead to 'grieving the Spirit'. But much of the sermons also contain a very great deal which is meant to warn, advise and guide those overwhelmed by the phenomena of the charismatic movement. If even a modicum of his advice had been heeded, there would have been less by way of casualties within the movement. I have met many such casualties with psychiatric problems, and it always grieves me that these Christians have never as much as heard of Dr Lloyd-Jones. They would have benefited greatly if they had read and absorbed his writings and taken note of his warm, concerned advice.

It seems self-evident to me that within the traditions which Dr Lloyd-Jones sought to found and encourage, there are now many deep splits. I am only concerned with how these affect the subject of my sketch. Some claim him as a great charismatic leader and listen to tapes which support that view. Others, perhaps the majority of his followers, love and honour him as a great preacher in the tradition of St Paul, John Calvin, George Whitefield and other evangelists who stressed God's sovereignty, man's desperate plight, and the work of Christ and His Spirit.

## The Problems of a Great Man as Politician

There was no doubt in the minds of anyone who knew him for any length of time that Dr Lloyd-Jones was a great man. His gifts of intellectual ability of the highest order, with both remarkable speed and strength in his intelligence, marked him out. He was always several steps ahead of his opponents in any argument. But though he sought to remain humble, he knew his own abilities and he knew that he might, like his greatest human hero St Paul, *glorify his office* as a preacher even while he also believed he was 'less than the least of all saints'.

His achievements were soon evident: he was a great leader of men, and with his remarkable gifts to lead came many perils. There is a phrase used sometimes of British Prime Ministers, that they are the *first among equals*. But when one looks among the men and women close to Dr Lloyd-Jones one does not find anyone of comparable stature. Many men he led were good, godly and learned, devoted to their work: but none was touched with his type of greatness. Did he find it easier to lead men who were willing to be followers and not to be in any sense equals or competitors? I was told that one or two men who spoke up in argument against him were referred to as 'Her Majesty's Opposition': but what does that say about the man who uses such language? I think it means one must be careful of offending a representative of majesty, of taking liberties with the man who sees himself in that regard as Prime Minister with a 'loyal opposition'. It is not a particularly happy or a Christian turn of phrase. Is it an attitude that we should welcome among men who were together as fathers and brethren, not simply leaders and led? It is so easy for us lesser people to find some strange fulfilment in following 'great men'.

The proverb says that the oak is a great tree, but not much grows in its shade. Even Iain Murray, in the second volume of over 800 pages devoted to the second forty years, finds it possible to admit that Dr Lloyd-Jones had not allowed his church officers at Westminster Chapel to learn to play their part in the church leadership. When he suddenly left in 1968 they had not developed the skills to manage without him, or to plan appropriately. It is noteworthy that unlike Dr G. Campbell Morgan when he had an assistant minister, the ministers who assisted Dr Lloyd-Jones had an obviously subordinate role as assistants.

Again sticking to facts rather than speculation, it seemed evident that on any scale with dominance at one end and submission at the other, Dr Lloyd-Jones was very high on the trait of dominance. Whether he required submission consciously is immaterial: that is what he obtained from any true follower. The forming of a party leads to party spirit. For Dr Lloyd-Jones the first chapter of the First Letter to Corinthians was very important. Why did he not then do more to prevent such party spirit developing? 'I am of Paul, I am of Apollos' soon became 'I am of Lloyd-Jones'. The fact that this was never stated, except by implication, made it all the more menacing for the future healthy development of his followers. All followers of great men, all of us who give in to the natural impulse to hero-worship, should never forget the last verse of the apostle John's first letter: *'Little children, keep yourselves from idols'*.

The sad thing is that so many seemed unaware that such a great man, when acting as a politician in church matters, lost something of his greatness by becoming the head of a party. He would speak of the men who followed him as 'his boys'. Of course one knows that calling them his boys was a real mark of affection, but it was also something else perhaps more sinister. To be a true boy meant never being allowed to grow up or to challenge effectively what the father said or did. It also meant, for a great many, idolizing Dr Lloyd-Jones as I did when I was a medical student. I once said, speaking rather lightly, to a person close to the great Doctor, that there was a time in my teens that I thought he not only knew everything, but was *right* about everything. The serious reply to my frivolous remark was: 'But I still believe that'.

It is one thing to believe in the infallible Word of God, quite another to believe that the words of a leader are infallible, or his conduct always right. The best men make mistakes, but I doubt if the true follower of Dr Lloyd-Jones ever attributed any mistake or misjudgment to the hero that they loved and worshipped.

**Personality and Temperament**

My aim in the previous studies in this book has been not only to avoid speculation, but also to draw some conclusions from the facts reviewed. I have tried to show how Martin Luther and John Bunyan were perfectionists who suffered a good deal in their youth from obsessional symptoms. The careful reader will have noted that a number of the others – J. B. Phillips, Christina Rosetti, Amy Carmichael and Gerard Manley Hopkins were also people with marked traits of obsessionality. Does Dr Lloyd-Jones have such traits also? When it was put to me on three separate occasions by two distinguished Christian psychiatrists that Dr Lloyd-Jones was a considerable obsessional, I was offended, as if my own father were being criticized. Then a devout and learned younger doctor said to me that if anyone by his style and writing showed his obsessional traits it was surely Dr Lloyd-Jones. Grudgingly I agreed, although I did not wish blemishes in my hero to be pointed out to me.

But of course, being over-conscientious or a workaholic is not a fault, it is simply part of many of the best peoples' temperament. No one can say that perfectionism (another characteristic) is a bad thing in itself – it simply adds to many difficulties when things have to be done in a set and 'perfect' way. With it goes a tendency to be rigid in the approach to problems, to be inflexible in moral or spiritual issues, and to have a great need to be *in control.* Such features are readily detectable in Dr Lloyd-Jones. One of the doctors I have mentioned asked me if I could not see that his over-emphasis on *'revival'* amounted to a form of obsessional thinking: I now believe he was right about that. But not everything about such a person as Dr Lloyd-Jones can be subsumed under a rubric of obsessive-compulsive traits.

I believe we must try and bear in mind his early upbringing and his experiences of loss in his own home – not only the fire from which he was saved at ten, but his oldest brother's death, and his father's bankruptcy. Losses such as that leave a lot of grief to be dealt with one way or another. A clinical psychologist would see Dr Lloyd-Jones sometimes using *denial* as a defence, but much more often using his powerful mind to raise defences by processes usually called *rationalization* and *intellectualization.* Such an observer would say that a young student would experience a great drive to work hard and succeed because of a need to compensate, and indeed to over-compensate, for what he might have felt to be deficits. Why did he always have to be right about everything, and why was he so combative, so aggressive? It was the only way he could cope with all that had happened, in my view.

Of course there was quite another side to him: his kindness and generosity, his willingness to offer help endlessly to those who needed him. His wit and humour gave rise to many stories which bear repetition but have been largely left out of my sketch. He was great fun to be with, and enjoyed company as any gregarious, extrovert Welshman would. He could be frivolous and light-hearted when the occasion called for it. When I first saw him playing table tennis at home, in a book-lined room, it was a revelation of this other side of him – though even then there was a fierce determination to win even at ping-pong. I read in his grandson's account that at croquet in his older daughter's home the same style became evident.

Reports of his early ministry indicate a more severe, rather threatening aspect: he would be quite outspoken about how Christians should dress and not provoke sexual conflicts. One good friend of mine was sitting near the front of a church wearing a canary yellow pullover: he sought to conceal it as the preacher waxed eloquent about his views on proper dress.

Because he was such a desperately serious person in his vocation, I do not think his sober, heartfelt and solemn attitude gave any offence. His long prayer in the church services at Westminster Chapel seemed to be very moving to many worshippers. His prayer of dismissal at the end of a service which including the phrase about 'our short uncertain life and earthly pilgrimage' seemed wholly apt, for he was a man who clearly lived his life in the light of eternity and laboured, in Milton's phrase 'as ever in my great taskmaster's eye'. He mellowed as he grew older and doubtless having six grandchildren with whom he was so happy to be, had as much to do with this as anything else.

**Character and Achievement**

As I have said in my introduction to this book, character is what we do with our temperament. There is no question that it was the godly and devout character of Dr Lloyd-Jones which was responsible for the great impression he made on those who grew to know him. He was in many ways more aware of his failings than anyone else, but he worked at them with a very firm and determined discipline, and with much success. Anyone who spent some nights at his home as I did as a student knew how naturally, for him, the matter of family prayers were; something that showed his wholehearted devotion as a Christian. He was still, in his mature old age, as determined not only to talk about Puritanism but to live it as he had been when he was only twenty five years of age. For him what he found in the teaching and the lives of those who had made such a contribution to English and Welsh life after the Reformation was a model of how to live out the Christian life.

I think it was from his pulpit that I first heard the words of Wordsworth declaimed from the *Ode to a Skylark*, which I have quoted in my epigraph to this chapter.

Type of the wise, who soar but never roam

True to their kindred points of heaven and home.

Dr Lloyd-Jones often soared. One nurse at Barts said to a friend of mine that 'he looked like a great bat about to fly off in that black Geneva gown'. But when he took flight, his wings were like those of an eagle, the traditional symbol, on a church lectern, of the word of God being carried. If he did sometimes soar like an eagle it was with his trust that under his wings were – at such times – the wind of the Spirit, the divine unction he always prayed to know. Of course it was not always so. I recall walking around a golf course with a friend whose adoration of the Doctor was even greater than mine, and he sadly reported to me that he had heard Dr Lloyd-Jones speak the previous week on 'Communication': he told me sadly that 'he never got off the ground'.

Part of his greatness was that as a preacher he followed his own description of how the Puritans preached: painfully, practically, powerfully. At his best he would prepare and take great pains over his preparation. He would aim to be practical in applying his message to that particular group of hearers. And he would look to God for the Spirit's unction to make his preaching powerful and as he said, 'that was not always given'.

His achievement was to use his genius in and for preaching and proclaiming in different ways, the Christian message. In doing so he was 'fighting with beasts at Ephesus' – he once borrowed St Paul's phrase as he then described his week's activities. He made an enormous contribution to restoring the intellectual and spiritual backbone of a generation of Christians who seemed to have lost it. He led from the front, and his innate combativeness was wedded to a courage which made him fear no one.

We have noted that he had a life-saving operation for cancer in 1967. I did not know until after his funeral that he had been suffering from another form of cancer, unrelated to the first, for many years. Such was his reticence, and his wish to endure suffering like a good soldier. He spoke a good deal about death: how Wesley had said 'Our people die well', and how the great Apostle Paul's words 'to die is gain' might be fulfilled. I often heard him say that if we wished to die like Paul we needed to live like him. It was not a morbid matter, but simply another aspect of his solemn, serious view of life. Much more might be said about how his native genius and God's grace were at work in Dr Lloyd-Jones and his many achievements, but space and time forbids a fuller estimate.

At his memorial service, perhaps inevitably, there was a reading from *The Pilgrim's Progress* which he had made so much of in his talk on Puritanism given fifty–five years earlier. The passage read was about Mr Valiant-for-truth towards the end of the book, which is a fitting way to take our leave of Dr Lloyd-Jones:

> 'When he understood it, he called for his friends, and told them of it. Then said he, I am going to my fathers, and though with great difficulty I am got hither, yet now I do not repent me of all the trouble I have been at to arrive where I am. My Sword, I give to him that shall succeed me in my Pilgrimage, and my Courage and skill, to him that can get it. My Marks and Scars I carry with me, to be a witness for me, that I have fought his Battles, who now will be my Rewarder. When the day that he must go hence, was come, many accompanied him to the River side into which as he went, he said Death, where is thy Sting? And as he went down deeper, he said, Grave where is thy Victory? So he passed over, and the Trumpets sounded for him on the other side.'

*Further Reading:*

Eighty of his books in print and 1,600 tapes of his sermons are available.

Iain Murray, *D. Martyn Lloyd-Jones* two volumes of authorised biography:

i. *The First Forty Years 1899–1939* 394 pp

ii *The Fight of Faith 1939–1981* 832 pp

Both published by Banner of Truth.

Iain Murray: *Evangelicalism Divided* (Edinburgh, Banner of Truth, 2000)

D. M. Lloyd-Jones: *The Sermon on the Mount,* (Leceister, IVP)

D. M. Lloyd-Jones: *Preaching and Preachers,* (London, Hodder, 1971 and reprints)

D. M. Lloyd-Jones: *Knowing the Times* Addresses (1942–1977), (Edinburgh, Banner of Truth).

D. M. Lloyd-Jones: *Spiritual Depression* paperback, various publishers

D. M. Lloyd-Jones: *The Puritans,* (Edinburgh, Banner ofTruth)

Christopher Catherwood: *Five Evangelical Leaders.* (Fearn, Christian Focus Publications, 1994 & reprints)

Christopher Catherwood:*From Wales to Westminster.* (Wheaton, Crossway 1999)

Christopher Catherwood: (ed) *Chosen By God.*(Highland Books 1986)

J. I. Packer, *The Collected Shorter Writings of J. I. Packer Vol. 4* (Carlisle, Paternoster 2000) This contains the two essays on Dr D. M. Lloyd-Jones by Dr Packer.

His two books of 'charismatic' sermons are *Joy Unspeakable* and *Prove All Things.* (Eastbourne, Kingsway – now printed as a joint volume.)

Many other books by Dr Lloyd-Jones include his many volumes on *Romans* and *Ephesians.*

Early works such as *Why Does God Allow War*? and *The Plight of Man and the Power of God,* are very valuable as showing the earlier Dr Lloyd-Jones.

# Postscript: 'Only Connect!'

> It did not seem so difficult ... She would only point out the salvation that was latent in his own soul, and in the soul of every man. Only connect! That was the whole of her sermon.
>
> E. M. Forster, *Howards End*

> Teach me your way, O Lord,
> and I will walk in your truth;
> give me an undivided heart,
> that I may fear your name.
>
> Psalm 86:11

> Continue to work out your salvation with fear and trembling, for it is God who works in you to will and to act according to his good purpose.
>
> Philippians 2:12-13

To find links between the Bible and the novel by E. M. Forster so recently filmed, may seem strange. I bring them together to emphasise the message: *only connect!* When grace comes into living contact with any one of us, it needs must change our lives. From Luther and Bunyan to C. S. Lewis, their lives and writings remind us of how the connections may be made. The many problems that may arise in the process of opening up our personalities to the influences of divine grace are also highlighted.

**The sanity of true genius**

Charles Lamb, in one of his *Essays of Elia,* maintains that true genius is found in a person who shows an 'admirable balance of the faculties ... He is not possessed by his subject, but has dominion over it.' An alternative view is that of Proust, that 'everything great comes from neurotics. They alone have founded religions and composed masterpieces.' These questions are reviewed by Anthony Storr in his book *Churchill's Black Dog.* I think the truth is in both extremes: that there is, indeed, a sort of balance in genius, but that the strains into which the person is forced in following his own course may cause breakdown and a lost balance, for a time, in mental or physical health. Madness, psychosis and losing touch with reality do not seem to be what happened to our eleven characters. Admittedly, Hopkins did say, 'My state is much like madness,' but there is an 'as if' quality of suffering, which he and the others surmounted, as they did their other difficulties, in order to do what they felt was their task.

One of the most important developments in modern psychiatry has been to look for 'meaningful connections' which help us to understand each other. The more we understand the loss of their mothers in Cowper and Lewis, and the lack of mothering and his lost mother-substitute in Lord Shaftesbury, the more we can make sense of their lives. If we know and understand these things, then such insights can be used to help those in our own day who suffer in similar ways.

I have not defined genius, using it here of any highly talented and gifted person. Genius used to be a word confined to the specially inspired writer, poet, artist, musician or scientist. It almost implied a sense of *possession* by a spirit, whose gift the genius received in a kind of divine ecstasy or madness.

I prefer the view that only a small part of genius is inspiration, and a great deal is perspiration. Much effort and hard work characterised all those about whom I have written. Yet the initial connecting flash of lightning inspiration, the vital connecting threads, may be needed for genius to function. Gauss, the celebrated scientist, could express this clearly when he wrote:

> Finally, two days ago I succeeded, not on account of my painful efforts, but by the Grace of God. Like a sudden flash of lightning, the riddle happened to be solved. I myself cannot say what was the conducting thread which connected what I previously knew with what made my success possible.

In my view, grace itself provides the connecting threads which link temperament and faith in a process that integrates the person into a 'whole': self mind, heart and will working together and producing the effects which we see written large in these lives.

This is not merely to repeat the modern view of holistic medicine and wholeness. It goes back to the ancient view of the psalmist: 'Unite my heart to fear thy name', or as the NIV has it: 'Give me an undivided heart, that I may fear your name' (Ps. 86:11). When St Paul writes of working out our own salvation, I accept the meaning given by some experts, that it implies working at our health, and includes the health of the church community too in the passage quoted (Phil. 2:12-13).

Our own lives, laying no claim to genius, may be on an infinitely smaller and unheroic scale, and I have often thought of the words which describe us as dwarfs being able to stand on the shoulders of these great figures of history. Yet the same linking and integrative processes may need to be at work to stop our tendency to keep our minds, our lives, in separate compartments.

**Head and heart together**

Great mental abilities alone are not enough for genius, for there is usually a sense of visitation that is necessary ('I want the one rapture of an inspiration,' says Hopkins), which usually involves the heart being moved to deeper feelings. When Bunyan asks his reader to 'lay my book, thy head, and heart together', he suggests a process of vital importance.

It may be thought that grace affects the feelings first and foremost, as George Whitefield would speak of the need for a 'felt Christ'. But the 'head' – the mind – must connect too, as the eyes of the understanding open to see and perceive the truth. Bunyan and Luther knew their systematic theology well, those beliefs so clearly set out in the great confessions of faith. But a dry-as-dust belief system was foreign to them, as to the others we have studied in these chapters. These Christians knew that the enlightening, illuminating faith was to shine in their minds to lead them to a Person, not a form of belief or a ritual statement. That Person was the living Christ, by whom grace and truth came, in whom the Word was made flesh. They might not have been able to say with the apostle John that 'That which was from the beginning, which we have heard, which we have seen with our eyes, which we have looked at and our hands have touched – this we proclaim concerning the Word of life' (1 John 1:1), but their faith led them to a similar experience.

A kind of miracle happens when our heroes find that the water of life, as Christ's gospel has become for them, is turned into a heady wine of doctrinal delight. As C. S. Lewis put it, the heart sings unbidden not with a devotional book but in reading some Christian treatise which speaks to the mind. This may of course become addictive, and systematic theology may be taken as a substitute for the real thing, life in Christ.

Perhaps we live today in a time when we fly from the mind, to urge Christians to seek experience, ecstatic phenomena and to have their feelings stirred up. Bunyan saw it all with the Ranters and the early Quakers; Luther with the ecstatic prophets of his day. There are, however, hopeful signs of a return to a more balanced life where heart and head act together in a better balance.

**Obedience: the Christian workout**

When all is said and done, it is clear that what is *done* is more important than what is said, believed or felt. 'Now that you know these things, you will be blessed if you *do* them' (John 13: 17) may not be our Lord's final word, but the accent on doing, on obeying, runs through Christian teaching. Obedience was a daily workout for our heroes. Luther and Bunyan faced their imprisonment and possible death as a matter of obedience, for their consciences forbade any compromise. For Hopkins and Rossetti obedience at the cost of personal fulfilment was paramount.

Shaftesbury seems to me a vivid illustration of what was taught in the terrible parable of the sheep and the goats in Matthew 25:31-46. He acted with a passionate conviction that visiting the sick (at a time when not many cared for the mentally ill) and feeding the hungry and doing all manner of things for the underprivileged and exploited was *'to do it for me'*. Likewise Amy Carmichael stayed in Dohnavur, South India, because of feeling compelled to obey the clamant demands to help children who were ritually sexually abused.

Cowper and Phillips wrote much, in spite of their depression and distress, and brought comfort and spiritual sustenance to millions. C. S. Lewis wrote often out of his suffering and his experience of grace, and his emphasis on obedience was among the strongest of all teachers. The obedience of faith may start with the mind bowing in submission, but it ends with a life of practical obedience to God. We may have to start, in Newman's phrase, having to learn the grammar of assent, but we go on to learn a whole language which expresses what the mind (including the imagination) and the heart comes to know. The heart has its reasons after grace has worked there which the non-Christian not only does not know, but attacks bitterly: hence the persecution of both servants and Master promised by Jesus.

The ultimate challenge that grows out of knowing more about the heroes of faith is not only to learn to know more, to stretch our minds and enlarge our hearts, but to do more in obedience to God's will. They would wish us to be more like Christ who learned from what he suffered, and through him to know more of the God whose service is perfect freedom.

# Index

Five
Leading
Reformers
Lives at a Watershed of History
Christopher Catherwood
Martin Luther
Thomas Cranmer
John Calvin
John Knox
Ulrich Zwingli
'a privilege to read.... a delight to recommend'
Ray Ortlund Jr.

# Five Leading Reformers

*Lives at a Watershed of History*

Christopher Catherwood

*'Christopher Catherwood, a writer abreast of ongoing historical study of the period and aware of the spiritual issues hanging on the chain of events, track five major players from the cradle to the grave: Luther, Zwingli, Calvin, Cranmer, Knox. Each in his way was a watershed figure, and Catherwood's vivid profiling of them will help to keep their memory green.'*

**Dr. J.I. Packer**
**Professor, Regent College, Vancouver**

*He shows how five men of very different personality and outlook could all be caught up in the same experience of a life transformed by the power of God.'*

**Rev Dr Gerald Bray**
**Samford Univerity, Alabama**

*'.. shows how their lives were touched by greatness from God, for He must be the ultimate explanation for the reformers' accomplishments. As I read, I was constantly making connections with our present-day situation.'*

**Ray Ortlund Jr., Senior Minister**
**First Presbyterian Church, Augusta, Georgia**

*'The author emphasises especially the political dimension of the reformation, and with it the emancipation of lay people. This is a religious biography with a message for today, lest we forget.'*

**David Wright**
**New College, Edinburgh**

ISBN 1 85792 570 6

william
hines
'easily read...
will stimulate your thinking'
dr jay e. adams
leaving yesterday behind
a victim no more

# Leaving Yesterday Behind

*A Victim no more*

William L. Hines

*'a refreshing source of help... demonstrates how to use biblical tools.'*

**Dr. Howard Eyrich, Briarwood Presbyterian Church , Birmingham, Alabama**

*'The style is readable, the content stimulating. I enjoyed reading it and heartily recommend it.'*

**Dr. K. Scott Oliphant – Professor of Apologetics, Westminster Theological Seminary**

-

*'Our Christian Publication reaches 100,000 readers and a worldwide internet audience... we specifically sought out Bill Hines alone to write a monthly Biblical counselling column... Bill has proven to us that he is that rare treasure – a compassionate Biblical counsellor with maturity.'*

**- John Dwyer, Editor, Dallas / Fort Worth Heritage.**

This is a profoundly practical book that can help you be released from the bondage of yesterday. It is the biblical answer to leading a full life.

Bill Hines has taught at Le Tourneau University, Trinity Bible College and Seminary and the Master's Divinity School. He is an ordained minister and board member for the International Association of Biblical Counselors. His other books include *Curing the Heart* (ISBN 1 85792 722 2) co-written with Howard Eyrich.

ISBN 1 85792 313 8

THOSE UGLY
EMOTIONS
How to Manage Your Emotions
Ken Campbell
"Dr Campbell is to be commended for
dealing with this all-important matter"
Jay Adams

# Those Ugly Emotions

*How to Manage Your Emotions*

Ken Campbell

Essentially you can be viewed in three different ways. The person **you** think you are, the person **other people** think you are and the person **God knows** you to be. So the first place we should go to in order to understand how to manage our emotions, is God's word. Because only God really knows who we are

Our real life has those uncontrolled times that we don't want others to know about, the times when we really dislike ourselves, those moments we even try to hide from God. Ken Campbell shows us where those 'ugly' emotions inside us come from and how to deal with them. This book is not lukewarm psychology dressed up as Christianity but a biblical way of dealing with our darker side. It is wonderfully practical but yet deeply spiritual and helps us get to grips with the thoughts, attitudes and behaviour that can drag us down.

*"..the book is simple to follow, easily read and should prove of benefit to all who read it."* **Evangelism Today**

Dr Ken Campbell has studied at universities in five different countries and pastored churches on both side of the Atlantic.

ISBN 1 85792 244 1

THE CHARACTER OF CHRIST'S DISCIPLES
PUT FORWARD IN THE BEATITUDES
TERRY L. JOHNSON
WHEN GRACE
TRANSFORMS
'The Beatitudes have found, in Terry Johnson, the expositor we have all been waiting for.' Alec Motyer

# When Grace Transforms

## *the character of Christ's disciples envisioned in the beatitudes*

Terry L. Johnson

*'The Beatitudes have found, in Terry Johnson, the expositor we have all been waiting for, and they become, in his hands, a statement of Christian ethics as profound as it is readable. He is as faithful in bruising as in uplifting, but, being a true pastor, even his bruises have a velvet and healing touch.'*

**Alec Motyer**

*My "Sermon on the Mount' note book is now crammed with* Johnsonisms—*pithy one-liners that get to the heart of what Jesus meant by adorning the righteousness of the kingdom of God. This is where preaching and teaching needs to go.'*

**Derek W. H. Thomas**
**Reformed Theological Seminary, Jackson, Mississippi**

*'...a clarion call to discipleship in depth.'*

**J. I. Packer, Regent College, Vancouver**

*'...shows us here a picture of what transforming grace looks like in the life of a believer, and he does so following Jesus' own description of his disciples in the Beatitudes. What a timely emphasis for a generation long on license and short on character.'*

**J. Ligon Duncan III**
**Council, Alliance of Confessing Evangelicals**

Terry explains each of the beatitudes, showing both **what they don't mean, and what they do**. His conclusions are strong, challenging, and immensely practical.

Let Jesus change your attitudes

Terry Johnson is the senior pastor of the Independent Presbyterian Church in Savannah, Georgia.

ISBN 1 85792 770 2

A Heart for Mission
Five Pioneer Thinkers
Jonathan Edwards, Cotton Mather, Richard Baxter,
Jan Amos Comenius, Count Zinzendorf
Ron Davies

# A Heart for Mission

*Five Pioneer Thinkers*

Ron Davies

Jonathan Edwards, Jan Amos Comenius, Count Zinzendorf, Cotton Mather, Richard Baxter

Many commentators agree that the Protestant Missionary effort really got under way in the late 18th century with the formation of the Baptist Missionary Society. Bearing in mind that the Reformation began in the early 16th Century the obvious question that arises is *'Why did it take Protestants nearly three centuries to act on Jesus' Great Commission mandate?'*

This book goes some of the way to explaining why. We are introduced to five Protestant, Christian thinkers who had a mind for mission, long before the Protestant world as a whole became aware of the need. From the celebrated Jonathan Edwards to the comparatively unknown Jan Amos Comenius, we see how these five men were ahead of their time. They influenced thinking about mission and their comments ultimately led to the missionary explosion which began at the end of the 18th century and which carries on to the present day.

*'For those who like to probe beneath the surface of missionary myths – read this fascinating book and be enriched, challenged and inspired.'*

**Chris Wright, Langham Partnership International**

*'May this book be used of God to move today's church to a greater self-sacrifice for the spread of the good news of Jesus Christ worldwide'*

**Martin Goldsmith, Author, former OMF Missionary**

Ron Davies has been thinking about mission for over 40 years. He has lectured at All Nations Christian College since 1964 and has been a visiting lecturer at several Seminaries in Eastern Europe and elsewhere.

ISBN 1 85792 233 6

# Christian Focus Publications

publishes books for all ages

Our mission statement -
STAYING FAITHFUL
In dependence upon God we seek to help make his infallible word, the Bible, relevant. Our aim is to ensure that the Lord Jesus Christ is presented as the only hope to obtain forgiveness of sin, live a useful life and look forward to heaven with him.

REACHING OUT
Christ's last command requires us to reach out to our world with his gospel. We seek to help fulfil that by publishing books that point people towards Jesus and for them to develop a Christ-like maturity. We aim to equip all levels of readers for life, work ministry and mission.

Books in our adult range are published in three imprints.

*Christian Heritage* contains classic writings from the past.

*Mentor* focuses on books written at a level suitable for Bible College and seminary students, pastors, and other serious readers; the imprint includes commentaries, doctrinal studies, examination of current issues, and church history.

*Christian Focus* contains popular works including biographies, commentaries, basic doctrine, and Christian living. Our children's books are also published in this imprint.

For a free catalogue of all our titles, please write to
Christian Focus Publications, Ltd
Geanies House, Fearn,
Ross-shire, IV20 1TW, Scotland, United Kingdom
info@christianfocus.com

For details of our titles visit us on our website
www.christianfocus.com